A Secret History of Consciousness

A SECRET HISTORY OF CONSCIOUSNESS

Gary Lachman

LINDISFARNE BOOKS

2003
Lindisfarne Books
an imprint of SteinerBooks
www.steinerbooks.org

Library of Congress Cataloging-in-Publication Data

Lachman, Gary, 1955-
A secret history of consciousness / by Gary Lachman.
p. cm.
Includes bibliographical references.
ISBN 1-58420-011-1
1. Consciousness—History. I. Title.
BF311.L19 2003
126'.09—dc21
2003002299

Printed in the United States of America

To Gerald Sorme, for all those books.

Contents

FOREWORD BY COLIN WILSON

—

When Rudolf Steiner was a teenager, he was irritated by a fellow student who professed to believe that human beings are nothing but machines, and asked him angrily why, in that case, he used the phrase "I think" instead of saying "My brain thinks." Of course, there was no way for Steiner to win the argument. Whatever he said, his friend could reply, "You are merely responding mechanically to a desire to win the argument," and if Steiner replied, "Then the same is true of you," would agree blandly, "That is what I am saying."

You could say that this infuriating old controversy is Gary Lachman's starting point in this book, for he feels much the same about the arguments of "philosophers" like Francis Crick and John Searle, but he does not devote much space to them, no doubt recognizing that readers who open a book called *A Secret History of Consciousness* are not going to spend too much time worrying about the twenty-first-century version of outdated nineteenth-century materialism. Presumably such readers have picked up this book because they are interested in the tradition that links figures as disparate as Steiner, Richard Maurice Bucke, Gurdjieff, Ouspensky, Schwaller de Lubicz, and Jean Gebser—in which case, they don't much care what Francis Crick thinks.

T.S. Eliot once criticized Bertrand Russell's essay "A Free Man's Worship" on the grounds that it was not for people who "hunger and thirst after righteousness" so much as for those who are content with a snack at the bar. Whether the thinkers discussed in this book "hunger and thirst after righteousness" is a matter for discussion, but one thing is certain: all of them undoubtedly hunger and thirst after *something*. And this is why I find them so fascinating, and why I read Gary Lachman's book with such deep interest.

It should be stated, before I go any further, that Gary Lachman is not—as the reader might suppose from the remarkable breadth of his knowledge—an academic, or even a psychologist. He is already well known to lovers of rock music as the guitarist in a seventies group called Blondie, and his song "I'm Always Touched by Your Presence Dear" was in the top ten. He tells the story of these years in his book *New York Rocker.* But during this period when he was a pop idol, all his spare time was spent reading philosophy and esoteric literature. And in 1983, he embarked on his own "search for the miraculous," visiting places like Gurdjieff"s prieuré in Fontainebleau, Chartres Cathedral, Glastonbury, Stonehenge, and other sacred sites. When I met him in the late 1980s, he was studying philosophy at California State University and working in the huge "metaphysical" bookshop The Bodhi Tree in Hollywood. He was working on an "occult" novel that I found fascinating. Then, in 1996, he moved to London and embarked on the career of a professional writer, writing *Turn off Your Mind: The Mystic Sixties,* and then *New York Rocker.* Readers of the present book will sense that his interest in the problem of the transformation of consciousness is immediate and personal.

Let me try to define the problem that preoccupies us both.

A small number of human beings differ from their fellows in feeling basically dissatisfied with what living in this world has to offer them. They suffer from the same kind of profound discontentment as Bunyan's hero, who could think of nothing but "What can I do to be saved?"

I must emphasize immediately that such people do not necessarily regard themselves as religious. Perhaps, like myself, they spent too much of their childhood bored to tears in church or Sunday school, and automatically react with hostility to the kind of bleating that clergymen indulge in. But whether they know it or

not, they are reacting to the same peculiar dissatisfaction that has
characterized truly religious people throughout the ages. They are
revolted and enraged by the hymn that declares:

> *The trivial round, the common task*
> *Should furnish all we ought to ask.*

As far as they are concerned, a life devoted to "the trivial
round" is not worth living.

Now, although such people strike most of their fellows as
rather peculiar, they always seem to form a certain small percent-
age of society, and have done so throughout the ages. Those who
were lucky enough to be born in Europe in, say, the thirteenth century, simply explained to their families that they wished to become
novices, and went off to the nearest monastery. And although they
were probably required to milk the cows and grind the corn into
flour, they had no objection to this "trivial round" of everyday
chores. For, as they listened to the chanting of the monks at even-
song, or took part in the Easter festival, they felt themselves to be
part of a world that satisfied a hunger of the spirit.

These natural contemplatives experienced disquiet when
reformers like Luther and Calvin and Hus denounced the Church
as corrupt, for the religious temperament is naturally conservative,
and feels no desire to challenge authority. They were not even too
concerned to learn that Canon Copernicus had propounded a new
theory in which the earth was no longer the center of the universe,
for Copernicus admitted that it was no more than a theory. But this
was not the end of the matter. Soon Galileo was declaring that
Copernicus was right and the Pope was wrong, while the respected
philosopher Descartes suggested that the only reliable way to arrive
at truth was through reason, and that although reason supported
the existence of God, the first step towards certain knowledge was
to "doubt everything." Then Sir Isaac Newton demonstrated that
the universe is a gigantic clock, which ticks on for all eternity without any help from God. And by this time, half of Europe had
become Protestant, and the old comfortable world of the thirteenth
century had been lost forever.

We can now see that, historically speaking, this had to happen. But it meant that those natural "misfits" and "outsiders" who had found their natural home in the Church no longer had anywhere to go. They had, in effect, become refugees, displaced persons. So when, in the 1880s, an Armenian-Greek named George Gurdjieff experienced the familiar dissatisfaction of the spiritual refugee, he had no idea where to start looking for a way of life that would satisfy that peculiar hunger that tormented him. It is true that he was deeply religious and, if he had been born a generation earlier, would almost certainly have entered the Orthodox Church, and ended his life with the reputation of a saint. But it was already too late for that. Instead, Gurdjieff wandered off to Egypt, then Abyssinia and Syria, then India, searching for a lost knowledge that he felt *had* to exist somewhere. And after many years of searching—he claims he was part of a group called "the Seekers after Truth"—he came to the conclusion that the answer he was looking for did not lie in some ancient monastery in the Himalayas. It lay rather "in the sphere of man's unconscious mentation," that is, in the depth of the unconscious mind.

Now—if I may speak personally for a moment—I came across Gurdjieff's name about 1950 when, in a bookshop in Kensington Church Street, I saw a squat, bulky volume entitled *All and Everything*. And since, ever since I reached my teens, I had been possessed by an absurd desire to know about every important idea of the twentieth century, I was deeply curious to know what Gurdjieff had to say that required well over a thousand pages. A glance into the book convinced me that he had no capacity for expressing himself in plain language, and I temporarily admitted defeat.

Not long after that, I found a volume called *In Search of the Miraculous*, by P.D. Ouspensky, in the Wimbledon public library, and was delighted to see that it was about the teaching of Gurdjieff. And since it seemed to be clearly written, I took it home and plunged in. But I soon found myself bogged down in obscure passages about "the ray of creation" and "octaves," and decided that, after all, this was not for me. Fortunately, a few weeks later, I came upon a volume called *Venture with Ideas* by Kenneth

Walker, and realised that this was a simple personal account of Gurdjieff and Ouspensky. And using Kenneth Walker as a key, I was soon making great strides with *In Search of the Miraculous*, and knew that I had stumbled upon one of the most important books of my life.

One of the things that impressed me most about Gurdjieff's teaching was his assertion that we are little more than machines. This is something I had felt obscurely since my teens, and it had crystallized when I read in T.S. Eliot's *The Family Reunion* the line: "partial observation of one's own automatism." I would have liked to be quite a different kind of person—self-possessed, focused, articulate—but my body and brain seemed to have a will of their own, and I sometimes felt that I was in charge of a shambling Frankenstein monster. Persuading him to do what I wanted was as difficult as driving one of those "dodgem" cars in an amusement park, which refuses to go the way you want it to.

But even when I outgrew the sense of clumsiness and awkwardness, I remained aware of this mechanical element in the human personality that I called "the automatic pilot"—the part of us that learns to type or drive a car or talk a foreign language. This I eventually came to call "the robot."

This robot is also responsible for something that preoccupied me greatly in my teens—mental illness. So many of those nineteenth-century figures I admired—van Gogh, Nietzsche, Hölderlin—had gone insane. And I could understand the mechanism. Every one of us is part "robot," part living entity, the "real you." Under normal circumstances, we seem to be about fifty/fifty. When you set out for work on a spring morning, you are more like 51% "real you" and only 49% "robot." Yet by the time you come home, you may be so tired that you drive home "automatically" and can hardly remember the drive—your robot has driven you home.

The problem arises when you feel overwhelmed with difficulties and complications, and you plod along mechanically, hardly recalling what it was like when you really enjoyed life. You cease to make the kind of effort that re-charges your vital batteries. You are now habitually more "robot" than "real you," and this is a highly dangerous state. For if we allow ourselves to slip down to the state of being 55% robot and only 45% real you, it is very hard to recover. Tiredness makes you pessimistic. Pessimism makes you tired. It is a vicious circle, in which it seems self-evident that living is bloody hard work, and that no one can be called truly happy. We cease to feel those flashes of sheer delight, those moments that Chesterton called "absurd good news" and Proust *"moments bien-heureux."* Life takes on the quality of a play by Samuel Beckett. (And it is surely a sign of how many people in our civilization live permanently in this state that Beckett is vaguely accepted as a "great writer.")

In short, although the robot is the most valuable servant we possess, he is also responsible for most of the things that are wrong with our civilization. And all these problems depend on the negative feedback mechanism—tiredness leading to depression, depression to more tiredness...

This explains why so much "modern thought" is tinged with gloom, from the psychology of Freud to the philosophy of Heidegger, Sartre, and their successors.

Yet, as Gary Lachman points out, not all serious thinkers end up in this pessimistic cul-de-sac. Abraham Maslow complained that Freud had "sold human nature short" and landed us in a radical underestimation of our own powers. He pointed out that all healthy and normal people have regular "peak experiences" (a close relative of Proust's *moments bienheureux)*. But he also made an observation of crucial importance. When his students began to talk to one another about their peak experiences, they began having peak experiences all the time. It is as if reminding yourself of their existence is enough to make them happen.

We have seen the same mechanism in Bucke's experience of "cosmic consciousness," which occurred after he had spent an evening with friends talking and reading Wordsworth, Whitman and Browning. The discussion had made him aware that he *ought* to be happy, and the happiness descended as he relaxed in the cab.

This raises an interesting question. If peak experiences are so natural, why do most people experience them so seldom?

The answer is fairly obvious. We don't spend most of our lives considering whether we are happy or unhappy. We spend them in practical considerations—catching buses, paying bills, watching the news. Happiness tends to come in moments of relaxation or withdrawal. Maslow describes a young mother who was getting breakfast for her husband and children when a beam of sunlight came through the window, and it suddenly struck her *how lucky she was*, and she went into the peak experience. Of course, she was lucky *before* it happened, but it took the sunlight to give her a "lift" that carried her into the peak experience.

The trouble, I concluded long ago, is that "close-upness" deprives us of meaning. We spend our lives peering at the present like a watchmaker peering at cogs and springs through his eyeglass. The result is rather like a shortsighted man in a picture gallery, who is forced to study the pictures from two inches away and so seldom gets the full impact.

The present acts like a bullfighter's cape, which prevents the bull from seeing the matador. Every time it charges, it is blinded by the cape. This is the perfect example of what Gurdjieff meant by mechanicalness. A really intelligent bull would fix the matador with its mind, ignore the cape, and charge at where it knows the matador to be. But most bulls are too mechanical to do anything so intelligent.

In the *moments bienheureux*, the matador stands back and drops the cape, and we can see things as they are, and plunge into the peak experience.

Of course, the trouble is not only "close-upness," but also the negativity that has somehow crept into our whole outlook on life. And the culprit here is *thought itself*. This has now been recognized by a school of psychiatry in America, of whom the leading exponent is a professor called George Pransky. He refers to it as the Psychology of Mind. In his book *The Renaissance of Psychology*, Pranksy describes how he was persuaded to attend a session at Salt Spring Island, off the coast of British Columbia. He was struck by the sheer cheerfulness and wellbeing of the participants. But what really impressed him was that the person at the center of this revival was an ordinary man named Syd Banks, not a psychologist or an academic, or even a minister. And Banks's insight had come upon him with absurd simplicity. He had been remarking to a friend that he felt unhappy, and the friend had replied, "You're not unhappy, Syd—you only *think* you are." And Banks stared at him with amazement and said, "What did you say?" as the incredible implications sank in. He suddenly saw that all our mental states are things we happen to "think" are so.

When George Pransky told me this story, I told him one of my own favorites. A man is on his way to borrow a neighbor's lawn-mower for the tenth time. He imagines the neighbor saying, "But why don't you buy one of your own?" and he replies, "It just isn't worth it." And his neighbor says, "Yes, but surely..." At this moment, he knocks on the neighbor's door, and as the man opens it, he shouts, "Oh keep your bloody lawnmower" and strides off.

This is an example of the kind of thing Banks means. It is our minds that create problems and inflate them.

But if we practise Gurdjieff's self-observation, we soon recognise that most of the things we think we see and understand are patterns created by our own minds, like faces seen in the clouds. And the cinema screen on which we project these shapes is the bull-fighter's cape, the present moment. If we could learn to brush the cape aside, everything would be different. For, as Blake realized, if the doors of perception were cleansed, everything would appear as it really is, infinite.

That is why, on the whole, I tend to be an optimist. As I study modern philosophy, from Heidegger and Sartre to Derrida and Lyotard, as I study modern literature, from Eliot's *Waste Land* to Beckett and Golding's *Lord of the Flies*, I see men who have convinced themselves that the faces they see in the clouds—and make the rest of us see—are objectively real.

Buckminster Fuller went straight to the heart of the matter with his comment, "I seem to be a verb." We come closest to understanding our own mystery when we grasp the meaning of this comment. If everyday consciousness shares the nature of sleep, then the problem is to "shake the mind awake."

Here, I would suggest, we have a fruitful starting point for this problem. In *Crime and Punishment*, Raskolnikov remarks that if he had to stand on a narrow ledge forever, in eternal rain and darkness, he would still prefer to do this rather than die at once. We can all understand just what he meant—that if someone put a gun to our heads and said, "Which is it to be? Do I blow your brains out, or will you choose the narrow ledge?" we would all cry, "Narrow ledge!" But what would we actually *do* on that narrow ledge?

The director of BBC music, Hans Keller, once described how he had been in Germany before the Second World War, when so many of his acquaintances were disappearing into concentration camps, and had prayed, "Only let me get out of Germany, and I swear I will never be unhappy for the rest of my life." And again, we can all see what he meant. But how could he actually set about keeping his promise?

Gary Lachman mentions in this book the story of how Graham Greene had temporarily escaped his own boredom by playing Russian roulette with a loaded revolver, and how, when the hammer fell on an empty chamber, he felt an overwhelming sense of delight, of relief. In that moment, he had actually *become* a verb.

But how do we set about "becoming a verb"? Shaw embodied his own answer to the problem in *Heartbreak House*, in Captain Shotover's phrase "The seventh degree of concentration." And we can see that a hammer clicking on the empty chamber of a loaded revolver would, indeed, bring about something very like the seventh degree of concentration.

In this remarkable book, Gary Lachman has approached this problem from many different angles. What all have in common is that they embody the idea that human consciousness is now evolving toward a new level. This is the basis of the teachings of Madame Blavatsky and Rudolf Steiner, and it reappears in Bucke, Gurdjieff, Ouspensky, Owen Barfield, Maslow, Schwaller de Lubicz, and Jean Gebser. And it also seems to me obvious that, as in the case of Maslow's students, we can only deepen our awareness of this step in evolution by talking and thinking about it. That is to say, a book like this is in itself an important step toward the evolution it discusses.

I stumbled upon an interesting insight several years ago—in fact, to be specific, in March 1987—after an accident involving a ferry called *The Herald of Free Enterprise*. Its captain made the mistake of allowing it to leave port with the car doors open, which was strictly illegal. A wave rolled into the ship, causing it to capsize with great loss of life. And as I thought about this, I found myself reflecting how easy it would have been to avert this tragedy, if only someone had walked up to the captain and threatened to report him if he did not order the doors closed before leaving port.

But then I became aware of the paradox. If the tragedy had been averted, *no one would have known*, and so no one would have felt happiness and relief. We can even imagine that, if one of the passengers had been a depressive, he might have thrown himself overboard on the return journey.

Reflecting on this makes me aware of what Gurdjieff meant when he said that what man needs to save him from the state of illusion in which he lives is an organ that would permit him to see the exact time of his own death. Let me add to that another reflection: that what we now need is an organ by which we can perceive the tragedies and miseries we might well encounter every day of our lives, but which we normally succeed in avoiding.

It may sound as if I am suggesting that we should spend our lives in a state of anxiety about possible disasters. But that is not at all what I mean. On the contrary, I am suggesting using the imagination actively—like Maslow's housewife—to grasp how lucky we are.

Forty years ago I compiled the first-ever "encyclopedia of murder." I tried to explain in the Introduction why I did not regard the study of murder as somehow morbid or sensational, because when you contemplate the idea of a criminal who has thrown away his freedom, you are galvanized into a recognition of the value of your own freedom.

For example, at the time I write this, a friend named Ira Einhorn has just been sentenced to life imprisonment on a murder charge. I am not now raising the question of whether he is guilty or not: only the fact that he is an intelligent man, who would certainly have better things to do with his life than spend it behind bars. And if I happen to be tired, or worried about some relatively trivial problem, and then I remember Ira's present predicament, I am instantly restored to an objective view of my situation. My own problems are reduced to a size that makes them almost invisible.

Gary Lachman believes, and I concur, that some basic changes have happened in human consciousness over the past four thousand years: the change to reflective self-awareness that occurred with what Julian Jaynes calls "the breakdown of the bicameral mind" around 1250 B.C., the change to "perspectival consciousness" at some time around 1336, when Petrarch climbed Mount Ventoux, and the astonishing change that occurred around 1750 with the birth of Romanticism.

If Gebser is correct, the greatest change is yet to occur. This is the change to "integral consciousness," defined by Georg Feuerstein as "consciousness that does not seek escape from the present."

That is why it seems to me that it is wholly appropriate that Gebser should occupy the place he does, at the end of this book, where the reader will be in a position to judge the remarkable extent of his contribution. For to grasp what is meant by integral consciousness is to have taken the most important step toward achieving it.

INTRODUCTION

Consciousness Explained

In 1994 Francis Crick, who with James Watson and Maurice Wilkins won the Nobel Prize for discovering the structure of the DNA molecule, published a book with the intriguing title *The Astonishing Hypothesis: The Scientific Search for the Soul.* That hypothesis, to quote from Crick, runs as follows:

> *You, your joys and your sorrows, your memories and ambitions, your sense of personal identity and free will, are in fact no more than the behaviour of a vast assembly of nerve cells and their associated molecules.*[1]

The average reader, awed by Crick's scientific credentials, may indeed have been astonished by this pronouncement and may have absorbed Crick's ambitious statement with little difficulty. After all, Crick had discovered DNA, and if the proteins locked into the spiral staircase of the DNA molecule can be responsible for life itself, then surely it is no great step to map out how other molecules could be the source of "personal identity" and "free will"—could, in fact, be the building blocks of "you" and "me." Indeed, for anyone aware of the history of science, Crick's hypothesis would not seem astonishing at all. For the past four hundred years, science has been trying to account for everything—including ourselves—in terms of atoms or molecules and the laws they adhere to, and Crick's "astonishing hypothesis" is merely part of a long attempt to excise all that is "merely subjective" from our account of the world.

But for some other readers, what may have been astonishing about Crick's hypothesis is that he expected anyone to believe it at all. For this group, "The Incredible Hypothesis" would have been a better title. Their immediate response to Crick's hypothesis, like my own, was probably a gut feeling that, for all his undoubted knowledge about molecular biology, when it came to explaining you or me he was no more qualified than anyone else. My joys and sorrows, memories and ambitions, sense of identity and feeling of free will are nothing but the products of nerve cells and molecules? Somehow, I just can't accept that. And even if it were true, wouldn't Crick's ideas about these things themselves be nothing more than the behavior of his nerve cells and molecules? And if that were true, why should I or anyone else pay any special attention to them? After all, nerve cells are nerve cells, and molecules are molecules, no?

Yet, as anyone familiar with the subject knows, "explaining consciousness" is probably the hottest item on philosophical and scientific agendas today, a surprising turnaround if you look at the history of academic psychology in the last century. For years the idea of discussing consciousness "scientifically" was unheard of. For most scientists, consciousness was, at best, an epiphenomenon, like the steam given off by boiling water. But today all that has changed. According to one biologist and neuroscientist, the 1990s were the decade of the brain, with the 2000s set to be the decade of consciousness.[2] Hundreds of journals and Web sites devoted to some aspect of "brain studies" publish thousands of research papers each year. Enter the keyword "consciousness" into the computer catalog at the British Library in London, where I am writing this, and you receive a list of more than one thousand titles, many of them published in the last five years. There are books arguing that consciousness can best be described as a kind of computer, books arguing that computers themselves will soon be conscious, and some, like Marvin Minsky's *The Society of Mind,* even arguing that they already are. Some neuroscientists argue that free will is located in a specific area of the brain (for Crick it is in a deep fold of the cerebral cortex called the anterior cingulate sulcus). Some, like Gerald Edelman, another Nobel Prize winner, deny that consciousness or the brain is anything like a computer, arguing that it is much more like a cerebral jungle in which different "neuronal ensembles" fight it out Darwinian style, the survivors being selected as members of "neuronal nets," one function of which is consciousness. Others, like Roger Penrose, agree that the brain isn't a computer and argue that no computer can ever be conscious, emphasizing that consciousness is deeply involved in both quantum mechanics and the intricacies of Gödel's theorem. There is even, as in the work of one influential philosopher of mind, a desire to "eliminate" consciousness altogether—a project that harkens back to the 1920s and the behaviorism of the psychologist J. B. Watson. Watson argued that he never saw any evidence for consciousness and hence concluded that it therefore did not exist—at least not in any scientific sense. This hard-to-swallow notion is the central thesis of *Consciousness Explained* (1992) by the philosopher Daniel Dennett, probably the most influential and certainly the strangest book in the "reducing consciousness" genre; its five hundred dense pages are devoted to the odd proposition that consciousness doesn't really exist. What does exist for Dennett are robot zombies—ourselves—who only *think* they are conscious and have subjective experiences ... but then *whom* does he want to explain consciousness to, if, like himself, his readers are not really conscious?

Exactly why Dennett wants to eliminate consciousness is unclear. Perhaps he shares the sensibility of Nicholas Humphrey, another thinker attempting to put the ghost of consciousness to rest (*Soul Searching*, 1995). Eager to jettison anything reminiscent of the "supernatural," Humphrey once remarked, "Unexplained subjective experience arouses an irritation in me."[3] Even after making allowances for scientific zeal, there is something disquieting about this statement. Curiosity, yes, wonder too. Awe, and even a nerdish desire to "know how it works." But irritation? Why should my enjoyment of a Beethoven string quartet—which, at heart, strikes me as a delightful mystery—bother Nicholas Humphrey? Why should subjective experience irritate anyone? Clearly such an attitude would not have much use for love if it had to explain the emotions of the person professing it. Why this troubling itch to explain our interior world, which ultimately means to reduce it to something wieldy, controllable—in short, to have power over it?

In *The Mystery of Consciousness* John Searle, a critic of Dennett and one of the leading academic thinkers on consciousness, remarks, "Future generations, I suspect, will wonder why it took us so long in the twentieth century to see the centrality of consciousness in the understanding of our very existence as human beings."[4] But any reader of the various wisdom traditions of the West and East, or of the large literature on consciousness that has emerged from the different "alternative schools" that have risen since the 1960s, will wonder why Searle believes we are just now finding out about "the centrality of consciousness." Ideas about consciousness and "altered states" have formed an underground current in Western thought since well before the nineteenth century. Only for academics like Searle is consciousness a new problem, and perhaps only for thinkers like him is it a "problem" at all. Although Searle thinks the idea of eliminating mental states is a mistake, his own thinking about consciousness has no hesitations about making sweeping statements that seem to reduce its stature. "We have to . . . start," he tells us, "with the assumption that consciousness is an ordinary biological phenomenon comparable with growth, digestion, or the secretion of bile,"[5] an analogy first proposed by the eighteenth-century French physiologist Pierre Cabanis. Searle has also likened consciousness to the process of photosynthesis,[6] an analogy he shares with Daniel Dennett. And in possibly the only thought on which he agrees with Dennett, Searle too believes that the sense of mystery is absent from our account of photosynthesis.[7] Soon, he believes, it will be gone from consciousness too.

How strongly Searle believes that we are on the brink of demystifying consciousness—and, again, by extension, ourselves—can be seen in the concluding chapter of *The Mystery of Consciousness*: "How to Transform the Mystery of Consciousness into the Problem of Consciousness." Throughout the book, Searle frequently repeats statements like "It is just a plain fact about nature that brains cause consciousness." "The problem of consciousness is the problem of explaining exactly how neurobiological processes in the brain *cause* our subjective states of awareness." "We know in fact that brain processes *cause* consciousness."[8] In fact, as David Chalmers of the University of Arizona, one of the few philosophers of mind who is not interested in "explaining" consciousness—and whom Searle singles out for a particularly hostile treatment—remarks, Searle repeats the dictum "The brain causes consciousness" like a kind of mantra.

But exactly how much brain we need for consciousness is itself an open question. In *After Life: In Search of Cosmic Consciousness,* a critical account of the near-death experience, science writer David Darling writes of some now largely forgotten but clearly remarkable cases of hydrocephalus, the condition known as water on the brain. In the cases he recounts, however, the people involved did not have water *on* the brain, but apparently had water *instead of* a brain. Nevertheless they functioned as perfectly normal, intelligent human beings. Darling speaks of two children born in the 1960s who "had fluid where their cerebrums should have been. . . . Although neither child showed any evidence of having a cerebral cortex, the mental development of each appeared perfectly normal."[9] In another case, a man with an IQ of 126, a graduate of the University of Sheffield with a first-class honors degree in mathematics, and by all accounts bright and perfectly ordinary, had no detectable brain. Identical twin girls with advanced hydrocephalus enjoyed above average IQs. In one case, an autopsy performed on a young man who had died suddenly revealed "only the most paltry rind of brain tissue." When the coroner expressed sympathy for the parents' loss, but offered that at least now their severely retarded son had found peace, the parents were dumbfounded, informing him that their bright son had been at his job only days before.[10] Although the paper reporting these cases received some attention at the time, it was subsequently forgotten, its findings just too contrary to the reigning scientific orthodoxy. Yet such cases at the very least suggest that the mantra "The brain causes consciousness" is perhaps not as incontrovertible as its adherents believe, and that, to put it crudely, the possibility of consciousness existing without a brain should not be completely ruled out.[11]

Searle, however, is adamant, believing that our sense of mystery about consciousness is a "genuine obstacle" to answering the "causal question" about it and that this sense of mystery will evaporate once we have a reasonably plausible explanation about how the brain causes consciousness. This hurdle is known as "the hard problem." How do firing neurons become subjective experience? How do Crick's physical molecules become curiously *meaningful* but intangible "things" like the scent of a rose, a nightingale's song, or the feel of your lover's touch? No one really knows, and as long as the slightest atmosphere of mystery remains about our subjective experience, there will always be individuals like me who believe that the entire scientific project of explaining consciousness is misguided. To us, explaining consciousness would be the same as "explaining" a Bach cantata or van Gogh's sunflowers. Who would want to? And, in any case, how *could* they be explained, and how would any such explanation be useful?

Not all contemporary explorers of consciousness share this vision of a demystified consciousness. There are a handful who don't believe that science can ever solve the "hard problem." Thinkers of this persuasion have been christened "mysterians" by their more optimistic brethren. David Chalmers, for example, insists that no matter how much we may learn about the brain, an "explanatory gap" still stretches between the various physical processes and our subjective experience. Purely physicalistic theories, Chalmers argues, cannot bridge the gap, and his own approach in many ways harkens back to ancient ideas of panpsychism, the notion, shared by premodern thinkers and by some twentieth-century philosophers like Henri Bergson and Alfred North Whitehead, that in some way *everything* participates in consciousness. Such views do away with the dreaded mind-body dualism by arguing that consciousness is not simply a property of brains, but exists in some form throughout creation. Most scientists and philosophers find this idea repellent, yet it is simply the opposite side of the coin of views like Dennett's that would do away with consciousness altogether. Strangely, for them it is more repellent to think that everything is conscious than to think that nothing is.

What really bothers "explainers" is that at bottom one can never "know," with the kind of certainty one can know a physical fact, that anyone other than oneself actually *is* conscious. We cannot see, touch, hear, smell, taste, or feel someone else's consciousness—nor our own for that matter. It is conceivable that an android could be designed that would, for all intents and purposes, appear conscious, yet have no subjective experience at all. There would be no way of knowing through the senses alone that this android was not conscious. All of its actions could be programmed in such a way that it would appear to be just like yourself, an individual with some kind of subjective experience taking place—metaphorically at least—inside its head. But there wouldn't be. Such a possibility, planted in a suggestible mind, can easily lead to a nasty case of paranoia. Yet some scientists skate fairly close to this edge. To my mind, this says more about the peculiarities of a particular "scientific" sensibility, hungry for absolute certainty, than it does about any "problem of consciousness."

—

This book is not about "explaining consciousness," nor is it in any way a "scientific" account of the brain or our interior world. There are many of these, excellent ones written by abler hands than mine. On the contrary, one of my motives in writing this book is to argue that the current monopoly on consciousness by scientists and academic philosophers is unfounded, and that a whole history of thought about consciousness and its possible evolution is left out of their "official" accounts. There is what I call a "secret history of consciousness," and in what follows I will try to bring some of this secret history to light. This is not to say that the scientific study of consciousness should be abandoned. That would be absurd and as reductive as the approaches to consciousness I have mentioned. What is important is to integrate what science tells us about the

brain and mind into a wider perspective, a larger image of humanity's history and a broader vision of its future.

In this book I focus on what we can broadly call the esoteric,
spiritual, or metaphysical tradition, although not all of the thinkers
discussed would place themselves within this camp. I have done
this because in that tradition consciousness, far from being
explained, is instead the central player in the drama. To put it simply, if in current scientific accounts consciousness is explained in
terms of molecules and neurons, in the countertradition consciousness itself is responsible for those neurons and molecules. For the
materialist, matter comes first, consciousness second; for the countertradition, consciousness comes first. And what is more, for the
countertradition consciousness is not a static "product" of the
brain, but a living, evolving presence whose development can be
traced through different historical periods. No one speaks of an
evolution of bile, in the sense that within it remain potentials and
possibilities yet to be discovered. For the secret history of consciousness, however, the paramount idea is that human beings *as
they are,* are not an end point of evolution and their consciousness
as it is, is not a final, randomly achieved state. For the secret history of consciousness the possibility remains that human beings
may evolve into something very different and that the form that
difference will take may be a new, broader, more expansive consciousness, manifestations of which have appeared in the past and
continue to appear in the present. What exactly that consciousness
may be like and how it may be achieved are some of the questions
this book will discuss.

———

The characteristics of this new consciousness have been known
for centuries. Mystics have spoken of them, and since at least the
1960s ideas of "higher consciousness" or "altered states of consciousness" have been part of our common language. Recently, science too seems to support their existence. In her book *SQ: Spiritual
Intelligence, The Ultimate Intelligence,* the physicist Danah Zohar
speaks of the work of the Austrian neuroscientist Wolf Singer,

whose specialty is what is known as "the binding problem." How does the brain fuse the disparate information coming from the senses into a comprehensible whole? Singer and his colleagues in Frankfurt studied visual perception and suggested that the neurological aspect of "binding" may lie in the synchronized firing of neurons in separate areas of the brain. Singer found that separate neurons located in different parts of the brain responsive to color, shape, and movement fire simultaneously at forty hertz, i.e., forty firings per second. Although many researchers doubt the importance of the finding, this neural oscillation at forty hertz seems to be associated with consciousness. Singer's work suggests there is a process in the brain that is itself antireductionist and is concerned with creating wholes out of parts, and hence with giving *meaning* to our experience. Without it the world would appear a random eruption of information: in other words, chaos. "Meaning" then is not something we import into the world, as some scientists and philosophers have argued.[12] There literally would be no "world" without it. Zohar further suggests the state of inner and outer unity experienced by practitioners of meditation is paralleled by the "unity" of oscillating neurons.[13] During meditation, brain waves become more coherent and are accompanied by the forty-hertz oscillations. The subjective experience of unity, Zohar points out, is accompanied by a physical unity in the brain. This simultaneous processing of information, she suggests, is an indication of a "third kind of thinking," what she calls our "SQ," or spiritual quotient, to differentiate it from IQ and recent ideas of an "emotional quotient." Rather than reducing our inner states to the behavior of molecules and neurons, or eliminating them altogether, Singer's work on synchronized neural oscillations lends a neurological support to perhaps our most valued inner state of all, the mystical sensation of unity.

Other researchers point in similar directions. The neuroscientists Denis Pare and Rodolfo Llinas have argued that consciousness, rather than being an epiphenomenon given off by firing neurons, seems to be an inherent property of the brain itself. Their research supports a view of consciousness and the mind held by mystics throughout the ages: that the world we perceive is actually shaped by our consciousness. Recognizing that the forty-hertz oscillations associated with consciousness occur during REM sleep, Llinas concluded that the only difference between our dreaming and waking states is that in waking states, the "closed system that generates oscillatory states" is modulated by incoming stimuli from the outside world. Consciousness, then, is not "caused" by sensory stimuli "writing" on the blank slate of the mind, as philosophers like John Locke supposed. It is an irreducible process in the brain itself. Although materialist scientists think a hard, unyielding reality pulls the strings of consciousness, the external world we perceive through our senses may really be a kind of waking dream, formed by a consciousness that happens to be aware of it.[14]

—

A very similar idea was proposed by a philosopher that probably very few students of consciousness are aware of. In his little-read *Essay on the Origin of Thought* (1974), which I discuss in Part Four of this book, the Danish philosopher Jurij Moskvitin proposed a theory of consciousness that is very close to Llinas and Pare's, and echoes the intuitions of dozens of mystical thinkers. For Moskvitin our consciousness of the outside world is a kind of hallucination, but one, as Llinas and Pare suggest, shaped by stimuli from the senses. Moskvitin was led to this conclusion not through studying the brain, but by becoming aware of unconscious processes in perception. Sitting in the sun on a spring day, he drifted into a dreamy, yet alert state of relaxation. With his eyelids almost closed, he became interested in the play of sunlight on his eyelashes and in the curious movement of what are called "floaters" on his retina, little "bubbles" on the surface of the eye, reminiscent of raindrops rolling down a windowpane. Focusing on these, Moskvitin became aware that the prismatic display caused by the sunlight passing through his eyelashes was not random, but formed geometric patterns, crosses, squares, and triangles. Watching the "strange and beautiful patterns" gave him "the feeling of watching something particularly significant"; he then realized that the patterns were not limited to the surface of his eye, but seemed to extend from his eye and to be projected by it to the outside world in the form of "sparks" and "cobwebs." He writes of seeing these "selective forms" taking shape as the external world, comparing it to the effect of a pointillist painting.

Moskvitin spent many hours studying these patterns, commenting on the curious states of mind that accompanied extended observation of the selective forms. He soon noticed that the attention required to observe the forms "was inseparable from a very particular mood . . . and gave rise to a sensation of pleasure and outbursts of the most remarkable thoughts." He also realized that "the patterns to which I had gained access were so similar to certain patterns in art, especially in religious art, or art . . . created by civilizations dominated by mystical experience, that I could not doubt that my experience was a very old one and widely known."[15]

Moskvitin believes that his selective forms are the work of the human mind and that they extend from "creating" the world we perceive through our senses to the creative insights of artists and scientists. They are, he argues, responsible for language, civilization, and human evolution itself. They are also responsible for dreams and hallucinations. Like Llinas and Pare, Moskvitin argues that in dreams, visions, hallucinations, and other altered states, the selective forms are, as it were, free, and it is through their unrestricted expression that novelty enters the world. He further concludes that all attempts to find our origin in the outside world must fail, since the opposite seems to be the case: the world has its origin in us. Human consciousness, he argues, is a kind of blind spot in the universe, a black hole at whose center we will find the mind. One of the aims of this book is to see if Moskvitin is right.

—

The study and exploration of consciousness, as opposed to the attempt to explain it, has a long and fascinating history. In the form of religious and spiritual practices it reaches back thousands of years—Hinduism, Buddhism, Christianity, Islam, and Judaism all have traditions centered on the investigation of interior states. But as a philosophical and scientific pursuit linked to the idea of evolution, its roots go back only to the late nineteenth and early twentieth centuries. Since the 1960s, ideas about "higher" and "expanded" consciousness have made many inroads into mainstream culture; yet few people who practice various forms of "consciousness technology" today are aware, I think, of the background to their interests nor know that some of the most influential people in academic and intellectual circles in the early part of the last century—like the philosopher Henri Bergson and the psychologist William James—were deeply involved in the study of mysticism and altered states of consciousness. In Part One, "The Search for Cosmic Consciousness," I go into some detail about the ideas and cultural milieu involved in these early journeys into the mind. The ideas about consciousness discussed at that time, like those discussed today, were not limited to a closed, restricted study; they broke out of the academy to touch on vital issues in social theory, the arts, anthropology, philosophy, psychology, and other important areas. At the beginning of the twentieth century, consciousness and its possibilities seemed to present humanity with a new future, with new potentialities, and—in a phrase that has come to mean something quite different for us—with a "new age."

During the same period, esotericism entered the main currents of modern thought. To be sure, for centuries the "esoteric tradition" had been a powerful source of ideas and inspiration, influencing many of the greatest thinkers of the West—as I note in the book, even as "modern" and "rational" a figure as Isaac Newton was as devoted to alchemy and other "occult" studies as he was to the scientific pursuits he is known for today. But I think it can be said that, within relatively modern times, until the appearance of Madame Blavatsky and Theosophy, esoteric thought functioned primarily as an underground current. By the early twentieth century this was no longer true, and as I try to make clear, it was precisely in reaction to the rise of modern ideas of evolution that that formidable Russian lady presented her remarkable teachings on humanity's cosmic destiny. For a brief period in the early twentieth century, scientific, philosophical, and esoteric ideas about the human being's possible evolution met in a heady mélange of insight and speculation. P. D. Ouspensky, who straddled the scientific and esoteric worlds, has a prominent role in Part One.

Another figure who straddled both worlds was Rudolf Steiner. In Part Two, "Esoteric Evolution," I examine some aspects of Steiner's ideas about consciousness in light of the influence on his thought of Goethe's phenomenology, as well as from the perspective of recent investigations into the curious condition of mind known as the "hypnagogic state." "Hypnagogia," so christened by its most thorough investigator, Andreas Mavromatis, is a unique state of consciousness, in between sleeping and waking. As I try to show, Mavromatis argues persuasively that in hypnagogia distinctions between the unconscious and the conscious, between dreaming and waking, break down, and that in the not-too-distant future, human beings may be able to experience both states *simultaneously*, in a kind of "duo-consciousness." That Steiner himself suggested something very similar, and that Mavromatis's work is based on an analysis of the structure of the brain itself, offers, I think, good evidence that such ideas are grounded in something more than mere speculation. Mavromatis argues that hypnagogic states are linked to the brain's "pre-cortical" structures, known collectively as the "old brain," and suggests that at an earlier time human consciousness may not have been the clear, distinct "waking state" it is today—an idea he shares with Rudolf Steiner.

In Part Three, "The Archaeology of Consciousness," I examine the evidence for the kind of consciousness our ancient and prehistoric ancestors might have experienced. If consciousness has evolved—a central theme of this book—then we have gotten to where we are today by passing through earlier stages. That these earlier stages are recapitulated in the consciousness of children—as Erich Neumann and other psychologists have argued—suggests that they are still a part of our "mature" psyches. By looking into our personal "prehistory," we may gain some insight into how consciousness might have felt in the past. The accepted view is that civilization and history began in 3100 B.C. with the unification of Upper and Lower Egypt. But there is much evidence to suggest that civilizations existed prior to this date, and that at some point a split occurred in human consciousness, precipitating the development of the ego and the world that we experience today.

What consciousness may have been like before this split, and what it may be like in the future, is the subject of Part Four, "Participatory Epistemology." Here I focus on the work of three thinkers whose ideas center around the latent potentials of the imagination. Owen Barfield shows that the history of language can tell us much about the evolution of consciousness. As he wrote in his last book, *History, Guilt, and Habit,* "Language contemplated is a mirror of my consciousness and its evolution."[16] Just as the external world of mountains and cities is made up of layers and layers of time, geological and historical, Barfield demonstrates how the language we inhabit—as fish inhabit water—is made up of different strata of consciousness. (And just as fish do not notice the water they move through, we, Barfield suggests, are hardly aware of the meaning of the language we use.) Jurij Moskvitin discovered something similar about our mechanisms of perception and the relationship of consciousness to the external world as a whole. As his work is practically unknown outside of a few readers, I discuss some of its basic themes at great length, particularly his, to my mind, convincing arguments against the intelligibility of any attempt to explain consciousness in purely materialist, scientific-rationalist terms. One of the few thinkers to appreciate Moskvitin's insights was Colin Wilson, who has grappled with the problem of consciousness for nearly half a century. In his ideas about "Faculty X" and our ability to escape the limits of the present and experience "other times and places," we get a glimpse of some of the powers, now dormant but possibly soon active, latent in the human mind.

Part Five, "The Presence of Origin," focuses solely on the work of one thinker, the cultural philosopher Jean Gebser. Although in recent years Gebser's work has gained a wider readership, he is still relatively unknown to many people interested in ideas about the evolution and history of consciousness. Gebser is best known to English-speaking readers for his mammoth work *The Ever-Present Origin,* first published in 1949 but translated into English only as recently as 1984. It is a demanding, daunting work that I discuss at some length, first because his ideas deserve to be better known; and second because they seem to me to be perhaps the most thoroughly argued and impressively documented case available for the evolution—or, as Gebser calls it, the "mutation"—of consciousness. (This is not to say that I think Gebser's account is "right," only that he presents highly persuasive and convincing evidence.) Throughout the book, where it seemed helpful, I have included some brief biographical material; in Gebser's case I have done so more than in others. His life is an inspiring and exciting embodiment of an idea too often ignored in our less naïve (read cynical) times: that philosophy is to be lived, not merely thought. That many more of us may be faced with this ennobling obligation, and how we may fulfill it, is the subject of the concluding words.

—

It may not be redundant to remark that the ideas about consciousness I discuss in this book are only a fraction of the many that have been thought, and whose implications and possibilities enrich our lives. Were I to include *everything* argued about consciousness, even beginning as recently as the consciousness explosion of the 1960s and '70s, this book would become either an encyclopedia or a lengthy but shallow survey. As with most things, personal preference and interest has guided me. The virtue of this is, I hope, a certain depth and passion; the vice is exclusion. The secret history of consciousness presented here is, of course, only one. There are many others. I look forward to as many as possible being brought into the light of day.

PART ONE

The Search for Cosmic Consciousness

CHAPTER ONE

R. M. Bucke and the Future of Humanity

In 1901 a book with the intriguing title *Cosmic Consciousness* appeared in Philadelphia in a limited edition of five hundred copies. Its author was Richard Maurice Bucke, a doctor and former medical superintendent of the asylum for the insane in London, Ontario. Although at first the book made little impression on the reading public, interest in its remarkable claim—that humanity was slowly evolving into a new, higher level of consciousness—attracted attention, and soon its readers included the psychologist William James and the esoteric philosopher P. D. Ouspensky. More than half a century later it had acquired even greater popularity. By 1966 *Cosmic Consciousness* had gone through twenty-six printings and had become, along with Hermann Hesse's *Siddhartha*, Aldous Huxley's *The Doors of Perception,* and J. R. R. Tolkien's *The Lord of The Rings,* part of the canon of works firing the imagination of a burgeoning counterculture.

Bucke's background was not what one might expect for the head of an insane asylum, nor, for that matter, the author of a book arguing that the human race was moving into a higher state of consciousness. Born in 1837 to English parents who soon after emigrated to Canada, Bucke left home at seventeen after the death of his stepmother and spent the next four years piling up enough adventures for a dozen enterprising young men. Crossing the bor-

der into the United States, he travelled across the country, working
at a variety of jobs. He was a gardener in Ohio, a railway man in
Cincinnati, and a deckhand on a Mississippi steamboat, before
finally signing on as a driver on a wagon train heading across the
Great Plains to the edge of Mormon territory, today part of
Nevada. The journey to Salt Lake took five months, and in the
1850s it was a dangerous business. For the last twelve hundred
miles there were no white settlements and the Indians, resentful of
the white man's incursion, were not particularly friendly. After this
Bucke crossed the Rockies, was attacked by Shoshone Indians, and
nearly starved, living for a time on flour and hot water. He then settled down as a gold miner. During an attempt to cross a mountain
chain in winter, his partner died, and Bucke himself was about to
follow when he was discovered by a mining party. Both of his feet
were frozen, and all of one foot and part of the other had to be
amputated. Bucke was twenty-one, and for the rest of his life only
occasionally would he be free from physical pain.

Yet Bucke had the optimism and determination associated with
the expanding United States in the nineteenth century, and this
same optimism led him to his master thought, the notion that
humanity was evolving into a higher form of consciousness. An
inheritance paid his way through medical school and postgraduate
work in England, France, and Germany. In 1864 he settled in
Canada and set up shop. By 1876 he had been appointed superintendent of an asylum for the insane in Hamilton, Ontario; the next
year he moved to London. He was appointed professor of mental
and nervous diseases at Western University. In 1888 he was elected
president of the Psychological Section of the British Medical
Association, and in 1890 was given a similar honor by the
American Medico-Psychological Association. By the end of the
century, Bucke was considered one of North America's foremost
"alienists"—the term used for doctors of the mind before "psychologist" came into use—and this standing among professionals
helped his extraordinary ideas about human evolution gain a hearing they might otherwise have lacked.[1]

Bucke's tenacity and application give the impression of a highly practical man, down-to-earth with an eye to business, suggesting

that the picture of him as a philosopher of a radical shift in human consciousness is somewhat incongruous—although the portrait of him in *Cosmic Consciousness,* with his flowing white beard and longish hair, does suggest the air of a prophet. Yet there was another side to Bucke. Growing up on a backwoods Canadian farm, he developed a sensitivity to nature and experienced a powerful curiosity about the basic mysteries of life. At about the age of ten he felt a strange ecstasy and longing about the notion of death, and was eager to discover if he could find answers to questions about "the beyond." Although for the most part uneducated at this time, he was a voracious reader of poetry and in later life was known to have memorized whole volumes of it. Bucke's father, a graduate of Trinity College, Cambridge, had himself mastered seven languages, and when he moved the young family from England to the wilds of Ontario he brought a library of some thousand volumes. Bucke grew up in an atmosphere of rugged hands-on experience softened by literary discussion; more than likely it was this that prepared him for his later work as a visionary and prophet.

The first sign of that vocation appeared in 1867 when a visitor to Bucke's home quoted some of the poetry of Walt Whitman. The effect was immediate. We do not know which of Whitman's expansive verses was recited, but Bucke was bowled over by it and from that moment considered himself the poet's disciple. The encounter prompted a wide reading in history, philosophy, and science, and for years afterward Bucke suffered "an unappeasable hunger for enlightenment on the basic problems."[2] Ten years later Bucke met Whitman and became a central figure in the circle around the poet, even treating him in his medical capacity, successfully, as Whitman later claimed the doctor saved his life. One of the volumes of poetry Bucke was reported to know by heart was Whitman's *Leaves of Grass,* a remarkable achievement by any standard.

Five years after his introduction to Whitman's poetry, Bucke had the experience that set him on his life's work and contributed to the language a phrase most people use without the slightest idea of its origin. In his thirty-fifth year, during a visit to England, he had his illumination. After an evening spent reading Wordsworth, Shelly, Keats, Browning, and, of course, Whitman, Bucke left his friends around midnight and settled into his hansom cab for the drive to his hotel. The night of poetry had left him calm, and his mind was full of the ideas and feelings stimulated by the evening's discussion. He felt himself in a state of "quiet, almost passive, enjoyment."

And then it happened:

All at once, without warning of any kind, he [Bucke wrote his account in the third person] found himself wrapped around, as it were, by a flame-colored cloud. For an instant he thought of fire—some sudden conflagration in the great city. The next instant he knew that the light was within himself.

Directly after there came upon him a sense of exaltation, of immense joyousness, accompanied or immediately followed by an intellectual illumination quite impossible to describe. Into his brain streamed one momentary lightning-flash of the Brahmic Splendour which ever since lightened his life. Upon his heart fell one drop of the Brahmic Bliss, leaving thenceforward for always an aftertaste of Heaven. Among other things he did not come to believe, he saw and knew that the Cosmos is not dead matter but a living Presence, that the soul of man is immortal, that the universe is so built and ordered that without peradventure all things work together for the good of each and all, that the foundation principle of the world is what we call love and that the happiness of every one is in the long run absolutely certain.

"The supreme occurrence of that night," Bucke said, was his "initiation to the new and higher order of ideas." Within the few seconds that his illumination lasted, as his cab carried him across a sleeping London, Bucke learned more than "in previous months or years of study," as well as "much that no study could ever have taught."[3]

Nowadays Bucke's experience would be chalked up to the brain's reported "God spot" or, less generously, to temporal lobe epilepsy.[4] For Bucke it was the first glimpse of the future of humanity.

We can assume Bucke discussed his experience among friends, certainly among the people who gathered around his mentor Whitman. But more than twenty years passed before he presented a version of it to his peers. In May of 1894, Bucke read a paper on "Cosmic Consciousness" at the annual meeting of the American Medico-Psychological Association. Later, in August of that year, in his presidential address to the British Medical Association in Montreal, he elaborated on his theme that a new consciousness had appeared sporadically throughout human history, and that its characteristics were becoming increasingly more common. These were signs, he believed, of a mental evolution that would eventually embrace all of humankind, transforming the species and lifting it onto an almost unimaginably higher plane. "Cosmic consciousness," Bucke believed, would one day be as common as our own self-consciousness is now. And just as the appearance of self-consciousness raised humankind out of the level of the brutes, so too cosmic consciousness would raise us incomparably higher than the human. Just how high cosmic consciousness would lift the race would be made clear seven years later, when the fruit of Bucke's extensive labors was made available to a reading public taking its first steps into the twentieth century.

Although the phrase "cosmic consciousness"—or its shortened version, just plain "cosmic"—would become an all-purpose password for members of the Age of Aquarius, it is interesting and salutary to see what exactly its originator meant by it. Bucke's account of his "illumination" was to become a classic example of what was later called "higher consciousness." Within it were the basic themes that would recur throughout a century-long discussion of the "evolution of consciousness": the conviction that "all is good," that the universe is not dead but living, that the human soul is immortal, and, most importantly, that the source of the illumination was not outside Bucke, but came from within himself. His vision of a living universe was brief, but it had lasting effect. Among other things, it later helped reconcile him to the early death of his son. In the dedication of *Cosmic Consciousness,* Bucke wrote, "Through the experiences which underlie this volume I have been taught, that in spite of death and the grave . . . you are not dead and not really absent, but alive and well and not far from me this moment."

The immortality of the human soul, though without doubt high on the list, was not the only thing Bucke's first taste of cosmic consciousness convinced him of. He saw the development of consciousness as a gradual ascent from simple sense perception to a broader vision encompassing the entire cosmos. From the bottom up there was, Bucke argued, a kind of inverted pyramid, beginning with the simplest awareness and broadening with each higher level. There is first what he called the perceptual mind, open only to sense impressions, at the level of what he called the lower animals. Next comes the "receptual mind" of the higher animals, resulting in simple awareness, the kind of consciousness a dog or cat may enjoy. Above this is the conceptual mind, which only human beings have and which produces our unique sense of *self*-consciousness, our awareness of ourselves, our egos, as separate entities in the world. One of the products of this form of consciousness is language, and, in a phrase that presages a discussion of language and consciousness later in his book, Bucke remarks, "Language is the objective of which self-consciousness is the subjective."[5] Possession of language, he argues, opens an unbridgeable chasm between ourselves and the animals, and a similar chasm separates the few who now experience flashes of the new consciousness from ordinary human beings.

Cosmic consciousness, the next level on the pyramid of awareness, "is a higher form of consciousness than that possessed by the ordinary man." It is a "consciousness of the cosmos . . . of the life and order of the universe," which includes an "intellectual enlightenment or illumination which alone would place the individual on a new plane of existence—would make him almost a member of a new species." And although its appearance then was still a rarity—indeed, in the last three thousand years Bucke was certain of only fourteen bona fide cases, although there were many more of what he termed "imperfect" examples—"our descendants will

sooner or later reach, as a race, the conditions of cosmic consciousness, just as, long ago, our ancestors passed from simple to
self-consciousness."[6]

The result of this, Bucke believed, would be an unalloyed
utopia, a veritable heaven on earth. Bucke's visionary streak was
not limited to his interest in mystical awareness. Along with cosmic
consciousness, he predicted other revolutionary changes for the
new century. "The immediate future of our race is indescribably
hopeful."[7] The two lesser radical shifts in human existence that
would accompany cosmic consciousness might not match it for
scope and effect, but they would nevertheless be tremendous. The
establishment of aerial navigation (just getting off the ground with
the Wright Brothers) would abolish national boundaries and make
large cities obsolete, allowing many to make their homes in the
mountains and on the seashore. And people would be able to enjoy
the benefits of the conquest of the air because the twentieth century, in Bucke's eyes, would see the rise and triumph of socialism.
Gone would be crushing toil, and the inequitable distribution of
wealth, and in its place would come a new economic prosperity and
social order. Such were the material conditions in which the rise of
cosmic consciousness would take place.

Aware of Bucke's millenarian dream, and of the realities of the
last century and of our own, we may feel it almost a blessing that
he did not live to see what the future actually had in store. His
utopianism was not unusual at the end of the nineteenth century.
At the tail end of the long innings of progress, the mixture of science and visionary prophecy that imbued the novels of Jules Verne
(soon to find a new voice in H. G. Wells) was taken up by writers
not only of fiction, but of sociology, science, and politics. The
beginning of the twentieth century saw a fantastic smorgasbord of
new ideas, an exciting, optimistic blend of radical politics, social
reform, occult beliefs, and evolutionary vision, which in the years
before World War One produced a heady, effervescent atmosphere in which almost anything seemed possible. Bucke's own
book was one of many arguing, in one way or another, that
humanity was maturing and was now able to take responsibility
for its own destiny.

Such sentiments were welcomed. In the last years of the nineteenth century, many were concerned about the deleterious atmosphere of the decadent *fin de siècle*. A decade before Bucke, the doctor, journalist, and later Zionist Max Nordau had risen to worldwide fame through his book *Degeneration* (1892), which argued
that the spirit of the age was rife with exhaustion, hysteria, ener-
vation, and narcissism, evident in work of obvious "degenerates"
like Nietzsche, Ibsen, Wagner, and Baudelaire. Earlier in the century, the book's dedicatee, Professor Cesare Lombroso (later an advocate of what would come to be called parapsychology), had
advanced a theory about the "criminal type" and its physiognomy,
and this Nordau applied to the art and literature of his time. A long
section of his book is dedicated to mysticism, and he would have
surely classified Bucke's experience as evidence of degeneration.
His attack was shallow and hysterical and prompted return fire,
most effectively in Bernard Shaw's brilliant essay "The Sanity of
Art" (1895). Yet concern about the "devolution" of the white race
and the threat to it from foreign influence, whether blacks or the
"Yellow Peril," informed much cultured discussion, and the attraction of a science of human betterment, in the form of eugenics, was
strong. Bucke's book, with its emphasis on an inspiring, optimistic
future, was embraced by a generation who felt that the cosmos
itself was pulling humankind up to a higher level of achievement.

Yet the new dawn was brief. By 1914 and the start of the Great
War, the belief in progress, advance, and the perfectibility of
humankind that had fueled the Enlightenment as well as more
eccentric doctrines like Madame Blavatsky's Theosophy, had col-
lapsed. Bucke himself died less than a year after the publication of
his book. In February 1902, after an evening discussing the theory
that Francis Bacon was the real author of the Shakespeare plays—
Bucke firmly believed he was—he slipped on some ice while gazing
at the night sky from his veranda; he fell, hitting his head violent-
ly against a pillar, and died almost immediately. The stars that
evening were exceptionally bright in the cold winter air, and one
hopes it was not a momentary flash of cosmic consciousness that
made Bucke lose his footing.

The argument of *Cosmic Consciousness* is simple. Having himself experienced the reality of this new form of consciousness, Bucke looked back through history to see if there were other examples of it. As already mentioned, he could, he believed, argue successfully that there had been at least fourteen cases of it, ranging from ancient times to his present, with several other near hits, as it were. Many of the names he includes in his list will be repeated in similar accounts of a kind of hereditary "chain of illumination," stretching down the centuries. Gautama the Buddha, Jesus, St. Paul, the Neoplatonic philosopher Plotinus, Jacob Boehme, William Blake, and, of course, Walt Whitman are all clear examples of full and complete cosmic consciousness. Some readers may not agree with Bucke's choices. Why, for example, is the novelist Honoré de Balzac a case of complete cosmic consciousness, while Emmanuel Swedenborg is classed with the "Lesser, Imperfect and Doubtful Instances"? Some of Bucke's other choices also seem questionable, as do some of his remarks about "primitive" and "backward" races, and his assumption that the Aryans form a recognized "higher type." But these shouldn't prevent us from grasping his basic thought that a different kind of consciousness has appeared in human beings throughout history, nor stop us from appreciating his efforts to provide us with examples. The term "Aryan" was around long before the Nazis appropriated it, and none of Bucke's examples of bearers of the new consciousness would have appealed to them as incidences of the "master race."

Although cosmic consciousness denies that life is a chance process occurring in a meaningless universe, Bucke's approach is basically Darwinian. A kind of survival of the fittest provides the physical and mental changes forming the foundation of cosmic consciousness. Just as the purely perceptual mind evolved into the simple consciousness of animals, and that consciousness was transformed into our self-consciousness, so our self-consciousness is now slowly evolving into a wider, more intuitive awareness. The trajectory is that of the simplest sensory awareness slowly widening to include the entire cosmos. Bucke argues that as we look back in history the instances of cosmic consciousness seem rare, but in more recent years have increased, and will continue to increase, just as our own self-consciousness was once the property of a few and is now the standard by which we gauge normality. He points to the development of the color sense and our appreciation of music as other examples of faculties once absent from humankind that we now take for granted. In an example that will be often repeated by other students of the evolution of consciousness, Bucke points out that the ancient Greeks knew of only three colors, that in both Homer and the Bible there is no mention of the blue sky, and that a similar lack of color words can be found in ancient texts like the Rig Veda and Zend Avesta. A comparable situation exists with the appreciation of fragrance.[8] Bucke's basic scheme is that the history of consciousness in the race is paralleled by that in the individual, so that faculties like color sense and musical sense appear in the individual at an age roughly analogous to their appearance in humanity as a whole. A chart on the "Psychogenesis of Man—Illustrated by a Few Faculties" provides the parallels.

We may find the chart simplistic and not entirely accurate. The idea that the "musical sense" appears at the age of eighteen seems unsubstantiated by the large number of child prodigies, and in my own experience my son had perfect pitch at age two and could carry several tunes. But the basic idea is clear. Cosmic consciousness is not a supernatural power bestowed on the elect few by the gods. It is a natural outgrowth of the evolutionary process. The individuals who could first discern brighter shades and finer hues must have stood out as freaks among their fellows, who saw the world in a drab monotone. As it is now, the individuals who today experience cosmic consciousness are a "family sprung from, living among, but scarcely forming a part of ordinary humanity, whose members are spread abroad throughout the advanced races of mankind."[9] The idea that a new race of human beings exists today side by side with the old humanity is one that we will find in other writers as the twentieth century progresses.

In individuals, the onset of cosmic consciousness occurs around the thirty-fifth year, an age that Dante, and later thinkers like C. G. Jung and Rudolf Steiner, thought particularly important. Other factors are necessary, and in spelling them out Bucke's rhetoric is, we must admit, flowery and sometimes off-putting.

Allowances must be made for the "copper-plated" style of the book as a whole, but Bucke's talk of the necessity for an "exalted human personality," "the singular perfection of the intellectual and moral faculties," and an "exceptional physique—exceptional beauty of the build and carriage, exceptionally handsome features, exceptional health, exceptional sweetness of temper, exceptional magnetism," strike us as the worst kind of spiritual snobbery.[10] Likewise his emphasis on the "necessary heredity." Bucke's earnestness is naïve and innocent of racial prejudice and stems, I think, from a simplistic association between physical health and spiritual advancement that is still common to much New Age thinking. (It is also merely the other side of the coin of Lombroso's belief that the "criminal mentality" could be detected by a recognizably "criminal physique.") Bucke often gives the impression that a likely candidate for cosmic consciousness would be a God-fearing, golden-haired bodybuilder, and in the face of such tedious perfection one often comes away hungry for a degenerate or two to liven things up.

Yet Bucke had certainly tapped into a powerful theme at the right time. Interest in what we call altered states of consciousness had indeed been strong throughout the nineteenth century. At the time Bucke published his book, one of the most popular writers on the subject was Edward Carpenter, who appears in Bucke's book as the most recent example of a full instance of cosmic consciousness. Carpenter was an interesting figure; influential in his own time, he is little read and less discussed today. He is a perfect example of the stimulating blend of progressive ideas, evolutionary vision, mystical doctrines, and radical lifestyle that characterized the pre–World War I version of the New Age. The author of Whitmanesque verse—Bucke points to his long poem "Towards Democracy" as a work in which "the Cosmic Sense speaks"—Carpenter was also homosexual and an outspoken advocate of what we would call today "gay rights" (Carpenter's own term was "homogenic love").[11] In From Adam's Peak to Elephanta (1892), an account of his travels in India, Carpenter gives an extended description of what he calls "consciousness without thought." He speaks of this "higher form of consciousness" in terms similar to Bucke's. If it does exist, Carpenter suggests, it is evolving and will evolve slowly over many generations, and its appearance will be just as miraculous as that of the first incidences of simple sense awareness and self-consciousness. In this new consciousness, the familiar difference between subject and object falls away, and Carpenter relates it to several themes that will be picked up later by the Russian philosopher P. D. Ouspensky, such as the "fourth dimension." And in another work he speaks of the new consciousness enabling him to see "the interior surfaces of all objects and things and persons." In this new consciousness he *is* the objects he perceives, and he perceives them in a new sense that is in effect all the senses combined into one, an intimation of the "intuition" that soon would be associated with the work of the philosopher Henri Bergson.[12]

Carpenter's speculations on "higher consciousness" were not a rarity. Although Bucke would probably have rejected them from his canon, accounts of drug use and their effect on consciousness became a popular literary form in the nineteenth century, most notably in Thomas De Quincey's classic *Confessions of an English Opium Eater* (1821).[13]

De Quincey's narrative of opium addiction, its visionary pleasures and hellish pains, became a much emulated investigation of the unfrequented avenues of human consciousness. In 1846 the French poet and novelist Théophile Gautier published an account of his experiences as a member of the celebrated Club des Haschischins, inaugurated in Paris by the physician and psychiatrist Jacques-Joseph Moreau de Tours. Modeled on a romantic version of the medieval Islamic sect known as the Assassins, who were believed to have used hashish in their initiation ceremonies, the club included among its members Charles Baudelaire, Gérard de Nerval, Alexandre Dumas, and Honoré de Balzac. (As Balzac was one of Bucke's fourteen "perfect" cases of cosmic consciousness, it is interesting to speculate whether Bucke was aware of Balzac's interest in hashish, as it would surely cast doubt on his possession of a singularly perfect moral faculty and exceptional health.) Most of the people involved in the club produced accounts of the resinous herb's effects, Baudelaire's classic essay *Artificial Paradise* (1851–60) rising above the rest for precision and scientific objectivity.

In 1857 a twenty-one-year-old poet and essayist from Poughkeepsie, New York, named Fitz Hugh Ludlow published, to much acclaim, his unabashedly derivative *The Hasheesh Eater, being Passages from the Life of a Pythagorean*. Ludlow was clearly aiming at becoming the New World's De Quincey, to whose opium-inspired phantasies he added philosophical insights originating in Emerson but enlarged by the effects of a large dose of the drug. And hashish was not the only substance offering metaphysical illumination. In 1874 Benjamin Paul Blood, a New York farmer, bodybuilder, and calculating prodigy privately published a highly eccentric account of his experiences under the gas nitrous oxide. In "The Anesthetic Revelation and the Gist of Philosophy," Blood claimed that inhalation of laughing gas revealed to him "the Open Secret . . . the primordial, Adamic surprise of Life." The philosophical implications of breathing nitrous oxide were first discovered by Sir Humphrey Davy in 1799 when, after inhaling four quarts of the gas, he experienced a sense of cosmic expansion, later distilled into the gnomic revelation, "Nothing exists but thoughts!" But since then, the gas's powers as a spiritual agent had been eclipsed by its efficacy in obviating the pain of a still-rudimentary dental procedure. Blood's vision returned the gas to its higher calling, and made the history of metaphysics obsolete, as it provided an immediate, intense, and unmistakable insight into the true nature of reality.

Blood sent copies of his pamphlet to as many influential people as he could think of, and although its message did not reach the world at large, it did fall into some appreciative hands. Some of these belonged to members of the newly formed Society for Psychical Research in England, who saw in Blood's ten-year self-experiment with nitrous oxide a possible means of exploring unusual states of consciousness with some scientific rigor. Another individual also interested in psychic phenomena and unusual states of being came upon Blood's revelation in a version of his account published in *The Atlantic Monthly*. The reader was so impressed by Blood's experience that he included an excerpt from "The Anesthetic Revelation" in his major work, which also discussed the remarkable theory of Dr. R. M. Bucke. The work was entitled *The Varieties of Religious Experience* (1902), and its author was William James.

CHAPTER TWO

William James and the Anesthetic Revelation

William James was a philosopher, psychologist, and scientist who appreciated the value of modern scientific method but deplored its tendency to declare types of experience and phenomena that eluded its methodology "unreal"—a prejudice that continues today in the work of "eliminative materialist" philosophers like Daniel Dennett. The types of experience and phenomena James had in mind could be roughly characterized as "mystical" or "supernatural." He was possessed of a singularly curious mind, and was as interested in the mechanisms of habit-formation as he was in the possibility of life after death. One of his core fascinations was the untapped potentiality of life. In an essay called "The Energies of Men" he examined the phenomenon of "second wind" and came to the conclusion that "we live subject to arrest by degrees of fatigue which we have come only from habit to obey." James argued that many people may soon learn to live at a higher level of energy and enthusiasm. Mind cures, positive thinking, hypnosis, telepathy: all found a curious investigator in James. Along with his friend and fellow philosopher Henri Bergson, James was committed to a serious investigation of psychic phenomena, and he was anxious to salvage convincing evidence of life's deeper meaning from a scientistic frame of mind determined to reduce it to the effect of molecules in motion. For science to be a true science and not a mere prejudice, it had to encompass *all* experience within its domain, not only what accommodated its methods.

James had a more-than-philosophical interest in limiting a reductive science's encroachment on religious territory, which, among other things, allowed for the possibility of free will. During a severe bout of depression, he gained control over his life and renewed his motivation through accepting the possibility of free will, his first act of which was to believe in it. Success in this endeavor prompted his notion of the "will to believe," which argued that the effectiveness of a belief is a good gauge of its value as "truth"—the essence of his "pragmatism." The core idea behind James's classic work *The Varieties of Religious Experience* (1902) is that "experience" is a more fruitful and solid foundation for religious belief than metaphysical systems or theological arguments, and that the experiences of visionaries and mystics, however irrational they may appear, cannot be dismissed in any account of reality purporting to be "total."

James recognized the need to develop a language that could accommodate the seemingly mutually exclusive claims of materialist science and immaterial religion. One philosopher, he knew, had done just that—the German arch-metaphysician Georg Friedrich Hegel, whose influence stretched across the nineteenth century and whose central work, *The Phenomenology of Spirit* (1807), is a massive narrative depicting the evolution of consciousness. Yet James's basic empirical bent prevented him from accepting Hegel's grand rationalism, and he was also unable to accept the Hegelian juggling act of maintaining contradictory assertions simultaneously. Yet this is precisely what he encountered in Blood's anesthetic revelation, which is rife with contradictory statements that in any normal discourse would cancel each other out. In Blood's vision, however, they act as a kind of propositional ladder, reaching to a higher, encompassing, all-inclusive reconciliation.

Never the armchair traveller, James decided to find out for himself. He made arrangements to inhale the gas. His account of his nitrous oxide experience is one of the classic mystical texts of modern times. It is also one of the funniest. One of its first benefits was to win him over to the Hegelian point of view. In his essay "On Some Hegelisms," James remarks, "I have made some observations of the effects of nitrous-oxide-gas-intoxication which have made me understand better than ever before both the strengths and the weakness of Hegel's philosophy. I strongly urge others to repeat the experiment."[1] The rest of the short essay is an account of how under the effects of the gas James experienced the reconciliation of opposites that Blood described as the essence of the anesthetic revelation. "I have sheet after sheet of phrases dictated or written during the intoxication," James wrote, "which to the sober reader seem meaningless drivel, but which at the moment of transcribing were fused in the fire of infinite rationality. God and devil, good and evil, life and death, I and thou, sober and drunk, matter and form, black and white, quality and quantity, shiver of ecstasy and shudder of horror, vomiting and swallowing, inspiration and expiration, fate and reason, great and small, extent and intent, joke and earnest, tragic and comic, and fifty other contrasts figure in these pages in the same monotonous way." A sample of his notes gives an idea of what went racing through his mind as the gas took effect:

> *What's a mistake but a kind of take?*
> *What's nausea but a kind of—ausea?*[2]

To the logical mind, such musings seem errant nonsense, and such was James's own feeling when he read back his notes in cold sobriety. What had seemed to him indubitable insights while under the gas were now mute, senseless maunderings. To a more pedestrian mind, this would have been enough to suggest that the sense of utter incontrovertible significance that accompanied inhaling nitrous oxide was merely an enlarged version of the sentimentality that washes over every drunkard. But James could not deny that what he saw during his own anesthetic revelation was in some important way true. Indeed, he knew himself that the "sway of alcohol over mankind is unquestionably due to its power to stimulate the mystical faculties,"[3] that it was the great exciter of the "Yea-saying" spirit, the emotional reconciliation that was the first stage of the stratospheric flights of logical leapfrog to which nitrous oxide had introduced him. "The keynote of the experience," he wrote, "is the tremendously exciting sense of an intense metaphysical illumination. Truth lies open to the view in depth beneath depth of almost blinding evidence."[4]

Ordinary consciousness, the logical, rational world that we take for granted and accept as a fundamental reality, was, James discovered, really only a provincial backwater. Through a slight adjustment, a bit of fine-tuning, a completely "other" kind of consciousness, claiming equal if not *more* reality, could be experienced. The import of his intoxicated jottings may have later faded, but one conclusion seemed inescapable. As he wrote in what became an often-quoted precedent for future explorers of the hidden mind, his nitrous oxide experiments convinced him that "our normal waking consciousness, rational consciousness as we call it, is but one special type of consciousness, whilst all about it, parted from it by the flimsiest of screens, there lie potential forms of consciousness entirely different." To the tough-minded reductionist scientists who wished to reduce consciousness to a negligible by-product—or, worse still, deny it altogether—James retorted, "No account of the universe in its totality can be final which leaves these other forms of consciousness quite disregarded."[5] The experience convinced James that the conscious person is continuous with a wider, fuller "self" of which one is usually unaware, but which is made present in moments of crisis, mystical illumination, or religious conversion; moreover, that "wider self" is itself conterminous with a "something more" that is active in the universe at large.

The similarity of James's thought to Bucke's conclusions is clear. What James brought to the discussion was an inkling of *why* "cosmic consciousness" is rare. He argued that one function of consciousness is to carve out of the vast sensory environment— what he called the "blooming, buzzing confusion"—a manageable, edited-down version. Only a limited amount of information reaches our conscious awareness, and for the very good reason that the majority of it is irrelevant. In a fashion similar to the philosopher Edmund Husserl, who argued that consciousness is "intentional," James argued that consciousness selects from the world at large elements that are of particular value and interest to it. Our minds are not, as the René Descartes believed, a mirror reflecting the external world, nor are they, as John Locke argued, "blank slates" passively written on by experience. Consciousness instead actively *chooses* from the mass of sensory information what it will attend to, rather as a radio receiver locks onto a particular broadcast and ignores the dozens of other signals washing over it. We need only observe the development of a child's awareness of the world to see that James is right. We do not come into the world with an interior mirror that accurately "reflects" the world outside. Our grasp of things is built up gradually, with much practice, and we can all remember when the world we now maneuver through with ease was once a frightening, bewildering mystery. One of the consequences of acquiring a mastery of our environment is that in the process of editing down the barrage of information, we also lose the feeling of the freshness of things that we associate with childhood. As the novelist John Cowper Powys wrote, "How magically sagacious is childhood in its power of arriving at boundless effects through insignificant means . . . how often the whole course of one's subsequent history becomes an attempt to regain this sorcery. . . . It is a criminal blunder of our maturer years that we so tamely, without frantic and habitual struggles to retain it, allow the ecstasy of the unbounded to slip out of our lives."[6] Hence the romantic nostalgia for lost youth.

CHAPTER THREE

Henri Bergson and the Élan Vital

The notion that the function of the brain is essentially eliminative is also associated with James's friend, the French philosopher Henri Bergson. Bergson himself was deeply interested in questions of consciousness, evolution, and altered states of being, and was for a time president of the Society for Psychical Research. It says much for the adventurous spirit of the early twentieth century that a public figure of Bergson's stature—he was a world-renowned philosopher and a national hero in his home country—could devote himself to pursuits our more narrow and intolerant climate considers laughable. Bergson wrote on dreams, "phantasms of the living," and in his last book, *Two Sources of Morality and Religion* (1932), capped off a career arguing for a "creative evolution" by stating bluntly that the universe was a "machine for making gods."

Bergson came to prominence with his first book, *Time and Free Will* (1889), in which he argued against the "spatialization" or "quantification" of time as it was perceived in Newtonian science and in our workaday "clock time." This kind of time, measured in discrete instants, is a product of the intellect, and for Bergson it falsified time's true nature, which, he argued, is a seamless, continuous process. Against spatialized clock time, Bergson wrote of what he called "duration," our immediate awareness of inner states. This immediate inner awareness, which we all experience, was, he believed, evidence of life's uniqueness. Psychological "facts," Bergson argued, are qualitatively different from physical ones, and hence consciousness is an irreducible given, not amenable to scientific determinism.

Like James, Bergson was concerned about the shallow scientistic vision that either treated inner realities as by-products of material processes or denied them altogether. He was not, however, antiscience; like James, he absorbed the most recent scientific developments and incorporated them into his work, which gave it a distinct character of grappling with concrete questions and problems, unlike the abstract Idealism left over from Hegel's heyday. Again like James, Bergson was a "philosopher of life," both in his absorption in biological questions and in his belief that for philosophy to have value, it must have some real effect upon our actions. In *Matter and Memory* (1896), Bergson took on the mind-body problem, arguing against the idea of "psychophysiological parallelism," which maintained that every psychological fact is determined by the physical fact that accompanies it. For instance, he argued that aphasia was not loss of memory per se caused by a physical lesion in the brain, but rather that the organic damage simply prevented the memory, an immaterial "fact," from being *expressed*, much as a broken television set prevents a program from being seen but does not affect the program itself. Hence Bergson came to the conclusion that consciousness *uses* the brain and is not, as contemporary philosophers of mind like John Searle assert, produced by it. It was insights such as this that drew Bergson into an interest in the paranormal and the "night side of nature."

Bergson developed his radical ideas about the role of consciousness and the brain into a complete evolutionary theory, presented in *Creative Evolution* (1907), his most widely known work. He accepted Darwin's by-then triumphant idea that the organic forms of the present had evolved out of much earlier forms over long periods of time. But like many other thinkers, Bergson was unsympathetic to the strict determinist interpretation of evolution that had gained scientific support and popular credence.[1] In its place he offered a vision of a creative impulse, the *élan vital* or life force, penetrating matter and driving evolution to higher forms of complexity and freedom. Bergson did, however, borrow one idea from Darwin's later interpreters. For Darwin, evolution proceeds through chance mutations that prove successful in the struggle to survive; such beneficial adaptations give an organism an advantage over its competitors. For Darwin's followers, the mind itself was just such an adaptation and evolved as a useful tool for dealing with the demands of the environment. The intellect, then, was a strictly *practical* device, and its use was solely limited to dealing with the necessities of staying alive. One imminently useful way of doing this was to "carve" out of the seamless flow of experience, seemingly solid, discrete, and stable objects occupying an extended space. It would be most helpful in the struggle for survival to recognize out of the "blooming, buzzing confusion" the tiger about to pounce on you, or the antelope you wish to eat. The difference between this kind of consciousness and a cosmic consciousness, open to the influx of the whole, is evident. The brain's function then, for Bergson, was to act as a kind of "reducing valve," limiting the amount of "reality" entering consciousness.[2] As he wrote in 1911, "The brain is the organ of attention to life," and the part it plays is that of "shutting out from consciousness all that is of no practical interest to us."[3]

Cosmic consciousness, then, can be seen as a perception of the world not limited by or filtered through the brain. And as most of us are compelled to "deal with" the world most of the time, it is clear why incidences of cosmic consciousness are rare. Yet one drawback to the brain's highly efficient ability to focus on necessities is that it "falsifies" reality, which, as Bergson earlier argued, is in truth a continuous flow of experience. The mind constantly takes snapshots, as it were, of reality, which enables it to orient itself amidst the flux. The problem is that science, which takes the most comprehensive snapshots, makes the mistake of confusing the photographs with reality itself.

We would, it seems, be left in a situation in which we are highly successful at dealing with the world, at the cost of losing contact with its reality. But, as Bergson argued in his essay "An Introduction to Metaphysics" (1903), the mind has another means of "knowing," aside from the rational intellect. This, he argued, was intuition. Just as we have an immediate, irreducible awareness of our own inner states, through intuition we have access to the "inside" of the world. And that inside, Bergson argued, was the *élan vital*. Through drawing back from our habitual gesture of "dealing" with the world, we can, as Edward Carpenter experienced, discover a kind of consciousness in which subject and object—we and the world—are "one." This consciousness, Bergson argues is not necessarily associated with the brain. He argues that we perceive "virtually" much more than what actually reaches our conscious awareness. This would make sense, since that awareness is subject to the highly efficient editing procedures of the brain, which limits the amount of input coming to it through the senses. The whole past, for example, Bergson believed "still exists, . . . is still present to consciousness in such a manner that, to have the revelation of it, consciousness has no need to go out of itself. . . . It has but to remove an obstacle, to withdraw a veil."[4] Such insights are the foundation for Marcel Proust's immense novel *Remembrance of Things Past,* perhaps the most determined effort to put Bergson's ideas into practice. The novel begins with the narrator "regaining" the past through the chance taste of a little cake dipped in tea. Suddenly he is flooded with a rich torrent of sensation, the memories of his childhood spent in the town of Combray. The "virtual" perceptions, held in check by the brain's reducing valve and now released by the memory that he had tasted such a cake in his youth, come washing over him, filling him with the vivid awareness of, in Colin Wilson's phrase, "other times and places." The narrator is swept into a version of Bucke's cosmic consciousness, aware that the stubborn, implacable, poker face of the present is a lie, and that his consciousness has access to a much wider range of time than he believed. This notion, of the perpetual "presence of the past," has wider implications for the evolution of consciousness, as we will see in our discussions of Madame Blavatsky, Rudolf Steiner, and, later, Colin Wilson's own work.

For Bergson, "the mental activity of man overflows his cerebral activity." A "close examination of the life of the mind," he argues, shows that "there is infinitely more in a human consciousness than in a corresponding brain."[5] Such a psychic overflow, he suggests, could be responsible for various paranormal phenomena. But as is the case with William James, Bergson's interest in psychical research, though sincere, was not central, and his real concern was with the meaning of human evolution. Bergson voiced a question that has been repeated by scores of other thinkers similarly dissatisfied with the strict materialist-mechanistic interpretation of evolution. If the "aim" of life is to successfully "adapt" to its environment, why did it ever go beyond the amoeba, which is practically immortal and has proved the successful adapter par excellence? Why has life gone on not only to adapt, which implies an essentially passive, reactive character, but to complicate itself more and more dangerously? An Einstein or a Beethoven is a far greater risk than a colony of single-cell eukaryotes floating in a warm, primeval soup. And why, if the brain is solely an "organ of attention to life," does it seem to possess a surplus of psychic energy and a multiplicity of states, far beyond the needs of simply dealing with the vicissitudes of a hazardous environment? Bergson argued that the defining characteristic of mind is that "it has the faculty of drawing from itself more than it contains."[6] This, for the materialist-mechanistic science that wishes to explain consciousness, is an impossibility. A machine only has as much energy as is put into it; when my car runs out of gasoline, it doesn't suddenly discover a fresh tank hidden away somewhere. Yet we all know from our own experience that there are moments in our lives when we seem able to call upon energies and resources we were hitherto unaware of; in his essay "The Energies of Men," William James cites several extraordinary examples of this phenomenon. From a strictly "adaptive" point of view, this is inexplicable.

For Bergson, the answer is that "life" is not simply concerned with humble adaptation, although, of course, adaptation is clearly a useful and profitable means of achieving its higher end. And that end, for Bergson, is a continual increase of freedom and a continual production of novelty. Bergson saw life as an immense current of consciousness, a spiritual force, brimming with potentialities, penetrating matter and organizing it, "colonizing" it, as it were, in the service of increasing its own freedom. Matter, resistant to life's impulses, impedes its advance and scatters its energies. Yet, as he argues in *Creative Evolution*, this current of consciousness seems to have been successful in at least three attempts to gain a foothold on matter: in the plant world; in the world of the insects; and in the vertebrates, who have so far culminated in ourselves.

For a complete explication of Bergson's theory, the reader will have to go to *Creative Evolution* itself. Suffice it to say that, for Bergson, in the plant world what life gained in its ability to transform available, constant energies into food—photosynthesis—it lost in its capacity for movement. The vegetable world has "fallen asleep in immobility,"[7] an idea, as we shall see, that Bergson shares with Rudolf Steiner. In the world of the insects, specifically in the ants, what life gained in social organization and cooperation, it lost in initiative and independence; here *instinct* rules supreme, and in as determinant a fashion as the so-called "laws" of physical science. The individual counts as nothing. Bergson points out that a species that can claim the entire Earth as its domain must be considered a successful, even "superior" species. This can be said of ourselves, but it can also be said of the ant. Yet, the ant shows little in the way of intelligence, being completely dominated by instinct; it is robotlike in the relentless carrying out of its routine. There seems little evidence of any possibility of the ant "evolving" into a new level of freedom, and any stray that might feel a spark of initiative would be ruthlessly eliminated by its fellows. It is not surprising that writers concerned about the increasing collectivization of human society have looked to the insects as living metaphors of their fears.

But if in both the plant and insect world life's initial impulse has congealed, in the vertebrates Bergson sees at least one channel of life's energy flowing in new directions. If in plants and insects life has "stalled," in the vertebrates there still remains the possibility of setting free "something which in the animal still remains imprisoned and is only finally released when we reach man."[8] For Bergson, humankind is the front line of evolution, the tip of the *élan vital*'s advance, the being in which the life force has most successfully organized matter to its own end of increasing its knowledge of itself and its freedom. Bergson does not say that humankind per se is the "goal" of evolution. His view is not teleological and posits no final end, which for him would deny life's essentially creative character and reduce evolution to the simple carrying out of a prearranged plan. But he does believe that in human beings the impulse to freedom, novelty, and self-direction has broken loose of the weight and restrictions of matter. Sporadically, perhaps, and with many setbacks and retrogressions, but it is in humankind that the force of life has achieved its greatest inroad into matter. That this is not a "once and for all" victory, and that the individual and society as a whole are subject to the automatism that plagues life's earlier expeditions, Bergson was well aware, and such concerns form the focus of his last book, *Two Sources of Morality and Religion*, in which he explores the antagonism between the static, closed society, and the open, dynamic one.[9]

That Bergson believed that human beings *as they are* are not the "end" of evolution is clear in his notion of a "creative evolution." What is achieved in humankind is a release of life's creative impulse, substantially free of the restrictions of the medium of its expression, namely matter. Life needs a secure foothold in matter so that it can concentrate on the real business of evolution: understanding and developing the mind. As long as the necessities of simply staying alive are paramount, life's advance is stalled: it's hard to write poetry on an empty stomach, and until it's filled the brain will focus on dealing with things, to the detriment of its perceiving of life's complexity. But when necessities are taken care of, then for Bergson the next phase begins. And that, he argues, is where we are today—or have been since, let us say, the rise of civilization.[10] Hence for Bergson, consciousness invaded matter to harness it to its own purpose, which is to increase consciousness, and the greatest expression of this is in the artist, the thinker, the mystic, and the saint.

Chapter Four

The Superman

Bergson did not write of a "superman." The examples he gives as expressions of the *élan vital*'s creative advance are familiar figures in history and although exceptional, are still within the bounds of the "human." But some twenty years before *Creative Evolution*, another thinker was brooding on the possibility of life "throwing up" a being that would be a step beyond its last creation. Like Bergson, Friedrich Nietzsche was a "philosopher of life." He also shared with Bergson the distinction of being a philosopher who could write eloquently, forcefully, and persuasively. But unlike Bergson, he was a more abrasive, destructive, and explosive thinker. And although they both shared the misfortune of having their ideas appropriated by fascism, the taint has since been washed out of Bergson's reputation, while for many Nietzsche is still mistakenly seen as a precursor and prophet of the Nazis.

Nietzsche did not see his *Übermensch*, or "superman," in terms of an evolution of consciousness; or at least he did not specifically write of him as such. For one thing, Nietzsche did not believe in a "spiritual reality," although his writing on "eternal recurrence" and the "will to power," with its indebtedness to Schopenhauer, suggest a mystical element often missed by his interpreters.[1] Nietzsche, however, did believe, as R. M. Bucke did, that the human race was giving birth to a "new" kind of human being, although he differs from Bucke in not seeing this as a "natural" outcome of Darwinian evolution. Like Bergson, Nietzsche did not see mere survival and adaptation as life's central concerns. He argued that only a distressed organism is worried about survival. A healthy organism wants above all to express its health, use its powers, and actualize its potential. Nietzsche condemned Christianity because he believed it valued weakness and timidity over strength and adventure. It was poisonous because its source was an active "hatred" of life, which posited a higher world in which those unable to meet life's challenge—the weak and timid—would find eternal peace, and a hell in which those who used their energies would find everlasting torment. Understandably, a Christian Europe found Nietzsche's ideas mad and was only too happy to chalk them up to the syphilis that eventually killed him. Sadly, although less than a century earlier people like William Blake had said pretty much the same thing, Nietzsche's own rhetorical brilliance worked against him, and his remarks about the "blonde beast" and the "good war that hallows any cause" were easily picked up by shallow thinkers and used to justify beliefs and ideologies that would have turned his stomach.

Nietzsche's conception of the superman was of an individual of such health, vitality, and zest for life that he would be able to affirm life *as it is*, joyfully, even in the face of its apparent absurdity and cruelty. And affirm it not only once, but eternally, as his doctrine of the "eternal recurrence of all things" implies.[2] Nietzsche imagined an individual so full of curiosity, expectancy, and a sense of adventure that he or she could do without the props that had hitherto supported humankind—religion, metaphysics, "the search for truth," the warm campfires of the herd—and could cast off into uncharted seas for unknown regions of experience. Nietzsche called for a "transvaluation of all values." That he himself often failed to meet the standards he set for his "free spirits" and "new philosophers" only says that he was, unavoidably, only "human, all too human," and not that those standards are false. His doctrine of self-creation, of finding a higher, deeper morality "beyond good and evil," and, above all, of affirming life in the face of his tortured, miserable existence, was to influence practically every major thinker and artist for decades after his death.

Nietzsche's notion of the superman would have the most immediate effect. A generation weary of Victorian restraint and prudery was eager for a doctrine that told them to cast off an obsolete morality and to think and live for themselves. His philosophy argued for a "higher morality" and a more severe self-discipline than that professed by the hypocritical Christians of his time. That this was often overlooked by individuals anxious to, as a later appropriator of some of his thought would put it, "do what they wilt,"[3] is unfortunate. But it is not an argument against his ideas, merely the recognition that they were used by shallow people to justify their appetites. Another reason for the popularity of the superman idea was the widespread success of Darwinism and the attendant notion of "progress." These suggested that the "march of life" had not come to a halt with ourselves and that before us lay a future pregnant with the possibility of some "higher" type, who would look back with a mixture of pity and disdain at their nineteenth-century ancestors, as they themselves looked back at the hairy ape. The idea soon seeped into the popular consciousness, enriching an emerging science fiction, fueling biological speculation (Bucke's, for example) and infecting sociological and political thought with often unappealing effect.

One area in which the biological doctrine of evolution, the visionary figure of the superman, and the notion that humankind was entering a new form of consciousness met was occultism. Here indeed was a heady and evocative brew. "The occult" had experienced a revival since the last quarter of the nineteenth century, but to say that it had experienced a revival is not to say that it had hitherto been absent. As scholars like James Webb and Joscelyn Godwin make clear, a current of occult interest ran through the Enlightenment, the Romantic revolution, and other cultural and political movements of the eighteenth, nineteenth, and twentieth centuries.[4] Prior to the rise of modern science in the seventeenth century, occultism formed a central part of the European intellectual curriculum; figures like Sir Isaac Newton, today seen as an archetype of the modern scientist, were as deeply—if not more—involved in occult studies like astrology and alchemy as they were in astronomy and physics. But with the rise of the Age of Reason, occultism went underground and became a subterranean stream, nourishing small enclaves and secret societies.

All this changed in March 1848, when strange phenomena began to occur in a farmhouse in Hydesville, upstate New York. Previous occupants of the house had been disturbed by strange sounds, and when the new tenants—the Fox family—moved in, the noises increased. They became so regular that the family grew accustomed to them, inviting neighbors in to listen. Eventually one of the young Fox daughters christened the "ghost" Mr. Splitfoot, and decided to see if she could communicate with "him." When the ghost replied, Katie and her sister developed a method of questioning him. They discovered he had been a travelling salesman who had been murdered in the house several years earlier, his body buried in the cellar. Subsequent excavation did indeed unearth the remains of a man. The age of spiritualism had begun. Soon after Mr. Splitfoot's debut, spiritualism swept across the United States, and not longer after that it crossed the Atlantic.

Katie and her sister went on to become "mediums," "channels" for the spirits who seemed willing to answer questions about the afterlife, the future, religion, or, more prosaically, the whereabouts of missing items. Other mediums appeared, and soon after the "raps" at Hydesville were first heard it seemed that the daylight world of common sense and cold, hard facts was facing a veritable invasion from another dimension. The spirits seemed to clamor for attention. Table turning and séances became popular pastimes among the Victorians. One of the most celebrated and well-documented mediums of the age was Daniel Dunglas Home, who was known to levitate, produce terrific crescendos, and hold live coals with no apparent effect, as well as perform dozens of other extraordinary feats as a matter of course. The new religion of spiritualism spread and gained adherents at such a rate that in 1898 the Roman Catholic Church condemned the popular practice of séances and mediumship, although it still allowed for the kind of "controlled" scientific investigation of the phenomena carried on by organizations like the Society for Psychical Research, founded by Fredrick Myers, Frank Podmore, and Edmund Gurney in 1882.

It was in this atmosphere of communication with the dead, remarkable powers, and fantastic but seemingly verifiable claims that a woman appeared who was to have tremendous influence, not only in the occult world, but in wider cultural and intellectual spheres as well. She was a flamboyant Russian, with a mysterious, colorful past. Her name was Helena Petrovna Blavatsky. We will have more to say about her further on. Here it is enough to say that the Theosophical Society, which she founded with Colonel Henry Steel Olcott in New York City in the summer of 1875, was responsible for giving spiritualism, as well as other occult beliefs and practices, an attractive intellectual cachet, linking them to notions of "ancient wisdom" and "secret teachings" lost to the materialistic West, but now regained and open to all who could see beyond the prejudices of modern thought.

Many accepted Madame Blavatsky's invitation. Probably the most famous was the poet W. B. Yeats, later a member of the most well known magical society of the nineteenth century, the Hermetic Order of the Golden Dawn. But other, less celebrated individuals were attracted to the appealing blend of spiritual exoticism and mystic wisdom offered by Theosophy. One such was a young, overworked schoolteacher from Leeds, Alfred Richard Orage, later known to the readers of the influential journal *The New Age* as the editor of genius A. R. Orage.

CHAPTER FIVE

A. R. Orage and the New Age

Orage is best known today to historians and students of the esoteric school known as the Fourth Way, whose central figure is the enigmatic Armenian teacher G. I. Gurdjieff. Orage came into Gurdjieff's circle in France in the early 1920s, after being introduced to his "system" through the lectures of P. D. Ouspensky. Later, after Ouspensky parted from Gurdjieff, Orage became

Gurdjieff's chief lieutenant and emissary, particularly in the United States. Ouspensky had worked with Gurdjieff in Russia and Turkey from 1915 to 1918, and although contact between them continued into the twenties, Ouspensky had by then effectively broken with Gurdjieff and followed his own path. In 1921 he arrived in London, feted as the best-selling author of a remarkable work of metaphysics, *Tertium Organum* (1912, American edition 1920), which we will be discussing shortly.

Ouspensky quickly established himself as a potent source of new and extraordinary ideas about the nature of human consciousness, and the audience at his lectures included such figures as T. S. Eliot, Aldous Huxley, Gerald Heard, and the occultist A. E. Waite. Orage had met Ouspensky some years before when the philosopher passed through London during his "search for the miraculous"; later, Orage published Ouspensky's "Letters from Russia" in *The New Age,* depicting the collapse of civilized life in Tsarist Russia in the throes of the Bolshevik Revolution. To many readers sympathetic to the Marxist "experiment," Ouspensky's account of famine, looting, murder, and widespread chaos was sobering.

Devoted to a dizzying variety of literary, philosophical, mystical, and political writing, the pages of *The New Age* introduced the work of the writer Katharine Mansfield, and counted among its contributors George Bernard Shaw, G. K. Chesterton and H. G. Wells. It was also clearly attuned to the coming "new man." In the first issue, Orage and his coeditor Holbrook Jackson announced their credo:

> *Believing that the darling object and purpose of the universal will of life is the creation of a race of supremely and progressively intelligent beings,* The New Age *will devote itself to the serious endeavour to co-operate with the purposes of life and to enlist in that noble service the help of serious students of the new contemplative and imaginative order.*[1]

Few advocates of the contemporary "New Age Movement" are aware of their distinguished predecessor.

Orage came into contact with Theosophy through his interest in Platonism and a hunger to escape the numbing dullness of his life as a schoolteacher. He was also a deep reader of Nietzsche. The story is that Orage was introduced to Nietzsche's work by a friend to whom he had given a copy of the Bhagavad Gita; the friend returned the gesture with an edition of *Thus Spake Zarathustra.* Orage spent the night reading the book and returned to his friend's door the next morning brimming over with Nietzsche's gospel.

All his life Orage had a taste for the mystical, esoteric, and "hidden"; it was natural that works like Blavatsky's *Isis Unveiled* and *The Secret Doctrine,* with their talk of ancient wisdom, secret knowledge, and hidden masters secure in their Himalayan monasteries, would appeal to him. For all their chaos and sheer improbability, which Orage was quick to comment on, Blavatsky's daunting tomes—together the two books contain more than 2,500 pages—offered readers like Orage a magnificent counterblast to the prevailing scientific positivism with its cramped view of philosophy and reductive picture of human beings and their place in the cosmos. If nothing else, Orage and thousands of other readers like him benefited from Blavatsky's work by being introduced through it to spiritual classics like the Bhagavad Gita, the Mahabharata, and other masterpieces of Indian thought. (It may seem odd that as the editor of an influential London literary journal and a critic of English literature, Orage referred to the Mahabharata more than any other work as a touchstone of literary style and quality.)

Orage also gleaned from his contact with Theosophy the conviction that our normal everyday consciousness was not the only consciousness available to us, and that humanity as a whole was slowly evolving into a new kind of being. Like R. M. Bucke, William James, and Henri Bergson, Orage believed that human beings had potential "other" forms of consciousness lying dormant within them, waiting to be explored. And like Nietzsche, he believed that those who managed to actualize these new forms would, in effect, become something more than human. Orage's Nietzschean take on Theosophical ideas soon set him apart from the rank and file members, and his innate scepticism made him critical of a slavish acceptance of some of Blavatsky's more outlandish

notions. In a series of lectures given in 1904 to branches of the
Theosophical Society in Manchester and Leeds, Orage brought
Nietzschean inspiration and Theosophical doctrine together under
the title "Consciousness: Animal, Human and Superhuman."
When the lectures were published in book form in 1907, they
established Orage as an important and insightful thinker on the
possibilities of an evolution of consciousness.

Orage begins his investigation with a remark that in some form
or other must occur to anyone who decides to seriously study consciousness beginning with the consciousness most available, one's
own: "The difficulty of discussing consciousness and its modes is
the difficulty of discussing ourselves."[2] In introspection, in observing and analyzing consciousness, there is the consciousness we
observe and the consciousness that does the observing. The two are
not the same, and the possibilities of an endless regression of
observers and observed, of an infinite hall of mirrors receding into
our inner depths, are at once intriguing and paralyzing. Orage rec-
ognizes this danger and admits at the outset that he knows that
what he will be speaking of will be only one part or aspect of consciousness. Just as our own selves perpetually escape complete
analysis, there will always be some part of consciousness lying outside the scope of observation. Definitions, too, will not help. As
Bergson later remarked, there is no need to define something we all
experience immediately and clearly, and in any case any definition
would be more obscure than the thing itself.[3]

For Orage the act of turning the mind in on itself, however
incomplete, is nevertheless salutary—something he will later return
to in his work on "self-observation" with Gurdjieff. The first thing
anyone interested in understanding the nature of consciousness
must do, he argues, is to develop the habit of withdrawing attention from the outer world, whose activities and objects draw
awareness like magnets. He must learn instead how to focus it on
the mind itself—an approach the phenomenologist Edmund
Husserl was developing in a different context around the same
time. Orage argues that we must abandon the prejudice that *our*
consciousness is consciousness in itself, and try to imagine what a
consciousness undifferentiated into either human or animal or any-

thing else would be like. Striking images lead us in the right direction: "The eye opening in darkness, the ear alert in silence"[4]—the possibility of perception without the perception itself. Not "this" consciousness or "that" consciousness, but consciousness with neither a subject nor an object—the "consciousness without thought," perhaps, that Edward Carpenter spoke of earlier. Stripping away the senses and our habitual inclination to act on their stimulus, one digs through layers of awareness to a kind of bedrock of "pure consciousness." What one then encounters is "a power of attention, a state of complete preparedness, a universal awareness, which only by the particularised activities of beings becomes defined and limited into specifically human, animal or vegetable modes."[5] This is Bergson's "life force" or Schopenhauer's "will" before it actualizes itself in any particular living being. Thus Orage argues that our own consciousness is but one form or manifestation of a "universal consciousness," which expresses itself in a variety of agents.

Orage's rigorous analysis of consciousness may have seemed austere fare to Theosophists used to talk of hidden masters, past lives, and karma, and his "dangerous" Nietzschean ethos of self-creation was soon to lead him away from the more earnest and idealistic Theosophical campfires. By the time of his lectures, Orage had found himself increasingly disenchanted with the occult ideas and practices that had once thrilled him, and more fascinated with the potentials of the mind itself. In an article written for the *Theosophical Review* in the same year as the lectures, Orage contrasted what he called the "occult arts" with "occult faculties," arguing that while the former obsess and "devour" people, resulting in "cranks," "occult faculties" free the mind, allowing it to soar into new dimensions. Intuition, insight, and imagination—the faculties in question—were, Orage said, "winged thought," "winged judgment," and "winged sympathy." These were preferable because unlike arts or knowledge, which can be forgotten, faculties, once acquired, are difficult to lose. What all three share is that each is a normal, everyday faculty raised to a higher power, and each partakes of what Orage sees as the kind of consciousness peculiar to the "superman," what he calls "ecstasy." This notion of a familiar "power" raised to a higher level forms the basis of Orage's thoughts on the evolution of consciousness.

In examining consciousness, Orage follows a three-tiered approach that in many ways is similar to Bucke's; in its essentials it also anticipates the more extended treatment that P. D. Ouspensky would provide in *Tertium Organum*. Orage argues that animal consciousness, like Bucke's "perceptual mind," is a kind of simple sensory awareness. Like a photographic plate, it receives impressions and retains images, but there is no consciousness of this, no awareness of awareness. Orage uses the analogy of a sheet of sensitive paper. Laid flat, this is a "one-dimensional" consciousness, "plane consciousness." It can pick up sensory impressions, even retain and store them, but it has no memory of them. Fold the paper once, and we arrive at human consciousness, which has memory and is aware of its awareness. It is, as it were, the paper photographing itself. This may occur with some continuity or only sporadically; we all fall into states of simple animal consciousness when our presiding ego seems to have disappeared, and the loss of this sense of "I" forms the basis of Gurdjieff's ideas of "self-remembering." Orage suggests that with a strong ego it is rather as if the paper were curved in on itself like a sphere, in which our awareness of our awareness achieves a kind of stability.

Now, just as human consciousness is animal consciousness raised to a higher level, superhuman or "cosmic" consciousness is human consciousness raised again. If animal consciousness is reflection and human consciousness the reflection of that reflection, then superhuman consciousness is a higher reflection still—consciousness of the ego by a higher "self." Again, the idea is that the mystical state, what Orage calls "ecstasy," is not something supernatural, nor is it a freak accident without significance for consciousness at large. It emerges out of a development of ordinary consciousness, which, as William James had said and Orage, in a different way, reiterates, is not "consciousness per se," but only one form of consciousness. And again as Bucke argued, the consciousness of the superhuman should differ from that of the ordinary human, as the human's differs from the animal's. For Orage "human consciousness is inferior to superman consciousness, just

as an embryo in an egg is inferior to the bird flying in the air."
Where for the animal the focus of consciousness is sense impressions and for the human is the awareness of these impressions in an
ego, for the superhuman the focus is in an observation of that ego.
"As the spectator of human consciousness, the superman would
have our interior world for his object."[6] This argues for an increasing "interiorizing" of consciousness, a deepening of our inner
world. Orage believed that such a change was happening in his
own time. "Doubtless, in evolved minds," he wrote, "the activity
of the inner senses is beginning slowly to predominate over the
outer senses. People do live more by their inner appreciations and
perceptions and ideas than by their outer perceptions." Trust and
confidence in our own ideas and perceptions leads to new powers
and faculties, and this sense of growth is the hallmark of human
consciousness itself, which is the embryo of the higher consciousness growing within us. That this process is in part at least directed by our own efforts is clear in Orage's Nietzschean remark that
"evolution is altogether an imaginative process. You become what
you have been led to imagine yourselves to be."[7] For Orage and
many readers of *The New Age,* what they imagined themselves to
be was the superman.

Who exactly the superman was, and how best to encourage his
appearance, was something Orage left up to his readers. In this he
was acting in a Nietzschean way. For him the imagination is the
main faculty whereby the superhuman relates to the world, and
where Bucke saw a change in human consciousness as the result of
powers outside human control, Orage called for a more active participation in the process. Like Bergson, he decried the emphasis on
the passivity of life fostered by Darwinian biology; and, like
Nietzsche, he believed that the "new consciousness" would emerge
out of the masses only in exceptional individuals, who were even
then forming a kind of secret fraternity, recognizing each other
through common ideals, passions, and beliefs. The "new consciousness" would stand outside human consciousness: such
"standing outside" is the essence of ecstasy.

The superman, too, would stand outside the society around
him, and would often be perceived as a freak, a criminal, a dan-

gerous character, a threat. Orage makes the Nietzschean point that as the bearer of a new culture the superman would act as a kind of "shepherd of minds," and this arrangement doesn't necessitate benevolence toward his flock. At the same time the popular image of a "master race" lording it over the rest of us is a myth, and the superman has more important things to concern himself with than exerting political or social power—such as exploring the new faculties and perceptions that emerge in his superconscious state. Central among these is a new, liberating relation to time and space. Sometimes, under the influence of art, love, or nature, people today can feel the ecstasy that is the birthright of the superman, an overpowering feeling of being above the normal limits of existence. In such moments, time and space seem to be beneath us, and we seem to exist in a different, higher dimension. Such a state would be a permanent condition for the superman; although we today have only fleeting glimpses of it, the possibility exists that the breakthrough can be made. There are no sure guidelines, and the way is dangerous. But for the "new man" that Orage recognized around him, the treasure is worth the risk.

CHAPTER SIX

Ouspensky's Fourth Dimension

One such "new man" was the Russian journalist, novelist, and philosopher P. D. Ouspensky. Born in Moscow in 1878, three years after Orage, Ouspensky is the archetypal seeker of wisdom; by the end of his life in 1947, he had become for many the dispenser of it. Ouspensky came of age in a remarkable period in Russian history, the so-called Silver Age of the *fin de siècle*, when mysticism, occultism, progressive ideas, and revolutions in art, politics, and life were the norm. The same period brought forth Madame Blavatsky and Gurdjieff, as well as controversial figures like Grigory Rasputin, poets like Andrey Biely and Valery Bryusov, philosophers like Vladimir Soloviev and Nicholai Berdyaev (both of whom wrote of the coming "God-Man"), musicians like the Theosophical composer Aleksandr Scriabin, and painters like Kazimir Malevich, whose Suprematism was heavily influenced by Ouspensky's ideas.

In the years after his tutelage under Gurdjieff, Ouspensky struck many as a rigid, taciturn ideologue, doggedly sticking to the letter of Gurdjieff's law. Few knew him as the romantic, convivial artist who frequented St. Petersburg's Stray Dog Café, hobnobbing with Anna Akhmatova or Aleksandr Blok, drinking vodka till dawn, immersed in the allusive world of Symbolist poetry. Ouspensky's later work, like *A New Model of the Universe* (published in 1931, though parts were written as early as 1905), the brief *The Psychology of Man's Possible Evolution* (1947), and his masterpiece, *In Search of the Miraculous* (1949), an account of his time with Gurdjieff, have a pessimistic air, a sense of the intense struggle and grim persistence Gurdjieff believed was needed in order to "awaken." But the book we will examine here, *Tertium Organum,* is altogether different. A young man's work, written during a time of intense inspiration and creative discovery, it is a fireworks display of metaphysical speculation, intellectual excitement, poetic insight, and evolutionary optimism. Like Orage, Ouspensky had steeped himself in Theosophical literature and had devoured Nietzsche. Also like Orage, the Ouspensky who wrote *Tertium Organum* is a man bitten by the superman bug.

Two obsessions directed and absorbed Ouspensky's life from his earliest years onward. One was the mysterious sensation of déjà vu, the strange feeling that "I have been here before." As early as the age of six, Ouspensky experienced with unsettling vividness "memories" of places he had not yet seen—at least in his present life. Later, after reading Nietzsche, the extraordinary clarity of his earliest memories became associated with the notion of "eternal recurrence," Nietzsche's idea that events in time repeat themselves over and over.[1] Obscure, difficult, and seemingly masochistic— one's defeats, embarrassments, and disappointments eternally repeated?— the idea was no mere hobby for Ouspensky, and in his last days his students watched as the tired, sick man dragged himself to favorite sites in order to impress the memory of them on

himself so that next time he would *not forget*. This obsession with
time also led him into other unusual areas, like the "fourth dimension," speculation about which was a popular pastime at the beginning of the twentieth century, much like our own recent craze
about "chaos theory" and "complexity."

The other obsession that haunted Ouspensky was his conviction that the everyday world was a fraud. In the introduction to *In
Search of the Miraculous,* he remarks that as a child he and his
beloved younger sister[2] had a favorite book called *Obvious
Absurdities.* In it were surreal pictures: a man with a house on his
back, a cart with blocks for wheels. Ouspensky later said that he
never understood why these were considered more absurd than the
rest of "ordinary life," which always struck him as false, and
equally mad. Early on the conviction was built up in him that nothing could come of following the paths already laid down in life,
and that the only possible way forward was of discovering some
new path, a new road hitherto undiscovered, that would lead out
of the false world of compromise, repetition, and security—what
he came to call by the Russian word *byt,* "deeply rooted, petrified
routine life." In this rejection of the narrow horizons of the commonplace and everyday, Ouspensky resembles practically every
romantic soul who preceded him. But unlike many, he actually did
something about it. Like the German writer Hermann Hesse, with
whom Ouspensky shared a recognition of the "new race" sprouting on the fertilized soil of a dying Europe, Ouspensky set out to
find an alternative to *byt.*[3] And like Hesse, for him this meant a
journey to the East.

Between 1907 and 1909 Ouspensky set off on the first leg of
his "search for the miraculous." Gurdjieff came across his writing
in 1913–14 and set his pupils the task of studying Ouspensky, with
the intention of drawing him into what was slowly becoming "the
work." But that was still in the future. Even before he had that
fateful meeting in a seedy Moscow café with the remarkable man
Gurdjieff, Ouspensky had embarked on a series of experiments
that to this day remain some of the most adventurous, fruitful, and
thrilling attempts to break through the artificial limits of human
consciousness and enter the worlds beyond.

Ouspensky's journeys to the East would in the end prove unsuccessful. Although through them he saw many remarkable sights—the Sphinx, the Taj Mahal, the piercing sapphire eyes of a statue of the Buddha in Ceylon—he returned to Russia skeptical of the romanticism that had fueled his wanderlust and aware that he had, after all, come back to square one. But if he did not find what he was looking for, one thing was given him: a taste of the expanded consciousness that he believed some men and women, scattered across the globe, were even then evolving into. In 1908, as he stood on the deck of a steamer crossing the Sea of Marmora in Turkey, Ouspensky had a sudden, fleeting experience of the higher consciousness he would spend the rest of life trying to achieve. He recorded the event in his notebook.

It was in the sea of Marmora, on a rainy winter day. In the distance, the high rocky shores were of all shades of violet, down to the palest, fading into grey and merging with the grey sky. . . . I was standing by the rail and looking at the waves. The white crests were running toward us from afar. A wave would come up, rear itself as though wanting to hurl its crest on the deck, then with a roar would throw itself under the ship. . . . I was watching this play of the waves with the ship and feeling the waves drawing me to themselves . . . drawing my soul to themselves. Suddenly I felt it go to them. It was only a moment, maybe less than a moment. But I entered the waves and, with them, with a roar, attacked the ship. And at that moment I became all. The waves—they were myself. The violet mountains in the distance—they were myself. The wind—it was myself. The clouds, hurrying from the north, the rain—were myself. The huge ship, rolling indomitably forward—was myself. . . . The mate on duty on the bridge was I; and two sailors . . . and the black smoke, billowing from the funnel . . . everything. It was a moment of extraordinary liberation, joy and expansion. A second—and the spell was broken.[4]

Ouspensky records that two years later the yellowish waves of the Gulf of Finland briefly brought the feeling back, but that it vanished almost as soon as it appeared.

It was, however, enough. His travels, as well as his wide reading in occult and esoteric literature—Eliphas Levi, A. P. Sinnett, Rudolf Steiner (who at the time was drawing a different Russian, the novelist and poet Andrey Biely, into his fold)—had convinced him that behind the façade of the everyday world lay another reality, the world, he believed, of "causes." It was the noumenal world of which newspapers, articles, politicians, and wars were only the effects, fleeting phenomena thrown up by the shifting face of time. But Ouspensky sought something more. He sought the infinite. And he was determined to find it.

Included in the library of esoteric books to which Ouspensky turned when his work as a journalist grew too tedious may have been Bucke's *Cosmic Consciousness*—certainly it would be a central text for *Tertium Organum*. William James may have been there as well. It is clear that Ouspensky read James, and it is also clear that the self-experiments he was about to undertake were at least in part influenced and inspired by James's own self-experiments with nitrous oxide. Although Ouspensky is never explicit about the use of drugs, from his account of his experiments it is almost certain they formed a central part of his undertaking. The descriptions of what he experienced suggest that for him, too, nitrous oxide was an entrance ticket into the potential "other" forms of consciousness. It is also possible he employed hashish. We must remember that at this time these substances were not illegal—indeed, nitrous oxide has never been—and that their use as a means of stimulating "altered states of consciousness," as well as the tradition of "self-experiment" in science, have long and respected pedigrees, whatever our own opinion of such expedients. Ouspensky was no drug addict, any more than William James was. He was a serious seeker of a greater reality than that perceived through the senses. In his little apartment in St. Petersburg, sometime between 1910 and 1911, he found it.

Ouspenky's experiments in charting the geography of higher consciousness are recorded in the extraordinary chapter

"Experimental Mysticism" in *A New Model of the Universe* and in his first major work, *Tertium Organum*. He had by this time already written a few books, notably his novel of eternal recurrence, *Strange Life of Ivan Osokin;* but it was *Tertium Organum* that established him as a writer of brilliance and as a profound thinker. It is unclear if Ouspensky read Bergson. He was fluent in French and for a time in his youth had travelled alone to Paris, which he loved, and it is possible that there he came into contact with Bergson's writings.[5] He may have known of Orage's short book, yet although both moved in Theosophical circles, and had met during the start of Ouspensky's "search," it was as a literary editor and not as a philosopher of the evolution of consciousness that Ouspensky knew of and respected Orage. To search for direct linkages between *Tertium Organum* and the works that preceded it may be an entertaining historical pastime, but it would tell us nothing we did not already know. Ouspensky did not have to be directly influenced by these works to have been obsessed with higher consciousness. The *Zeitgeist* was full of it; the idea was in the air. Ouspensky brought its various strands together and, in a season of novalike inspiration, produced perhaps the single most effective counterblast to the desiccating doctrine of positivism, whose stranglehold held fast the progress of thought.

The basic theme of *Tertium Organum* is the need to pass beyond the artificial limits to knowledge erected by the inadequate logic of positivist science. To this day that science asserts that there is no greater significance or deeper *meaning* to life than that provided by its material explanation—which in effect means that there is no meaning or significance to it at all—and it was against this numbing assessment that Ouspensky brought his considerable talents and incisive intellect to bear. To recognize that our normal everyday consciousness is only one mode of consciousness and that the physical world we perceive through it is its product, to grasp that behind this world lies another world, totally different from our own, a world, as Ouspensky called it, of the "miraculous"—such was the aim of *Tertium Organum*. The book's title means the "third organ of thought," beyond Aristotle's and Francis Bacon's, although, as Ouspensky points out, this "third organ" was known to the ancients who preceded them. As witnesses for this revelation Ouspensky called on the fruits of his travels, his many years of study, and his own recent attempts to scale the heights of higher consciousness. Art, nature, Theosophy, higher space, infinity, non-Euclidean mathematics, Kantian philosophy, reflections on animal psychology, sex, the anesthetic revelation, Nietzsche, mysticism, poetry, and much, much more are marshalled in order to support Ouspensky's central insight:

> *There is no side of life which does not reveal to us an infinity of the new and the unexpected if we approach it with the* knowledge *that it is not exhausted by its visible side, that behind this visible side there lies a whole world of the "invisible," a whole world of new and incomprehensible forces and relations.*[6]

Ouspensky came to understand that this world was a gigantic hieroglyph, a symbol for a higher, more intensely meaningful world that lay beyond it but radiated its significance through the most mundane items. Of this insight Ouspensky had personal experience. During his experiments, he took a break from probing the edges of the comprehensible and sat on his sofa, smoking a cigarette. Flicking the ash, he looked with wonder at his ashtray. Suddenly he saw this humble object as the center of a vast radiating web of meanings and relations. In a rush of recognition, everything to do with the ashtray flooded his consciousness. Who had made it, its use, the material from which it was made, the history of tobacco, the whole long development of humankind's ability to mold its environment. Fire, flame, and the match he had just struck: each seemed a hitherto unopened window on the world, through which he now looked with wonder and amazement. So great was the truth now washing over him that Ouspensky knew he had to capture it. Later, when he returned to the world of everyday awareness, he looked at the note he had written. It read, "A man can go mad from one ashtray." Like "Think in other categories," the other one-liner he salvaged from his metaphysical forays, it shares with William James's nitrous oxide jottings the exasperating inability to translate more than a hint of the depths of understanding that loomed before him.

One of the metaphors Ouspensky used to convey the import of his experience was "the fourth dimension." Einstein and the mathematician Hermann Minkowsky are called on for support, but the central inspiration here is the work of the English mathematician C. H. Hinton. In the 1880s and 1890s, Hinton wrote a series of books in which he speculated on the existence of dimensions beyond our familiar three of length, height, and depth.[7] His work influenced writers like E. A. Abbot, whose *Flatland* (1884) depicts a visit by a being of three dimensions to an inhabitant of only two, and H. G. Wells, whose *The Time Machine* (1895) is heavily indebted to Hinton's *Scientific Romances* (1884–1885).

In Abbot's book, the two-dimensional square perceives its three-dimensional visitor, a sphere, in the only way it can, as a circle, flat like itself. Ouspensky adopts this as his analogy for how a devotee of positivist science must perceive any manifestation of the "miraculous." Just as the square cannot conceive of any dimensions greater than those it possesses, and so finds the sphere's remarks about a third dimension incomprehensible, so too the positivist scientist—or, for that matter, the average person of "common sense"—cannot grasp the possibility of any meaning or significance to the phenomena of the world beyond those already accepted. Things are as they are: a rose is a rose is a rose, and any suggestion that there is anything more to it is simply nonsense. Abbot's book is mainly a satire, but Hinton had a more positive aim. He believed it was possible to train the mind to perceive the higher dimensions he speculated on. One method of doing this was to imagine a four-dimensional cube, what Hinton called a "hypercube" or tesseract—it is even possible he coined the word.[8] Hinton even designed an actual "hypercube" to be sold along with his books. It was made up of eighty-one individual cubes, each painted a different color. The idea was to alternate the order of the individual cubes and to memorize each arrangement. Eventually the entire construction could be visualized, in each of its different orders. The practice is reminiscent of the Renaissance "art of memory," as well as of various exercises in perceiving the aura or astral plane popular at the time. Along with these, Hinton's "cubes" were a favorite pastime of the late-Victorian occult demimonde.[9]

In *A New Era of Thought,* from which Ouspensky drew heavily, Hinton wrote, "Space is the instrument of the mind." This was in 1888, a year before Bergson would make the same argument in *Time and Free Will.* Hinton based his idea on the work of the philosopher Kant, who argued that space and time were categories through which the mind perceived reality—with the corollary that there is no reason to believe that they have any real existence outside of the mind. The world "in reality" might be spaceless and timeless—a condition referred to by many mystics and in more recent years argued for by many scientists. For Kant, space and time are, as it were, the pincers with which we grasp the world, and they leave their indelible mark on it—so much so that we can never know what the world is like when we are not grasping it with our tools. For Kant and for most of the philosophers that followed him, the *Ding-an-sich,* or thing-in-itself—the world, that is, when it is not perceived by us—remains forever unavailable. We can never see what things look like when we are not seeing them, for to do so would be to see them, and this would create the very condition we wish to avoid. For the sensitive-minded, the idea that we can never know what reality is "really" like is shattering. One such was the German writer Heinrich von Kleist. After reading Kant, Kleist lost all faith in knowledge, adopted a radical scepticism, and sunk into a profound depression, eventually killing himself as part of a suicide pact with an incurably sick woman. Aside from a few exceptions—Hegel, Alfred North Whitehead—this radical epistemological scepticism remains the central assumption of modern philosophy.

Yet Hinton believed that the reaction Kleist had to Kant was unnecessary. Most commentators on Kant have assumed that his assertion that space and time are the means by which we perceive the world argues that they in some way *falsify* the world, that they are barriers to our ever really "getting at it." But there is no reason to assume this, and the pessimism that follows from it is unjustified. If space and time are the means by which we perceive the world, then it follows that if we can somehow increase or amplify our use of them, our perception of the world will also be increased, just as the landscape I perceive through a telescope is made clearer when I adjust the focus. I would not say that the telescope "falsifies" the landscape. Indeed, there is good reason to believe that without such means of perception, there is no "world," only the raw material for one, a notion we will return to in our chapter on participatory epistemology. The world of space and time is not, then, an *illusion;* it is merely a *limited perception,* something altogether different. If we assume that what we see of the world is limited by our understanding of space and time, and that these limits are not necessarily fixed, we can use our existing perceptions as starting points for deeper, more inclusive ones. Rather than bemoan our separation from a reality we can never know, and hence make no efforts to know it, we can begin to develop our powers of perception, and try our best to grasp something of the mystery of the world.

Such, in any case, was Ouspensky's belief, and to my mind his argument is very convincing. Ouspensky's chapters on the mathematics of the "fourth dimension" may be doubtful—he was not, after all, the mathematician he is described as being on the dust jackets of his books; this was an early mistake by his first English translators, subsequently repeated. Nor do his chapters on animal perception hold up.[10] But this is unimportant. What remains is his central insight. As William Blake had before him, in his state of expanded consciousness Ouspensky saw the world in a grain of sand, and heaven in a wild flower.

> It seems to us that we see something and understand
> something. But in actual fact we have but a dim sense of
> all that is happening around us, just as a snail has a dim
> sense of the sunlight, the rain, the darkness.[11]

A horse on the Nevsky Prospect was an "atom" of a "great horse," a dog an "atom" of a "great dog," and human beings "atoms" of the "great man." Although they were in a material sense the same, in his heightened state Ouspensky saw that in the "fourth dimension"—in the world, that is, of meanings—the wood of a gallows, of a cross, and of a ship's mast were *different*. He saw differences everywhere. The stones of a prison were not the same as those of a factory, nor those the same as ones of a church, although a chemical analysis would detect no difference. Calling on a Platonic analogy, Ouspensky pointed out that the shadows of a hangman, a sailor, and a saint may look identical; no physical analysis of the shadows could detect a difference between them. Yet these shadows are formed by radically different men, completely different objects. It is only the shadows that are alike. And, he pointed out, positivist science is concerned only with shadows, mistaking them for reality. Ouspensky walked the streets of St. Petersburg filled with a sense of the numinous. It was as if some fourth-dimensional Dutch boy had pulled his finger from the dike, and the waters of significance came forth in a torrent. And what Ouspensky saw most was that there was something wrong with our ideas of time.

In one of his expanded states, Ouspensky had a vision of the *Linga Sharira*, our four-dimensional "time-body," the "long body of life." The term comes from Indian philosophy by way of Madame Blavatsky. Ouspensky realized that at any time our picture of ourselves or of others is limited by the moment in which we see it, but that the "real" individual is one's life *extended through time*. Like Bergson, Ouspensky was aware that all we can study at any separate moment is a "snapshot" of a person's life, never the whole of it, which, like the rest of the world, is a constant process. And, of course, each snapshot is different. From birth to death, we are in a condition of constant change. (I see this in my children, and already miss the one-year-old in my son who is now three.) Yet beneath the visible alteration to our physical body, there remains something that endures: the image, the form of the person. That image and form is the *Linga Sharira*, which, Ouspensky believed, exists in a kind of Eternal Now. The key to higher consciousness, Ouspensky understood, lay in a changed perception of time, in an ability to escape the limitations of the present moment and see deeper into the past and future. Just as what is "behind" us or "before" us is still "there" although we no longer occupy its space, in his heightened state Ouspensky could see that the past, which we believe to be obliterated, still exists, and that the future, which in our "normal" state we believe has not yet happened, is already taking place. We are so used to the idea of "now" being the only time we can be aware of that the idea that the past and the future are in some way "with us" seems absurd. Yet for Ouspensky this awareness was the same as being able to see ahead of or behind himself. Clearly this is an extended version of Orage's "ecstasy," the powerful sense of being above space and time. Like Orage, Ouspensky believed that this kind of awareness, although still exceptional, was becoming less and less rare. And also like Orage, Ouspensky thought the people in whom this new perception was emerging formed a "new race." In short, superhumans.

Ouspensky's ideas on the "superman" and the "new race" are collected in his remarkable chapter "Superman" in *A New Model of the Universe* and in the final chapter of *Tertium Organum*, where he engages in an extended discussion of Bucke's theories. Here there is talk of "cosmic consciousness" and other mystical states. But with Ouspensky's superman, a new perception on the evolution of consciousness enters the picture. Like Orage, Ouspensky was a Nietzschean; and, like Bergson, he has many doubts about the adequacy of the Darwinian version of evolution. His Nietzscheanism appears in his denial of Bucke's democratic vision that cosmic consciousness is a natural, more or less automatic or inevitable outcome of the evolutionary process and that over time it will produce an entire humanity possessing the new consciousness in the way it now possesses self-consciousness. In contrast, Ouspensky argues that the appearance of the new consciousness is not part of the general "development" of humanity. It is limited to individuals—not, it must be made clear, by any outside authority, but by their own interests and values. Any evolution of consciousness must be achieved through our own efforts, chiefly through the development of a culture that encourages and nourishes the new consciousness, in contrast to what Ouspensky saw as the philistinism and barbarism then prevalent in Western civilization. Ouspensky had none of Bucke's ebullient optimism about the immediate future, and, as his "Letters From Russia" show, he viewed socialism as a central evil, a levelling of all values to the lowest common denominator, more or less sanctioning philistinism as the norm. By today's standards, Ouspensky was definitely not politically correct.

The other criticism he makes of Bucke is that he leaves out the possibility that evolution may operate through several independent streams or strains simultaneously. For Ouspensky, evolution may make many detours, sudden starts and stops, and changes of direction. He argues that the paleontological record does not reveal a neat, orderly progression from "primitive" forms to us; rather it tells a story of abrupt jumps, leaps, and "sports." It portrays the rapid appearance and disappearance of forms and cannot be understood as depicting a stately "ascent" from earlier organisms to twentieth-century humanity. For Ouspensky, evolution is not the single, orderly, unbroken process of development it is usually understood to be. It is rather a series of different, varying experiments carried out by what he calls the Great Laboratory.[12] Each of these experiments aims at creating a being that can be self-evolving, no longer dependent on the submerged consciousness of the species or race for its direction, but capable of independent action and thought. So far, the only experiment that can be considered in any way successful in this direction is the human being. As with Bergson, it is the human being that carries within itself the greatest potential for freedom and novelty. That potential, however, will not be actualized automatically.

In the chapter "Esotericism and Modern Thought" of *A New Model of the Universe,* Ouspensky discusses many ideas that have today gained a new currency, such as the possibility that civilization appeared much earlier than we have hitherto believed, as well as the idea that there have been several civilizations before our own.[13] One of the central themes of this and other chapters is the idea that there is no such thing as a "natural" or "mechanical" evolution—that is, what is generally considered evolution, the Darwinian notion of chance mutations, adaptation, and "survival of the fittest." Again, by definition all evolution is guided, has aim and purpose, otherwise it is mere "change." In animals it is nature, the Great Laboratory, at work. In human evolution, Ouspensky saw signs of what he called the Inner Circle, an esoteric center, from which the ideas, tools, and knowledge of civilization emerge. As he writes, "There exists no evolution which begins accidentally and proceeds mechanically. Only degeneration and decay can proceed mechanically. Civilization never starts by natural growth, but only through artificial cultivation."[14]

This idea of an Inner Circle strikes us as particularly dubious today, smacking of conspiracy theories and dictatorial demigods, even though neither of these, in fact, applies to what Ouspensky is talking about. At a time when the majority of thinkers smugly believed that the civilization and culture of nineteenth-century Europe was the "aim" of evolution—this meant capitalism and mechanistic science—Ouspensky was one of a few voices arguing against this complacency, and offering instead the humbling thought that civilizations much higher than our own may have already risen and fallen in the past. The idea of a "secret society" guiding human affairs may be hard to swallow, but recent years have seen a resurgence of the notion that the civilization of ancient Egypt—which orthodox archaeologists argue had no precedent— may possibly have been inherited from a previous civilization, which some have suggested was Atlantis. And again, Ouspensky is in no way Eurocentric in his discussion of civilization and its evolution. He makes clear that during periods of barbarism in European history, civilization may have flourished in South America, Africa, Asia, or Polynesia. Likewise, his conception of a "new race," however awkward the phrase seems to us, is not to be understood in racial terms. He recognized signs of the emerging new consciousness in all the peoples he came across in his travels in Europe, North America, India, the Near and Far East.[15] (It was in fact in the Europeans of his time that this idea met with the greatest resistance.) What is crucial for Ouspensky is not race—not in fact "nature"—but "nurture," cultivation, the root of our own idea of "culture." The new consciousness, if it is to occur, must be cultivated.

The cultivation he argued for would not, he knew, come from the intelligentsia of his time. As far as he was concerned, they were little more than sophisticated barbarians. If the new consciousness was to be nurtured, and if civilization was to be saved, help would have to come from somewhere else. That "somewhere else" was esotericism. And it is to this we must turn in our next section.

PART TWO

Esoteric Evolution

CHAPTER SEVEN

The Bishop and the Bulldog

In 1860 a debate took place at Oxford University between Bishop Samuel Wilberforce and the biologist T. H. Huxley. The subject was evolution. It was only a year since Charles Darwin had published *The Origin of the Species,* and the bishop intended to squash the controversial idea once and for all. As hardly needs pointing out, he was not successful. It was not for nothing that Huxley was known as Darwin's "bulldog."

Bishop Wilberforce was an orthodox, conservative man, and his blustery rhetoric expressed the anxiety, fear, and sheer incomprehension that affected a generation whose world had been turned upside down. Darwin had proposed an explanation radically different from the one most people accepted for the appearance of the variety of life-forms on the planet. Until then it was generally agreed, at least in the Western world, that God had created the heavens and the earth at some definite point in the not-too-distant past. The exact year Creation had taken place had even been worked out: In the seventeenth century, based on the chronology in the Bible, Archbishop Ussher had calculated that it must have happened in 4004 B.C. Darwin changed all that.

That Bishop Wilberforce, Huxley, and everyone else had descended from apes was, of course, a difficult notion to accept. But what was equally disturbing was that Darwin's idea of evolu-

tion called for a universe very different from the one people of that
time had grown up with. Darwin's idea called for a gradual change
from one species to another over vast spans of time, much more
than the mere five or six thousand years Archbishop Ussher would
allow. The kind of changes Darwin spoke of required millions of
years, great gulfs of time that were beyond most people's imagination, and still are even today.

That these changes took place without aim or purpose was bad
enough; as Samuel Butler would soon point out, Darwin had "banished mind from the universe." But he had also done something
else. He had made the universe a very strange place. Science is
about acquiring more and more knowledge about the world, and
in "explaining" our appearance by way of our simian ancestors,
Darwin had perhaps provided some deeper insight into ourselves.
But he did so by making the rest of the universe more *un*-known.

Although today evolution is associated with his name,
Darwin's "idea" was not really new. In 1721 the French philosopher Montesquieu, famous for his *Persian Letters*, had proposed
that a few early species had multiplied into the present ones and
that the differences between species could increase or decrease over
time, a process he called "transmutation." One of his contemporaries, the naturalist Georges Buffon, suggested that the horse was
related to the ass. By 1760 the great Swedish taxonomist Linnaeus
had come to the conclusion that species could vary. In 1790 the
poet Goethe—who considered his scientific writings more important than his poetry—had published his *Metamorphosis of Plants*,
in which he argued that all existing plants had derived from a common ancestor.[1] And in 1809 Jean-Baptiste Lamarck had designed a
kind of "evolutionary tree," beginning with tiny animals and continuing on to ourselves; he had also suggested a means by which
changes in species took place, proposing that giraffes, for example,
had "evolved" their long necks by what he called "the inheritance
of acquired characteristics." In the past some giraffes wanted to
reach the leaves higher up in trees and made the effort to do so.
What they gained in size by stretching was passed on to their offspring, who in turn made similar efforts and also bequeathed to

their offspring similar benefits, and so on, until we arrive at the long-necked giraffes of today.

For a long time Darwin's ideas and Lamarck's ideas seemed equally possible, and as no one ever saw "evolution in action," there seemed no way to prove who was right. But at the end of the nineteenth century when the German zoologist August Weismann showed that the genes passed on from parent to offspring were unaffected by characteristics acquired by the parent—a doctrine known as "the continuity and unalterability of the germ-tract"—Darwin's version won out.[2] Strangely, at the same time that Darwin was meditating on the "survival of the fittest"—a phrase the philosopher Herbert Spencer had coined a decade earlier—the naturalist Alfred Russel Wallace had hit upon the idea of "natural selection" independently, through a reading of the economist Thomas Malthus's *Essay on the Principle of Population*. Wallace magnanimously allowed Darwin to reap the glory of their "discovery," although in some key respects, Wallace could not accept all of Darwin's conclusions. He rejected, for example, the idea that our higher mental and spiritual faculties could be explained in terms of natural selection, believing that some nonphysical agency had to be involved. It is perhaps for this reason, as well as the fact that Wallace was an ardent spiritualist, that he has been gently airbrushed out of most discussions on evolution.

Although many minds fought a rearguard action against the rising idea, evolution seemed destined for success. For years the notion that *change* was central to the world had been making headway. Less than a century before Darwin published his findings, the American and French Revolutions had altered societies irrevocably. The philosopher Georg Friedrich Hegel, who believed that history is the work of the unfolding of Spirit, emphasized "becoming" rather than "being" and was profoundly influential; for one thing, his work had a deep effect on Karl Marx, whose own ideas would lead to massive social and political changes in the twentieth century. And the Industrial Revolution, which had changed not only people's lives but the landscape, had contributed the notion of "progress" to the collective consciousness.

What was different about Darwin's idea was his explanation for how the changes he spoke of came about. He had indeed "banished mind from the universe." There was no need for it. The mechanisms of supply and demand could account for everything. No will was necessary, no effort, and, most disturbingly, no God. Only three things: the relentless pressure of survival; the possibility of random mutations which occasionally produced an organism better suited to survive and hence more able to leave offspring; and time.

The time Darwin needed came from his friend and mentor Charles Lyell, the father of modern geology. In 1830 Lyell, a Scotsman, had published his *Principles of Geology,* in which he argued that all the features of the Earth's surface had been produced by physical, chemical, and biological processes taking place over vast periods of time. The processes Lyell spoke of could not have operated within the span allowed by Archbishop Ussher. Or rather, they could, and in fact were operating, but they did so at such a slow tempo that five or six thousand years would account for little visible change.[3] To arrive at the Earth as Lyell knew it required millions of years: "deep time." Deep time gave Darwinian evolution the leeway it needed to work. Given these vast aeons, it was possible that small, chance changes, building up over millennia, could account for the variety of organisms scattered across the planet. They could even account for the rise of one organism in particular, the only one, it seemed, that was concerned about its origin: the human being.

CHAPTER EIGHT

—

Enter the Madame

Darwin was not the only one interested in human origins, or in the possibilities opened up by the vast prospects of time revealed by

Charles Lyell. At the same time that T. H. Huxley was decimating Bishop Wilberforce at the Oxford debate, a woman who would present the first full-scale attack on Darwinian evolution—as well as on the whole edifice of scientific materialism—was travelling through the Caucasus, living among native tribes, and developing control over her strange paranormal powers. Fifteen years later, and on the other side of the world, she was the head of a new mystical movement. Two years after that, she made her literary debut, which, if sheer size and sales are any indication, had a great impact. In two volumes, the book's densely packed 1,270 pages covered an immense range of material, from magic, kabbalah, and psychic powers to ancient races, secret teachings, and Hindu philosophy. It spoke of Christ, Buddha, and the mysterious Comte de St. Germain. Its basic premise was that magic, or "the occult," is not hocus-pocus but a true science, based on profound knowledge of the secrets of nature, lost to modern humanity but known to the ancients and to a few highly evolved human beings—adepts—then existing on the planet. It also presented an outline of cosmic and human evolution vastly different than that offered by modern science. The first printing of one thousand copies sold out in ten days. A review in the *New York Herald* called it "one of the most remarkable productions of the century." The book's title was *Isis Unveiled* (1877), and its author was the inimitable Helena Petrovna Blavatsky.[1]

A century after the publication of *Isis Unveiled,* Theodore Roszak, the historian of the 1960s counterculture, remarked, "In the years following publication of *The Origin of the Species,* HPB [as she was known to her followers] was the first person to aggressively argue the case for a transphysical element in evolution."[2] This accomplishment is easily forgotten when we look at the book today, as well as at her later and even larger work *The Secret Doctrine* (1888). Both seem enormous heaps of disorganized erudition, full of startling insights, but riddled with plagiarisms, crank ideas, and unsavory notions on race. It takes an effort of historical imagination to grasp the electrifying effect they had on a generation that had had the wind taken out of it by the revelations of Darwin.

Blavatsky's eccentric books fed a hunger gnawing at the nine-teenth-century soul.

Darwin was not the century's only dark prophet, for a decade before *The Origin of the Species* the physicist Rudolf Clausius had cast a pall over the age with his formulation of the second law of thermodynamics. Summed up in the notion of "entropy"—the increase of disorder or "waste" in a closed system—Clausius's "law" led to the doleful recognition that the universe would even-tually run down into what was then called its "heat death." All of its highly organized energy would dissolve into a featureless cosmic soup. This outcome was inevitable, given the "facts" uncovered by science. Physicists even predicted when the Sun would burn out. Minds sensitive to this were prompted to reflect on the purpose of existence. If the end was certain chaos, what was the point? It was in this climate of cosmic pessimism that spiritualism came to prominence, and along with it Madame Blavatsky.[3]

In the years before she appeared as a voluble critic of scientif-ic materialism, Blavatsky led what is commonly called a colorful life. Before she founded the Theosophical Society with Colonel Henry Steel Olcott in 1875, she had been, among other things, a piano teacher, the manager of an artificial flower factory, a circus bareback rider, a journalist, a world traveller, and a medium. It was in this last capacity that she first met Colonel Olcott when both were investigating the reports of a series of "materializations" at a farmhouse in Vermont. Olcott was struck by the Madame's bear-ing—particularly her blazing red Garibaldian shirt. He introduced himself, and less than a year later they founded the Theosophical Society in New York City.

Although originally centered on the by-now familiar spiritual-ist routine, the society soon moved in another direction. Blavatsky herself was bored with the spiritualist business and could casually toss off "apports" and "manifestations" other mediums labored at. These, she felt, were ultimately unimportant. Her calling lay else-where. It was not the message of the spirits that she was destined to proclaim, but the hidden wisdom of the ages. Lost for centuries, obscured by the false doctrines of materialism and an incomplete science, it was now revealed to her in copious detail by an incontrovertible source.

She was, she told Colonel Olcott, in contact with higher intelligences. These were the Hidden Masters, adepts who guide the evolution of humankind from secret monasteries secure in the forbidding heights of the Himalayas. They had chosen her as their spokeswoman to bring their teachings to the masses, in order to prevent the modern world from sinking deeper into the spiritless doctrines of matter. Proof of this claim came in the form of the famous Mahatma letters, which the Madame would materialize out of thin air, to the amazement of Colonel Olcott—and the contemptuous remarks of others.

In her own day Madame Blavatsky was a formidable figure and often in the news, but today, outside of occult, Theosophical and New Age circles, she is remembered, if at all, as one of the many mediums who preyed upon the gullible and bored in the last years of the nineteenth century, and as the founder of a dotty religious cult. Her "exposure" by Richard Hodgson, a member of the Society for Psychical Research, showed her up as a fraud, and although this exposure itself has been questioned repeatedly, Blavatsky has gone down in most of the history books as a colorful, eccentric crank. Peter Washington's astringent and entertaining *Madame Blavatsky's Baboon* (1993) is a good example of the mainstream view of her and Theosophy.

Yet Blavatsky's contribution to esoteric thought is considerable, and perhaps so fundamental that it is difficult to recognize it. It is true that works like *Isis Unveiled* and *The Secret Doctrine* are great hodgepodges and that, as many have pointed out, there is less a definable "Theosophical philosophy" than a collection of beliefs and ideas brought together under the term. Nevertheless some of those beliefs and ideas are so central to the various strains of mystical thought forming a countertradition to mainstream scientific materialism that it is important to remember just what they are.

Perhaps the central idea of Theosophy is that of the fundamental unity of all existence, an idea, certainly, that modern science itself adheres to, but with one important distinction. Whereas science grounds this unity in "matter," or some form of physical "stuff"—atoms or some subatomic particle—for Blavatsky, this unity of being is predicated on consciousness. One basic, primal being, preceding any of its manifestations, is shared by everything, from atoms to God. In its "positive" aspect, this being is consciousness; in its "negative" aspect, it is substance, which forms the subject of consciousness, that which consciousness is conscious of. (In this formulation, Blavatsky's metaphysics are very similar to Hegel's.) This being so, each individual thing is at the same time all things as well as absolute being—an idea we find in philosophers like Alfred North Whitehead and physicists like David Bohm. This idea of the fundamental "oneness" of things is so basic to mystical thought that it would need a separate book to trace all its appearances in all its varieties since Blavatsky popularized it more than a century ago. Needless to say, she absorbed it from Indian philosophy, although the idea had been percolating in Western thought for some time—we find it in Schopenhauer, Hegel, and the Transcendentalists. But Blavatsky got it across to thousands of readers who might not otherwise have bothered with metaphysics.

A corollary of this idea is that the universe, as R. M. Bucke recognized, is alive. There is no such thing as "dead matter." The picture of the universe as a vast space peppered here and there with blind, inert matter, which just by chance has "evolved" on our planet into what we call "life," is the complete opposite of the truth. Life is not the exception; it's the rule. That the universe is one conscious, living being is a grand elaboration of James Lovelock's Gaia hypothesis, yet Blavatsky predated his popularizing of the idea by more than a century.[4]

Another central theosophical thought is that the human being, the highest form of life that we know, is a microcosm that encompasses in its being all the forces operating in the universe. The human being is not, as we are told again and again, merely one "thing" among others, but is in truth a "little universe." In contrast to modern science which sees them as passive, accidental creatures acted upon by physical forces beyond their control, human beings for Blavatsky house within themselves all of the energies available in the universe, and are capable of using these at will. Magic is the knowledge of these energies and the ability to use them, a discipline known and employed by the ancients, but lost to us with the rise of modern science.

The cosmos itself, for Blavatsky, is not a static, once-and-for-all event, but is ever changing. For a generation anticipating the "heat death" of the universe, Blavatsky held out the idea that the universe had been created and destroyed countless times, in an unending cycle of birth and death—an idea we ourselves can draw on for comfort when we contemplate the Big Bang that supposedly started it all and the possible Big Crunch we may be heading toward. She also postulated that our universe is only one of an infinite number of universes, another idea that has gained some scientific currency, mostly through the work of the physicist John Wheeler, but that found its way into science fiction books and films decades before he made it "scientifically acceptable." Eternity for Blavatsky is "the playground of numberless Universes incessantly manifesting and disappearing,"[5] and the human soul itself is involved in this ceaseless ebb and flow, incarnating and evolving through all forms of manifestation, from the smallest atom to the Godhead.

With her belief that "our universe is only one of an infinite number of universes,"[6] Blavatsky countered the deadening influence of the second law of thermodynamics and its frightful prospects of the death of the cosmos. And with her ideas on cosmic evolution, she took on Darwin, and advanced an idea that would echo in popular culture in various forms throughout the next century. Contra Darwin, Blavatsky declared that we were not descended from the animals, but were in fact created by higher beings that incarnate on our planet for the express purpose of guiding human evolution. In the early days of humankind, a "Great Being" appeared and, with a group of "semidivine" beings, formed a kind of nursery for future human adepts. Human development began, Blavatsky declared in *The Secret Doctrine*, not through the vagaries of chance and the pressures of survival, but through the agency of the highest and best from other worlds. Almost a century later this idea would reappear in various forms in the late 1960s, in the bestselling but absurd fantastications of Erich von Daniken and in the film collaboration between Stanley Kubrick and Arthur C. Clarke,

2001: A Space Odyssey. Both shared with Blavatsky a desire to bring mind in some form back into the origin of humankind. Far from feeling any debilitating mea culpa over being human, as some current "spiritually correct" teachings suggest, Blavatsky prophesied that all planets "are, were, or will be man-bearing," an idea that in a different form was put forward recently by the physicist Frank Tippler.

Blavatsky's account of the creation and evolution of humankind and the universe was based on several sources: knowledge given her by her Hidden Masters, the Mahatmas; an ancient work called *The Book of Dyzan,* written in the secret language called Senzar; and the Akashic Record, a kind of spiritual videotape record of the entire history of the universe. The Mahatmas have been questionable ever since Richard Hodgson's "exposé," and the kabbalist scholar Gershom Scholem argued that the stanzas from *The Book Of Dyzan* were based on an obscure seventeenth-century kabbalistic work. But the Akashic Record has fared better since Blavatsky first made public some of its revelations. The Sanskrit word *akasa,* on which it is based, means "ether" or "space," and the idea of some immaterial medium housing otherwise inaccessible memories—memories not immediately available to consciousness—has surfaced in different ways since Blavatsky's day. Jung's "collective unconscious" seems a variant of it, as does Rupert Sheldrake's "morphogenetic fields," and the idea has resemblances to Bergson's notion that we perceive more "virtually" than we are "actually" conscious of, as well as his belief that there is more in human consciousness than what is stored in the brain. It is also, of course, in line with Ouspensky's realization that the "present" we perceive is only a section of a fuller time dimension including the past and the future. As Blavatsky herself remarked, "Time is only an illusion produced by the succession of our states of consciousness as we travel through eternal duration."[7]

Regardless of our reservations about its validity, Blavatsky's vision of human and cosmic evolution is thrilling, and in many ways resembles a later vision of future ages, the evolutionary science fiction epics of Olaf Stapledon.[8] Existence oscillates between two phases, the days and nights of Brahma, *manvantaras* being the cosmic days and *pralayas* the cosmic nights. In the beginning—or at least in the most recent beginning—there was, as in most accounts of creation, chaos, formless and void, an absolute nothing, something very much like the stage of nonexistence that present-day cosmologists postulate "existed before" the Big Bang. Then the vibrations of eternity awaken to new life and a new *manvantara* is entered upon. The primordial essence separates itself into seven Rays that shape the created universe. These Rays are in reality intelligent beings, the *Dhyan Chohans*, and, through the use of *Fohat*—a kind of universal energy—they fashion a new cosmos. Our own world is the result of a kind of cosmic condensation, with stellar matter passing through a kind of whirlwind, which eventually collects into the nebula that will become our solar system and the Earth itself. The Earth is destined to progress through seven "Rounds," or periods of cosmic evolution. Seven is a central number for Blavatsky, as it is for a later reader of the Akashic Record, Rudolf Steiner. Not only does the Earth work through its sevenfold evolution—we are currently in the fourth Round, a placement that Steiner will adopt as well—but the human race also passes through a series of seven "Root Races." In both cases the trajectory is from an initial spiritual condition, through increasing solidification, to a growing and eventually liberating etherealization.

It is in the fourth Round that human beings appear on Earth. Four of the seven "Root Races" have appeared before our own, and two will follow. The first Root Race, which would scarcely appear human to us, inhabited a continent called the "Imperishable Sacred Land." This first race were in fact pure spirit, being without bodies, a condition shared by the second Root Race, the Hyperboreans. After the "Imperishable Sacred Land" was destroyed by a cataclysm—prompting curiosity about the aptness of its name—the second race inhabited a land near the North Pole. In those days—several hundred million years ago—the axis of the Earth was not tilted as it is today, and the climate of the Pole was mild.[9] The third Root Race had its home on the continent of Lemuria—fragments of which remain today as Australia and Easter Island. Not until eighteen million years ago, a comparatively short time in Blavatsky's cosmic history, did beings resembling us appear.

It was during the beginning of the fourth Round that the Higher Beings descended to the Earth. Their descent into physical bodies and the pleasures of material existence gave rise to the legend of the Fall. It was during this time that separation of the sexes took place; previously the first and second Root Races reproduced through forms of parthenogenesis. It was during the later half of the third Root Race that sex as we know it developed. This race met its end when the continent of Lemuria, which spanned what is now the Pacific, sank after a catastrophic fire.

The next race to emerge did so on Atlantis. Eight hundred and fifty thousand years ago, the fourth Root Race appeared on the fabled island continent, first spoken of by Plato in the *Timaeus* and subsequently the subject of hundreds of books. Possessing bodies, four senses (sight, hearing, touch, and smell; taste would appear with the fifth Root Race), the Atlanteans were the most "human-like" race so far. Masters of psychic powers and technology, they were in many ways more advanced than us; they had airships and could manipulate electricity and other forces. The Atlanteans, however, had a taste for black magic, as well as for some unsavory sexual practices. According to Blavatsky, gorillas and chimpanzees, rather than being the forebears of humanity, were the product of the unwholesome union between decadent Atlanteans and certain "she animals." The idea that apes and other animals are not the "raw material" out of which *homo sapiens* emerged, but are instead evolutionary cul-de-sacs stemming off from the main branch of human development, is one that would be picked up by several esoteric thinkers who followed. (Tragically, in the hands of some fanatical racial theorists it would be applied to various "inferior races," with inhuman results.)

Some of the Atlanteans were giants, which explains the colossal scale of some ancient architecture like Stonehenge and the pyramids. The Atlanteans, however, abused their power and knowledge, and the race sank into decadence as the continent itself began to sink below the waves. A last lingering portion, Poseidonis, remained to the very end, disappearing a mere eleven thousand years ago. It was these final days of Atlantis that gave rise to the legends of the Great Flood.

Not all the Atlanteans met their doom; some travelled to what would become Egypt, some to the Americas. But they were soon overshadowed by the rise of the fifth Root Race, the Aryans, who, until the close of the nineteenth century, remained a kind of evolutionary avant-garde. Each Root Race breaks down into seven Sub-Races—it would be too complicated and repetitious to follow all of them—and the fifth Sub-Race of the Aryans are the Anglo-Saxons. Blavatsky believed that the sixth Sub-Race was being born on the western shores of the United States in the last decade of the nineteenth century. Two more races will appear after the Aryans perish—as Lemuria burned, and Atlantis sank, the Aryans are due to meet their end through some sort of gigantic earthquake, a shifting of the planet's crust.[10] Exactly what will happen after that is anyone's guess, but as Blavatsky told her followers, the adepts who had appointed her as their spokeswoman were working to guide humankind through its cosmic maturity.

However, not all the recipients of Blavatsky's cosmic wisdom were willing to wait patiently for developments.

CHAPTER NINE

Doctor Steiner, I Presume?

In the same year that Madame Blavatsky published *The Secret Doctrine*, 1888, an unprepossessing young scholar gave a lecture to the Vienna Goethe Society on "Goethe as Father of a New Aesthetic." The scholar had made a modest name for himself a few years earlier as the editor of the great German poet's scientific writings for an immense compilation of his work in the German National Literature series. The young man had been twenty-one at the time, and the job had given him entrée into the literary and intellectual circles he had long wished to penetrate. It may seem surprising that the responsibility for editing Goethe's scientific work—which ran to several volumes—would have been entrusted to a young student, but the general opinion among the intelligentsia was that Goethe's scientific forays were both worthless as science and dreary as literature, and it is more than likely that no one of any higher standing wanted the job. The young scholar, however, snapped at it. In Goethe he had found confirmation of the insights into the relation between the human mind and external reality that had come to him often as he contemplated nature. Not long after editing Goethe's writings, he wrote his first book, *Theory and Knowledge in Light of Goethe's Worldview* (1886). It did not catapult him into fame, but it did establish him as a serious thinker on the curious problems of epistemology, the difficult study of how we know what we know. It also led to other work. Earlier in 1888, the young man had taken up the post as editor of a weekly political newspaper, the *Deutsche Wochenshrift,* but his tenure there did not last long. Politics was not his forte, and, in any case, the romantic idealism that inspired him was not quite what the Viennese reading public had in mind. Unabashed, he left the journal after six months. But his interest in Goethe remained, as did his enthusiasm. Both were to stay with him as the heart of a philosophy that would reach from the hallowed halls of Weimar to the lost secrets of Atlantis and the visionary future of the human race. The young scholar's name was Rudolf Steiner.

Rudolf Steiner was born in 1861 in Kraljevec, in what was then part of Austria-Hungary, and is now Croatia. Given his contemplative nature, there could hardly have been a more suitable environment for him to spend his early years. Mountains and green expanses were his playgrounds, with long walks in the nearby forests providing ample time to study nature and her creations. The young Steiner was also drawn to the electric telegraph that his father operated for the Southern Austrian Railway, and to the trains that ran on the line. At that time the telegraph was the cutting edge of technology, and train travel itself was still in its infancy.[1] The inquisitive young boy could turn from the inspiring heights of the nearby Alps to the complex workings of modern electronic communication. Rudolf Steiner started life at a meeting point between science and the beauties of nature, and the need to balance this polarity remained with him throughout his career.

Early intellectual influences came from mathematics and reading Euclid, and a fascination with practical mysteries, such as how the raw material delivered to a nearby textile factory was transformed into the finished product, instilled a deep hunger for down-to-earth, hands-on experience in the young boy. Such practical matters played a central part in Steiner's later career—as architect, agriculturalist, educator, and homeopath—and need to be kept in mind when considering his other talents as a seer and visionary.[2] An early reading of Kant prepared him for his later philosophical struggles. But there were other experiences as well, ones not altogether common for growing boys. Like Madame Blavatsky, early on Steiner showed a propensity for peculiar psychic powers. Once, while sitting in a room at his father's train station, the young Steiner saw a strange woman open the door and come in. She looked, he thought, like other members of his family. Standing in the middle of the room the woman looked at young Rudolf and said, "Try to help me as much as you can—now as well as in later life." Then she walked toward the stove and vanished. Steiner hesitated to tell his parents of the strange woman, fearing they would not believe him. But the next day he saw that his father was upset and discovered that a female relative had killed herself; the suicide had taken place at the same time that Steiner had seen the strange woman.[3]

There were few Steiner could speak with about this strange experience, and it was not until he was eighteen that he met someone with whom he could share his insights into the spiritual world. Although Steiner does not tell us in his autobiography, his student Emil Bock later discovered that the humble, poor herb gatherer Steiner had come to know was named Felix Koguzki. Koguzki was not a very articulate man, but he shared the young Steiner's spiritual sensitivity. On a train they shared once a week to Vienna—where Steiner by then was studying and Koguzki took his herbs to sell—the herb gatherer listened with sympathy to the young man's talk about the spirit world, and from his own simple but intense piety he could answer him. It was the beginning of the long development of spiritual self-confidence that preceded Steiner's first public expression of his insights in his fortieth year.

There was one more fateful encounter. Not long after meeting Koguzki, Steiner had conversations with someone who to this day remains unknown. All we know of him comes through the few references Steiner makes to him in his autobiography. He had as humble a position as the herb gatherer, but his influence on Steiner was more intellectual. Steiner's conversations with this strange man helped plant the seeds of what would later flower as one of the most successful and influential alternative teachings in the world today.

But one more ingredient was needed. It is unclear exactly when Steiner first became interested in Theosophy. He joined the Theosophical Society in 1902, and soon after became the head of its German branch, as well as the editor of an esoteric journal, *Lucifer*, later called *Lucifer-Gnosis*. But his interest in Theosophy more than likely began several years earlier, in 1888, when he became acquainted with Friedrich Eckstein at the Griensteidl Kaffe in Vienna. Eckstein, a wealthy patron of the arts, was Blavatsky's most important Viennese follower, and it is more than likely that he spoke of her and Theosophy to the earnest young scholar— Eckstein even records that at one point the young Goethean asked him to explain exactly what Theosophy was about. Eckstein had brought a copy of A. P. Sinnett's *Esoteric Buddhism* (1884) back with him from a trip to England, and soon after Steiner read it in its German translation. Around the same time, Steiner frequented the salon of the feminist Marie Lang. She and her husband were both ardent Theosophists, and conversations with them eventually convinced Steiner that, although the talk of Hidden Masters was too simplistic, there was a core spiritual knowledge in Theosophy that warranted serious study.[4]

CHAPTER TEN

◠

From Goethean Science to the Wisdom of the Human Being

By 1913 Rudolf Steiner had broken with the Theosophical Society, ostensibly over Annie Besant's attempt to promote Jiddu Krishnamurti as the latest incarnation of the master Maitreya. Steiner combined his psychic sensitivity, his insights into Goethe's worldview, and the evolutionary framework of *The Secret Doctrine* into a remarkable account of human and cosmic evolution. He named his new teaching Anthroposophy, the wisdom of the human being.

It may seem that Goethe and Atlantis are the unlikeliest of bedfellows. But what Steiner discovered in Goethe was an effective antidote to the prevailing assumption that human consciousness was "cut off" from reality, that our subjective, interior world has no direct relation to nature and the external world, and hence no access to "truth." For this point of view, all we know, and all we can ever know, is what is going on "inside our head," and if we are interested in knowing the "truth" about nature, we must look to science (although the obvious fact that scientists too have everything "inside their heads" is conveniently ignored). As we saw in our discussion of Ouspensky and *Tertium Organum,* this notion was associated with the philosophy of Kant, who argued that the *Ding-an-sich,* or "thing-in-itself," is forever beyond our reach.

Ouspensky proposed one solution to this curious situation: enhance our appreciation of space and time in order to perceive more of the world. Goethe took a different but related approach. He was extremely wary of metaphysics and sceptical of any purely abstract thinking that divorced human beings from harmonious interaction with nature. He had an unshakeable bedrock faith in the senses and was forever upbraiding his fellow Germans for their, to him, debilitating addiction to "ideas." This is not to say that Goethe was a mere sensualist with no interest in ideas. Indeed, it is

an idea that led Steiner to find in Goethe a countercurrent to
Western materialist science. However, this idea came to Goethe not
through the detached thought-spinning of a mind abstracted from
experience, but from his conscious and imaginative *participation* in
the observation of nature. The kind of truth that would arrive at
the conclusion that reality is forever beyond our grasp was for
Goethe no truth at all, nor would that "reality" be of any use.

For Goethe truth is "a revelation emerging at the point where
the inner world of man meets external reality. . . . It is a synthesis
of world and mind, yielding the happiest assurance of the eternal
harmony of existence." This is so because "there resides, in the
objective world, an unknown law which corresponds to the
unknown law within subjective experience."[1] Goethe did not come
to this conclusion through poetic meditation, but through the rigorous practice of scientific observation—which, for a poet like him,
often meant the same thing. The "idea" mentioned above was
Goethe's *Urpflanze,* the archetypal plant from which all others are
derived, the subject of his botanical study *The Metamorphosis of
Plants.* The details of his observations needn't concern us here, but
what is curious and unusual about this "idea" is that Goethe
claimed that it was not solely a product of his head—of detached
abstract thinking—but was actually *perceivable* by closely observing a plant in the process of growth. The trick is to observe it not
with the cool detachment of the scientist, careful to exclude any
subjective element from the observation, but with the imaginative
warmth and ardor of an artist. In this way Goethe claimed to have
actually *seen* the *Urpflanze* itself, and it is only in this way, he says,
when human imagination "participates" in the external world, that
truth, or at least any truth worth having, emerges. Admittedly, this
is a radical departure from the idea of truth, and the place of
human consciousness in relation to it, that has held center stage for
the last three centuries.

One of the targets of Goethe's criticism was "transcendental
philosophy," epitomized in the philosophy of Kant. The other was
modern science or, perhaps more accurately, the "scientism" that
was then emerging and has since become our own dominant sensibility. Goethe found both ultimately debilitating and antilife

because both were founded on abstraction at the cost of experience. His approach was phenomenological: what were important for him were the *actual phenomena of our experience*—blue skies, green grass, white clouds. Kant, as we have seen, argued that there is good reason to suspect that these things may not exist in reality—as, that is, things-in-themselves. Science undermined a faith in the immediacy of our experience in a similar way.

We can characterize the advance of science as the sole arbiter of truth by seeing in it the gradual expulsion of human consciousness from its object of study. This began when Galileo split—"bifurcated," in Alfred North Whitehead's phrase—reality into two camps, which for convenience we can call the quantitative and the qualitative, or, following Galileo, *primary* and *secondary* qualities. *Primary* qualities were all those things that could be measured with certainty and that would remain constant, regardless of how they were perceived by an observer: position, speed, mass, etc. *Secondary* qualities were those things that were "purely subjective," meaning the sensual aspect of experience: the blazing reds of a sunset or the refreshing caress of a breeze. Primary qualities were primary because they could be accurately and repeatedly measured. And because they could be measured they were considered "real"—which meant they existed "objectively," on their own, independent of human subjectivity. Secondary qualities—which in effect are what we mean by "the world" (we are usually more interested in the sensuous aspect of a tree than in its mass)—were by definition "unreal," or, as the cliché goes, "merely subjective."[2] Thus, where we, as sensuous interpreters of reality, see a glorious sunset and feel the mystical awe that often accompanies this experience, the ideal "objective" observer—some recording device or other—would perceive "reality" in the raw: a collection of colorless electromagnetic waves refracted through the Earth's atmosphere.

Although Goethe the poet was concerned about the threat to poetry that such a development suggested—he knew that the beauties of nature, both the natural phenomena themselves and our subjective response to them, would lose their primacy as they were methodically "explained" by science—what troubled him more deeply was that such an idea of truth would eventually leave humanity as the master of a spiritually void reality. For there was no doubt that science "worked." Today we are convinced of this as never before. But it is also true that we are more alienated from ourselves and from our world than at any other time in history. The truths this science was uncovering were inimical to us because they extracted human consciousness from the world and pushed it further and further back into a narrow corner, while opening up a "reality" that was as dull and dead as it was pointless. Truths such as these stood the whole idea of the value of truth on its head, a recognition Nietzsche would bring to its ironic and paradoxically logical conclusion later in the century. Truth, for Goethe, is only of value if we can harmonize it into our total being. The abstract concepts of a detached objective science were not of this sort. More dangerously, they advanced people's power to manipulate nature without advancing their capacity to appreciate her. Goethe, a more robust soul than Nietzsche, met the challenge head on and sought to beat the scientists at their own game by showing that human consciousness is an integral part of truth—most famously in the color theory he developed contra Newton. The success he had can be measured by the fact that his scientific writings—which he considered more important than his poetry—were left in the hands of the unknown twenty-one-year-old Rudolf Steiner.[3]

By the time Steiner began to develop the ideas that would take shape as Anthroposophy, the scientism Goethe wished to counter had long been established as the "official" guarantor of truth, a position it now holds unrivaled a century later. There had of course been many warning voices. William Blake, Goethe's more obscure contemporary, spoke of the "Satanic mills" blackening England's green and pleasant land. Others followed—Madame Blavatsky, as we have seen, was one. By the end of the nineteenth century a veritable chorus had risen up against the juggernaut of material progress and scientific rationalism. Yet science and the scientific sensibility were so successful that they could absorb these criticisms and relegate them to impotent sentimentality, while pointing out their own undeniable concrete achievements. To have any influence on the times, something more than poetry was needed: science had to be fought with science. And this is what Rudolf Steiner decided to do.

———

The science Steiner had in mind was the rigorous investigation and exploration of consciousness. This meant understanding how our own consciousness arrived at where it is today. Goethe was important for Steiner because in his pursuit of the *Urpflanze* Goethe pointed to a relationship between the inner and outer worlds that had existed in the past and that Steiner believed would exist again, in a different way, in the future. With a poet's intuition and a scientist's scrutiny, Goethe had hit on the crucial insight that human consciousness was not, as Descartes and those who followed him believed, a passive mirror *reflecting* an external world whose "laws" determined it with ironbound necessity; consciousness, rather, was a cocreator of that world. Or, as Steiner would say in an early work on Goethe, speaking of our relationship to the external world: "Man is not only there in order to form for himself a picture of the finished world; nay, he himself cooperates in bringing the world into existence."[4]

Steiner believed that our modern consciousness is not the only kind of consciousness. He knew that although we take it for granted and assume that the consciousness we experience is consciousness per se, throughout history human beings have perceived the world in ways much different than the way we perceive it. Steiner, like Madame Blavatsky, accepted Darwin's idea of evolution, realizing that, like everything else in the world, consciousness, too, has evolved. But also like Blavatsky, he argued that Darwin and his followers had grabbed the stick at the wrong end: matter or material pressures such as survival had not produced spirit—our subjective, interior world. It was rather the other way around: the material world we perceive through the senses is a creation of consciousness as it unfolds in its evolution. The "spiritual science" Steiner devoted the last twenty-five years of his life to advancing was an elaborate, detailed, and inspiring—if often intellectually challenging—account of that evolution.

Steiner had made an early attempt at communicating his belief in the primacy of thought and thinking. But in an age given over to explaining inner experience by anchoring it in the brain's chemical exchanges, a work of subtle epistemology like *The Philosophy Of Freedom* (1894)[5] was bound to have little effect. Even qualified thinkers like Eduard von Hartmann, author of the once immensely influential *The Philosophy of the Unconscious* (1869), had no insight into the book's importance. Yet its basic message, that thought and the conscious ego behind it are the real expressions of an irreducible spiritual freedom, is one that is as important to grasp today as it was a century ago.

Steiner begins the book with a fundamental philosophical question, whose answer will determine the importance of any questions that follow: "Is a human being spiritually *free*, or subject to the iron necessity of natural law?"[6] Put this way, it is clear that it is only as a "spiritually free being" that we can engage in any kind of true thinking at all. A computer, however great its speed in processing information, never "thinks," because it operates according to a set of rules dictated by its program. It cannot choose *what* to think. But once we seriously engage with a question or intuition by making the gesture of inner effort, then we are in touch with that part of ourselves that is truly free, because it is only from that "free" part that such effort can arise. (Bergson, we remember, said that the force of mind has "the faculty of drawing from itself more than it contains.") In the great German philosophical tradition, Steiner spends more than two hundred pages methodically and powerfully arguing that human beings are indeed "free" and that through the rigorous observation of our *thinking* we can become aware of ourselves as conscious, spiritual entities.

Steiner's arguments are not difficult to follow; they do, however, demand a serious, flexible, and alert mind. The curious thing about *The Philosophy of Freedom* is that in actually accompanying Steiner in his step-by-step exposition we become aware of our own thinking as an *activity*, which is precisely the experience Steiner wants us to have; it demonstrates better than any argument the reality of our freedom. The book's subject is the very activity we engage in as we try to understand it. It is a book about thinking, and it succeeds, not when it "convinces" us of its arguments, but when, by prompting us to think about our own thinking, it triggers the very experience it is trying to describe.[7] Steiner demonstrates that the physical world which materialist science argues is the true root of "spirit" is itself a product of spirit. As William James and Henri Bergson would argue around the same time, without the selective activity of the mind there would be no "world," only a formless chaos. Or, as Steiner put it in another work, "The content of reality is only the reflection of the content of our minds. . . . We receive from reality only the empty forms."[8] When neuroscientists observe the brain and its chemical reactions—the physical basis of thought—they are also observing *their own thought*. Consciousness is there, because it is only through consciousness that any observation can take place: we can never get at some "purely" material stuff, because any such stuff would of necessity be part of our mental world. Matter itself is an *idea*. And when the materialists reply that all this is poppycock, they rely on arguments—that is, thoughts and ideas—to do so. Even the thought that thinking can be explained by reducing it to brain processes is itself something more than those processes—it is, as Steiner would patiently point out, a thought.

This leads to another central observation: our thoughts are not arbitrary, negligible epiphenomena taking place in our heads, with no relation to the world. They are as much a part of the phenomena of the world as the flowers and leaves of plants. Common sense tells us that the world is "complete" without your or my thoughts, which are "tacked on" to it, solely inside our heads. But Steiner tells us that we have no right to think this. "Doesn't the world bring forth thinking in human heads with the same necessity that it brings forth blossoms on the plant?"[9] If you plant a seed in the earth, it will send out roots and stem, blossoms and fruit. If you contemplate the plant, as Goethe did in search of the *Urpflanze*, it will bring forth concepts. Why, Steiner, asks, aren't these as much a *part* of the plant as its leaves? This organic relation between inner and outer worlds also does away with the notion that we are forever cut off from the reality that lies behind our perceptions. Transcendentalism is right to believe that there is some greater reality than what we experience through the senses, but that greater reality is not some inaccessible thing-in-itself; it is our own inner response to the world, the concepts we bring forth to *complement* and fulfill bare sense perception.

From all of this Steiner arrives at the centrality of the conscious ego, the "I," an emphasis that runs counter to a great deal of "anti-ego" thought popular in our time. Contrary to philosophies as disparate as poststructualism and Jungian psychology, as well as to various scientific attempts to explain it in molecular, Darwinian, or other determinist ways, Steiner declares the human ego, the "I," to be the aim of the entire world process. That process is the evolution of consciousness. This emphasis on the ego was shared by two of Steiner's predecessors, the philosophers Johann Gottlieb Fichte (1762–1814) and Max Stirner (1806–1856).[10] But Steiner takes the ego into areas neither of his philosophical antecedents had anticipated.

Practically everything Steiner wrote or lectured about is rooted in his conception of the evolution of consciousness. And although a beginning reader may rightly feel daunted by the prospect of so many volumes, the basic ideas, although highly challenging to modern scientistic sensibilities, are relatively easy to grasp—which is not to say they are simple. But Steiner had the system builder's penchant for taking a core idea and extrapolating from it and elaborating on it until it encompassed the world. As a brief survey of his work shows, he applied his central theme to a dizzying number of subjects: reincarnation, art, education, diet, architecture, agriculture, history, healing, to name a few. As I mentioned, Steiner adopted the importance of the number seven from Theosophy. Like Blavatsky, he taught that our world evolves through seven planetary incarnations; but he goes on to relate these to our seven "bodies," as well as to the seven levels of consciousness we and the world will pass through during our cosmic evolution. Also like Blavatsky, Steiner speaks of Hyperborea, Lemuria, and Atlantis. More immediately significant for our purposes, are the seven "post-Atlantean epochs" that follow the sinking of the fabled continent, the fifth of which we are currently experiencing.

Like Madame Blavatsky, Steiner too was a reader of the Akashic Record. But there was a difference between their accounts. The reason for this, Steiner claimed, was that Blavatsky read the Akashic Record haphazardly, while in a state of trance; Steiner, however, had developed a method of perceiving it while retaining full consciousness. With his emphasis on the central importance of the conscious ego, he had little faith in mediumship or trance states, arguing that penetrating other spheres is of little use if one lacks the clarity of mind to observe them accurately. One result of this is that Steiner's accounts have a precision unlike other reports of the Akashic Record.

Exactly what Steiner *did* when he "read" the Akashic Record is a matter of conjecture, although there are some indications. In his book *Rudolf Steiner Enters My Life*, Friedrich Rittelmeyer remarks that when people came to Steiner for spiritual advice he would arrange to sit where he could avoid looking into the light. Then he would lower his eyes and make a "certain deliberate adjustment of his being." Rittelmeyer remarks, "With Rudolf Steiner there was no question of trance. One looked into the *super-conscious*, not into a dark, dreamy subconsciousness. . . . He seemed to pass without effort into the higher states of consciousness; or rather it was as if both states of consciousness, that of sense perception and of spiritual perception, were there for him freely and naturally. "[11]

If, as is clear, Steiner was adamantly against trance states, then one asks what exactly was the "deliberate adjustment of his being" Rittelmeyer refers to? One possibility is that Steiner had developed a method of entering what are known as "hypnagogic states."[12] We will return to this idea shortly, but first we need to take a look at exactly what Steiner "saw" when he "read" the Akashic Record.

Chapter Eleven
—

Cosmic Evolution

According to Steiner, our present solar system has evolved out OF three previous stages, which he, with a perhaps unfortunate choice of terms, calls Old Saturn, Old Sun, and Old Moon. (He uses "old" to differentiate these ancient "planets" from the current celestial bodies bearing these names.) Although Steiner uses astronomical terms, he did not believe that these ancient "planets" existed in what we would call material form. He sees the Saturn stage as characterized by *heat* and the Sun stage by the addition of *air*, or gas, while during the Moon phase *water*, or liquid was introduced. Only in our present Earth stage, which represents the ultimate stage of materialization, do the planets appear in their solid physical forms. Following Earth, there will be three more planetary incarnations: Jupiter, Venus, and Vulcan, which will involve an increasing spiritualization. The entire process is under the guidance of what Steiner calls the "spiritual hierarchies," who serve in his system the same function as Blavatsky's *Dhyan Chohans*.[1]

After reaching the Earth stage of evolution, what we might call the beginnings of creatures like ourselves took shape, although, at this point, human "bodies" were more like gas than anything else. Steiner follows Madame Blavatsky in speaking of Hyperborea and Lemuria. Major cataclysms took place during these periods, such as the extrusion of our present Sun and Moon from the Earth, a point on which Steiner differs considerably from current astronomy. The Moon had to be removed, Steiner tells us, because once the Sun had broken off, the "hardening" forces of the Moon threatened to solidify human beings prematurely. After Lemuria came Atlantis, and it was here that our physical body was perfected. Following the destruction of Atlantis, Steiner tells us that the human race evolved through what he calls the post-Atlantean epochs. There are seven of these in all; currently we are in the fifth post-Atlantean epoch, with two more to follow. Each is devoted to the perfection of a certain stage of consciousness, related to one of our nonphysical bodies. The first post-Atlantean epoch began in 7227 B.C. and lasted until 5067 B.C. This was the Ancient Indian epoch and its "mission" was the development of the etheric body. The second post-Atlantean epoch—the Ancient Persian epoch— focused on the perfection of the astral body, and lasted from 5067 B.C. until 2907 B.C. The third post-Atlantean epoch, the Egypto-Chaldean, began in 2097 B.C. and lasted until 747 B.C. It was concerned with developing what Steiner calls the "sentient soul." With the descent and crucifixion of Christ during the fourth post-Atlantean epoch—747 B.C.– A.D. 1413—the detached, objective "I" was brought to perfection. This is known as the Greco-Roman–Christian epoch, and its mission was the development of the "intellectual soul." During this period the Earth reached its most "material" state; the process of "hardening," which began during the Lemurian phase, reached its peak—or, more accurately, its nadir—and the return trip to the more spiritual states began, Christ's crucifixion being the exact midpoint of the entire process. The current epoch, the fifth, began in 1413 and will last, Steiner tells us, until 3573. It is called the European-American epoch and its goal is the perfection of the "consciousness soul." Each epoch has its own presiding spirit, or *Zeitgeist*, the current one being Michael, whose mission is to guide us to regain our spiritual perception without losing the powers of independent thought and critical observation we have acquired through our "descent" into matter. In Michael's mission to help us "recognize the supersensible in the immediate sense world,"[2] we can recognize the Goethean science that lies at the heart of Steiner's project. Unfortunately, some of the spiritual hierarchies seek to impede our evolution, and throughout its history, Lucifer and Ahriman have tempted human beings away from their true destiny.

This brief and sketchy run-through can give only a bare hint of the complex events Steiner "saw" as he read the Akashic Record. The entire process, from Old Saturn to our present state and beyond, is aimed at developing our *independence* from the spiritual powers presiding over the affair. This seems odd, until we realize that what is essential for Steiner is our capacity to *freely* embrace those powers. Earlier ages and, indeed, whole planetary incarnations, enjoyed a greater and more intimate participation with the spiritual forces than we do. But the consciousness associated with these periods was not *free* in the sense we are today. Again, one might ask, Why, if in earlier times conditions were more "spiritual," did spirit, or consciousness, become more "material"? Steiner replied to this in *Cosmic Memory*: "It requires a higher power and capacity to direct denser forms of substantiality than to control those less dense."[3] Spirit descended into matter in order to develop its power of *control*. It was only by slowly "detaching" itself from its source that consciousness could return to that source and yet retain its own being and independence. In earlier times, the kind of clairvoyance, spiritual sight, and other paranormal abilities that we find exceptional were commonplace. This was one of Steiner's arguments against trance-states and mediums like Madame Blavatsky: they were a kind of "throwback" to an earlier, atavistic state of consciousness. Given the trajectory of human evolution, a philosopher like Bertrand Russell, for all his scepticism and abstract rationality, was a more apt example of the appropriate stage of human consciousness in the modern world. Yet, for all its incisive power, Russell's desiccating intellect had to be transcended as well. As Robert A. McDermott remarks, "This entire cycle . . . has had as its primary task the perfection of the physical, rational, and ego powers of humanity in combination with the spiritual powers possessed by the Atlanteans and those born in the early epochs of the present cycle."[4] All of Steiner's thinking has this character: an earlier stage, once passed through, is not abandoned, but is instead integrated into the next stage.

Steiner encapsulated his teaching on our previous states of consciousness in a series of lectures given in Munich in 1907; now available under the title *Rosicrucian Wisdom*, they present perhaps the best short introduction to his ideas.

In the Saturn condition, consciousness was in a very dull, deep state, which Steiner calls "deep trance consciousness." Mediums are familiar with this state; in it, all other conscious activity is deadened, and those exhibiting it appear to be virtually dead. In the Saturn condition, the mind is unaware of its immediate surroundings, but conscious of what Steiner calls "cosmic conditions." This is not the same as Bucke's "cosmic consciousness." It is a "deep trance consciousness" that seems to be a curiously insensible state, a condition of a kind of dull "universal awareness." The mineral world, Steiner says, still experiences such a state, and if we could speak to minerals, they would tell us what things were like on Old Saturn.

On Old Sun, consciousness existed in a kind of perpetual sleep, the deep, dreamless sleep we experience today. It is still rather dull, but by comparison with Old Saturn consciousness it is relatively clearer. On Earth today, the plant world shares this sleep state—we remember Bergson's remark that the vegetable kingdom had "fallen asleep in immobility."⁵ If plants could speak, Steiner tells us, they could tell us what conditions were like on Old Sun.

On Old Moon, consciousness was what Steiner calls "picture consciousness." We can best understand it, he says, by considering our own dreams. In comparison with our clear, waking-state consciousness, dream consciousness is still quite dim, but compared to Old Saturn and Old Sun, it is much better defined. Nevertheless, instead of a clear perception of an object in a physical world external to us, which is what we get in our waking-state, picture consciousness encounters only symbols and representations, as in dreams. On Old Moon, instead of seeing another human being's physical body, we would perceive a kind of aura, and from its colors we would know whether the being was a friend or not. Old Moon consciousness also lacked our clear-cut sense of time and space, again as is the case in dreams. On Old Moon, images were not "fixed" to objects as they are for us—Steiner speaks of colors and forms hovering "freely in space." This Old Moon consciousness strikes me as very important, and we will return to it shortly.

What we know as "consciousness" first appeared on our present Earth. This is our familiar clear, rational consciousness. Its central characteristic is the awareness of a solid, well-defined physical world that appears external to us. It is the world "out there," which we generally assume exists as it appears to us, *whether or not we are conscious of it* and, indeed, whether or not we exist at all. This external world appears to us to be completely independent of our consciousness, a point we will return to later. Although we

can withdraw our awareness of the external world and focus it on
our thoughts, memories, or imagination, the images associated
with these "inner objects" are generally not very vivid, unlike
images in dreams, and most of the time our waking state is concerned with "dealing" with events in the outside world. That, in
fact, is our gauge for determining whether or not someone is sane.
An inability or disinclination to acknowledge the world outside our
own subjectivity is generally a characteristic we associate with
madness.

Beyond our everyday waking state, Steiner foresees three further states of consciousness, which he links to the future incarnations of the Earth as Jupiter, Venus, and Vulcan. He calls the next
level of consciousness Imagination, in which our clear, waking consciousness is combined with the picture consciousness of Old
Moon. This is what consciousness will be like during the Jupiter
incarnation. After that, during the Venus incarnation, the state of
consciousness Steiner calls Inspiration will appear. This is waking
consciousness and picture consciousness, *plus* the consciousness of
Old Sun. Finally, in the Vulcan incarnation, the last three states will
be joined with the consciousness of Old Saturn, in the state Steiner
calls Intuition. But unlike the initial "dull" Saturn condition, this
universal consciousness will be perceived in a clear, waking state,
and so may be much more like the "cosmic consciousness" Bucke
spoke of.

Of these different levels of consciousness, the one that strikes
me as the most interesting is the one Steiner calls Imagination.
Being the next level in line, it is the one we would have a good
chance of experiencing. And having said that, it strikes me that we
already *do* experience it, because it is not only in dreams that the
curious conditions Steiner associates with Old Moon consciousness
appear. They are also associated with what are known as "hypnagogic" states.

CHAPTER TWELVE

Hypnagogia

The literature on hypnagogia was relatively thin until 1987, WHEN Professor Andreas Mavromatis of Brunel University published the first full-scale account of this strange state of consciousness. In *Hypnagogia: The Unique State of Consciousness Between Wakefulness and Sleep,* Mavromatis maps out the philosophical, psychological, paranormal, and neurological implications of this weirdly suggestive state of mind. Each of us experiences hypnagogic states at least twice a day, but most of us have little awareness or knowledge of them. As the title indicates, hypnagogic hallucinations—visual, audial, even sometimes olfactory—occur at the onset of sleep. When they occur as we are waking, they are called *hypnopompic.* (There is some debate over whether the actual experiences differ in any significant way, but the terms simply relate to whether one is entering or leaving sleep.) Mavromatis establishes that in states of hypnagogia we can become aware of generally "unconscious" processes, such as dreams, while remaining conscious. Allowing for oversimplification, a shorthand definition of hypnagogia is that it is "dreaming while awake." However, these dreams are not simple "daydreams." As Mavromatis shows, in hypnagogia we can "see" sometimes utterly bizarre images and visions with an unsettling clarity, while remaining perfectly aware of the "outside world." Mavromatis also relates hypnagogia to paranormal experiences such as precognition, synchronicities, and clairvoyance; to creativity; and to psychological and spiritual growth. He also discusses the interest in them shown by other esoteric thinkers, such as Ouspensky and the Scandinavian philosopher Emmanuel Swedenborg.[1] If, as is clear, Steiner maintained the importance of retaining rational consciousness while "reading" the Akashic Record, then some form of hypnagogic state may have been his means of doing so. There is even the possibility that a kind of consciously induced hypnagogic state may be what Steiner has in mind as the next stage in the evolution of consciousness.

As Mavromatis and others have pointed out, the images and pictures that appear in states of hypnagogia are almost always "auto-symbolic"—they represent either the physical or psychological states of the persons experiencing them, or their thoughts as they drifted out of consciousness. People experiencing hypnagogic hallucinations often shift in and out of a "normal" sense of space and time. They see strange landscapes, and entire adventures can unfold in a few moments. Mavromatis conducted experiments in controlled hypnagogia and discovered that under certain conditions subjects were able to focus on the hypnagogic imagery while at the same time maintaining a clear awareness of the external world, even to the point of carrying on a conversation. Mavromatis also discovered that it was possible to induce particular imagery in some subjects through mental suggestion—in other words, that hypnagogia could be telepathic, and that it even could be shared among several subjects.

In the fascinating chapter "The Old Versus the New Brain," Mavromatis argues that hypnagogia is linked to the subcortical structures of the brain, which are known collectively as the "old brain." During states of hypnagogia, he claims, the usually dominant neocortex—the evolutionarily recent and specifically "human" part of the brain—is inhibited, and much older structures, such as the reticular brainstem core, hippocampus, medulla oblongata, and thalamus, "take over." Cortical brain activity is associated with clear, logical thought and with the perception of a well-defined "external" world. When such activity is inhibited—during sleep, for instance, or in states of deep relaxation—the older brain structures dominate. These structures are more attuned to inner experience and to a "prelogical" form of thought that uses imagery, symbols, and analogy rather than language and clearly defined concepts. If we remember that Steiner claimed that Old Moon or picture consciousness is an older form of consciousness, then much of what Mavromatis says about the activity of the old brain during hypnagogia seems suggestive.

For example, Steiner says that in picture consciousness "human beings lived entirely in such pictures as they have in modern dreams, but then they expressed realities." These pictures, however, "hovered freely in space." Steiner uses our perception of the color blue as an example. In picture consciousness, blue "was not resting upon objects. . . . The form of beings with a colored surface could not have been perceived at that time." Instead an inhabitant of Old Moon would have seen "a freely hovering picture of form and color." Steiner uses the example of salt, saying that when we see salt on a table today, we see it as a granular object of a definite color occupying a specific space. Picture consciousness, however, would perceive it as a freely floating color and form.[2]

Mavromatis suggests that the function of cortical consciousness is to "stabilize" and "objectify" sensation: "Consciousness as such does not reside in the cortex, but in the old brain; it is the specificity of consciousness that the cortex is concerned with—it provides sequential-temporal and spatial relationships, it particularizes and individualizes existence."[3] Given that in picture consciousness sensation is neither stable nor objectified, but, as Steiner says, "free floating," the kind of consciousness preceding the development of the cortex must have been something like the kind Steiner describes. Mavromatis also links subcortical activity to "paranormal" phenomena like "blind sight" and "paroptic vision," the curious ability to "see" without the use of the eyes. Unlike "normal" sight, which is focused and directed linearly—we speak of a line of sight—paroptic vision is spherical, meaning that it can "see" in all directions equally; it also seems to be able to detect colors beyond our ultraviolet limit.[4]

Mavromatis also speculates that consciousness began with a single "nuclear" sense out of which the later specific senses developed. This nuclear sense was synesthetic, meaning that it was a form of perception in which all of our later differentiated sense perceptions were combined. Rather than having our present sensory specificity, in which colors are clearly differentiated from sounds, taste from scent, and so on, this primitive "nuclear" sense would have been a kind of general "awareness," probably tactile in character, lacking the kind of sharp *differences* between things we now know. This primitive nuclear sense strikes me as similar to the "dull" universal awareness of Old Saturn referred to by Steiner.

Mavromatis's conjecture that consciousness proceeds from a diffuse synesthetic state to the perception of an external world containing well-defined objects is strikingly like Steiner's outline of the evolution of consciousness through the sequence of planetary incarnations. And if, as Steiner argues, the development of "supersensible" perception is achieved through a "return" to an earlier stage of consciousness while maintaining clear, rational awareness, then Mavromatis's remarks on hypnagogia warrant serious consideration.

For instance, if, as Mavromatis maintains, synesthesia is characteristic of earlier stages of consciousness, then one is surprised to discover that synesthetic phenomena are precisely what the person developing supersensible perceptions experiences.[5] In a series of lectures on music given in Berlin in 1906, Steiner remarks that as the initiate proceeds in developing "supersensible perception" one of the signs of success is that his or her dream life changes. From the usual chaos of symbolic representations, the initiate enters a world of "flowing colors and radiant light beings."[6] This, Steiner says, is the "astral world." Curiously, he remarks that the astral world is always present and surrounds us continuously, and that only the presence of our everyday consciousness prevents us from perceiving it. Similarly, Mavromatis tells us that the subcortical structures responsible for hypnagogic phenomena are always active, and it is only the dominance of the neocortex that obscures their work. (Just as the stars are always present in the sky, and it is only the brilliance of the Sun that obscures them.)

After sufficient training, resulting in a transformation of the state of deep, dreamless sleep, the initiate enters a second higher world. In this world, which Steiner calls *Devachan,* a world of "resounding tones" permeates the color world of the astral. At a deeper level of the Devachan, these tones begin to be heard as words. Steiner goes on to say that all of us experience these different worlds as we pass through sleep; the difference between a noninitiate and an initiate is that the initiate undergoes these experiences consciously. Mavromatis records that colors, tones, and words are all experienced during hypnagogic states, oftentimes in startling combinations. Similarly, Steiner remarks in *How to Know*

Higher Worlds that one of the first signs of advance on the path of initiation is that one begins to be conscious in one's dreams. One of Mavromatis's descriptions of the hypnagogic state is that it can be characterized as either being awake while dreaming or dreaming while awake. He goes on to relate hypnagogia to what is described in Tantric Yoga as the "Fourth State," "the half-dream state," which is the junction of all the states—waking, sleeping, and dreaming. Maintaining awareness while in this state is essential, because by doing this the student will ensure the "continuity of consciousness unaffected by sleep."

Curiously, this "intersection" of states is paralleled in the anatomy of the brain responsible for it. Mavromatis points out that the thalamus, which he conjectures is the "center of consciousness" and the probable source of hypnagogic phenomena, is anatomically linked to the reptilian brain (central core), limbic system (paleo-mammalian brain), and the cerebral hemispheres—the three "houses" of the "triune" human brain. He suggests that each of the "three brains" has a consciousness and a logic of its own, and that the "consciousness" of one level would appear very strange to that of another.[7] In hypnagogia, he argues, the dominance of the cortex is inhibited through the onset of sleep, or through deep relaxation, allowing the "consciousness" of the other brains to appear. Usually, cortical consciousness is completely absent as we fall asleep, so we pass into these other states unawares. But if a minimum level of cortical arousal is maintained, then the consciousness of the old brain can be observed. This can be done, Mavromatis suggests, in meditative states which are characterized by the activation of the thalamus and other old-brain structures, and during which the practitioner is on guard against "falling asleep."

—

The thalamus is also important, Mavromatis argues, because located within it is the pineal gland, that tiny organ the philosopher Descartes believed to be the seat of the soul, whose function is still somewhat of a mystery today. Dating back to the Devonian and Silurian periods, the pineal gland is extremely old. One of its earliest functions in primitive reptiles was as a kind of eye located in the top of the head, and in some contemporary vertebrates, including ourselves, the pineal gland is still photosensitive. In human beings, the early "pineal eye" appears in the initial stages of embryonic life; it soon disappears, but its associated gland remains. And this, like the ancient eye, is sensitive to light.

Recently, one crucial function of the pineal gland has become clear: it is the only gland in mammals that produces the amino acid melatonin, which is important in the production of the neuro-transmitter serotonin. Melatonin is also involved in the synthesis, release, and levels of serotonin in the hypothalamus, as well as in the synthesis and distribution of other neurotransmitters in other parts of the brain. Melatonin is also linked to skin color, and this function is associated with the pineal gland's sensitivity to light.

An excess of light and stress tends to inhibit the production of melatonin, resulting in a decrease in the size and weight of the pineal gland. Darkness and relaxation have the opposite effect, increasing the synthesis of melatonin as well as the pineal gland's overall activity. Melatonin itself has a calming effect on the nervous system, and it is thought that its production is increased through meditation or deep relaxation, creating a kind of positive feedback: meditation stimulating the production of melatonin, which increases feelings of calm and detachment, which lead to greater production of melatonin, and so on. That the pineal gland is located precisely where ancient Vedic literature places the "third eye," whose function is "spiritual vision" and whose opening results in "enlightenment," offers some hard, neurological evidence for a belief too often relegated to fancy and superstition. Mavromatis likewise remarks that in the Vedic tradition the spiritual vision provided by the third eye was once available to human beings and has only been temporarily lost, its return at a higher level guaranteed through our spiritual evolution. The similarity with Steiner's teaching need not be stressed, and Mavromatis himself suggests that the conscious participation in hypnagogia, with its access to other realities and "earlier" forms of consciousness, is a good candidate for the next step in human evolution. He also relates the pineal gland and its unique function to the occult and esoteric symbolism of the scepter of Hermes. In the twin snakes coiled about a rod crowned by a winged cone, Mavromatis sees the integration of our conscious and unconscious minds, united by the unique state of hypnagogia.

The means of inducing hypnagogia, or more precisely, of becoming aware of the hypnagogic imagery that is continuously emerging into consciousness, is also suggestive of Steiner's method of "reading" the Akashic Record. That Steiner sat "where he would not be obliged to look against the light," and the "deliberate adjustment of his being, often accompanied by a lowering of the eyes," suggests the darkness and the relaxed, meditative state conducive to the activity of the pineal gland.[8] Such states promote the "minimum degree of arousal without active thinking" that Mavromatis argues are essential for conscious awareness of hypnagogic imagery. In such meditative states the thalamus and other old-brain structures become active and cause the cortex to "idle." The old brain then "declares its independence" from the cerebral cortex. Yet the "minimum degree of arousal" prevents cortical consciousness from disappearing completely and promotes the peculiar characteristics of hypnagogia.

An old-brain structure like the hippocampus, for example, is concerned with maintaining the distinction between perception and internal imagery. Yet if at the point of sleep, or during self-induced states of relaxation, the "minimum degree of arousal" is maintained, then the function of the hippocampus can be inhibited, and internal imagery may be experienced as external perception. Given the exceptionally detailed and vivid accounts of human and cosmic evolution presented in Steiner's lectures, one comes away with the impression that these were things he *saw*, almost as if there was a kind of continuous film running in his consciousness.[9] Again, as the "older" forms of thinking associated with hypnagogia are preverbal, it is not surprising that Friedrich Rittelmeyer remarks that he "often noticed that at the beginning of a conversation it was not easy for [Steiner] to find the right words. One said to oneself then that he had surely been occupied with his spiritual investigations and needed a few seconds for the transition to the world of purely physical existence. He tried to find the appropriate word, missed it, and stopped."[10] The passage from subcortical to cortical consciousness was not yet complete, and words, the currency of the cortex, were not yet easily at hand.

Rittelmeyer offers other good evidence that hypnagogia was at least a part of what Steiner envisioned as the next stage in the evolution of consciousness. As quoted above, Rittelmeyer remarks, "It was as if both states of consciousness, that of sense-perception and of spiritual perception were there for [Steiner] freely and naturally." This "double consciousness" is precisely what Steiner saw as the characteristic of our coming Jupiter consciousness, which, we remember, is our current waking rational consciousness *combined* with the picture consciousness of Old Moon. Such double consciousness is also what Mavromatis sees as an evolutionary potential. "The ability to retain consciousness of one's surroundings while dreaming," he writes, "is a definite evolutional advance over sleep dreaming: it enables a person to retain control over his external environment while investigating his internal terrain. An individual may, then, learn to oscillate in and out of hypnagogia to any desired degree. . . . Learning to balance oneself in hypnagogia lies along evolutionally normal and natural directions." Such a development, he concludes, sees hypnagogia not as merely a *regressive* state—as hyper-rationalists view any loosening of rational control—but as a *progressive* one "in which the various aspects of consciousness and the bipolarity of rationality-nonrationality are brought to a synergetic relationship."[11] Again, that Steiner's recapitulation of previous levels of consciousness is practically identical with this hardly needs stressing. As we will see, such a "return to advance" is very much in line with another theorist on the evolution of consciousness, the German philosopher Jean Gebser, whose ideas on the "structures of consciousness" have much in common with Steiner's visions of cosmic evolution.

—

Mavromatis remarks, "Hypnagogia gives rise to the insight that there are many realities and that what we call wakefulness merely constitutes one of them,"[12] a sentiment echoing William James's classic pronouncement on the subject. He goes on to suggest that our so-called waking state is hardly any less of a dream than the kind we experience during sleep. This, as hardly needs pointing out, is a perception shared by practically all mystical, occult, esoteric, and spiritual traditions. It is only in relatively recent times—taking place, perhaps not merely coincidentally, within the period Steiner calls the fifth post-Atlantean epoch—that our three-dimensional solid waking world has appropriated sole ownership of the category "reality." This world of space and time we all know so well is the gauge by which we judge the validity of other possible worlds. But if, as Steiner through his cosmic vision and Mavromatis through his neurological research suggest, this all-too-familiar world of solid objects and passing time is the product of a particular kind of thought, then it stands to reason that a different thinking may indeed produce or reveal a different kind of world.

This indeed does seem to be the case. Mavromatis remarks that dreams and hypnagogic phenomena take place in their own kind of space, not limited by the constraints of our known three dimensions. Hypnagogia can be shared; it can be telepathic; it can be precognitive; and, if we are right in relating it to Rudolf Steiner's reading of the Akashic Record, it can reach back in time. Given the archaeology of consciousness presented in the structure and function of the brain, this last proposition should not seem at all preposterous. If, as Mavromatis suggests, the task of the cerebral cortex is to stabilize and objectify existence in order to present to consciousness a more wieldy and easily manipulated world—which, we remember, is precisely what Bergson suggested—then a consciousness with its roots in other, older parts of the brain may indeed present a very different kind of world, a world perhaps less constrained by our present ideas about space and time, subject and object, or past and future.

However, there does seem to be a kind of "hierarchy of consciousness" implied in the structure of the brain itself; otherwise, why would evolution take the dangerous step of developing risky self-consciousness at the expense of infallible instinct? Yet, as Mavromatis points out, consciousness itself does not "reside" in the cortex, and a purely cerebral consciousness would lack the depth and texture supplied by the old brain. The kind of objective consciousness exemplified by rigid, impersonal rationalists who deny any meaning or value to the world is perhaps a good approximation of a purely cortical awareness; perhaps even closer would be the kind of consciousness some scientists claim to have "generated" in computers. And if the cortex is to be accorded greater value because it is the most recently evolved organ of consciousness, then surely the next step should be granted even greater preference. Rational-cortical consciousness, then, would be seen as one stage in an ongoing evolution of consciousness—which is precisely how both Steiner and Mavromatis do see it.

But if this evolution of consciousness can be seen in the structure of the brain itself, as I believe Mavromatis has shown, then the next question is, Has it left any other trace? Is there any other evidence for the kind of evolution Steiner and other thinkers have claimed? Short of discovering Atlantis itself, is there any other sign that something along the lines of what Steiner and Mavromatis have suggested has actually taken place? In short: is there a "fossil record" of the mind? We approach this question in the next section.

PART THREE

The Archaeology of Consciousness

CHAPTER THIRTEEN

The Invisible Mind

In studying the history of consciousness, we are immediately faced with a unique difficulty. Unlike paleontology, where the outlines of ancient life-forms are open to study, in trying to understand what a consciousness prior to our own may have been like we run into the fact that there are no "fossil remains" of previous consciousnesses available for our inspection. We cannot dig through strata of earth and piece together the remnants of early minds, nor collect fragments of ancient consciousness into a likely arrangement. This is so because of the simple fact that the mind, consciousness, is not material. It does not occupy space and, in a very real sense, it is not constrained by the limits of the present moment. Consciousness can range through the past or peer into the future at a moment's notice, just as it can focus on a galaxy millions of light years away as easily as it can observe what is taking place right before its eyes. Yet it is this very freedom from materiality that makes consciousness difficult to study.

If I want to understand something about the history of the Earth, I can go to the Museum of Natural History here in London and walk through the physical remains of past ages. The outline of a sixty-five-million-year-old ammonite, the skeleton of a mastodon, shards of prehistoric pottery, and pieces of Neolithic tools are there to speak to me of their time and age. But I do not see an ancient consciousness on display behind the glass. There are no minds preserved in formaldehyde nor ideas stuffed and presented in a mock-up "natural setting." And even if I accept the reigning notion that consciousness is caused by brains, I am still in the same predicament. Brains indeed are material objects, but they are exceedingly delicate ones, and none remain from ancient times for us to study. So we have little way of knowing if the brain of, say, the ancient Greeks was in any significant way different from our own, and if this could have possibly given them a different consciousness.

No, the fact of the matter is that the only consciousness available to us today is our own. And although many scientists believe that by studying the physical "hardware" of the brain—neurons, chemical transmitters, electrical exchanges—they are studying consciousness, this is not really the case. I can make a complete physical analysis of a compact disc containing Mozart's piano concertos, just as I can do a chemical breakdown of my copy of Tolstoy's *War and Peace*, but in neither case would I approach the music or the novel. The surface of the compact disc and the ink and paper of the book are the means by which the music and the novel manifest; if I destroy them, I will only have destroyed one means of the music's and the novel's manifesting. Neither the music nor the novel will have been touched, and I can easily purchase other copies. It is even true, I believe, that if somehow *all* copies of Mozart's piano concertos and Tolstoy's *War and Peace* were destroyed, neither the music nor the novel would be touched. Both have their real existence in the consciousness of their creators, and once given to the world they now exist in a shared world of ideas, which is also immaterial. Something of the same is true, I believe, of all attempts to explain consciousness by studying its physical correlates. A particular neural net may be active when I contemplate a sunset or meditate on the idea of freedom, but that neural net is no more my experience of the sunset or my profound thoughts about personal liberty than the pixels making up the letters on my computer screen are the words in this document.

Consciousness, our entire interior world of thoughts, feelings, dreams, beliefs, hopes, fears, ideas, imagery, and everything else, can neither be weighed nor measured, nor in any way handled in the same way we treat physical objects. Consciousness is not big, small, round, square, hot, cold, heavy, or light. Everything else in the world we encounter and deal with through our senses. Whether or not Rudolf Steiner is right about the evolution of consciousness, most of us do live our waking lives with our awareness focused almost exclusively on the outer world. This is a world of solid, palpable objects that we do our best to either manipulate or avoid. We either touch them with our hands or devise machines to do this for us. We are very good at this, and practically everything we meet with in our day-to-day lives can be handled in this way. But not consciousness. We can neither pick it up nor put it down, bring it toward us nor move it out of the way. Of course we say that we "weigh" thoughts or "grasp" an idea, but these are simply metaphors. In fact most, if not all, of our ways of speaking about consciousness and the mind are metaphorical. Thoughts "race." We speak of a "stream" of consciousness. We say that someone has a "closed" mind, that someone else has a "bright" idea, and wonder what is going on "inside" yet another person's head. But on closer inspection we realize there is something odd about all of this. No thought has ever "raced." There is no "stream" of consciousness. One's mind is neither "closed" nor "open." And no idea, however bright, has ever illuminated a dark room. The only thing "inside" people's heads is a brain. If we were absolutely literal and opened someone's skull, we wouldn't find thoughts or ideas, only cerebral spinal fluid and gray matter. These are all ways of speaking about a very curious thing, the mind. And what is perhaps most strange about this curious thing, is that it is at once the most intimate and the most distant thing about us. What could be "closer" (again, a metaphor) to us than our "self"? And yet, what can we say we know about it?

—

In *Living Time,* the psychologist Maurice Nicoll, a disciple of P. D. Ouspensky, makes the curious remark that we, our "true selves," are really invisible. We can see people's faces, hear their voices, watch their movements, and feel their touch, but we never actually see *them*. And the same is true of ourselves. I can see my face in a mirror and hear my voice on a tape recording, but is that *really* me? No, Nicoll says. The "real you" is that stranger who inhabits your inner world (another metaphor) and who, from time to time, you get a glimpse of (another metaphor) but more often take for granted. We may think that this talk of an "invisible you" is itself a metaphor, but there is at least one experience of our "invisibility" that we all share. From around our second or third year until our old age and death, we feel this sense of "I" inhabiting that metaphorical space behind our eyes. In the passage from that small child to a weary septuagenarian or octogenarian, the physical body goes through an immense number of changes, with some very visible results. In fact, we know that the very cells of our bodies, and the atoms and molecules making up those cells, have changed many times over during our lifetimes, and that in all truth we are not the same "bodies" we started out as. But there is a curious persistence in our interior selves. They, of course, change too. But who hasn't looked at a weathered middle-aged face in the mirror and thought, "But I still feel as if I am in my twenties"? And who hasn't raged against the ravages of time, whose trail we see in every wrinkle and feel in every aching bone and creaking joint, and felt that this scarecrow of old and tired flesh is not the "real you"? That "real you" is not that aging body, trapped in the currents of passing time. It is *something else*. What that "something else" is, is consciousness.

Now, having said all this, you might wonder how I can contemplate writing anything about the evolution of consciousness if consciousness itself is such an elusive thing. If consciousness has evolved, how can we possibly know? In the 1920s the school of psychology known as Behaviorism took the "invisibility" of consciousness so seriously that it argued that precisely because no psychologist had ever "seen" consciousness, it therefore did not exist. For Behaviorists, there was no "interior world," no "ghost in the machine," only behavior—which, like everything else science studies, can be observed and measured. And, as I have mentioned earlier, Daniel Dennett, one of today's leading philosophers of consciousness, has argued along similar lines. So, the very immateriality of consciousness has led some very influential thinkers to argue that it is something that simply doesn't exist.

Clearly, this view can't be right. Consciousness exists. You, reading these words, are aware of it, just as I am, writing them. As Bergson said, consciousness is something we are aware of so intimately and immediately that it requires neither proof nor definition. The immateriality of consciousness is not an argument against its existence. It is instead one of its characteristics—perhaps its most central one. It argues very persuasively that we are beings who inhabit two worlds: one of space and time and matter and motion, and another of something we used to call "spirit" but today feel more comfortable calling "psychic" or "mental," or, in this case, "consciousness."

But having said that consciousness is not material, it doesn't follow that it has no *relation* to matter. As we saw in the first part of this book, for philosophers like Bergson consciousness has "invaded" matter, entered it, "colonized" it for its own purposes. These metaphors may seem too aggressive for contemporary sensibilities, but they do suggest the sense of struggle and striving we associate with spirit. Matter is inert. A stone will stay in the same spot indefinitely unless something or someone moves it. It is essentially passive. A stone will not get out of the rain or move out of the path of an approaching object. Physicists tell us that what appears to be solid, motionless, "dead" matter is really an incalculable number of atoms, vibrating at an inconceivable rate. But this is not what we see and it is not how we interact with it. The stone is, we say, an *in*animate object. Living things, on the other hand, *are* animated. They move. Plants grow, animals move about in search of food. Yet, like the stone, plants and animals are made of matter. On an atomic or subatomic level they are perhaps ultimately not very different, but on the level of molecules and larger bodies such as cells, they are. Plants, animals, and people are matter with *something else*. For esotericists like Rudolf Steiner, that something else is what is known as an "etheric body." For philosophers like Bergson and Nietzsche, that something else is "life," "spirit," the "life force." Consciousness is not material, but in some strange way, it can enter matter and organize it for its own purposes.

———

What has all of this to do with studying the evolution of consciousness? Well, one way of doing this is the approach that Bergson took: studying "evolution" itself. Consciousness or the *élan vital*—in Bergson the two are the same—enters matter at an early stage, as early as three and a half billion years ago, and builds it up into finer and more complex bodies: into "organisms," which are "organized" life-forms. It is only living matter that we say is "organized"; we even speak of the "organs" of the body. A stone is not "organized"; it is, in Alfred North Whitehead's term, an "aggregate." The difference between the two is that if we take a large stone and break it in two we then have two smaller stones. But if we take a living thing—a plant or a person—and do the same, we do not have two smaller organisms. We have disrupted the organism; we have "dis-organized" it and, in doing so, have killed it.[1] The stone, on the other hand, is not "hurt." We merely have smaller lumps of the same thing.

By studying the forms of organized matter, the variety of living things in the evolutionary "stream," Bergson and other thinkers, like Teilhard de Chardin, chart, as it were, the *movement* of consciousness through matter. They show how consciousness has adapted matter to its ends, where it has been successful, where it has failed, and hence, they provide a kind of "map" of the "flow of consciousness." But if, as thinkers like Ouspensky suggest, with human beings the Great Laboratory (another metaphor for the "life force") has been very successful in organizing matter, then the character of the "flow" changes. If, as these thinkers claim, in human beings (or at least in *some* of them) the Great Laboratory has succeeded in creating an organism that can continue to develop *through its own efforts*, then it is no longer the *direct* control of matter that is the aim. Consciousness now begins to push its first sprouts through the dark loam of the "unconscious." For, even though I have been using the term "consciousness" throughout as the name of the agency behind evolution, we are not to assume that early life-forms like trilobites or contemporary ones like sunflowers are conscious in the way that we are. Slowly, and with many setbacks, that indefinable yet unmistakable condition we call "self-consciousness" begins to emerge in human beings. And at this point, the evolution of consciousness takes a turn. Now it is focused no longer on the direct penetration and control of matter, but on the growth and development of the interior world of these new self-evolving creatures. And it is through them that a new relationship with matter develops. These agents of the life force now begin to interact with it in a new way, through what they will later call art, science, and religion—in a word, culture. Now it does become possible that a stone cut in half is not merely two smaller stones. If that stone has felt the hand of a sculptor, fashioning it into a tool or into an effigy of a deity, it becomes "organized." A broken hand axe is not merely two smaller stones, just as a toppled statue is not merely rubble. The hand axe and the statue are matter imbued with spirit—no longer as a force or energy entering matter, as is the case with living things, but as the imprint of human imagination. It is the mind pressing itself upon the material world. And it is through these "mindprints," that we can trace the further evolution of consciousness.

CHAPTER FOURTEEN

—

Cracking the Egg

Exactly when the mind began to leave its trace on the physical world is unknown. When did that spark of spirit ignite the latent powers of imagination in the earliest human beings? When did we take those first fledgling steps out of instinct and unconsciousness that would lead to the Buddha, Beethoven, and landing on the Moon? When did we first begin to climb out of the millennia of kinship with our animal ancestors and regard the world illuminated by the dawn light of self-consciousness? When, in other words, did we first become human? No one knows. And it is quite possible that no one will ever know with any certainty. The search for some exact date when self-consciousness first appeared seems futile; the problem of what would count as evidence is alone enough to put off even the most dedicated researcher. It is nevertheless the single most important development in human history, and it is unlikely that it has left no trace. The roots of consciousness reach deep into the rich soil of the preconscious, and when we look this far back into human history and prehistory we invariably enter the realms of myth. As Erich Neumann and Marie-Louise von Franz have shown, practically all creation myths—stories explaining "the creation of the world"—can be read as accounts of the rise of consciousness out of the primal depths of the unconscious.[1] To give only one example, in the Judeo-Christian tradition one of the "names of God" is "I AM THAT I AM," the basic statement of self-awareness. And the first act of creation was the appearance of light, where before there was only darkness, chaos, "formless and void," an apt description of a state of unconsciousness or preconsciousness.

But it is not only as a manner of speaking that we can look at the emergence of consciousness as the emergence of a world. Up until around the age of two, children do not distinguish any break between themselves and the outside world. Until that point, there is in truth no "world" for them, in the sense of some "thing" other than themselves set against their awareness. They exist in a kind of seamless unity with the world beyond their bodies, what Neumann has called the "uroboric" condition, taking the term from the alchemical symbol of the snake with its tail in its mouth, an archetypal emblem of totality. At this stage the psyche and what will become "the world" exist in a kind of blissful but unconscious unity. One has only to observe a baby at its mother's breast to understand what Neumann means. Neumann—and, as we will see, other thinkers, like Jean Gebser—believe that early human beings existed in a similar condition with the Earth, and it is still a debatable question just how much of a "world" in the way that we experience it exists for animals. There is good reason to believe that animals are "in" the world in a way that we are not—in any case, there seems little evidence that animals ever feel the kind of existential terror we sometimes feel at the recognition of a strange, alien *otherness* set against our own existence, nor the awe we feel at a night sky or magnificent sunset. Myths like the exile from the Garden of Eden do not depict the punishment of a vindictive God meted out to disobedient creatures. Rather they show the painful rupture of this unconscious bliss by the rise of consciousness. The shame Adam and Eve feel at their nakedness is the awareness that they are no longer merely unconscious natural creatures, but have crossed over the threshold into consciousness. Suddenly the warm buoyant unity of the primal garden is shattered, and they find themselves separate beings, facing a strange world. For better or worse, they are no longer merely animals.

In Neumann's view, shared by other psychologists like Melanie Klein and D. W. Winnicott, the expulsion from the garden is not only some primal historical event, nor merely an archetype embedded in the human psyche. It is a trauma experienced by every human being who hatches from the uroboric egg of infancy. As Neumann writes, "Detachment from the ouroboros, entry into the world, and the encounter with the universal principle of opposites are the essential tasks of human and individual developments."[2] These "tasks" form the challenges of the hero's "journey," and they are not merely the narrative material for ancient myths. Each of us, insofar as we become *individuals*—following the path of what Jung called "individuation"—must face these challenges. They may seem of small consequence today, as most of us have little memory of a time when "we" did not exist. But as Neumann writes, "Trite as it seems to us, the logical statement of identity—'I am I'—the fundamental statement of consciousness, is in reality a tremendous achievement."[3] (Having seen this awakening take place in my own sons at around the age of two, I can attest to its profound significance.) And on a broader scale the tasks must be faced by humanity as a whole, and what is generally known as the "rise of civilization" is our collective coming to maturity. How much and in what way we have been successful, or at what stage of arrested development we may be stuck, are questions each of us must address individually.

Neumann also echoes an idea that we have already encountered in Rudolf Steiner and in a different way in the work of Andreas Mavromatis, and that we will again find in the philosophy of Jean Gebser. The rise out of uroboric unity is not a simple jettisoning of a childlike "oneness" with nature. As Neumann writes, "Man's task in the world is to remember with his conscious mind what was knowledge before the advent of consciousness."[4] This has echoes of Plato's notion of knowledge as memory; it is also reminiscent of Steiner's vision of a future consciousness that is a recapitulation of our ancient Moon consciousness yet with full rational awareness, as it is a restatement of Mavromatis's conception of hypnagogia as a "descent" into the old brain while maintaining the wakefulness of the new. This psychic balancing act looks easy in print, but it is extremely difficult in practice and gives rise to what I call the "Goldilocks syndrome," a situation in which the individual or collective mind teeters between an excessive rationality on one hand, and a plunge back into the unconscious on the other, only rarely hitting on the middle ground where it is "just right." (In *Turn Off Your Mind: The Mystic Sixties and the Dark Side of the Age of Aquarius,* I examine one such oscillation: the "occult revival" of the 1960s.)

The available evidence suggests that the appearance of self-consciousness is a relatively recent event. Given this, the balance seems heavily weighted on the side of the unconscious. We may find it difficult to grasp that for millennia our ancestors lived in a state similar to what we enjoy as infants. Yet as Neumann and other thinkers suggest, the pull toward the unconscious is strong, and there is no final, decisive entry into full consciousness—or, at least, there is none at our present stage of development. To achieve consciousness is a struggle, and to maintain it is a burden. Many of us are prone to throw off its load and return to the less demanding conditions of the unconscious—hence the widespread drug and alcohol abuse too common to our time, as well as other, more dangerous manias involving sex and violence. Again, this shouldn't be misunderstood as arguing for consciousness and against the unconscious. Relaxing with a glass of wine or losing ourselves in a book or film are also ways of loosening consciousness and opening up to deeper parts of ourselves. The question is one of balance. To avoid life's realities by sinking into drug abuse is not the same as the pleasant shift in awareness the judicious use of alcohol engenders, nor is a rigid, absolutely "rational" way of life the same as taking responsibility for one's actions and decisions. In life, as in the fairy tale, getting it just right is not always easy. And the fact that self-consciousness is relatively new makes it even harder.

—

Just how recently self-consciousness appeared is, as we have seen, a difficult question to answer. Anatomically "modern" human beings first appeared in Africa at least 100,000 years ago, but somehow we find it difficult to conceive that these early ancestors had a consciousness like our own; theorists like Neumann and Jean Gebser argue that their mental world was probably much more like an animal's, still close to nature in the uroboric embrace. According to the standard account, *Homo sapiens sapiens*— "behaviorally" modern human beings, i.e., ourselves—emerged 60,000 years later, around 40,000 years ago, in what has been called a "cultural big bang." During this late stage in the Upper Paleolithic (Old Stone Age), the first shoots of art, religion, magic, technology, and social organization are said to have appeared, and these are the boundaries between creatures like ourselves, and our earlier ancestors. But even here our interior world and theirs must have been very different. Early *Homo sapiens sapiens* looked like us, and, in many ways, acted as we do. But whether they *thought* as we do is another matter.

Although it is difficult, if not impossible, to pinpoint exactly when self-consciousness appeared, one sign of it would certainly have to be the beginning of a written or symbolic record, what we have come to call "history." As Erich Neumann writes, "So long as an apperceptive ego consciousness is lacking, there can be no history; for history requires a 'reflecting' consciousness, which by reflecting, constitutes it. Hence the time before history must be indeterminate chaos and nondifferentiation."[5] Which seems to be saying that the "I" and "history" should appear at the same time— or perhaps the "I" first, with history by definition following short-

ly after. Which is to say that before the "I" there can be no history, and there can be no history without some reflection of that "I."

In fact, if one thinks about it, it is difficult to avoid the idea
that the "I" *is* that reflection: a "self" *is* its own reflection, or at
least it is difficult to see how there could be a self without that
reflection. As A. R. Orage argued, self-consciousness is like photographic paper turned in on itself. It is difficult to see how a "self"
could have awareness of itself without something reflecting that
self back. Having a "self," *being* a "self"—"selfing," if I am
allowed to coin a word—seems to be a kind of "duo" or "double"
consciousness, and we are reminded of the "double consciousness"
in relation to hypnagogia discussed in the last section. For some
metaphysicians, God's "reflection" is the world. In human beings,
that something, that reflection, is "history."

But if history is a clue to the appearance of self-consciousness,
when did it begin? It is commonly accepted that history as we
know it began with the "birth of civilization" in the Fertile
Crescent some 5,000 years ago. Traditionally, the date and place
for the start of civilization and hence history is around 3100 B.C. in
Egypt, the event being the unification of Upper and Lower Egypt
and the beginning of the dynastic period. The famous Palette of
Narmer, which depicts the first king of the First Dynasty subjugat-
ing a victim by a blow to the head with his mace of authority, sym-
bolizes the event. As one scholar remarks, this image has been
reproduced in countless books on the "origin" of civilization, and
has been called "the first page of the first chapter of the written history of Egypt." Any standard textbook on the history of civilization will agree. And yet, such a view partitions into two hugely
unequal portions the time that the human species in some form—
from our earliest ancestors to ourselves—has existed on the planet.
The earliest known stone tools found in Africa date back to 2.4
million years ago and are believed to have been made by *Homo
habilis,* the earliest known member of our own genus. The time
between this ancestor fashioning its paleolithic implements and
King Narmer bringing his mace down on his pitiful subject, and
hence starting civilization (although the fact that it started off with
such a "bang" raises doubts about how civilized it actually was),

amounts to about ninety-five percent of the time something remote-ly "human" walked the Earth. Civilization, from Narmer on, amounts to about five percent. If we associate self-consciousness with the start of history and the rise of civilization, then it is easy to see how recent an arrival it is. For the overwhelming majority of "our" time on the planet, self-consciousness, at least as we know it, did not exist. Small wonder that the fledgling ego has a hard time of it resisting the pull back into its darker, less demanding past.

Some scholars however have questioned this division, as well as what they see as the unequal value and attention the two parts have received. If the historical period comprises only five percent of our time on the planet, it has made up for this by drawing at least nine-ty-five percent of the attention and praise. "Prehistoric" has come to mean a variety of negatives; when we picture complete destruction, we speak of being bombed "back into the Stone Age." Civilization on the other hand, its few discontents excluded, is the epitome of the desirable, and essentially means "progress," in the sense of techno-logical advance—although, this, of course, is as limited and narrow a definition as the one given for "prehistoric." Not all archaeolo-gists are satisfied with this dichotomy, nor with the definition of civ-ilization on which it is based, but for many years the possibility of an ancient, "lost" civilization predating our own was as inadmissi-ble as the idea that we may not have descended from apes.

———

Such an idea, of course, is a standard theme in much esoteric thought. We have seen it already in our discussion of Madame Blavatsky and Rudolf Steiner. In the early 1960s, it gained a wide popularity through Pauwels and Bergier's book *The Morning of the Magicians* (1963). This argued, along with a dozen other eccentric theses, that there was evidence of a "prehistoric," technologically advanced civilization thousands of years before our own, whose source seemed to point to outer space. By the late 1960s this idea fuelled the best-selling but highly dubious work of Erich von Daniken and his imitators, and enjoyed a wide readership among the counterculture through the work of John Michell. A Platonic philosopher, mathematician, and student of sacred geometry,

Michell argued in books like *The View Over Atlantis* (1969) that places like Stonehenge, Glastonbury, the Sphinx, and other sacred sites were linked through a network of "ley lines." These were lines of magnetic or "spiritual" force crisscrossing the planet, whose existence was known to the ancients. Thousands of years before the rise of Western civilization, Michell's ancients understood the Earth's hidden forces and built a civilization around them, based on astronomy, sacred geometry, and harmony with nature. A similar idea has informed a spate of more recent, highly successful books arguing that civilization is much older than the official account; the work of Graham Hancock and Robert Bauval, for example, who suggest that the Sphinx may have been built as early as 10,500 B.C., has been especially influential.

For the hippies in the early 1970s who read John Michell's books and flocked to places like Glastonbury, his ley lines were a portent of a New Age; for some critics, they were the standard utopian dream, the Golden Age served up with tie-dyed trousers and patchouli oil. In more recent years, however, the idea that "civilization as we know it" is not the sole claimant on that title has received strong support from researchers whose theories cannot simply be rejected as pipe dreams. Increasingly, there is reason to believe that the period we call "prehistoric" was not one long doldrum until the rise of civilization.

Chapter Fifteen

—

The Lost World

In the 1980s the late Marija Gimbutas became a controversial figure in the world of archaeology, and later in culture at large, for her belief that a matriarchal Stone Age civilization based on a worship of a Great Goddess predated the so-called origin of civilization in Egypt, and existed in Europe between 7000 and 3500 B.C. Peaceful, nonhierarchical, and living in harmony with nature, the civilization of "Old Europe" was centered, she claimed, on social responsibility, artistic creation, aesthetic achievement, nonmaterial values, and a respect for the generative powers of the female, leading to an ecologically sound society fostering equality between the sexes. Flourishing during long periods of stability, the various farming communities making up Old Europe erected temples, developed skills in ceramics and metallurgy, lived in spacious houses, and even had a kind of sacred script. Artisans produced a remarkable number of goods, and early trade routes enabled a wide exchange in shells, marble, copper, obsidian, and other materials. Çatal Hüyük, in the southern part of central Anatolia (Turkey), is the showcase site for Gimbutas's theory, a remarkable prehistoric "town" founded some 8,000 years ago, estimated to have supported a population of 7,000 people. Wall paintings, sculptures, and statuettes support the theory that the inhabitants of Çatal Hüyük worshipped a Great Goddess, and there is good reason to believe that the important rituals associated with her were performed by women, with men taking part in secondary roles. Men in general seem to have occupied a subordinate position in the society of Çatal Hüyük; male images have been found in the iconography of the site, but they are usually subsumed by the more dominant figure of the feminine. Similar temples and sites also devoted to the Goddess and worship of the feminine have been found in Malta, Slovakia, Serbia, Moldavia, and the British Isles. All attest to Gimbutas's view that a widespread Goddess-oriented "civilization" existed in Europe some three thousand years prior to the unification of Egypt.

But according to Gimbutas, this holistic Golden Age of high aesthetic achievement and sexual equality came to an end between 4300 and 2800 B.C. During this period, the peaceful, feminine-centered civilization of Old Europe suffered incursions from a Proto–Indo-European culture that would eventually overrun and dominate it. Originating on the steppes of Russia, the Neolithic Kurgan culture espoused values that were the complete opposite of Goddess worship. Horse-riding warriors, the Kurgans shattered the stability of Old Europe with devastating weaponry, and a male-centered, patriarchal religion based on the worship of a sky god. The Kurgan warriors toppled the worship of the Goddess, reducing her and her fellow female deities to secondary positions as wives of the new male pantheon. Sexual inequality, aggression, and linear and dualistic thinking—all, needless to say, elements of our own culture—leveled the older culture, which eventually died out, its stable, holistic way of life based on the cycles of nature shrinking to mere folklore and superstition.

Although it was popularized by writers like Riane Eisler (*The Chalice and the Blade*, 1987), Gimbutas's vision of an ecologically, politically, and sexually "correct" prehistoric civilization crushed by androcratic male warriors whose values went on to shape the Western world increasingly marginalized her among her archaeological peers. Perhaps inevitably, it was seen as more of a blueprint for a feminist utopia than an actual reconstruction of a past culture. This is unfortunate. Although Eisler, perhaps understandably, presents a simplified picture of what she sees as the need to regain the values of a "partnership" culture lost to our "dominator" one, Gimbutas's work in uncovering this lost past is exemplary and adds an essential dimension to our self-understanding.[1] The fact that she was not alone, that other thinkers have argued persuasively for the existence of a Goddess-oriented prehistoric civilization, adds weight to what too often seems in the work of some of its advocates an exercise in wishful thinking.

In a series of brilliant books written in the 1970s and 1980s, the psychologist Stan Gooch argued that prior to the appearance of our direct ancestor, Cro-Magnon man, Neanderthal man (*Homo sapiens neanderthalensis*) lived in what we would have to call a kind of "civilization."[2] Neanderthal man, who appeared about 100,000 years ago, has come to stand for an assortment of negatives: brutishness, stupidity, a general animal-like existence. In fact, Neanderthals had a larger brain than ours, their skulls showing a 1400-cubic-centimeter capacity, compared to our own average of 1300. This, Gooch argues, is mainly due to the larger size of the Neanderthals' cerebellum, a subcortical structure that in his view served as a kind of early cerebral cortex, but one that provided

Neanderthals with a significantly different consciousness than our own—a point we will return to shortly.

The Neanderthals had stone and bone tools, and showed an interest in ornamentation, but what is truly remarkable about these ancestors is that they had a profound religious and ritualistic sense. At a Neanderthal site at La Quina in the Dordogne, seventy-six absolutely perfect spheres were found, as well as a carefully shaped flat flint disk some twenty centimeters in diameter. There seemed no apparent utilitarian use for these objects, which, however, could indicate some form of Sun or, more to the point in Gooch's view, Moon worship. There is evidence that the elderly in Neanderthal groups were cared for, indicating some sense of respect and veneration, and the dead were ritually buried, usually decorated with flowers and often with food and other offerings, suggesting a belief in some form of afterlife. But what is most striking about Neanderthal culture is that their dead were often painted, sometimes *covered,* in red ochre, a name given to the iron ore hematite, a source of red pigment. Red ochre mines discovered in southern Africa dating back to 100,000 years ago give some idea of the importance this mineral had for the Neanderthals. It is estimated that a million kilograms of the ore had been mined from one of the oldest sites. Ochre is not a food and it was not used as a material in construction. Mining a million kilograms suggests a cooperative effort involving many generations. As the ore was used solely for religious and ritualistic purposes, this argues that they were powerful motivating forces in Neanderthal life. Gooch believes the ochre had such a powerful attraction because of its resemblance to blood—menstruation cycles were an important part of Neanderthal "religion," he argues. Yet strangely, although they possessed red ochre as well as black manganese dioxide, another source of pigment, which they formed into "crayons," there has so far been no report of Neanderthal cave art. They do not seem to have been "self-symbolic."

Gooch believes that the Neanderthals' large cerebellum made them what we would call "psychic," and that this made them sensitive to hidden forces as well as to natural phenomena like magnetic fields, useful for dowsing—an idea that seems to support John

Michell's ancients and their understanding of ley lines. Gooch believes, like most orthodox paleoanthropologists, that the Neanderthals were exterminated by our direct ancestors, the Cro-Magnons about 25,000 years ago. But, disagreeing with the standard account, Gooch also believes that Cro-Magnon males mated with Neanderthal females, and that their issue was—ourselves. In this view we are a "dual" being, bringing together in an often uncomfortable union two diametrically opposed mentalities and consciousnesses (once again an instance of "double consciousness"). Where Neanderthals were intuitive, "socialist," nature-oriented, and devotees of the Goddess and the Moon, Cro-Magnons—like the Kurgan warriors who devastated Old Europe—were logical, hierarchical, male-oriented, and believers in a solar sky god. One central difference between Neanderthals and Cro-Magnons was that the former were what we today might call sex addicts: according to Gooch, the Neanderthals had an almost insatiable lust, and it was this, perhaps more than any other reason, that enabled their women to gain dominance. Cro-Magnons, apparently, were altogether more continent creatures.

Classic Neanderthals were short, hairy, barrel-bodied, and nocturnal, with large, perhaps bulging eyes (physical characteristics, Gooch suggests, resulting from a successful adaptation to Ice Age conditions); Cro-Magnons were tall, slender, relatively hairless like ourselves, and diurnal. They were also highly efficient killers. In what must have been one of the most ruthless and sustained acts of genocide in human history or prehistory, Cro-Magnons wiped out what they must have considered an ugly subhuman animal. Yet, argues Gooch, the Neanderthal lives on, contained within our skulls. Like Andreas Mavromatis, Gooch sees the subcortical cerebellum, our inheritance from Neanderthals, as the source of our "other self," the unconscious, the "ancient adversary" with which our rational, cortical consciousness is in perpetual conflict. Yet again like Mavromatis, Gooch sees the rare moments of reconciliation as the precursor of a new kind of consciousness, the brief glory of "just right," when the Goldilocks of awareness hits on the successful proportions of "old" brain and "new."

But our "dual consciousness" is not the sole blessing (or curse, depending on how you look at it) that our Neanderthal ancestors bestowed on us. Their subcortical consciousness gave them a profoundly different view of the world—as we would expect, remembering what we know of hypnagogia—and, if Gooch is right, it is possible that with the Neanderthals we have some evidence of a kind of "Old Moon" culture, although, to be sure, the points of similarity do not tally with Steiner's vision exactly.[3] Neanderthals, Gooch argues, were Moon worshippers, and their "Moon culture" was so extensive and widespread that he is prompted to speak of a "Neanderthal empire," radiating out from central France, and reaching Africa, Siberia, and Turkey.[4]

Yet before we start thinking of some Golden Age of pre-Eden harmony, Gooch tells us that this "empire" included some practices we today would find highly dubious: orgiastic group sex, for one (which may not strike many of us as too bad),[5] but also other, less titillating pastimes such as human sacrifice, ritual cannibalism, and drinking blood. Racial memories of devotions such as these have lodged in our consciousness; they appear as an assortment of dark figures—vampires, bogeymen, goblins, and the yeti, as well as classical figures like satyrs, centaurs, and the Minotaur. Esoteric wisdom as found in the teachings of the Kabbalah, and other "occult" systems such as Rosicrucianism are, Gooch argues, unavoidably garbled echoes of the original Moon knowledge. He also makes a persuasive argument that a considerable number of common superstitions—unlucky thirteen, lucky seven, touching wood—as well as holy days such as Christmas and Easter, are all highly corrupted (from the ancient point of view) remnants of the universal Moon religion once practiced by our Neanderthal ancestors.

Here I have given only a bare fraction of the massive evidence Gooch presents to support his theory. His vision of a Neanderthal "Moon Empire" may not entirely convince, but if we are left questioning in some instances, others are striking in their implications. One such is the widespread and apparently inexplicable reverence shown to a rather faint and certainly unspectacular constellation known as the Pleiades or Seven Sisters. In a fascinating chapter of *Cities of Dreams,* Gooch sets forth the evidence that this undistin-

guished group, made up of fourth-magnitude stars—not particularly brilliant—was not only known to our ancient ancestors, but
appears in the mythology of many disparate peoples, and in exactly or nearly exactly the same context. For example, for the ancient
Greeks, the story went like this: Orion the hunter came upon six
sisters and their mother one day in a wood. Burning with lust, he
chased the sisters through the wood for five years, whereupon Zeus
took pity on the girls and changed both them and Orion into stars,
hence the constellations of Orion and the Seven Sisters. Strangely,
a very similar myth exists among the Aborigines of Australia.
Wurrunna the hunter was out in search of game, when he too came
upon a group of seven girls. He grabbed two of them and took
them as wives on the spot. However, the trees in the forest took
pity on the girls and suddenly grew to a tremendous height; the five
free sisters climbed to the sky, as did the other two, thus escaping
Wurrunna. The same story, Gooch tells us, appears in different
forms in other mythologies as well. The Pleiades are *always* known
as the Seven Sisters, and they are *always* hunted. Likewise, they
always escape, either through magical means or through the inter-
vention of a god. Now, there is nothing whatsoever in the bare
appearance of the Pleiades that should suggest they are women,
and certainly nothing to tell us they are hunted. Yet this is the story
time and again. The Pleiades also have the unchallenged distinction
of being the *only* constellation noted and named by *every* culture
on the planet, past or present. Why should a faint group of stars
that, as Gooch remarks, would not be recognized by the average
person have such importance?

Gooch proposes that the Pleiades gained their unique importance in world mythology because some 30,000 years ago, just at
the time when our Cro-Magnon ancestors were wiping them out,
Neanderthals were tracking the rise of the Seven Sisters as the har-
binger of spring.[6] The Moon-worshipping Neanderthals would
have been very knowledgeable of the heavenly motions, and, as
worshippers as well of the Goddess and her procreative powers—
which, for Gooch, were all an aspect of the Moon—they would
have been especially keen on noting the arrival of the vernal equinox. Gradually, due to the precession of the equinoxes, the coinci-

dence of the rising of the Pleiades and the arrival of spring faded, and in any case, as Gooch points out, the Cro-Magnons, who inherited the Neanderthals' "wisdom," would have had other things to deal with, like the new Ice Age. So the astronomical knowledge of the Neanderthals would sink into myth—where we find it today.

—

Whether or not this indeed points to a "Neanderthal empire," Gooch does receive support from other scholars. In his fascinating book *Lost Civilizations of the Stone Age* (1998), the Oxford prehistorian Richard Rudgley echoes Gooch about the odd status of the Pleiades, along with discussing other remarkable "anomalous" findings. Like many prehistorians, Rudgley was troubled by the apparent abruptness with which "civilization" was supposed to have begun. He was dissatisfied with the standard story of Narmer's mace starting off everything with a bang in Egypt, as well as with the most popular, though not academically accepted, alternatives: Atlantis or the "ancient astronaut" accounts. Rudgley asked a simple question: Why couldn't the roots of civilization be found in the period we call prehistoric?

He found that they could and his book is a persuasive collection of evidence showing that students of the history of civilization may soon have to rewrite their textbooks. *Lost Civilizations of the Stone Age* amasses a remarkable amount of material arguing for the high culture and civilization of people we usually consider our unquestioned inferiors. Rudgley cites the evidence for a Paleolithic (Old Stone Age) language reaching back 15,000 years, far earlier than Sanskrit or the Proto–Indo-European language dating to between 4000 and 6000 B.C., commonly considered one of the "ur" languages from which our modern tongues have evolved. Indeed, similarities between the languages of such different areas as southern Africa, the Amazon rain forest, and Europe point to the possibility of an even older Mother tongue called Proto-Global, believed by some prehistorians to have emerged around the same time as the first behaviorally modern human beings, 40,000 years ago. It is argued that the rise of this world-tongue, from which, its advocates claim, all the planet's diverse languages group emerged (numbering between 5,000 and 10,000, depending on your criteria), may have been responsible for the "sapiens explosion" that eventually led to us.

Rudgley also brings together the evidence for Stone Age mathematics, medicine (including trepanation), surgery, dentistry, writing, pyrotechnology, even a kind of Upper Paleolithic pornography. Some of his most fascinating accounts are of the use of psychotropic substances among the inhabitants of Old Europe. Opium was domesticated by farmers in the western Mediterranean area by around 6000 B.C., and the use of cannabis can also be traced back to the Neolithic period. There is even evidence that it was used by the Kurgan people who were alleged to have overrun the farmers of Old Europe; a burial site in Romania dating from the third millennium B.C. and belonging to the Kurgans was found to contain a ritual brazier in which the remains of charred cannabis was discovered.

The taste for altered states of consciousness seems to have a long history. In *The Long Trip: A Prehistory of Psychedelia* (1997), Paul Devereux suggests that the curious forms found in Neolithic cave art at sites like the island of Gavrinis off the coast of Brittany may be the result of our Stone Age ancestors' use of psychedelic substances. One curious thing about this site and others like it is that the forms—swirling, curvilinear lines, resembling nothing so much as giant fingerprints—are very much like the kinds of patterns associated with what are known as "entopic forms," the swirls and curls of light produced by rubbing one's eyes. They are also often seen at the point of sleep and are, as we might expect, associated with some types of hypnagogic experience. As I recounted earlier, the philosopher Jurij Moskvitin came upon his discovery of what he called "selective forms" by focusing on the strange patterns he detected on the surface of his retina. He associated these patterns with religious and mystical art, and suspected that his experience was probably a very old one, known to human beings for ages. The patterns on Gavrinis suggest this is the case and are also perhaps more evidence that early human beings had a consciousness similar to what we experience during hypnagogic states.[7]

Some of the most remarkable material in Rudgley's book deals with Stone Age science, specifically what we would call astronomy. It has been known for some time that megalithic sites like Stonehenge, Callanish in Scotland, and others were erected as Neolithic observatories. Since the 1960s, the work of the aeronautical engineer Alexander Thom, the astronomer Gerald Hawkins, the prehistorian Alexander Marshack, and those who followed them has made respectable the notion that our so-called prehistoric ancestors had mathematical, engineering, and astronomical capabilities equal to, and in some instances exceeding, our own. Marshack, for example, was fascinated by a series of markings he recognized on some pieces of bone dating from the Upper Paleolithic. After examining them under a microscope, he realized that at least one group of markings formed a kind of calendar, charting the phases of the Moon. During a visit to Callanish, Thom realized that the main north-south axis of the stones was aimed directly at the Pole Star. He also knew that at the time the stones were erected, the Pole Star was not in its present position, which meant that to align the stones to geographic north without the Pole Star as a guide would have been an extremely complicated business, requiring a highly sophisticated engineering ability—not the sort of thing usually granted the "primitive cavemen" who were supposedly responsible for the site. Gerald Hawkins took the measurements and alignments of Stonehenge and ran them through his computer. The result confirmed the idea advanced earlier in the twentieth century by the astronomer Sir Norman Lockyer that Stonehenge was a kind of astronomical clock. The conclusion from all of this evidence was that the prehistoric people who had built these sites were not ignorant, brutish savages, but possessed talents and skills we can only call civilized.

This astronomical talent seems to have appeared at a very early stage. The construction of Stonehenge began around 3100 B.C., about five centuries before the pyramids—at least according to the standard account. But Marshack's bone depicting the phases of the Moon was 35,000 years old. The Moon is undoubtedly the largest object in the night sky that we can view with the naked eye, and it does go through a series of easily recognizable changes, so it is not too difficult to imagine Neanderthals or Cro-Magnons making a rough calendar of its phases. But a faint group of stars is another matter. Rudgley does not mention Stan Gooch or his theories, but he does point to the same remarkable role the Pleiades had for our ancestors. Discussing the work of the Russian prehistorian Boris Frolov, Rudgely echoes Gooch by remarking on the curious fact that this unspectacular star group is known as the Seven Sisters to native people in areas as far apart as North America, Australia, and Siberia. Frolov and Rudgley both discount the possibility of this being mere coincidence—and by their remarks one assumes they also dismiss, as Gooch does, the idea that some form of Jungian "archetype" or expression of the "collective unconscious" can account for it. But if this is not a coincidence, the alternative is startling. Without going so far as to propose a "Neanderthal empire," Rudgley remarks that the only other possibility is some common heritage between these widespread groups. If that is the case, then it must reach back before the time the New World was first occupied, around 12,000 years ago—and even farther still, to before the peopling of Australia, which most authorities date at about 40,000 years ago. So, Rudgley suggests, both the observation of the Pleiades and their christening as the Seven Sisters must have taken place as early as 40,000 years ago. As he dryly remarks "This is something which is extremely awkward for most widely accepted views of the history and knowledge of science."[8]

―

Understandably, the idea that Neanderthals were not only observing the Pleiades but christening them as the Seven Sisters some 40,000 years ago, and that this informed a common heritage later shared by people as diverse as North American Indians and Australian Aborigines, is difficult for the standard view of paleoanthropology to accept. But this is not the only oddity about our past that the accepted view of prehistory has had to contend with.

According to that account, around three and a half million years ago an apelike creature called *Australopithecus afarensis* took the evolutionary step that would eventually lead to us. The famous "Lucy" and "first family" discovered in Ethiopia by the anthropologists Donald Johanson and Tom Gray in 1974, and dating back to 3.5 million years ago, are of this type. Then, after another million years, *Australopithecus africanus* appeared, the hominid ancestor discovered by Raymond Dart in the 1920s. Sometime around 2.2 million years ago, *Homo habilis*, "tool-making man," arrived, the earliest-known member of our genus. After him came *Homo erectus*, who lived from 1.6 to .5 million years ago and was the first to move out of Africa, spreading to the temperate zones of Asia and Europe. And around 500,000 years ago the earliest populations of *Homo sapiens* made their first appearance on the planet. Four hundred thousand years later—100,000 B.C.—Neanderthal man was active in Europe and western Asia, and by 40,000 years ago *Homo sapiens sapiens*, the eventual inheritors of the Earth, first arrived.

Now, at around 500,000 years ago something happened that, in terms of standard Darwinian evolutionary theory, shouldn't have. Suddenly, the human brain grew at such an accelerated rate that many scientists speak of a "brain explosion." *Homo erectus* had a brain capacity of 600 to 800 cubic centimeters; present-day human brains average around 1300 cc. In a mere 500,000 years the brain expanded to almost twice its size. Prior to this the brain had stayed between 600 to 800 cc for something like two million years. This is certainly ample time for the mechanisms of Darwinian selection to have made some changes, yet the period is characterized by an evolutionary standstill. Many anatomical features remained the same. There was some slight improvement in tools, but nothing more. One writer even speaks of the time as characterized by "an almost inconceivable stagnation and conservatism." But then came what we can call a cerebral "big bang," because most of the brain's rapid growth circa 500,000 B.C. had to do with the cerebrum, the layer of neural tissue sitting atop the "old" subcortical structures. From *Homo erectus* developing the stone tool technology known as Acheulian we get, in something like an evolutionary blink of an eye, Plato, Shakespeare, Beethoven, and Einstein. Science, as the cliché goes, cannot account for this.

Another evolutionary anomaly ignored by most orthodox pale-oanthropologists is the unaccountable presence of what seem to be fossils of anatomically "modern" human beings in time periods when they are not supposed to have existed—rather like discovering a laptop computer amidst a heap of *Homo habilis* remains. In a controversial book published in 1993, Michael A. Cremo and Richard L. Thompson presented a kind of archaeological "book of the damned." *Forbidden Archaeology* is a nine-hundred-page study of the science of palaeoanthropology, from its inception to the present, focusing on the odd bits and pieces of evidence that do not fit into the standard account. The result is something like an *X-Files* approach to the study of human evolution.

Cremo, admittedly, is a devout member of the Bhaktivedanta Institute, an organization formed around the teachings of Swami Prabhupada, the guru of Krishna Consciousness, who for a short time in the late 1960s occupied the position of spiritual guide to the Beatles after the post had been vacated by the Maharishi Mahesh Yogi. This, of course, is enough to make Cremo persona non grata among professional archaeologists, and one has to admit there is the possibility of bias in his approach. According to Hinduism, human beings like us have walked the planet for enormous periods of time, the *yugas* spoken of in the Bhagavata Purana, a commentary on the ancient Vedic hymns. (We, incidentally, are in the tail end of the Kali Yuga, a period of decline that is supposed to presage a new Golden Age.) Even so, Cremo and Thompson collected a disturbing amount of evidence suggesting that much of what may have upset the archaeological applecart has been conveniently left out of the official story. The core of their study focuses on various findings reported during the late nineteenth and early twentieth centuries that seem to contradict the Darwinian account of evolution. Since Thomas Huxley's debate with Bishop Wilberforce, that account had become the reigning orthodoxy. I can only touch on the material they provide, but these few examples should give an idea of the sort of thing that has been swept under the "official" archaeological carpet.

For example, in one instance from the 1870s, bones from an extinct three-toed horse called *Hipparion* were discovered, and it was clear that they had been fractured in order to extract the marrow. What made them odd was that the fractures appeared to have been made by a stone tool, not by animals. One group of bones excavated from the site and showing the same fractures dated back to at least five million years ago—much earlier than "Lucy" and her family. In another example from around the same time, sharks' teeth found in a layer dating back to two and half million years ago displayed fine holes that seemed clearly bored through them, making the teeth resemble ornaments for a necklace, something not associated with the hominids present at that time. In yet another case, in the 1860s, the head of the Geological Survey in Portugal, a man named Carlos Ribeiro, discovered flint tools in a layer of limestone dating back to the Pliocene and Miocene, two and five million years ago respectively, much earlier than the accepted view of when such tools should have been present. In each of these cases—and Cremo and Thompson's book is filled with hundreds more—the anomalies were either ignored, rejected, or qualified in order to fit into the standard account of human evolution.[9]

Cremo and Thompson are not the only ones who pondered the possibility that beings anatomically very much like us walked the Earth millions of years before they are supposed to—at least according to the official view. In 1978, at Laetoli, a site twenty miles south of Olduvai Gorge in Tanzania—a place made world-famous by the work of the anthropologist Louis Leakey—Mary Leakey, her son Philip, and a member of their expedition named Peter Jones came across a remarkable discovery. They found several sets of footprints left in volcanic ash that dated to about 3.5 to 3.8 million years ago. The footprints were those of hominids, and they indicated that their makers walked upright. But what was truly remarkable about these remains was that the footprints were typically human. Mary Leakey spoke of "unique evidence, of an unimpeachable nature" which established that "our hominid ancestors were fully bipedal a little before 3.5 million years ago." "The essentially human nature and the modern appearance of the footprints were quite extraordinary."[10] Years earlier her husband, Louis Leakey, began his career by investigating an equally unusual discovery made by a German geologist named Hans Reck. At

Olduvai Gorge in 1911, Reck came upon an anatomically human skull in a layer of earth at least 800,000 years old. According to the accepted view, this should not be the case. Darwinian theory argued that any remains that old should not be "human," and any that were human, could not be that old. Although Alfred Wallace, the cofounder of the theory of natural selection, believed that human beings as we know them existed as far back as the Tertiary Period (ten to fifteen million years ago), the "missing link" between ourselves and apes was thought to be not more than 500,000 years old. So Reck's skull was either that of an apelike creature, or it was much younger than he believed. Twenty years later, in 1931, Louis Leakey visited the site with Reck and investigated the strata where the skull was found. It was clear to him that indeed it was nearly a million years old. It seemed that some creature not so vastly different from us was occupying the Earth at a time it should not have; Leakey had pushed our presence on the planet back by nearly a million years, and the experts, of course, were not happy about this. He later raised much controversy by his contention that some two to three million years ago, *Australopithecus* and *Homo habilis* coexisted, a belief that was contested but that his son Richard Leakey also advanced. Some support for this view was provided by Donald Johanson and his discovery of Lucy and the First Family. *Australopithecus afarensis*, Johanson's name for his find, was not, as far as we know, a toolmaker, yet tools were discovered along with Lucy and her "family." If they hadn't made them, who had? One possibility is *Homo habilis*, which would push its presence on Earth back by at least a million years.

—

If nothing else, these anomalies suggest that the neat and orderly account of the "ascent of man" from early apelike ancestors to ourselves is not as foregone a conclusion as the experts would claim. And while it does not argue that alternative accounts such as Madame Blavatsky's and Rudolf Steiner's are therefore correct, it at least gives us room to speculate, without feeling that we are merely whistling in the dark. One thing that does suggest itself is that notions of a "multiple evolution" of the kind offered in different ways by Bergson and Ouspensky cannot be simply ruled out. If the idea of an uninterrupted linear progression from some ancient hominid ancestor to us fails to account for these various anomalies, then we are justified in, as Ouspensky would put it, "thinking in other categories." Human beings, or someone very much like them, may have been around for much longer than we have supposed. If that is the case, another question arises. If beings like us have been around for such a long time, why didn't they build a civilization like ours much earlier? Even if we put aside the possibility suggested by Mary Leakey's footprints discovered at Laetoli that a human-like being walked upright around the same time as Lucy and the First Family, and concentrate on much more recent times like, say, the last 50,000 years, we are still left wondering, why civilization as we know it dates from only 5,000 years ago.

Neanderthals were observing the movement of the Pleiades some 40,000 years ago and giving this faint group of stars a name that would last for millennia. Five thousand years later, our ancestors were charting the phases of the Moon. By 8,000 B.C.—10,000 years ago—the people of Old Europe had erected Çatal Hüyük and other Goddess-oriented sites and, if we accept Marija Gimbuta's account, developed a culture of nature worship and aesthetic and social sensitivity. Soon after come the megalithic observatories like Stonehenge and Callanish. All of these activities suggest intelligence, reason, knowledge, and technical skill. In fact, one anthropologist examined Stone Age tools dating from some 330,000 years ago using tests devised by the psychologist Jean Piaget—famous for his work in child psychology and cognitive theory—and declared that the people who had made them were as intelligent as ourselves. And yet, even with all these attributes, the very qualities necessary to create "civilization" as we know it, the prehistoric world remained very different from our own.

The question that raises is: Why?

Chapter Sixteen

Noncerebral Consciousness

One answer to the question why civilization did not begin earlier is that it is highly likely the consciousness of our prehistoric ancestors was very different from our own. Given what we have heard from Stan Gooch and Andreas Mavromatis, this is to be expected. If our own cerebral cortex dates back to the brain explosion of 500,000 years ago, we can imagine that the consciousness of the hominid ancestors who left their footprints at Laetoli some 3.5 to 3.8 million years ago was probably not very much different from that of the animals. *Homo habilis* developed tools, and *Homo erectus* had enough curiosity to leave the homeland of Africa and explore new lands—driven, of course, by a variety of environmental factors. But for something like three million years, our ancestors were in many ways as rooted to the earth as the trees they once lived in.

With the brain explosion this changed. Whatever may have caused the change, it shifted our ancestors' awareness. They began to use some of their intelligence and to notice the world around them. And some of the things they saw were the Moon and the stars. Of course they had seen them before, but now they looked—different.

One of the things we must grasp about our "premodern" ancestors is that they were "in touch" with nature to a degree we find difficult to imagine. And this remained true even after the "brain explosion," but there was a difference. *Homo habilis* and *Homo erectus* were more than likely "in" nature in the same way that animals are today. But with the brain explosion *Homo sapiens*—Neanderthals and later Cro-Magnons—began to experience a certain "separation" from the world. This is a point we will explore further in our discussion of Jean Gebser's work. Suffice it to say here that at this time our ancestors began to recognize patterns in nature and to become aware of the relationships between them: the movement of the Pleiades, for example, and the arrival of spring. Or the phases of the Moon and the menstrual cycle—as Stan Gooch suggests.

But this would seem to say that the prehistoric mind was merely a dim version of our own, not that its consciousness itself was different. Yet there is reason to believe that what prompted our ancestors to chart the phases of the Moon was something more than their attempts to devise a kind of primitive calendar—and in any case, their sense of time was very likely not like our own. Bergson, we remember, argued that the brain's function was essentially eliminative, and by the brain he meant by and large the cerebral cortex. And Andreas Mavromatis, as we have seen, suggests that "cortical consciousness" is aimed at stabilizing and objectifying sensation.

This prompts us to ask some obvious questions. What is it exactly that the cerebral cortex is "eliminating"? And what kind of sensations is it "objectifying"?

One theorist who has speculated on the nature of "noncerebral" consciousness may offer some useful suggestions. He also happens to be associated with one of the most celebrated archaeological anomalies of our time: the true age of the Sphinx.

———

Before the mid-1990s the name René Schwaller de Lubicz was known, at best, to a handful of intrepid but eccentric scholars, whose interest lay in the esoteric side of ancient Egypt and the often-impenetrable mysteries of alchemy. With the publication of Graham Hancock's best-selling *Fingerprints of the Gods* in 1995, Schwaller became known to millions as the man who claimed that the Sphinx was thousands of years older than had been suspected. It was not, he argued, built around 2500 B.C. as the official view held, but had been constructed much earlier, as early, perhaps, as 10,500 B.C. Hancock was not the first to bring Schwaller's fascinating theory to light. His remarkable ideas about the age of the Sphinx had been pointed out several years earlier in John Anthony West's brilliant book *The Serpent in the Sky*. West's central theme was one that has been a mainstay of esoteric thought ever since Madame Blavatsky: that the civilization of Egypt—which, we remember, started "abruptly" in 3100 B.C. with King Narmer's mace—is in fact thousands of years older than the official view upholds. Moreover, West also pointed out there was good reason to believe that rather than appearing "overnight" out of the darkness of predynastic Egypt, the archaeological marvels that we associate with Egyptian civilization, like the Sphinx and the pyramids with all their mathematical and engineering genius, may indeed be the remains of a civilization that existed for millennia before Egypt, a civilization that we may, for convenience, call "Atlantis."

The Serpent in the Sky, is, in fact, a study of Schwaller's ideas about the profound mathematical and symbolic aspects of the wisdom of ancient Egypt; like Schwaller's own books, it reached a relatively small audience, generally those interested in these or similar aspects of what has come to be known for better or worse as New Age philosophy. When West's book first appeared in 1979, the "New Age" was still a marginal affair, although Marilyn Ferguson's *The Aquarian Conspiracy* (1980) was about to uncover a broad grassroots interest in ideas about consciousness and spirituality. By the time of Hancock's book, New Age consciousness had spread, creating a large audience eager for ideas and insights offering some sense of meaning in a predominantly materialistic, rationalistic culture. As in the occult revival of the 1960s, the notion that a highly advanced civilization rich in spiritual insight and cosmic knowledge had preceded our own, but was unknown to modern science, satisfied a felt need. This time, however, the creators of that civilization did not come from outer space, and the evidence for their existence was more convincing than the inaccuracies and fabrications of Erich von Daniken and the like.

The story of Graham Hancock's investigation into the true age of the Sphinx is best told in *Keeper of Genesis* (1996, U.S. edition *The Message of the Sphinx)*, cowritten with another archaeological detective, Robert Bauval (author of *The Orion Mystery,* 1994). The story is too involved to go into here, but basically Hancock, author of a best-selling book about the lost ark of the covenant, was intrigued by Schwaller's remark (which he came across in West's book) that except for its head, the Sphinx showed clear signs of water erosion. This was something no Egyptologist had noticed before—or perhaps some had but had decided not to mention, for good reason: the observation would upset the standard archaeological record and explode the accepted date for the beginning of civilization. The fact that Schwaller de Lubicz was a maverick student of ancient Egypt, who also practiced alchemy and had a penchant for secret societies and right-wing politics, meant that his ideas were not immediately accessible to the average archaeologist. What was known of them was considered the work of a crank.[1] (The title "de Lubicz" was given to Schwaller by the Lithuanian poet and diplomat O. V. de Lubicz Milosz for his efforts on behalf of the Lithuanian people in the aftermath of World War I.)

Schwaller made his remark about the water erosion on the Sphinx in one of his last books, *Sacred Science,* published in 1961. Although it was aimed at a "general" audience, it is still a difficult work, and, like his other, even more unwieldy books, it remained relatively unknown. So amidst the wealth of Schwaller's equally eccentric notions regarding ancient Egypt, the one that could be *scientifically tested* lay unnoticed for years.

Until John Anthony West. West realized that if it could be confirmed that the Sphinx had suffered water erosion, archaeologists would have to start rewriting their textbooks. He sought help from scholars, including geologists, archaeologists, and Egyptian specialists. When it became clear that he was interested in arguing that the Sphinx showed signs of water erosion, they backed away. The notion seemed too cranky and occult, another addition to the grab bag of esoteric ideas that had accumulated around Egypt since the eighteenth century. Finally, in 1989, West approached Robert Schoch, a professor at Boston University. Schoch is a geologist and paleontologist whose specialty is the weathering of soft rocks, precisely like the limestone the Sphinx is made of, so he had the exact expertise needed to make a geological assessment of its erosion marks. His conclusions corroborated Schwaller: the erosion marks on the body of the Sphinx were made by water— not, however, by flooding, as Schwaller thought, but by rainfall.

This is startling because the "official" date of construction of the Sphinx is 2500 B.C., yet the kind of rainfall needed to cause the erosion marks hadn't happened in bone-dry Egypt since at the very least 7000 to 5000 B.C.—and this is a conservative estimate. The erosion marks push the construction date back by several thousand years, to a time when the only tools available to the local Neolithic hunter-gatherers were some flint and bits of stick. No engineers, no mathematicians. A major anomaly, to be sure.

As if this wasn't bad enough, Hancock and Bauval argue that the Sphinx and the plan for the pyramids, if not their actual construction, actually date back to 10,500 B.C. and that the entire Giza complex is a monument commemorating what is known in the ancient Egyptian religion as *Zep Tepi,* "The First Time." Using computers to trace back the precession of the equinoxes, Hancock and Bauval discovered that circa 10,500 B.C. the Sphinx, the Nile, and the ground plan for the three great pyramids all mirrored, with a startling accuracy, the night sky over Giza, specifically the constellation Leo, the Milky Way, and the belt of Orion. All three feature prominently in Egyptian religious beliefs. (And for what it's worth, we recall that for both the ancient Greeks and the Australian Aborigines, Orion is the hunter chasing the Seven Sisters.) "The First Time," *Zep Tepi,* occurred during the Age of Leo—some 12,000 years ago—a period even more prehistoric and backward, at least according to the official account, than the 7000–5000 B.C. of Robert Schoch's estimate. It also happens to be a likely time period for the fabled sinking of Atlantis . . . In either case, given the accepted account of humanity's "ascent," there is no way anything like the Sphinx could have been constructed at that time.

—

But the true age of the Sphinx is only one of the many mysteries surrounding ancient Egypt that Schwaller investigated. And as startling as it is for us—and shocking for the archaeological establishment—it is not the most important of his central ideas. Clearly it supports his fundamental belief that Egyptian civilization is much older than academic Egyptologists claim. But more than being an archaeological anomaly, what is important about the Sphinx is what it *says* about that civilization. And for Schwaller, what the Sphinx tells us is that the core of ancient Egyptian culture was a fundamental insight into the "laws of creation."

The evidence of the Sphinx, the pyramids, the stupendous Temple of Luxor, and the magnificent stones of Karnak—all of which, Schwaller argues, are much older than we suspect—forces us to admit that the people responsible for them possessed a spiritual insight and cosmic genius of which we have little awareness. In the face of these tremendous works we "moderns," he argues, must admit the existence of "a humanity both inspired and prehistoric," something the academic standard-bearers are loath to do.[2] Everything about Egyptian civilization, from the construction of the pyramids to the shape of a beer mug, Schwaller claimed, was motivated by a central metaphysical vision about the nature of cosmic harmony and an awareness of humanity's place in the evolution of consciousness. Not something we generally associate with cavemen dragging their girlfriends around by the hair.

The kind of mathematical, astronomical, and engineering genius evident in the Sphinx, the great pyramids, and other Egyptian monuments has been recounted by numerous writers—a reader might start with Hancock and Bauval, and then turn to John Anthony West's and John Michell's work. That the great pyramids embody profound geodetic and celestial insights, and that they are constructed with an engineering finesse that is difficult, if not impossible, to repeat, even using the most advanced "modern" techniques, has been known for some time.[3] The history of "pyramidology," in which everything from flying saucers to biblical prophecies has been associated with the ancient Egyptian builders, is an absorbing, amusing, and enlightening study; sadly, it falls outside our present pursuit. But if the remarkable scientific knowledge of the builders of the Sphinx and the great pyramids is challenging to our standard model of the "progress" of civilization, what is even more disturbing is the notion that whoever constructed these works of genius had a consciousness radically different than our own.

This consciousness Schwaller called "the intelligence of the heart." He believed that through a "harmonic coincidence of the ambient cosmos," the ancient Egyptians were "able to know the forces that bring about the becoming of things." This "knowing," however, was not a "knowing by learning," but an immediate, unreflective grasp of the fundamental laws of existence.[4] Lost to us moderns because of our emphasis on rational, logical thinking— the function of the cerebral cortex—this "intelligence of the heart" was communicated by the ancient sages through the rich symbology of their monumental structures.

As we have seen, the most fascinating and disturbing fact about ancient Egypt is that, like the Greek goddess Athena, it appears suddenly, fully grown. There is no apparent development or evolution of the Egyptian style: hieroglyphics, technical skill, and architectural mastery are there, all of a piece, seemingly out of nowhere. It is precisely this fact that has led some theorists, like Schwaller, to suggest that these accomplishments are an inheritance from an earlier civilization. Whatever the case, it is evident that there is a profound difference between our own sensibilities and those of the people responsible for these works. Contact with this ancient world produces an eerie feeling, the proximity of, to our mind, a very strange and alien consciousness. One reason for this, Schwaller remarks, is that the Egyptian monuments exhibit the "cohesion of a style which does not speak to the ordinary sentiments of man and leaves no place for sensuality."[5]

A similar assessment can be made of Schwaller's own work, which is austere and uncompromising in the extreme. Yet his basic idea can be extracted from its imposing setting: that the ancient Egyptians, and the people who came before them, saw the world in a way very different from how we perceive it.

Schwaller's basic insight is not that different from Bergson's, whose influence he came under during his time as a student of the painter Henri Matisse. Like practically everyone else in the early part of the twentieth century, Matisse was deeply influenced by Bergson's philosophy of "intuition"—and Bergson's later remark that the universe is "a machine for making gods" is a sentiment Schwaller would later wholeheartedly support. After Bergson, a reading of Einstein, Max Planck, Niels Bohr, and Werner Heisenberg suggested to Schwaller that the strange world of quantum physics and relativity opened the door to a universe more in line with the cosmologies of the ancients, and less compatible with the Newtonian clockwork world of the nineteenth century. Bohr's "complementarity" and Heisenberg's "uncertainty principle" were particularly influential on Schwaller's investigations of the true meaning of Egyptian hieroglyphics.

Niels Bohr ended the debate over the nature of light—whether it was a particle or a wave—by opting for a position that saw it as both, with one definition complementing the other. And Heisenberg argued that we cannot know both the position *and* the speed of an elementary particle, since pinpointing one obscures the other—hence the "uncertainty." What these non-Newtonian notions suggested was that "reality" exceeds our logic's ability to grasp it. Complementarity and uncertainty demand a stretch of our minds beyond the either/or of syllogistic logic—something that Ouspensky had argued for way in advance of the popularity of what became known as the new physics. Both ask us to hold mutually exclusive ideas together, the basic principle behind Zen koans. The result, Schwaller knew, could be an illogical but illuminating insight.

Such insights, he argued, were behind the mind that created the hieroglyphics, in which the "simultaneity of opposite states" plays a central role. Schwaller called this practice *symbolique,* a way of holding together the object of sense perception and the content of inner knowing in a kind of creative polarity—a process that sounds remarkably like hypnagogia. When Egyptians saw the hieroglyph of a bird, he argued, they knew it was a sign for the actual, individual creature, but they also knew it was a symbol of the "cosmic function" the creature exemplified—flight—as well as all the myriad characteristics associated with it. (Again, we are reminded of Ouspensky and his experience of the ashtray.) Hieroglyphs did not merely designate: they *evoked.* As Schwaller wrote in *Symbol and the Symbolic,* "The observation of a simultaneity of mutually contradictory states . . . demonstrates the existence of two forms of intelligence."[6] One form is our familiar rational, scientific intelligence. The other is the intelligence of the heart.

Schwaller believed that the appearance of the new physics indicated that humanity was moving toward a massive shift in awareness—an idea, we shall see, shared by his near contemporary Jean
Gebser. Schwaller related this shift to the precession of the
equinoxes and the coming Age of Aquarius. But he knew that science alone could not provide the deepest insights into the true character of the world. For this a completely different kind of consciousness is necessary. This belief led to his study of theosophy
and esoteric knowledge. In particular it led to alchemy and his
meeting with the mysterious individual known as Fulcanelli, one of
the great figures of myth in our time. One result of Schwaller's
alchemical studies was his belief that in esotericism a concrete,
objective knowledge unknown to modern science could be found.
Schwaller rejected Jung's idea that alchemy was a purely psychic
affair, a working out of the complexes and "projections" of the
alchemist's unconscious. He knew that alchemy was a spiritual
practice involving the consciousness of the alchemist—it was, or is,
as we shall see, a form of "participating" with nature. But it also
involved objective insights into the nature of matter. This insight
into the reality of objective knowledge fueled Schwaller's later
investigations into Egyptian civilization.

One form of this objective knowledge came to Schwaller in
1926 during a series of "channeled" communications he received
from a higher intelligence. He called the voice that spoke to him
"Aor," which means "intellectual light" in Hebrew. (It was also,
incidentally, the mystical title he took after an initiatory experience; later, students who gathered around him in Suhalia, his
alchemical community in Switzerland, would call him by this
name.) These "inspirations" revealed to Schwaller the true significance of time, space, measure, and harmony. The basic message
was to "think simply," to abstract oneself from time and space.
"To cultivate oneself to be simple," he wrote, "and to see simply is
the first task of anyone wishing to approach the sacred symbolism
of Ancient Egypt." "Thinking simply" is necessary because "the
obvious" blinds us—"the obvious" being our perception of the
world via cerebral consciousness alone, which divides, analyzes,
and "granulates" experience—all of which is another way of

expressing Bergson's insight about "static perception." Schwaller
would later discover that the ancient Egyptians associated this static perception with the evil god Set. Its opposite, the intelligence of
the heart, was linked to the god Horus.

—

Schwaller formulated his central ideas about ancient Egypt during his studies at the temple of Luxor. On his first visit in 1937, he
was impressed with a tremendous insight. The temple, with its
strange, "crooked" alignments, was, he was certain, a conscious
exercise in the laws of harmony and proportion. He called it the
Parthenon of Egypt and searched the temple for evidence of the
"golden section," or phi, a mathematical proportion believed to
have been discovered by the Greeks.[7] If it was embodied in Luxor,
that would prove the Egyptians knew of it much earlier. Schwaller
did find evidence for phi, and also for much else: the precession of
the equinoxes, the circumference of the globe, the secrets of pi. But
what struck him forcibly was his insight into the essence of
Egyptian consciousness. The Egyptians, he believed, saw the world
symbolically. Nature for them was a kind of "writing" conveying
truths about the metaphysical forces behind creation, the *Neters,* as
the Egyptian gods are called. Viewing the world *from the inside* in
this way gave them access to their profound mathematical and
astronomical knowledge—knowledge not available to "cerebral
consciousness" until centuries later. Luxor was a kind of living
organism, a colossal compendium of esoteric truth, whose every
detail, from its total design down to its very material, voiced a central revelation: the insight that the Conscious Man, the Pharonic
King, was the goal of cosmic evolution. According to Schwaller, the
Egyptians believed that each individual type in nature is a stage in
a kind of cosmic embryology, whose culmination is the human
being. The different species developed different "cosmic functions"—the *Neters,* which we translate as "gods." The Conscious
Human, far from descending from the animals, is the apotheosis
and integration of their "cosmic functions." We have seen that a
similar idea was shared by Madame Blavatsky, Ouspensky, and
Bergson.

The essence of this evolution has to do with what Schwaller calls "functional consciousness," which, with all respect to his profound insight into ancient Egypt, seems very much like Bergson's "intuition." "Functional consciousness" is a way of knowing reality from the "inside," and Schwaller believed that the culture and religion of ancient Egypt—the two were really the same—were based on this "inner knowing," which is very unlike our own "outer" oriented one. The ancient Egyptians, he argued, were aware of the limitations of purely cerebral consciousness, the Set mind that granulates experience into fragments of space and time. Granulated experience produces our familiar world of disconnected things, each a kind of "island reality," a fragmentation that in recent years has come to be called the "postmodern condition." From this perspective, when I look at the world, I see a foreign, alien landscape, which I can only know from the "outside," by taking it apart and analyzing it. But in doing so I tear bits and pieces of the world out of their context, rupturing the whole. The result is that I may be able to analyze the fragment in great detail, but it is no longer living, vital. As Wordsworth said, "We murder to dissect." It is not too much to say that since the seventeenth century and the rise of scientism—the application of scientific method to phenomena outside its scope—much of the world has wound up on the dissecting table.

The ancient Egyptians, Schwaller believed, saw the world in another way, and we have good reason to believe they were perhaps the last people to experience reality as a totality. As Schwaller wrote in his difficult work *Nature Word*, "The Universe is wholly activity." In a section called "The Way," he advises his readers to "leave all dialectic behind and follow the path of the Powers."

> *Tumble with the rock which falls from the mountain.*
> *Seek light and rejoice with the rosebud about to open: . . .*
> *labor with the parsimonious ant;*
> *gather honey with the bee;*
> *expand in space with the ripening fruit.*[8]

All of these injunctions are classic examples of the kind of "knowing from the inside" that Bergson had in mind in his talk on intuition. In this way, we participate with the world, rather than hold it at arm's length, objectifying it, as modern science is prone to do. In this sense, Schwaller's injunctions are also expressions of the "participatory consciousness" we will discuss in a later chapter.

CHAPTER SEVENTEEN

The Split

Clearly, if Schwaller de Lubicz is right, the ancient Egyptians, and the hypothetical civilization that preceded them, had a relationship with the world profoundly different from our own. And while the achievements of the ancient world are awe-inspiring and without doubt worthy of respect, those of the modern world are also considerable. The ancient Egyptians never saw pictures from the Hubble telescope—but there is a good chance they would not have felt the need to build one. If they were as "at home" in the cosmos as Schwaller suggests, they would have felt no need to explore it— it was there for them, immediately, in their "unreflective grasp of the fundamental laws of existence." And if you have a strong intuitive knowledge of something, you feel no need to make the effort to explain it. Take language, for example: we all know how to *use* it, but most of us would be hard pressed to explain in detail how or why it *works*. And those of us who *do* ask questions about it are usually seen as a bit odd.

If Schwaller is right, there is good reason to believe that the "humanity both inspired and prehistoric" that preceded us had a similar relation to their knowledge about the cosmos. Feeling the living presence of the Neters, they would not have understood a desire to know *why* the universe is the way it is. The question itself would not have made sense to them. While this may have prevent-ed them from developing the kinds of problems we face in the modern world, both environmental and psychological, it also had its drawbacks.

In *From Atlantis to the Sphinx,* Colin Wilson suggests that it may have been precisely their closeness to the cosmos that prevented our ancestors from evolving. They simply felt no need to. Since everything was at hand, evolution, which is the result of challenge and curiosity, was left without a prompt. In this sense, being kicked out of the Garden of Eden was probably the best thing that could have happened to Adam and Eve. Had they remained in the cozy, uroboric embrace of Mother Earth—or God's graces—they would never have felt the need to develop their own abilities and potentials. Wilson also speculates that early human beings, even as late as the ancient Egyptians, existed in a kind of "communal consciousness," a unitary mind that we experience briefly during mass events like rock concerts and football games, which the Egyptians "tapped" in order to perform some of their engineering marvels, such as lifting the twenty-ton stone blocks that make up the pyramids. Such group experiences fill the solitary ego with a sense of power and connect it to something greater than itself—the basic drive behind religion.

Most of us enjoy such immersions in collective consciousness, at least occasionally. During them we are no longer a vulnerable, insignificant atom, but part of a vast, vital "whole." To want to experience such feelings is perfectly normal; it is part of being human, and, on a smaller but even more intimate scale, is the central attraction of love. But such collective consciousness can also be used for less-than-desirable purposes, as was made clear during Hitler's years in power, when mass meetings like the Nuremberg rallies fused the separate consciousnesses of the crowd into a single, group mind. Such a mind can indeed be powerful, but it is not always intelligent, as any kind of mob hysteria makes clear. And even when it does not grow demonic, a group mind has a curiously static quality. For a variety of reasons, intelligence, genius, and insight are profoundly individual, and what the mass mind may gain in power and "wholeness," it lacks in innovation and adventure. (Attendees at any conference or board meeting can attest to this, and the fact that more and more "creative" decisions are now made by committee suggests a current distrust of the authoritative individual.)

Creation is a solitary affair. A mind that feels close bonds with those around it may never suffer from anxiety or cosmic loneliness, but it may also never feel the spur to satisfy its own needs through creative effort. Insecurity, angst, a sense of being "myself, alone" may at times be unbearable; they are also the flipside of courage and determination.

But how did the split occur? How did we get from a collective mind, at one with the cosmos, led by the directives of a sacred, spiritual king, to ourselves, island egos adrift in a strange, alien universe? The process probably began long ago, long before the reign of the Pharaohs and the building of the pyramids and the Sphinx. Cro-Magnons lived in a vital, magical world, as the cave art at sites like Lascaux and Altamira shows. But they were just that bit less immersed in the cosmos than their Neanderthal predecessors. According to Stan Gooch, Cro-Magnons had all the qualities we attribute to our "rational" selves. Our rational, logical, "masculine" traits, focusing on dealing with an external world—what Gooch calls "system A"—are our inheritance from the Cro-Magnons and are a direct outcome of the growth of the cerebral cortex. "System B," our mystical, intuitive, "feminine" qualities, related to our interior world, derive from our Neanderthal ancestors—who, Gooch tells us, had a much larger cerebellum, the subcortical "little brain" that may have been evolution's first choice for an organ of self-consciousness. So Cro-Magnons, and the hybrids that emerged from their mating with Neanderthal females—ourselves—had at least one foot out of the Garden. Clearly the Kurgan horsemen, who Marija Gimbutas argues overran the Goddess-oriented civilization of Old Europe, seem to have been less peaceful and harmonious, no longer suckling at Mother Earth's breasts. The communal society of sites like Çatal Hüyük suggests that their inhabitants may have shared something like the collective consciousness of ancient Egypt, while the hierarchical structure of Kurgan clans, as well as their emphasis on a solar sky god, argues for a society held together by fear and authority.

We shouldn't think, however, of the Cro-Magnons or Kurgans as being individuals in the sense that we are. More than likely the sense of self-consciousness we experience was dim in them, if present at all. They were still part of the group. But the split from the whole, from the totality, had begun. Linear thinking, which posits cause and effect, and which Gooch and Gimbutas argue was typical of both the Cro-Magnons and Kurgans, functions by separating one group of events from the totality in which they are embedded. It posits a "past" and a "future," rupturing the ever-present "now" which, in its totality, contains both in a timeless whole. (Nonlinear, "acausal" knowledge systems, like the I Ching, function by accepting that at any time a part of the whole is representative of its entirety, much as a small portion of a hologram nevertheless contains its entire image.) Cro-Magnons practiced magic, painting images of their prey on the walls of their cave. By doing this they exerted their *will* upon the world. They wanted to *influence* events in the future, not merely take things as they came. And by doing this they had taken a step *out* of the whole.

Clearly, then, we shouldn't think of the split as a sudden, solitary event—a singularity as it is called in physics. Rather it was something that occurred over time. But there were obvious signs that something had changed. According to a recent book, one such occurred on the eastern shores of the Mediterranean sometime between 1700 and 1500 B.C., with the invention of what we know as the alphabet. The Phoenicians are traditionally given the honors for this, but there is evidence of an earlier alphabet, and more than likely credit for developing this revolutionary tool should be shared by several groups who inhabited the lands between Egypt and Mesopotamia in the second millennium B.C. Whoever may be responsible, Leonard Shlain argues in *The Alphabet Versus the Goddess* (1998) that with the rise of the alphabet, the old image-oriented, holistic, nonlinear Goddess consciousness embodied in Egyptian hieroglyphics was jettisoned in favor of a new device which "shifted the perceptual mode by which people understood their reality, deflected the thrust of gender politics, and changed the course of history."[1]

Cultures that adopted the alphabet made remarkable achievements: monotheism, codes of law, democracy, the sanctity of the individual, economics, and the development of science, philosophy, and drama. But, Shlain tells us, there was a flipside. The "abstraction" from the whole that made the alphabet possible also opened the door to the abuse of nature, war, imperialism, racism, and sexism. For all its undoubted advantages—I would not have written this book without it and you would not be reading it—literacy has not been an unalloyed boon for humankind, and certainly, according to Shlain, not for womankind. It has been much more like a Pandora's box—which may be merely another of the kind of antifeminine remarks it has engendered.

Shlain argues that by focusing on this abstract, linear means of communication we have become a left-brain-dominated civilization, at the expense of our right brain and the nonlinear, holistic, participatory consciousness typical of the matriarchal, Goddess-oriented societies that preceded literacy. Literacy, Shlain suggests, is a predominantly male device, fostering a detachment from nature and a devaluing of the nonmasculine. His argument is well put and convincing, and, for an inveterate reader and writer like myself, disturbing. For example, he points out that the Phoenicians, who supposedly invented the system that, more than anything else, our humanist civilization is based on, are not particularly good missionaries for the ABCs.

> One might expect that the inventors of the alphabet would have excelled culturally, or that the creativity that inspired the alphabet would lead to other significant advances. Yet the only area in which the Phoenicians can be credited with innovation is in the art of naval design. . . . The most vivid descriptions of the Phoenicians come not from their own pens but from their enemies, the Romans. In the final stages of the Roman siege of Carthage, the Phoenicians threw several hundred children, drawn from the finest families, onto the stoked fires with the bronze belly of their god Moloch. This cruel deity could only be appeased by human sacrifice.[2]

Shlain says that such cruelty, has sprouted throughout history in lands fertilized by the letter, along with patriarchy, a hierarchical social structure, and a rejection of nature, and infers that it stems from the invention of the alphabet itself. This is because "all forms of writing increase the left brain's dominance over the right."

> *As civilization progressed from image-based communications, such as pictographs and hieroglyphs, to non-iconic forms, such as cuneiform, written communication became more left-brain oriented. An alphabet, being the most abstract form of writing, enhances left-brain values the most. . . . Unlike icons, which often evolved from images of things, an alphabetic word bears no resemblance to the object or action it symbolizes.*[3]

As the popular literature on split-brain theory has made widely known, the left cerebral hemisphere is oriented toward language and logical, linear thinking, toward analysis, and toward "dealing with the world." It is, in the jargon, the "scientist." The right hemisphere is geared toward patterns; it sees the world holistically, sensually, and has little sense of time, being quite content to inhabit a perpetual "now." It is the "artist." The alphabet, by focusing consciousness on an abstract means of conveying *information,* loses the felt *reality* of what it is communicating. The hieroglyph of a bird still looks like a bird. The word "bird" doesn't look like anything; it bears no direct relation to what it is symbolizing. In other words, it seems that literacy is as far removed from Schwaller's intelligence of the heart as we can get.

Shlain's argument warrants serious consideration, as does his belief that with the rise of the Internet and our electronic culture we are moving away from the linear-bound thinking of the book to a kind of renaissance of the image. This, he suggests, will foster a more feminine, harmonious, and holistic consciousness. His forecast in many ways resembles that of Marshall McLuhan in the 1960s; it also suffers from the same drawbacks. Whether an "image-based" culture is in itself preferable to a "literary" one, and whether indeed the Internet is as nonlinear and nonliteral as he suggests, are questions we will return to in a later chapter. But it is clear that Shlain has certainly pegged one of the major shifts in the history of consciousness, and one of the ways, perhaps the central one, by which we have arrived at minds like our own.[4]

———

Shlain's date of 1700–1500 B.C. seems fairly recent for the birth of self-consciousness, but the work of another theorist argues that consciousness as we know it appeared even later, only as recently as 1250 B.C. In *The Origin of Consciousness in the Breakdown of the Bicameral Mind* (1976), the Princeton psychologist Julian Jaynes argues that until the later part of the second millennium B.C. human beings did not possess the kind of "interior world" that we do. They were not, in effect, self-conscious. Jaynes finds evidence for this bizarre theory in Homer's epic poem *The Iliad*. Composed in the eighth or ninth century B.C., *The Iliad* depicts events in the Trojan War during the time of the Mycenaean civilization some six or seven centuries earlier. Jaynes writes, "The picture then is one of strangeness and heartlessness and emptiness. We cannot approach these heroes by inventing mind-spaces behind their fierce eyes as we do each other."[5] Simply put, he argues that *The Iliad* contains no words for internal states of mind. The heroes of *The Iliad*, as well as the people living at the time its events took place, could not "look inside" themselves as we do. They did not ask themselves, "Hmm, what shall I do today?" or "What do I think about this?" Instead, when they needed to know what to do they listened to "voices" they heard in their heads, voices they believed came from the gods. Jaynes tells us they really came from the right brain.

Curiously, the inspiration—literally—for Jaynes's theory was a hypnagogic experience, this one auditory. One afternoon, when he had been thinking hard about the problems in his book, "particularly the question of what knowledge is and how we can know anything at all," he had a remarkable experience.

My convictions and misgivings had been circling about through the sometimes precious fogs of epistemologies, finding nowhere to land. One afternoon I lay down in intellectual despair on a couch. Suddenly, out of an absolute quiet, there came a firm, distinct loud voice from my upper right which said, "Include the knower in the known!" It lugged me to my feet absurdly exclaiming, "Hello?" looking for whoever was in the room. The voice had had an exact location. No one was there! Not even behind the wall where I sheepishly looked. I do not take this nebulous profundity as divinely inspired, but I do think it is similar to what has been heard by those who in the past claimed such special selection.[6]

If Jaynes had read Wilson Van Dusen's enlightening little book *The Natural Depth in Man* (1972), he would have known that his hallucination was not merely a "nebulous profundity," but a valuable insight, clearly related to what he had just been thinking about so desperately. Including "the knower in the known" is a fundamental precept of the "participatory epistemology" we will be discussing shortly. Jaynes, unfortunately, was a convinced materialist, and he uses his experience as evidence for his belief that the gods of the ancients were merely similar hallucinations, which our ancestors only mistook for messages from divine beings. Wilson Van Dusen has shown, however, that rather than being sheer nonsense, the kinds of voices one hears during states of hypnagogia often have very insightful things to say.

Just as the imagery seen in hypnagogia can depict profound truths, these voices can be autosymbolic, commenting on one's state of mind, or on the thoughts one has focused on while drifting into sleep. That Jaynes ignored the content of his hallucination is unfortunate, but not surprising, given the reductionist, scientistic bent of his thinking. Van Dusen, a clinical psychologist, with an equal scientific training, thought otherwise.

Much of the hypnogogic area looks simply like cute images and odd sentences being tossed around in one's head until one asks precisely what the individual was thinking of at that same moment. Then it begins to look like either a representation of the person's state or an answer to his query.

> *. . . I was trying to pick up hypnogogic experiences and heard, "still a nothing." I wasn't getting much and it said as much. While I was trying to see in detail how hypno-gogic experience forms I heard, "Do you have a comput-er?" I was getting very sleepy in the hypnogogic state and heard "The usual snoofing." At the time the odd word "snoofing" sounded like a cross between snooping (trying to snoop on the hypnogogic) and snoozing (getting sleepy). . . . I was thinking of the richness of the process and heard "My liberal arts course." While meditating on a pain in my head I heard "Nonmaterial!"[7]*

Clearly, although Jaynes failed to recognize it, "Include the knower in the known!" belongs in this category. For the rest of his book, although he has much to say about hallucinations, especially about the voices heard by schizophrenics, he goes no deeper into his own experience.[8]

Jaynes's theory is that until around 1250 B.C., human consciousness was "bicameral." Bicameral simply means two-chambered, and what Jaynes refers to are the right and left hemispheres of the brain. He argues that until 1250 B.C. the two hemispheres were independent, functioning as two separate minds within one skull, and supports his theory with findings from split-brain research. Since the discovery of the "division of labor" between the two hemispheres was popularized in the 1980s, much of the material on the "two brains" has become widely known. But the most remarkable discovery is that in a very real sense, two minds do inhabit our heads. Neurosurgeons operating on individuals suffering from epilepsy often sever a knot of fibers called the corpus callosum, which connects the two cerebral hemispheres, hoping this will stop the spread of the epileptic "storm" from one hemisphere to the other. It works, but the procedure has a curious side effect. For some unknown reason, the right side of the body is controlled by the left cerebral hemisphere, and the left side by the right. A person with a severed corpus callosum who bumps into something with the left side—connected to the right brain—*does not know it.* This is because our "I," the verbal, linguistic ego, is housed in the left brain. And so "it," connected to the right side of the body, did not bump into anything. Other equally disturbing examples of this remarkable phenomenon can be found in the literature. Jaynes argues that until 1250 B.C., *all* human beings were like people with severed corpus callosums. And instead of being able, as we are, to look inside ourselves and carry on inner dialogues, the people of an earlier time heard voices, telling them what to do. They believed the voices were the voices of the gods, but Jaynes argues they were really hallucinations coming from their "other mind," the right brain. So, faced with a certain situation, say, crossing a deep river, or going after game, they would ask "the gods" for their advice. This, Jaynes argues, is the true root of religion. The gods are voices in the head.

This sounds like an unbelievable idea until one looks at the evidence he collects to support it. He has amassed too much to recount with any detail, but through a study of ancient texts, the archaeological record, split-brain research, and the development of language, he concludes that human beings of the second millennium B.C. and earlier simply did not possess what we call an "interior world." The chapter on "The Mind of Iliad" is, to my mind, the most convincing.

But if Jaynes is right, then what happened in 1250 B.C. to change this? He suggests that several crises—natural catastrophes, wars, massive migrations, raids on coastal cities by marauding pirates—created a time of such stress and upheaval that people were forced to react much more quickly than they were used to, and this eventually broke down the wall between the chambers of the mind. Previously, life followed well-worn routines, and they needed to consult the gods only infrequently, when confronted by some novelty or unusual situation. They could petition the voices and wait for their reply. Often, Jaynes remarks, they may have had to do this several times. En route to build a dam downriver, our bicameral ancestors may have forgotten why they were there, and may have had to ask the god for instructions each time the purpose of their journey slipped their mind. But with volcanic eruptions (Jaynes cites the destruction of the island of Santorini sometime between 1470 and 1170 B.C.; the devastation is believed to have been greater than a nuclear explosion), such leisure was no longer possible. Add to this wars, social collapse, famine, and pirates, and it is clear that the old bicameral mind would be sorely tested.

Some of Jaynes's most impressive evidence is from literature and inscriptions that come directly after the "breakdown." In 1230 B.C., Tukulti-Ninurta I, tyrant of Assyria, had a stone altar made that tells the tale. On the face of the altar, Tukulti himself is shown kneeling before the *empty* throne of his god. As Jaynes remarks, "No king before in history is ever shown kneeling. No scene before in history ever indicates an absent god."⁹ A cuneiform tablet from about the reign of Tukulti dots the i's and crosses the t's:

> *One who has no god, as he walks along the street,*
> *Headache envelops him like a garment.*

Another tablet laments the departed voices:

> *My god has forsaken me and disappeared,*
> *My goddess has failed me and keeps at a distance.*
> *The good angel who walked beside me has departed.*¹⁰

Other tablets from around the same time repeat a similar lament.

One foreboding sign of a change in consciousness around this time is the rise of cruelty, something we have already seen in the context of the rise of the alphabet. A century after Tukulti-Ninurta, the Assyrian tyrant Tiglath-Pileser I (1115–1077 B.C.) began one of the bloodiest campaigns in human history. One clear sign of a shift in human beings' relation to the gods is that, unlike previous kings, Tiglath-Pileser does not join his name to that of his god. But a more startling indication is the sheer brutality of his reign. "The Assyrians fell like butchers upon harmless villages," Jaynes writes, "enslaved what refugees they could, and slaughtered others in thousands. Bas-reliefs show what appear to be whole cities whose populace have been stuck alive on stakes."¹¹ Tiglath-Pileser's laws carried the bloodiest penalties known to history, even, Jaynes tells us, for minor offenses. Jaynes believes this reign of terror is a result of the breakdown of the rule of the gods, an attempt to hold a crumbling civilization together by sheer fear. Remembering Cro-Magnons' extermination of Neanderthals, and the Kurgan warriors descent on Old Europe, the disturbing thought is that self-consciousness itself is rooted in bloodshed and atrocity.

And yet, although the historical facts that Jaynes calls on to support his theory are undeniable, it is difficult for us to accept that before the end of the second millennium B.C. human beings simply did not have "insides"—were, as Jaynes depicts them, automatons, directed by the hallucinated voice of a god or dead king. That their consciousness differed from our own is clear—that, in fact, is the central argument of this book. But that they were as bicameral as Jaynes suggests somehow seems too extreme. It is difficult to imagine automatons designing and constructing the Sphinx or the pyramids, although, again, I believe their self-consciousness was not as acute as our own. We can even agree with Colin Wilson, who suggests that it is not our ancestors who were bicameral, but ourselves, stuck, as we seem to be, in our left-brain cerebral consciousness, with little access or appreciation of the intuitive, participatory powers of the right—or of our cerebellum, as Stan Gooch would argue. The "unreflective grasp of the fundamental laws of existence" that Schwaller saw at work in the monumental structures of ancient Egypt seems a far remove from Jaynes's mindless zombies, prodded by the barked commands of a dead king. It does, however, seem much more like the kind of insights offered by right-brain consciousness. And as the left brain is geared toward "dealing" with things, the "withdrawal" of right brain awareness—for whatever reason—would find human beings alone in a world that had suddenly become alien. No longer supported by an unconscious bond with nature, and faced with a host of problems, the new left-brain consciousness would surely look for the easiest way to handle difficulties. It may seem an odd way to put it, but cruelty may be nothing more than a shortcut devised by a consciousness suddenly thrown into a threatening world.

Jaynes is right, however, to see the change in consciousness as a departure of the gods. His theory is that the bicameral voices were made up of "stores of admonitory and perceptive experience," the echoes of the commands of the elders of the clan, much as the haranguing voices heard by schizophrenics are often those of an overbearing parent or spouse. This "experience" was then transmuted into articulate speech, which then gave them their commands. The gods, then, were "a mere side effect of language evolution."[12] When their voices were no longer heard, they had gone.

As self-consciousness and language are directly related, this makes a kind of sense. As we have seen, R. M. Bucke said as much as early as 1901. But other thinkers who have looked into the relation between language and the evolution of consciousness have not been as dismissive of the gods as Jaynes. In the next section we will see how, for at least one thinker, it may be that through language itself something like the gods may return.

PART FOUR

Participatory Epistemology

CHAPTER EIGHTEEN

The Shock of Metaphor

Owen Barfield, who died in 1997 at the age of ninety-nine, is perhaps best known for being the close friend of C. S. Lewis. With Lewis, Charles Williams, and J. R. R. Tolkien, Barfield is also known for being a member of the Oxford literary group, the Inklings. To a smaller but by no means less dedicated audience, he is probably the most articulate interpreter of the ideas of Rudolf Steiner. But before he became the most literate and philosophical of Steiner's many apologists, Barfield had made a small reputation for himself in 1926 with the publication of his first book, *History in English Words*. As the title suggests, the book deals with history and language, but not in the way one might immediately think. It was not "History *and* English Words," but "History *in* English Words"—meaning that history could be found *within* the words themselves. As Barfield wrote,

> *In our own language . . . the past history of humanity is spread out in an imperishable map, just as the history of the mineral earth lies embedded in the layers of its outer crust. But there is this difference . . . : whereas the former can only give us a knowledge of outward, dead things . . . language has preserved for us the inner, living history of man's soul. It reveals the evolution of consciousness.*[1]

What Barfield meant by "the evolution of consciousness" can be best understood by his brief remark in a later book, *Romanticism Come of Age* (1944). Here he called it "the concept of man's self-consciousness as a process in time." This he distinguished from what is known as the "history of ideas." In the history of *ideas,* an ancient Greek, for example, and a postmodern American have very different ideas about the world, but both are held to *perceive* the world in the same way—with the understanding that our ideas, informed by modern science, are closer to the truth. There is no question of a difference between our *consciousness* and that of the ancient Greek, only between the ideas "inside" it. When we open our eyes, we see the same world that the Greek saw—it's just that we have better ideas about it.

For Barfield this is totally wrong. Not only do our ideas about the world differ, but the world the ancient Greek saw and the one we see are not the same. Our consciousness is very different from that of an ancient Greek—or from that of a Greek of late antiquity, or someone from the Middle Ages. Not only our ideas about things, but also our *consciousness* of them, have evolved over time, and the record of that evolution lies in language. And whereas the standard view of evolution has a consciousness much like our own, confronting a preexisting, external world made up of distinct, independent, impermeable objects, the record left by language, Barfield argues, suggests something different.

Barfield came to this study, he tells us, at an early age. The inspiration was, of all things, a Latin lesson. During an instruction in the accusative case, the young Barfield came upon the sentence *Cato, octoginta annos natus, excessit e vita,* which, he saw, could be translated as "Cato, at the age of eighty, walked out of life"— meaning that Cato, the great Roman orator, died at eighty. What struck him was the felt *change* he experienced when he realized that the drab fact of Cato's dying could be expressed *figuratively,* that is, in a metaphor—in this case, that of Cato "walking out of life." It was not only the pleasant sensation of appreciating a neat turn of phrase, although the aesthetic aspect of the recognition appealed to him; it was also that this way of expressing things and grasping them (another metaphor) somehow increased his *knowl-*

edge and *awareness* of life. As he would later phrase it, it "changed one's consciousness a little."[2] He realized that language *in itself,* and not only the facts or ideas it is used to convey, could be enjoyed; moreover, focusing one's attention on it led to some interesting results.

These results increased when Barfield began to look more closely at poetry, something he had developed a great love for in his teens. He came to the conclusion that, as in his Latin lesson, metaphors were at the heart of his appreciation. This power of using language figuratively, of, as it were, making "pictures" with it, affected him deeply. The world became a more profound, a more *meaningful* place when seen through the lens of the great poets. They made it more *alive,* and at the time Barfield was discovering this, such enlivening was rare. It would not be long before the suffocating atmosphere of linguistic analysis and logical positivism would stifle the Western mind. And in poetry itself, an anti-Romantic modernism had taken center stage, ushered in by T. S. Eliot's *The Waste Land* (1922), a profoundly urban, almost prosaic work depicting a world of fragments, far removed from the sudden gripping sense of *hidden meanings* that Barfield's reading was revealing to him.

This revelation, Barfield realized, was possible because of the poets' use of language. It was not only that they said interesting things and that their subjects were interesting in themselves (and as the poetry that affected Barfield most deeply was lyric poetry, the subjects were invariably the poets themselves, their moods and feelings); it was the way their use of language affected his *consciousness* that appealed to Barfield. They did not just *say* that the world was full of hidden meanings, they *showed* this to be so. This effect was so pronounced that Barfield wrote a book about it.

Published in 1928, *Poetic Diction* explored this curious ability of poetry to change its reader's consciousness, to effect, as Barfield put it, a small increase in knowledge and wisdom. The pleasure afforded by lyric poetry, he argued, came about precisely because of this change. When the metaphors the poets used were fresh and new, the "shock" of seeing sunrise as the "rosy fingered dawn" (Homer) or of feeling one's soul to be a lyre (Shelley) contrasted with one's prosaic understanding of these things, and, for the brief period that the shock lasted, one enjoyed a kind of "double consciousness." Years later Colin Wilson, in his little book *Poetry and Mysticism* (1968), would also argue that this "duo-consciousness" was at the heart of aesthetic and mystical experiences, citing Ramakrishna's *samadhi* at the sight of a flock of white swans passing before a dark cloud, and at a less ecstatic level, the domestic bliss of curling up in a warm bed with a good book, aware of the cold rain pattering against the window: the essence of both experiences is contrast, another form of the double consciousness discussed earlier.

Barfield recognized, however, that the pleasure in metaphors is, of course, fleeting. With repeated readings, the "newness" evaporates, although the wisdom granted by the change in consciousness can be retained—at any rate, one hopes it is, and it is this belief that informs the idea that reading great literature "humanizes" us. But the shock fades. So Barfield also discovered that metaphors grow old. They become, to paraphrase Emerson, "fossilized." ("Language," Emerson said, "is fossil poetry.") Metaphors, Nietzsche remarked, are like coins whose faces become worn down by use. We handle metaphors everyday but no longer experience the shock they must once have produced. Today we hardly recognize them at all, or if we do we see them as clichés or simply manners of speaking. (The technical term is "trope," a "turn of phrase," which is itself a kind of metaphor: in which direction do phrases "turn"?)

At the beginning of the last section I examined a few of the many metaphors we use to talk about the mind. We all use them, quite unconscious of the fact that they *are* metaphors, and I believe we would find it extremely difficult to talk about the mind in any way other than metaphorically. In the paragraph above I speak of pleasure being "fleeting" and of newness "evaporating"—yet pleasure does not run, nor does novelty dry up, except only metaphorically. I mention this to bring our attention to the fact that we all use figures of speech that at one time must have seemed wonderfully new and unusual, but that we now hardly notice. (This is why we look for striking new metaphors in writers.) It is only an extremely literal mind that finds metaphors "difficult," just as a similar kind of mind sees no difference between a myth and a lie. When I was a child, there was an old comic routine in which the straight man took literally every metaphoric phrase of his partner, who was soon in tears, desperate to express himself. If he mentioned some old affair as "water under the bridge," the straight man asked, "Which bridge?" If he referred to some easy task as "taking candy from a baby," the straight man accused him of child molesting. Trying to communicate without metaphors is extremely difficult and invariably frustrating. The one language I can think of in which it can be done is mathematics, and this is possible because it reduces content to the bare minimum.[3]

It was this "aging" of metaphors that prompted Barfield to his next phase of study. If language, as Emerson said, is "fossil poetry," then as we look into the history of language, the fossils should become "more alive." And this is precisely what Barfield found. He recognized that it was not only poetry that could effect a change in consciousness. Our everyday language at an earlier stage of its development could produce a similar effect. This is because as we go further and further into its history, language becomes more figurative, more metaphoric, more like poetry than it is today. Barfield discovered that reading literature from an earlier period produced the same shock as did reading poetry, and this led him to formulate a theory about why the shock should be produced. It came about, he argued, from our coming into contact with a consciousness *different from our own*. (Schwaller de Lubicz, as we have seen, felt the same about our reaction to the monuments of Egypt.) A similar phenomenon takes place when learning a foreign language, as I can attest from my own fumbling attempts at learning German. The mind grasps what all good translators know: that there is no direct substitution of one language for another, because even though they may speak of the same thing, different languages express a different way of seeing the world. In Barfield's case, this insight came from looking at the history of his own language, English.

What is thought-provoking about this is that, in the case of poetry, one expects the poet to try to use language in an evocative way. Poetry in this sense is a special case. But the language Barfield was reading was the language of prose, which is supposed to be straightforward, descriptive, expository; what he found, however, was that this language produced the same effect. And if the effect is produced by a consciousness *different* from our own, that meant the writer of the prose had such a different consciousness. Further, since this was not a special case, it also meant that the everyday consciousness of the time in question was itself different. And this meant, for Barfield at least, that consciousness must *evolve.*

This evolution, Barfield came to see, moved from a more metaphorical way of seeing the world to a less metaphorical way, from, as the German scholar Erich Heller put it, an age of Poetry to an age of Prose.[4] It could also be seen as moving from a more "concrete" consciousness to one that is more "abstract." And again, evidence for this hypothesis seemed to lie in language itself.

—

"It is a commonplace . . . that, whatever word we hit on," Barfield wrote in *Saving the Appearances,* a book we will look at in detail further on, "if we trace its meaning far enough back, we find it apparently expressive of some tangible, or at all events, perceptible object or some physical activity. . . . Throughout the recorded history of language the movement of meaning has been from the concrete to the abstract."[5] Given this, the standard understanding of the evolution of language, Barfield argues, is that all words referring to something spiritual or abstract have their origin in *literal* meaning. So when we refer to a "spirit" enlivening the physical body, what we are talking about is something like breath. We find this, for example, in the Hebrew *ruach* and the Greek *pneuma,* both of which designate an "indwelling soul," but also the volatile character of air. Such considerations have led some theorists to suggest that *all* words that are supposed to point to some kind of "spiritual reality" are merely metaphors, "ways of speaking" and "turns of phrase," that have been mistaken to indicate some actual "intangible" entity. Indeed, one theorist even went so far as to call mythology, with its talk of gods as the source of natural phenomena, a "disease of language." A similar sensibility was at work in the years Barfield was writing his book, with linguistic analysis and logical positivism arguing that the traditional concerns of philosophy, the great questions of metaphysics, were simply the result of a misunderstanding of language. (Wittgenstein, who started this trend, famously remarked that philosophy was a sickness from which philosophers needed to be cured.)

It was clear to Barfield, as it was to thinkers like Nietzsche and Emerson, that modern language, with its abstract terms and nuances of meaning, is, as he wrote, "apparently nothing but an unconscionable tissue of dead, or petrified, metaphors." The deeper we dig into language, the more metaphors we find. But, as Barfield continued his study, he realized there was something wrong with this idea. Etymologists, like the famous Oriental scholar Max Müller, believed that early speech began with very simple, literal words and phrases for tangible, perceptible things. Then, with the "dawn of reason" (itself a metaphor), our early ancestors began to use these phrases "metaphorically," to describe inner and outer experiences. Barfield even jokingly suggests that Müller has to posit some early generation of "amateur poets" who supplied their fellows with a whole catalog of clever turns of phrase, and that the habit hasn't left us since. If we take this theory to its logical conclusion, Barfield argues, the result should be that today, after millennia of metaphor building, we should all be spouting poetry whenever we speak. And likewise, we should, being so much more sophisticated, find poetry from earlier times rather *less* poetic. Neither of which, of course, is true. In fact, quite the contrary seems to be the case: our common language has a flat, "matter-of-fact" character, and it is this that led Erich Heller to say that we have moved from an age of Poetry to an age of Prose. And hence our attraction to the "classics." Homer still thrills like nothing else, and it is precisely because he does that we still read him. In fact, as Barfield found, rather than finding earlier poetry and language *less* figurative than our own, we find the opposite to be the case, and we read older and ancient writers because of the richness of their language. Anyone familiar with modern poetry, which is little more than a kind of truncated prose, will see the difference immediately.

Müller and his followers erred, Barfield believed, by adopting an unquestioned Darwinian approach to the history of language.

Just as simple organisms became more complex over time, so too, they believed, language evolved, from simple "root" words denoting tangible "things" into our highly abstract and metaphorical speech. The only problem with this, Barfield argued, is that the evidence from language itself suggests something different.

What the history of language tells us, he argues, is that our ancestors didn't use language in the way Müller and other earlier theorists believed, because they didn't see the same world Müller saw. Müller and practically every theorist after him projected the world as perceived by late nineteenth- (or early twenty-first-) century Europeans into the past—which is why the only account of the history of language he could give was one that followed a Darwinian idea of "progress." The same is true of various accounts of the "prehistoric world," a world, that is, before the arrival of human consciousness—a point we will return to shortly. Barfield's arguments suggest that all ideas about the prehistoric world, from paleontological textbooks to films like *Jurassic Park,* are, at the least, questionable because, as Barfield put it, they project a picture of that world as it would be seen by a consciousness alive *today.* We have no way of knowing what that world looked like to a different consciousness because we have no record of a consciousness from that time. Even the fossils and other traces we have discovered are limited in what they can tell us, since it is *our* consciousness that classifies and organizes them into the schemata of ancient life.

The kind of world our ancient ancestors saw—and which, Barfield suggests, our more recent ancestors continued to see—was not the well-defined, "objective" external world made up of distinct, independent, impermeable "things" that we bump up against everyday. It was not a world in which a Cartesian *res cogitans* existed on one side of an ontological borderline, with *res extensa* on the other. It was not a world in which such boundaries existed, nor one in which epistemological conundrums troubled the heads—literally—of philosophers. It was a world, he suggests, in which human consciousness "participated" and from which it was not, as it is today, separated by an invisible wall of alienation. What Müller misunderstood as "metaphoric" was an ability to see the "inside" of things (remember Bergson and Schwaller), just as we now are aware of our own "inside"—our minds. Accounts of nature spirits; folk tales and myths about fairies, nymphs, and sylphs; legends of gods walking the Earth—all are rooted in this "participatory consciousness." This was the kind of world that the great poets saw; and, as Barfield discovered, it was also the kind of consciousness that Rudolf Steiner claimed was experienced by early human beings. Barfield called it "original participation."

Chapter Nineteen

—

The Participating Mind

Barfield's ideas about "participation," or, as I have called it, "participatory epistemology," run throughout his work. But the most concise expression of them can be found in a book he wrote nearly thirty years after the publication of *Poetic Diction*. Both *Poetic Diction* and *History in English Words* received high praise, and Barfield contributed to the leading literary journals of the time, but it wasn't his destiny to make a living as a writer—an uneasy task in any age. Forced by financial pressure to enter his family's law firm, he dropped out of the literary scene in the 1930s, only occasionally publishing articles in philosophical journals. Then, after retiring from law, he made an impressive comeback in 1957 with a deceptively short book, *Saving the Appearances: A Study in Idolatry*.

Saving the Appearances begins with some reflections on a common phenomenon: a rainbow. While a rainbow lasts, it appears to us as a great arc of many colors, spanning rooftops and hills, somewhere out there in space. We have all seen rainbows and enjoyed them. We also know they are not quite like other things. Although we have been told many stories about what we may find there, we know we can never get to the "end of the rainbow." If we ran out and tried to reach it, it would be gone. Now, Barfield asks, bring to

mind everything you've ever heard about a rainbow and ask yourself a simple question: Is it *really* there?

Most of us, I think, would say, "Yes, it *is* 'really there.'" But
then, what do we mean by "really"? Well, although we know that
rainbows only appear in showery weather, and that they are a
result of a peculiar arrangement of the raindrops, the sunlight, and
our vision, we say they are "really there" because we aren't the
only people to see them. Others do too. If I see a rainbow in the
sky, usually my first reaction is to point it out to my companion—
I can even remember the pleasure I had pointing one out to my son,
who recognized it for the first time with great delight. We also
know that people before us have seen them too, and their experiences have been recorded in literature. So although a rainbow is
not "there" in the same sense as, say, a tree is, it is still, for most of
us, *there*. Yet if, for example, someone were to claim to see a rainbow on an absolutely clear day, or at night, and we were confident
that person was not simply lying, then we could say that in this
case the rainbow was *not* "really there." It was, we would say, a
hallucination.

So a rainbow that we all see is "really there," whereas one that
only one person sees is not. This applies to anything we may consider a hallucination, although, to be sure, there have been reports
of something called "mass hallucination," such as the appearance
of the Virgin Mary at Fatima and some UFO sightings, but for the
time being let us put these considerations aside.

But then, Barfield asks, let us consider something else that we
say is "really there." Let us look at a tree.

A tree, we know, is made of organic, cellular material, built up
into wood, leaves, branches, roots, perhaps flowers. Unlike a rainbow, if we reach out to touch a tree, we can. We can hear the wind
rustling its leaves, can grip its sturdy branches, can perhaps smell
the fragrance of its blossoms, and, if we like, can even taste its bark
or its fruit. The tree is as "there" as anything could be. Solid, indu-
bitably present. Whatever the weather, rain or shine, a tree is part
of our objective, external world. Its appearance does not depend
on anything except our having our eyes open.

And yet we also know that the very material of which the tree is made is itself made of other things, of molecules, which are made of atoms, which are made of subatomic particles, which are made of even smaller elementary particles, which themselves are made of . . . well, something that is increasingly difficult to describe using the idea of a "thing." Charges of energy, probability fluctuations, quarks, leptons, and a host of other increasingly arcane "entities" (hundreds of them have been discovered), some of which are said to exist for only the most inconceivable fraction of time, while others are said to move from future to past and not, as most of us do, the other way around. This world of "elementary particles" (to use a convenient term) is, science tells us, what is "really really there," and, as we recall with Galileo's distinction between primary and secondary qualities, it has been telling us something along these lines for nearly the last four centuries. The most accurate way of expressing how modern physics—meaning the "new physics" beginning with Einstein and quantum theory—sees the world is to say that the only "really real things" are mathematical equations. The old model of an atom with a nucleus around which orbit electrons—a kind of miniature solar system—has been obsolete for decades, as has the idea of trying to "model" the behavior of these mysterious non-things. Today models and metaphors are used mostly to convey some idea of the discoveries of physicists to laymen (having worked as a science writer, I have some idea of how the process operates). And most models and metaphors are misleading. When popular science writers talk of atoms as the building blocks of the universe, they are perpetuating a misconception. The universe is built of no "thing"—except perhaps mathematical formulae, something the ancient philosopher Pythagoras suggested some millennia ago.

But then, how do we get to a tree? When I see it, I do not see electrons "buzzing" (a metaphor; they don't) or elementary particles making prodigious quantum leaps (a popular misconception).[1] What I do see is a tall, stout, multilimbed, leaf-bearing growth of a general green, gray, and brownish color. And so do you. How is this so?

Barfield makes the analogy that particles are to a tree—and to everything else as well—as raindrops are to a rainbow. And just as rainbows are really there because we all see them, so too trees are really there because we all see them. But both, Barfield says, are "representations." Our mind, our consciousness, "re-presents" the raindrops and the particles, in the first place as a rainbow, in the second as a tree. The difference between hallucinations and things that are really there is that in the former the representation is solitary while in the latter it is collective. A rainbow is, in Barfield's words, a "collective representation." So is a tree—and the rest of the world, from stars to seashells, as well.

This is curious, because, as most of us will agree, in some odd way a rainbow, which we say is "really there," is "really there" in an *unusual* way, whereas a tree is "really there" in a *usual* one. Those of us not put off by such metaphysical chatter can accept that the rainbow is a representation, formed by the raindrops, my vision, and the sunlight. But a tree seems a different story. We might even be inclined to give a tree a good, strong kick—as Samuel Johnson once did a stone, in order to refute Bishop Berkeley's contention that it was, in essence, just in his mind. But such a tactic would no more eliminate the question of the tree being a representation than Doctor Johnson's aching toes did Berkeley's philosophy.

Let's retrace our steps a bit.

—

Earlier I remarked, "We can characterize the advance of science as the sole arbiter of truth by seeing in it the gradual expulsion of human consciousness from its object of study." While this is true, paradoxically there has also been an increasing *involvement* of human consciousness in our understanding of "the world." Kant, we know, argued that the most fundamental "givens" of our experience—space, time, causality—were provided by the mind, by our "perceptual apparatus." Later philosophers, like Edmund Husserl, argued that perception is "intentional," that, unlike the Cartesian mirror, consciousness somehow "reaches out" and grabs the world, rather than simply reflecting it, an idea that, in different ways, we have seen in the thinking of William James and Bergson. Yet, scientists, particularly those of a strong materialist bent, continue to speak of an objective *outside* world, unadulterated by the influence of the mind—they even speak of the mind as being the product, or epiphenomenon, of purely material forces. And ever since Descartes the aim of physics, seen as the most authoritative of the sciences since it dealt with the "really real" things of the world, has been to finally discover the most "real" of the "really real" things—those basic "building blocks" that popular science writers are always talking about.

Yet breakthroughs in physics in the early twentieth century made it clear that in some baffling way the mind "participates," as Barfield phrases it, in the world, and that the great nineteenth-century ideal of the detached, objective scientist, coolly *observing* the virgin processes of an external world, was a myth. We know now that the very act of observation alters the phenomena under scrutiny. As Morris Berman writes, "The major philosophical implication of quantum mechanics is that there is no such thing as an independent observer."[2] Werner Heisenberg's Uncertainty Principle is perhaps the most popular formulation of this insight. Heisenberg said, as mentioned earlier, that we can know either the position or the momentum of a particle, but not both. He explained how this is the case by imagining the following situation. Imagine a microscope powerful enough to observe an electron. Light travels down the microscope to illuminate our particle and enable us to see it. But this light is itself made of particles, which have enough energy to knock the electron under observation out of its position. The experiment, then, has itself altered the situation it wishes to test. There is no longer, as in the classical model, a clear boundary between the observer and the observed—something Julian Jaynes's hypnagogic hallucination tried to apprise him of when it suggested he "include the knower in the known." We can never peek fast enough to see what the world is like when we are not looking at it. "We are," as Berman again remarks, inescapably "sensuous participants in the very world we seek to describe."[3] The whole idea of a nature "in itself" seems increasingly less intelligible, and this is especially so in the discipline that started by trying to wrench "nature" free from the muddying effects of consciousness. Physicists now know that consciousness itself is part of their measurements. "What we observe," Heisenberg wrote, "is not nature in itself but nature exposed to our method of questioning."[4] Again, as Morris Berman writes, "The great irony of quantum mechanics is that . . . the Cartesian attempt to find the ultimate material entity, thereby 'explaining' reality and ruling out subjectivity once and for all, resulted in discoveries that mocked Cartesian assumptions and established subjectivity as the cornerstone of 'objective' knowledge."[5]

That this "participation" of consciousness with the world opens the door on several taboo subjects, such as magic, "the occult," and parapsychology is obvious, and is something we shall return to. For the moment, however, let us get back to Barfield and the tree.

—

The "real" tree is made of elementary particles. The tree we see is a representation formed by our consciousness. So far, we are on firm scientific ground. The world around us, from mountains and clouds to street signs and shopping malls, is also made of particles, and what we see is the representation of that world created, somehow, by our minds, our consciousness. But, as Barfield points out, there is a slight problem with this. The science that tells us the world we see is a representation created by our consciousness also has something to say about the kind of world that existed *before* there was a consciousness—at least, before there was a consciousness like our own. It tells us what the world was like ten million, twenty million, five hundred million, a billion, or several billion years ago. And with its remarks about what may have been the case prior to the supposed Big Bang, it even tells us what the world was like *before* there was a world.

With the exception of this last highly speculative exercise, the kind of world that science tells us existed long before there was a consciousness to represent it seems, in all of its descriptions, to be quite like a world *with* a consciousness like our own representing it. The arrangement of things may be different—the continents may be fused together as one, the seasons may have been unlike our own, volcanoes may have fumed incessantly and earthquakes rocked continuously. But all of this is still fundamentally the kind of world we would have seen had we been there to see it. Except we weren't. No one was. There were, according to science, no human beings alive at the time. Hence there was no human consciousness around to represent the particles of which the world at that time, just like our own world, was made. There were no senses. No touch, no smell, no hearing, no taste, no sight. And yet, science insists that the "prehistoric world" was just like our own world. There were different animals, and different plants, and the landscape was different. But it was a solid, objective, independent, three-dimensional *external* world, just like our own.

But if the solid, objective world that we see is a representation of the "really real" particles of which it is made, then how, given there was no consciousness like our own around to represent it, could such a solid, objective world have existed in "prehistoric times"? And by "prehistoric" I mean a time much earlier than those discussed in the last section. We might want to say instead "prehuman" or "preconscious," even "preorganic." We know that, in the case of a rainbow, if there were no sunshine, no raindrops, or no human consciousness, there would be no rainbow. In the case of a solid, three-dimensional world, there is only one necessary ingredient: human consciousness. As there was no human consciousness in prehistoric times, the conclusion seems to be that there couldn't have been a solid, three-dimensional world either. There *may* have been "unrepresented" particles, but we have no idea, and *can* have no idea, what they may have looked like, because for them to look like *anything* they would have to have been represented, which they were not. The situation is, admittedly, baffling, but the poet William Blake summed it up two centuries ago: Where man is not, he wrote, nature is barren.[6]

All of this strikes us as difficult to grasp, but we must remember that all Barfield has done is follow some of science's dictums to their logical conclusion. If what "really" exists are elementary particles, and if the world we see is a representation of those particles created by our consciousness, then a world without that consciousness would not be so represented. Imagine a world that was all rainbow. Then subtract one of its necessary ingredients. That is the world before human consciousness.

This being the case, what follows from it is highly suggestive. One thing it suggests is that we need to distinguish, as Kant did, between a world "in itself," what Barfield calls the "unrepresented," and a *represented* world relative to our consciousness, what he calls the "phenomenal world." And this, as has been pointed out, is a crucial difference. If "we have chosen to form a picture, based very largely on modern physical science, of a phenomenal earth existing for millions of years before the appearance of consciousness," and if that "same physical science tells us that the phenomenal world is correlative to consciousness," then clearly our ideas about how that phenomenal world evolved need to be reexamined. For one thing, it follows from this that "the period during which the *phenomenal* earth has been evolving is probably much shorter than is now generally assumed."[7] This indeed is a radical idea, and one that has hardly been taken up by contemporary evolutionists. But what is even more radical is the fundamental shift that Barfield's argument effects in our understanding of the relation between the world and human consciousness. Barfield argues that, as we have seen, the history of language suggests that at an earlier time consciousness "participated" in the world and was not, as it is now, a kind of ghost, hovering above it. We will return to this part of his argument shortly. This loss of participation happened over time, and it is only in our relatively recent "modern" period— the period since Descartes split the world in two—that it has reached its end point of complete separation. It was not too long after this that human beings began to investigate the phenomenal world—created by their own consciousness—for answers to questions about their own origin, putting the cart before the horse in as fundamental a way as possible. (This "material world," divorced from the consciousness that creates it, is the "idol" in the subtitle of Barfield's book.) This, Barfield suggests, is a pity because

if the impulse to construe as process the record of the rocks
and the vestiges of creation apparent in the natural order

> *had come either a little earlier, before participation had*
> *faded, or a little later, when the iconoclasm implicit in*
> *physical analysis . . . had really begun to work, man might*
> *have read there the story of the coming into being, pari*
> *passu, of his world and his own consciousness.*

This is so because "it is only necessary to take the first feeble steps towards a renewal of participation . . . in order to see that the actual evolution of the earth we know must have been at the same time an evolution of consciousness."[8]

The world we see, Barfield is saying, is the way it is because our *consciousness* is the way it is. If our consciousness were different, the world would be too.

CHAPTER TWENTY

—

The Tapestry of Nature

The history of language is important, Owen Barfield argues, because it reveals a consciousness and a world unlike our own. In our world, consciousness is considered to be firmly located in our head, "produced" by the chemical and electrical exchanges of a three-pound mass of organic matter called the brain. But this was not always held to be the case. The ancient Egyptians, we have seen, spoke of an "intelligence of the heart" and located the seat of consciousness there. The priests who performed mummification were careful to preserve the heart and other internal organs, but cared little about the brain, drawing it out in pieces through the nostrils and discarding it. The Greeks likewise placed consciousness in a different part of the body than we do, locating it in the diaphragm, what they called the *phrenes*. From this we get words like "frenzy," to be out of one's mind, and the discredited nine-teenth-century science of "phrenology," the study of mental char-acteristics through analyzing bumps on the skull. Aristotle, the first empirical "scientist," did not think much of the brain, believing its main purpose to be a kind of "cooling system" for the blood.

Scientists today may argue that all this shows is that our ancestors had some very bad ideas. Barfield argues that it tells us more than this: it tells us that people of an earlier time *saw* the world in a way radically different from the way we see it. And if this is so, then it is possible that the figurative character of older language may not be the result of a generation of ancient poets spinning out reams of metaphors. It may have been that the world itself was more *alive* then, and that the poets were only communicating what they saw—although perhaps this use of "seeing" is itself a metaphor more appropriate for our own Cartesian age, which emphasizes the *distance* between consciousness and the world and likes to keep the world at arm's length. Our ancestors' experience may have been much more *visceral*, much more of a felt contact between their inside and the world's.

Our own modern, and by now postmodern, alienation, the abstraction from the world that we all take for granted, is at least partially rooted in the rise of perspective and the radically different experience of space that generated. We will return to this in a later chapter, when we discuss the work of Jean Gebser; for now it is useful to point out that in earlier times something as basic and as unquestioningly accepted as our actual physical *place* in the world—not our social or economic standing, but our location as a physical object—was not the same as we experience today. When I leave my room and go "outside," I have a dim sense of a kind of open "space" stretching out to the horizon, and I move within that space as a kind of independent point. But, Barfield suggests, this sense of our spatial environment, which we take for granted as "given," was not always the case and is a product of our having grown up in a Cartesian/Newtonian worldview. However, "before the scientific revolution the world was more like a garment men wore about them than a stage on which they moved." Compared with us, independent points moving about on a Cartesian grid of other independent material objects, the people of that time "felt themselves and the objects around them and the words that expressed those objects, immersed together in something like a

clear lake of—what shall we say?—of 'meaning,' if you choose."[1]
They were somehow "blended into" their environment—although
they would never have used as abstract a word as that for the world
they were immersed in. They were part of "nature," figures in its
living tapestry, and not, like us, hard, independent atoms that rattle around with everything else in a kind of open-ended box.

In a fascinating chapter entitled "Medieval Environment" in
Saving the Appearances, Barfield attempts to convey what a world
that consciousness still participated in would have been like. It is of
course too long to quote in full, but some extracts will give an idea
of what he means. He asks us to place ourselves inside the skin of
the "medieval man in the street." If we look at the sky,

> *We do not see it as an empty space. . . . If it is daytime, we
> see the air filled with light proceeding from a living sun,
> rather as our own flesh is filled with blood proceeding from
> a living heart. If it is night-time, we do not merely see a
> plain, homogenous vault pricked with separate points of
> light, but a regional qualitative sky, from which first of all
> the different sections of the great zodiacal belt, and sec-
> ondly the planets and the moon (each of which is embed-
> ded in its own revolving crystal sphere) are raying down
> their complex influences upon the earth. . . . We take it for
> granted that those invisible spheres are giving forth an
> inaudible music. . . . We know very well that growing things
> are specially beholden to the moon, that gold and silver
> draw their virtue from sun and moon respectively, copper
> from Venus, iron from Mars, lead from Saturn. And that
> our own health and temperament are joined by invisible
> threads to these heavenly bodies we are looking at. We
> probably do not spend any time thinking about these extra-
> sensory links between ourselves and the phenomena. We
> merely take them for granted.[2]*

Looking at the sea, Barfield goes on, medieval people saw one
of the four elements, Water. They knew that it, along with Fire, Air,
and Earth, had an invisible aspect, which they experienced in their

own selves as the "humours" making up their temperament. Through them they were linked to the stars as well, since the signs of the Zodiac were each linked to one of the elements. If they saw a stone fall to the ground, it did not do so because of some mysterious "occult" force called "gravity," but because it *desired* to be in its rightful place. Their world in general was a much more *living* world than ours, a world in which they were microcosms within a macrocosm, with each different part of themselves linked to the macrocosm in a very specific way. They did not, as we do, feel isolated from their "environment." They were, as Barfield comments, not like islands, as we are, but much more like embryos.[3]

One clear indication that the medieval consciousness was much more participatory than ours is the practice of alchemy. Clearly, a great deal of alchemy was merely a futile attempt to create actual physical gold, but as any student of its history or practice knows, this was not the heart of the discipline. As C. G. Jung was to rediscover centuries later, a central theme of alchemy was the union of the alchemist's mind with the material being worked on. Although, as we have seen, Schwaller rejected Jung's interpretation, and many modern historians and practicing alchemists believe Jung put too much emphasis on the psychological aspect, it is impossible, I think, to spend much time studying accounts of alchemy without coming away believing that the key to this mysterious practice was precisely some form of the participatory consciousness Barfield is speaking of. The central sense that comes from studying the baffling writings and diagrams that have come down to us from the alchemists is that they saw the world as a living, active entity and not, as we do, as dead, neutral stuff. They didn't *manipulate* matter, as we do, but sought to arrive at some interaction, or better still, *communion* with it. All the long, complicated, and, to our mind, tedious and pointless preparations and distillations were not "science" as we know it, but a means of bringing mind and matter into some equilibrium, of creating some medium of communication between the two, or, perhaps, of enhancing and perfecting the communication that already existed. Alchemy, as one maxim ran, "speeds up" the processes of nature. And that the aim of this "speeding up" was not merely to create riches is clear from another alchemical maxim, *Aurum nostrum non est aurum vulgi, tam ethice quam physice*: "Our gold is not the common gold, as much moral as material." It is difficult for us to conceive of gold, or any other material, as having a "moral" aspect, but this was something quite clear to the alchemists. And that the alchemists themselves were involved in the alchemical changes—were, perhaps, the central goal of those changes—is clear in a saying attributed to the alchemist Gerhard Dorn: "Transform yourselves into living philosophical stones." We are reminded here of Schwaller's dictum, "Tumble with the rock which falls from the mountain. Seek light and rejoice with the rosebud about to open."

This "communication" between the world and the mind was, of course, not limited to the alchemists. It was inherent in the Hermetic tradition that they drew on and added to. It is, as mentioned earlier, at the heart of all "occult" views of reality. "The secret that lies at the heart of the occult view," writes Morris Berman, "is that the world is sensual at its core; that is the essence of reality. . . . When the Indian does a rain dance, for example, he is not assuming an automatic response. . . . He is inviting the clouds to join him, to respond to the invocation."[4] And the notion of an Indian rainmaker "inviting the clouds" to join him in his dance suggests that what is at the heart of the occult worldview is a kind of mimesis, an "acting like," which is clearly a form of metaphor. We see the same idea at work in magical cave art, in different forms of sympathetic magic, and even in forms of healing such as homeopathy. At bottom, each of these examples, as well as many others, say the same thing: that the human mind does not exist in isolation from the world, but is linked to it in ways few of us are aware of.

At this point we should make clear that the reason we are unaware of the links between our consciousness and the world is that these are formed and operate mostly unconsciously.[5] We do not, as I'm certain many readers have already said to themselves, go around saying, "Hmm, all right. I think I'll represent *that* bunch of particles as a tree, and *that* bunch as a mountain." We do not "participate" with the conscious part of our minds. Much of "New Age" philosophy amounts to the saying "Create your own reality," but it is not as simple as that. I cannot suddenly turn my bedroom into the Grand Canyon, or even a doorknob into gold, simply by saying, "My mind creates reality, so c'mon now, change!" What I *can* do is become aware of the unconscious processes *involved* in participation. What is different now about human consciousness is not that it no longer participates in the world, but that we are no longer *aware* of that participation. Human consciousness has risen out of its earlier state of intimacy with the world and now sees it as something completely cut off from itself, rather as if a novelist forgot that he or she was the creator of the people and scenes depicted and saw them as totally independent, and yet somehow went on writing the novel *unconsciously*. (Or, better still, it is like what we all experience when we dream: we are immersed in the adventures our minds create, yet are unaware of ourselves as their creator.)

Earlier human beings were not so much aware of the processes of participation as of the "participated world" itself, a world with living elements, nature spirits, gods, and all the rest. They *felt* themselves a part of the world, with an intimacy we probably only feel, aside from mystical experiences, in our childhood and, if we are lucky, when in love. This is why Barfield says it is pointless to ask questions about the origin of language, which to him is like asking about the "origin of origin." Language didn't come about as a way to imitate, master, or explain nature, as is generally assumed, because "nature" as we understand it did not exist until language did. To Barfield the polarities mind/world and language/nature are a result of a splitting up of "original participation." To understand language, Barfield tells us, we must imagine ourselves back to a stage at which human consciousness hadn't yet separated from its unconscious background. At that point there was no "nature" and no "consciousness," but the kind of cosmic intimacy Erich Neumann calls "uroboric."

Although this intimacy seems desirable to us in the isolated twenty-first century, it also had its drawbacks. An inhabitant of Çatal Hüyük might not have felt the kinds of psychic pressures that a postmodern Londoner does, but as Morris Berman remarked,

"To be constantly immersed in Great Mother consciousness is hardly the best state the psyche can be in."[6] For consciousness to grow, her psychic apron strings had to be cut. Even in more recent times, that sense of connection to the cosmos we find enviable in the medieval mind could not last. A figure on a tapestry, no matter how beautiful it may be, is fixed. The same "closeness" that embraced medieval men and women, and held their ancestors even more firmly, also limited their freedom. Like Rudolf Steiner, Barfield argues that, however regrettable, the loosening of our consciousness from what he calls original participation was necessary for human beings to become free, independent individuals, capable of returning *consciously* to a state of participation. In other words, the development of the ego, even in as radical a form as Cartesian scepticism, was necessary. However much we may daydream of how pleasant it may have been to live in medieval times, and however much we may pine the loss of the paradise of the Garden, it is our destiny to break free of these earlier forms of participation and to become fully aware of our own contribution to the phenomenal world.

It is important that we do this, and not only for the possibility of enjoying a rare and, as Barfield discovered from his study of poetry, psychically nourishing experience. To be sure, as I can say from my own experience, the shock of feeling one's inner world to be directly and intimately linked to the outer one is vitalizing, to say the least. And, to a certain extent, we all experience something of this sort already: anyone who has been baffled by a curiously apt synchronicity knows there is more to our relation with the world than what the science that denies these experiences suggests. Absorbed in a book, a film, or a piece of music, our mind stretches out beyond its normal confines, its fixation on the here and now, and "participates" with deeper meanings and relations, becoming aware of, as Colin Wilson phrases it, "other times and places." Becoming more attuned to these moments is a practice that can enhance both our psychic and physical health, as, contra Descartes, we now know there is no absolute boundary between the two. But Barfield suggests that once we become aware of our role in representing the world, a responsibility is incumbent upon us, a responsibility, I would say, of the imagination. We have to remember that Barfield is *not* saying, "It's all in the mind." We do not "create reality." There clearly is a reality "outside" us. What we do create is our representation of it, and it is to this we are responsible. It has become quite common in our postmodern time to think that "reality" is up for grabs, and the attitude engendered by this thought has been, on the whole, a kind of frivolous cynicism. If reality can be anything we want it to be—and that is the message of the new cybertechnology—then it can't be anything that important. This creates the "been there, done that, got the T-shirt" jadedness in which everything, regardless of its degree of significance, is made simply image, simply surface, as there is no longer any depth. (It is curious that both postmodernism and New Age philosophy have battened onto the "create your own reality" ideal with equal superficiality.)

Yet Barfield, writing decades before either the New Age or the rise of the cyberworld, makes our responsibility for the phenomenal world the pivot of his insights into participation. "If the appearances are, as I have sought to establish, correlative to human consciousness, and if human consciousness does not remain unchanged but evolves, then the future of the appearances, that is, of nature herself must indeed depend on the directions which that evolution takes."[7] This quotation requires a second reading. If, as we have argued, our minds are responsible for the phenomenal world, for trees as much as for rainbows, and if, as Barfield has shown—successfully, I think—our minds evolve, with the corollary that they are *evolving still*, then the fate of the phenomenal world, of which "nature" is part, is not only in our hands, but *in our minds*. We can be "environmentally correct," Barfield is saying, not just through such useful and necessary practices as recycling, purchasing organic food, avoiding waste, protecting the ozone layer, and saving the rain forests—all of which are important ways we can fulfill, as Rudolf Steiner called it, our "responsibility to the Earth"; neither I nor Barfield is saying that we can or should avoid this side of our responsibility. But he is saying that we have a perhaps deeper, more immediate responsibility. One of the most baffling as well as suggestive things Rudolf Steiner said was that the future *physical* body of the Earth will be determined by the kinds of thoughts people think now, just as the physical Earth we know today has been shaped by the thoughts of the past. This is the kind of remark that leads people with a superficial knowledge of Steiner to believe he was simply a crank, but given what Barfield has made clear about the relationship between the mind and the phenomenal world, it makes a profound and troubling sense. As both Steiner and Barfield argue, the evolution of consciousness has been from an immersion in the world to, with us, a complete separation from it, in order for us to experience freedom. Where earlier humankind participated unconsciously, we now have the possibility and responsibility to do so consciously. As Barfield wrote, "The future of the phenomenal world can no longer be regarded as entirely independent of man's volition."[8]

To me, this suggests that we need to become aware of both the unconscious processes involved in participation and of the effect our imagination may have on the world. Nature-oriented individuals may bristle at Barfield's claim that nature herself is a representation, formed by the mind. Indeed, some radical ecologically minded people claim that since humankind itself is responsible for despoiling the planet, the Earth would be better off without us. While I in no way condone the rampant exploitation and abuse this planet has been subjected to, I do think that in many ways such sentiments share the same "idolatry" as the very technology that they hold responsible for the problems. They see a fair, "pure" nature that would exist without human beings, and envision in their own way a "prehuman" Golden Age before the arrival of us unthinking despoilers. Again, we do have a responsibility for taking care of the Earth, just as we have a responsibility for taking care of our children. But we don't believe—at least I don't—that our children would be fairer or purer or better off if we were not around.

In many ways, that vision of a Golden Age of an "untouched" Earth is a product of human imagination. Nature is as much erupting volcanoes and colliding stars as it is peaceful meadows and flowing brooks. And, as Barfield points out, the whole idea of "nature" as we now appreciate it is very much a product of the minds of the Romantic poets he loved to read. In the eighteenth century, nature was a thing either to avoid or to control. On his celebrated trip to Scotland, Samuel Johnson famously complained about all the mountains and lakes his carriage had to go around; and the idea of a garden then was of a well-sculpted topiary. Our place was in civilization, not the wilderness, "The proper study of man is man" was the accepted wisdom. It wasn't until the next century and the shift in consciousness known as the Romantic movement, which we will be looking at shortly, that nature wild and free became something to be sought out and appreciated. Again, I am not saying that trees and hills and clouds and streams did not exist; of course they did. But they were not for the people of that time what they have become for us—symbols of a kind of unconstrained freedom and lost innocence, slipping by now, it seems, into guilt. The fact that people today pay large sums and make great efforts to get to places that people of two centuries ago would have assiduously avoided, says something about the influence of the human mind on what we call "nature."

In a very real sense, nature as we understand it did not come into being until 1798, when William Wordsworth and Samuel Taylor Coleridge published their *Lyrical Ballads*. Of course there were others: Rousseau, for example, and Goethe. But it was Wordsworth and Coleridge who brought the actual *presence* of "nature"—Wordsworth's "unknown modes of being" and his "impulse from a vernal wood"—close to the common person. Coleridge had a profound influence on Barfield's thought, equal, probably, to that of Steiner, and it is clear that Coleridge had "participation" in mind when, thinking of our relation to nature, he wrote in "Ode to Dejection," "We receive but what we give / And in our life alone does Nature live."

CHAPTER TWENTY-ONE

~

Thinking about Thinking: Jurij Moskvitin and the Anthrosphere

When Barfield impresses on us our responsibility for the future of the phenomenal world, he has in mind not only the way we "see" nature, but also the way we "represent" it. He has a useful terminology to describe the processes involved in participation. He speaks of "figuration," "alpha-thinking" and "beta-thinking." Figuration is the actual process of representation, of transforming raindrops and sunshine into a rainbow, and elementary particles into a tree. It takes place unconsciously. Alpha-thinking is the kind of thinking that we all engage in, and that scientists do to a much more acute and disciplined degree. It is, as Barfield puts it, "thinking about" our representations, taking them, as it were, at face value as independent, objective "things" in a wholly external world. All technology, all the achievements and advances of science are made possible by this kind of thinking, but it completely ignores, or, more to the point, is unaware of, the contribution of our minds to what it is "thinking about." Our thinking about a tree, botany, agriculture, ecology, and so on, until we get to physics and elementary particles, are all examples of alpha-thinking.

Beta-thinking is something else. It is thinking about the representations *as* representations, thinking about how our minds form the objects of the phenomenal world. Thinking, that is, about thinking itself, as Rudolf Steiner did in *Intuitive Thinking as a Spiritual Path: A Philosophy of Freedom*. It is this kind of thinking Barfield has in mind when he speaks of a "renewal" of participation. It is this kind of thinking that watches the unconscious at work. It is as much an imagining and a watching as a thinking.

We have already seen some examples of this in our discussion of hypnagogia. One of the clearest examples I know comes from a little-known work I mentioned in my introduction, *Essay on the Origin of Thought* by the Danish philosopher Jurij Moskvitin.

Moskvitin's aim in writing his book is to explore what he calls the Anthroposphere. What Moskvitin means by this unusual name is the world created by human consciousness, and for him this includes everything from cave paintings to the theory of relativity. Although it is clear that the Anthroposphere exists within or parallel to the world of nature, a reader of Moskvitin's book soon grasps his basic insight: we all live in a world that is much more "human" than "natural." From the minute we awake, we are all in an immediate contact with a world created by human effort, which has its roots in the human mind. Practically everything around us, from can openers to cars to the computer I am using to write this book, as well as the language I am writing it in, is part of the Anthroposphere.[1]

Now, this may not seem a particularly profound insight, and as it is not central to our theme here, I will forgo elaborating it, at the risk of not doing Moskvitin's book justice. But what is important to our discussion is how Moskvitin arrived at his insight, because it brings him to the recognition—which we have already seen in Owen Barfield—that even what we call the "natural world" is a product of the human mind.

Moskvitin believes that the ideas and insights that are the source of the Anthroposphere originate sporadically in the minds of a few individuals, and that the results of these are then *copied* by the rest of humankind. "The qualities that we consider . . . particularly human and by which we differ from the other animals— i.e. our capacity for memory, reflection, and imagination—are not naturally the property of all men, nor due exclusively to the influence from the social environment, but . . . are derivatives of some particular and rare function, the effects of which are spreading in society and apportioned among all men by means of a principal of imitation." Given this, his book is an "attempt to trace the roots of language and civilization to the region of hallucinatory experience, dependent on mechanisms innate in the psyche and physis of man."[2]

This indeed seems like very deep water, but a simple example can show what Moskvitin means by a "principle of imitation." Many of us drive cars, but not all of us invented the internal combustion engine. The same is true of television, writing, algebra, or the practice of meditation. Someone, at some point, was the first to see the significance of these things. Whenever I want to cook a meal, I don't have to rediscover fire, nor do I have to reinvent the wheel each time I'm in the mood for a bicycle ride. Someone else has already done this, and I profit from his or her insight by "imitating" the initial discovery. And as the value of one discovery can be appreciated by many people, there are fewer "discoverers" than there are "appreciators." Not all of us have written the Jupiter Symphony. Mozart did. But we all can enjoy it.

What is striking about Moskvitin's idea is that he traces the roots of human creativity to, as he says, "the region of hallucinatory experience." We have already seen how important hallucinations were to Julian Jaynes's ideas about consciousness, as well as their role in hypnagogic experience. Moskvitin also sees them as crucial; they are, as I have quoted him saying above, responsible for language and civilization itself. He argues that the great creators and inventors of the Anthroposphere were individuals who, under some form of psychic stress, managed to release powerful imaginative forces from deep within the mind. He calls these experiences "mutative points in the evolution of civilization," and they are to him "the reactions of men exposed to conditions that bring about the collapse of their normal psychical setup, forcing the mind . . . to retreat from a position of externally directed attention and back towards a state of mirroring its own inner recesses."[3]

The result of this experience, which could as easily lead to madness as to creative insight, might be an important discovery, or a work of art, or a new religion or vision of human society.[4] Moskvitin ranges over history, finding impressive examples to support his thesis, citing individuals as distinctive as the Neoplatonic philosopher Plotinus, the poet William Blake, and Nietzsche, as well as Gurdjieff, Ouspensky, and Rudolf Steiner. It was perhaps these references to "occult" thinkers that made mainstream critics shy away from the book; it appears to have been published to no notice whatsoever. I first read it in 1984; ten years later, I had an opportunity to write an article on Moskvitin, and checked the book out of the same university library to refresh my memory. In the decade that had elapsed, no one else had taken it out; the book-marks I had left behind were still in place.

Moskvitin calls these imaginative forces "selective forms," and he came upon his idea after observing these processes at work. His book, he says, is the outcome of a long period in which he found himself drawn to meditating not so much on *what* he thought, but on *how* he thought. "I began to realize," he writes, "that behind much of our intellectual activity . . . lie mental processes to which we normally do not have access, but which are nevertheless prior to and indispensable for any kind of intellectual activity."[5] In other words, Moskvitin accidentally hit upon a method of engaging in what Barfield calls "beta-thinking," and the experience led to a perception of the mechanisms of "figuration." Moskvitin's experience led him to believe that this focusing on the mind's own activity is the trait common to all creators of the Anthroposphere.

As I mention in the introduction, Moskvitin found himself quite by accident in a position in which he was able to observe the mechanisms of perception. Having once achieved this by chance, he set out to do it consciously, which led to some peculiar insights. For example, one of the first things he discovered was that what he felt to be "himself" and his thoughts, that is, his rational, conscious ego, was actually the thing to be observed—which raises questions of who then was doing the observing? The effort required to maintain this observation produced a sensation of pleasure and a surge of unusual thoughts. Another thing it produced was an awareness of a kind of "film" or "screen" or "mosaic" with the "most strange and beautiful patterns," which seemed spread across his field of vision. This mosaic would appear in the hypnagogic states that his observations produced, "states of mind when consciousness is kept somewhere halfway between the waking state and dream." As I write in the introduction, Moskvitin then became aware of a strange phenomenon. He began to see curious sparks and smoke-like forms, which "upon close and intense observation became the elements of waking dreams, forming persons, landscapes, strange mathematical forms." (These sparks and smokelike forms bear a remarkable similarity to the patterns and traces formed by the recorded movement of electrons and other subatomic particles.)

The sparks, Moskvitin writes, reminded him of "the tips of waves glittering in the sun," which on prolonged observation appeared to be "strange rings and nets moving swiftly over the waves."[6]

As I mention in the introduction, Moskvitin became aware of perceiving odd geometric patterns, which he associated with religious art or the kind of visions common to mystical experience—triangles, crosses, squares, and other ornamental shapes.[7] Over time, these patterns seemed to assume three-dimensional forms and, as he writes, were *projected* onto the "external" world by the eye itself. The sparks, smokelike forms, glittering rings, and nets that he observed appeared to Moskvitin to be actually building up that "external" world, and he compared the experience to the effect of a pointillist painting. Observed close up, the work of a painter like Signac, for example, seems a chaos of dots and patches of color, but when we step away and see it from a distance, we recognize it as a still life or landscape. The mind orders the riot of colors and random shapes into a pattern, and Moskvitin was observing this process at its most fundamental level. We can also compare the process to what happens when we look at what are called Rorschach blots, shapeless blobs of ink used in psychological tests, onto which the mind projects patterns.

It may seem difficult to accept that the world we see is a kind of cosmic Rorschach test, but it is easy to observe our own "pattern making" propensity in action. We all remember how, as children, we saw pictures in the clouds floating overhead, how one looked like a bird, another perhaps a face. Earlier I quoted the novelist John Cowper Powys on children's "power of arriving at boundless effects through insignificant means." This is so because children have yet to learn that there is some impassable barrier between themselves and the world: they, it, and their mind still form a whole. Powys himself displayed a powerfully "participatory" mind, able in his novels to enter the consciousness of animals, plants, even stones and old, crumbling walls, as well as planets and stars. He often writes from the point of view of an old, abandoned fence post, or of algae on a pond. Another novelist also keenly aware of this ability to project consciousness into the world "outside" was Hermann Hesse. In *Demian,* Hesse's hero, Emil Sinclair,

is taught by his mentor, the musician-magician Pistorius, to observe
the strange patterns and faces his unconscious projects onto a fire.
Hesse's novel is a kind of fictional account of what Jung called "the
individuation process," and the aim of Pistorius's teaching is to
show the young Sinclair that there is a whole world inside him that
he is unaware of. It is an example of what Jung called "active imagination," which is basically a kind of controlled hypnagogia. It is
also an initiation into an awareness of how much our own minds
participate in the world we see.

Moskvitin takes this awareness a step further. It is not only that
we project patterns onto natural "chaotic" forms, like flames,
clouds, flowing water, or, as Leonardo da Vinci famously did,
stains or cracks on a wall. Moskvitin, like Barfield, is saying that
we "project" the phenomenal world itself. Moskvitin came to see
that there was no fundamental difference between the patterns and
"waking dreams" he was observing and the so-called real world.
Both are, as it were, made up of the same "stuff." The only difference is that in dreams, visions, hypnagogia, and other "altered
states," the pattern-making power of the mind is not constrained
by the information coming to it through the senses.

As we have seen, Rudolfo Llinas and Denis Pare, two of the
key people working on the brain today, are in complete agreement
with Moskvitin—although it is doubtful they, or anyone else working in the field, has ever heard of him. Yet the agreement is striking. Llinas and Pare argue that the only difference between dreaming and waking is that while we are awake the closed system that
generates the brain's oscillatory states—the synchronous firing of
neurons—is modulated by incoming stimuli from the outside
world. When we dream (and we must assume this includes hypnagogia and other forms of nonwaking consciousness as well), that
"closed system" is free of these stimuli and is then not limited in
the kind of mental experience it can create. Moskvitin's wording is
different, but in all essentials the insight is identical: "If we remember that the essential difference between what we call the real
world and the world of imagination and hallucination is not the
elements of which we build them up but the sequence in which
these elements appear . . . then it follows that the sequences direct-

ed from without represent a limitation of the otherwise unlimited combinations of the selective forms released at random from within."[8] Both Moskvitin's and Llinas and Pares's work can be seen as confirmation of Barfield's aphorism that "interior is anterior." Our inner world of dreams and visions comes *before* the outer one of sensory stimuli. The poets have always known this.

This is as radical a departure from the *tabula rasa* picture of the mind that has dominated "scientific" psychology for the last three centuries as we can get. For that view of our mental worlds, we are all, as John Locke said, "blank slates," until written upon by stimuli from the outside world. What Llinas and Pare have concluded through neurological research, and what Moskvitin arrived at through introspection and observation decades earlier, is that this picture is untrue. We are not empty CDs, waiting for experience to make its mark on us. Philosophers like Plato, novelists like Hesse, psychologists like Jung, and the entire hermetic and occult tradition of the West have been saying the exact opposite of this. In a very real sense, we are microcosms, containing an entire world within our psyches, a world in many ways much richer than the "real world" we are taught to gauge our possibilities by. For the scientific view of the mind, dreams, visions, hypnagogic experiences, and the like are so much mental rubbish, relegated to the psychic dustbin. It is the external waking world that counts, and our insides, if they are allowed at all, are merely a kind of reflection of what takes place "out there." This strict rationalist-mechanistic view of the human mind, which sees us as little more than automatons pushed and pulled by outside forces, and which has profoundly influenced not only psychology and philosophy, but Western politics for the last three centuries, is quite simply wrong. As Colin Wilson, one of the few influential thinkers to have come across Moskvitin's book, sums up its insights, "The external world that our eyes reveal to us is just a limited version of the larger inner world."[9]

—

Moskvitin knew that if we follow this insight to its logical conclusion, the consequences are profound. Perhaps most disturbing is the change it effects in our attitude toward reality. Poets and artists

from the Romantic movement to our own day have always felt that
the "real world" is somehow not as real as it seems. They have
always been moved by sudden glimpses of "another world," one
not constrained by the limitations of space and time and the dull
resistance of matter. As we have seen, Ouspensky's *Tertium
Organum* is only one of a canon of works arguing for the preemi-
nence of mind over matter. That "this world" of the senses is maya,
illusion, and that beneath its hard surface lies a living, vital, magical world, is a belief common to all mystical and occult philosophies. Moskvitin knows this, and in his experience of the selective
forms, he believes he has hit on the key to understanding this
perennial belief. "All sensations recorded in literature of the 'unre-
ality' of this world," he writes, all notions "that there is a 'painted
veil' before our eyes preventing us from seeing things as they really are, all the metaphors that we are blind and that we may awake
refer to such experiences of the actual composition of the phenomenal world, of how our senses are glued to something of which we
can know only what it calls up in ourselves."[10]

If this is the case, then the world we see when we open our eyes
is, as Andreas Mavromatis suggested, as much a "dream" as the
visions we see when we are asleep. And if this is so, it certainly is
suggestive that our relationship to these different but similar
"dreams" is practically the same. In our dreams we are unaware
that *we* are the creator of our strange nightly visions and adventures.

Yet the same is true of the world we see each day. I may not be
the creator of the "unrepresented" particles of which the material
world is supposedly made, but I certainly am the creator of my *representation* of those particles, just as I am the creator of the rainbow I see during a rain shower. And just as I may occasionally
dream that I am dreaming—have, that is, a "lucid dream"—and
experience a sudden sense of power and expanded consciousness,
so too in my waking state, I may occasionally recognize that *I* am
the author of the marvellous world I see around me, and experience a radically different relationship to that world.

For one thing, I may become briefly aware of my mind as an
active power, and not, as it usually appears to me, a passive reflec-

tion of the "real world." Anyone who has experienced lucid dreaming and has learned how to control it to some extent knows the feeling. In his chapter on dreams in *A New Model of the Universe*, Ouspensky writes of his experiments in changing and altering his dreams, and speaks of discovering a "hidden artist" in his unconscious mind; other writers have recorded the same sensation. But the same can be true of our "waking state." Artists and writers know the difference between the times when they are intensely focused on a work, and the times when they are not. We know the difference between the times when we feel bored and listless, when everything seems drab and uninteresting, and those other times when our minds catch fire from some fascinating idea or absorbing story. If we can observe ourselves during those moments, I believe we will recognize that a good part of our delight comes from the fact that we have remembered that our minds are active and living—or at least are supposed to be. And it is moments like this that are the strongest arguments against the Cartesian "mirror" theory of knowledge, much more than any epistemological conundrum. No mirror reaches out and "grabs" the world or sets off a chain reaction in itself when one idea triggers another and then another. No mirror goes out of its way to find new and unusual things to reflect. And no mirror contains more than the image of what is before it. To paraphrase Bergson, we can say that if the mind is a mirror, then it is one that has the curious power of showing more than it reflects: it is a mirror that can produce its own images; it is not merely a blank, shiny surface, waiting for something to stand in front of it.

CHAPTER TWENTY-TWO

The Black Hole of Consciousness

Recognizing the active character of the mind led Jurij Moskvitin to one of his most profound insights, which we might call the "black hole" theory of consciousness. It has some similarities to the famous "undecidable" theorem proposed by the mathematician Kurt Gödel. Simply put, Gödel showed that in any rigidly logical mathematical system, there are propositions that cannot be validated—proved or disproved—on the basis of the axioms *within* that system. To be proved or disproved, such propositions would have to refer to something *outside* the system. There were, Gödel proposed, no absolutely closed systems. There is always something in the system that points to what is beyond it. In the simplest instance we can readily see that we cannot, say, use logic to validate logic, because to do so we would have to assume the validity of what we are trying to validate. The axioms of logic cannot prove themselves.

Moskvitin says something similar about the relation of the mind to itself and to the universe, and what he says seems a strong argument against there ever being an explanation of consciousness in strictly materialist terms. He begins with a simple observation. If the phenomenal world, the world we perceive through our senses is, as he, Barfield, and others argue, relative to our consciousness, then we must think of it more in terms of being *our* world, *our* universe, than *the* world, *the* universe. What we call reality, he writes, "is not necessarily the whole universe, for the simple reason that it is limited by the human organs of perception. . . . There is not the slightest reason why *our universe* should be the entire universe."[1] We can only know of the world what we can grasp of it through our means of perception, and so what we know of the world is shot through and through with elements of ourselves. Different means of perception, like a different consciousness, might reveal a different world. Nearly two centuries before Moskvitin wrote his book, William Blake had the same insight. "How do you know but every bird that cuts the airy way, is an immense world of delight, closed to your senses five?" he asked.

"Our world," then, for Moskvitin, is a slice of a totality to which we can never have full access. And since our world is only a part of this totality, formed by our organs of perception, it is pointless to look for the origin of that world in its own elements. This would be like looking for the author of a novel in the novel itself, or the painter of a picture in the picture itself, or the dreamer of a dream in the dream itself. The "origin" of our world lies *outside* that world, just as the author of a book lies outside the book. This is not to say that we can't look for the origin and causes of elements *within* that world, just as we can look within a story for the motivation of its characters. This, in effect, is what science does. But the world itself, like the story itself, cannot be explained by its constituents, just as Gödel showed that propositions in a logical system cannot be proven by the axioms of that system. Any explanation must refer to something *outside*. And if this applies to "our world" as a whole, it also applies to ourselves. As Moskvitin writes, "It is absurd . . . to look for an absolute cause, a source, of our existence in a world the appearance of which depends on the existence of a spectator which is exactly ourselves. . . . What is perceived can never be the perceiver." A flashlight can never shine on itself; it can illuminate everything but its own source of light. The attempt to illuminate itself can only lead to an infinite regress. "We shall have an infinite series of increasingly subtle attempts to grasp the essential principle in ourselves, but the ultimate point is beyond our Tantalic grasp—the ego is transcendental. An unknown point will remain forever, and just as there is a blind spot in the eye at the point where all the retinal tissues are uniting into a mainline leading to the brain, there is a blind spot in the mind."[2]

It is through this "blind spot"—or black hole, as I call it—that we are connected to what Moskvitin calls the "absolute universe." "The thing that created us, our cause . . . cannot possibly be contained in the slice that lies before our eyes. . . . The true cause must be something more complete than the selection made by our organs of perception."[3] Beyond "our world" lies another world, the totality, the world of what Ouspensky called "the miraculous." Mystics, occultists, and metaphysicians have given it an assortment of other names: Gnostics speak of the *Pleroma*, Kabbalists of the *Ain Soph*, Neoplatonists of the One. Each, however, speaks of the same thing. Scientists, Moskvitin points out, will not be happy with this observation, because they want to get at the source of "the real world," which they believe is the world they see, and pin it down once and for all. But they cannot do this because, "There will forever remain an unknown zone of ultimate causation, created by, and coinciding with that in ourselves that will forever remain unknown—the blind spot in the mind."[4] In other words, there is some part of us that is not part of the phenomenal world, and it is this unknown part that is itself the cause of the phenomenal world. And since that is the case, the unknown part *cannot be explained* in terms of the phenomenal world of which it is the creator.

The aptness of Gödel's theorem to our own relation to the world will be clear in this last quotation from Moskvitin:

> *A mind looking into a world external to itself will receive a picture of a world in which there are some phenomena that cannot be explained in terms of the laws generally ruling in that world. The reason is that a mind—any mind— is creating its world by means of a process of selection. The thing that will be missing in that world . . . is the law governing the total system because the mind is a part of the total system, and what it cannot perceive is itself. . . . The world as we see it is determined by the structure of what to us appears as its smallest components. To move deeper in this direction is to change the world.*
>
> *. . . [T]he total system of which the point (consciousness) is itself an element will forever remain unknown to the point. It is itself governed by a system of which it can never grasp the totality. . . . Fully to grasp and understand what it is in itself would be to grasp the totality. Therefore there will in itself forever remain something unknown, and so there will remain something unknown in the world that it perceives as external to itself. That unknown will appear as life. The increasing approach to the unknown—the blind spot in itself—is the creation of life itself.[5]*

It is curious that Moskvitin says that to "move deeper" than the "smallest components" of "our world" would be to change that world. This seems to be saying that the mind can alter reality itself. Over a century of documentation concerning the reality of the "paranormal" seems to corroborate this suggestion, and anyone willing to investigate the material will find sufficient evidence for the belief that in repeated cases the mind has clearly exerted a power over, or exceeded the constraints of, matter. Several good histories of the paranormal exist, and it would be pointless to repeat their findings here. In my own experience the clearest and most convincing evidence has been in the form of precognitive dreams and synchronicities, too exact and meaningful to be explained by coincidence—which, in any case, explains nothing at all.[6] But more immediate than the possibility of the "hidden powers of the mind" are the potentials of our unconscious power of "figuration," which we are considering here. This strikes me as immensely important, and it is this Barfield is concerned about when he speaks of a "responsibility of the imagination."

If our unconscious minds are the creators of the phenomenal world, then it certainly seems incumbent upon us to understand just what our unconscious minds are about. And in order to do this, before anything else we would have to become aware of the *reality* of our unconscious minds. Certainly, the phrase "the unconscious" has been around for decades and is a part of our common vocabulary, but the fact that a part of our minds is not under our conscious control, and that it plays a very large part in determining our lives, is still something people talk about more than actually grasp. We speak glibly about Oedipus complexes and archetypes, and there are reams of books on every aspect of psychoanalysis, dream interpretation, hypnotherapy, and whatnot. But we are talking here about something deeper than our personal unconscious, that basement full of childhood traumas and antisocial appetites.

In the 1950s there was a science fiction film called *Forbidden Planet*, an intelligent adaptation of Shakespeare's *The Tempest*, set on another world. A scientist, who lives alone on the planet with his beautiful daughter, has discovered the remains of an ancient super-race, part of which is a machine capable of amplifying the powers of the mind a hundredfold. When an expedition sent to check up on the scientist's research arrives, he resents their intrusion, as well as the attention the crew gives his desirable daughter. Curiously, the arrival of the expedition coincides with the strange appearance of a mysterious invisible creature, a monster of enormous strength and ferocity. Several crewmembers are killed and much equipment destroyed before it becomes clear that the monster is a *creation of the scientist's unconscious mind*, amplified by his experiments with the super-race's "brain machine." Along with the amplification of his intellect and powers of reason, there has been an equal amplification of his dark, irrational urges. Resentful of the invasion on his privacy and jealous of the young crewmembers, he has unknowingly called forth a monster to fufill his secret wishes.[7]

We are all, I would say, in the same position as the scientist in *Forbidden Planet*. We all have to become aware of how much our own minds are responsible for the world around us. And this means becoming aware of how much our own imagination is involved in shaping the world we see. We have already seen how the imagination of poets like Wordsworth and Coleridge helped create the idea we have of "nature" today. This doesn't mean we should all become poets, but it does mean that if we wish to become aware of participation as a living reality, we will have to make a particular kind of effort. As Barfield writes, "Participation as an actual experience is only to be won today by special exertion; . . .it is a matter, not of theorizing, but of imagination."[8] We have seen some examples of this "special exertion" in Goethe and in Moskvitin's observation of the selective forms.

But, Barfield warns, simply "imagining" more is not enough. He points out that although since the Romantic movement the imagination has been considered a "good" in itself, this is not really the case. It can equally be "bad." For a generation held back by the rationalist mentality of the Enlightenment, an unfettered imagination would understandably seem an unquestioned good. But such constraints have long been broken, and for years now there has been little check on the creations of the human mind. It is also true that even a cursory glance at the products of the imagination over the last two centuries will reveal an increasing obsession with the dark side of the mind.

When Barfield was writing he had in mind the efforts of the Surrealists. He was concerned that with the accelerated rate of evolution, the kind of world their wild obsessions depicted might move from their paintings onto the larger canvas called "real life."

As the changes that have taken place in merely the last three hundred years show, the transformation of the human mind, and hence, of its "representations," has speeded up, and Barfield was concerned about what this meant for the future. The Surrealists were, of course, interested in the workings of the unconscious, and some, like André Breton and Robert Desnos, explored the curious world of hypnagogia. But the Surrealists, like the psychics and mediums of the nineteenth century, believed that any product of the imagination—or the "spirit world"—was by definition "good," and that any conscious control or inhibition was "bad." This led to the paranoid landscapes of Salvador Dali, as well as the now highly unreadable reams of Surrealist automatic writing. Barfield knew that much of the Surrealist aesthetic was mere affectation, but he also knew that some was not, and those for whom it was genuine, he argued, must actually *see* the world in that way. Half a century earlier, Arthur Rimbaud, the "bad boy" of Symbolist poetry, threw himself into a systematic "derangement of the senses" in order to escape the confines of "bourgeois" normality. Many followed him, and a history of the imagination since the mid–nineteenth century could be seen as a history of our deepening obsession with the bizarre, gruesome, and inhuman. By the 1930s, Rimbaud's systematic derangement was the height of fashion, and it has since gone on to be adopted by advertising. The "pictures of a dog with six legs emerging from a vegetable marrow or a woman with a motorbicycle substituted for her left breast" that concerned Barfield are now casually absorbed, along with much worse, by the consuming public through a variety of means.[9]

And, as Barfield said, those who appreciate these kinds of images are willing to make the effort to see the world in that way. Eventually, over time, they *will* see such a world, and, if Moskvitin's "imitation" theory of evolution is correct, so will many others. Today, with the formidable movie industry and our ability to "morph" reality or to create it "virtually," the wedding of unfettered imagination and technology can result in something like *Star Trek*'s "holodeck," which our hunger for raw sensation and aesthetic shock will use to fashion environments like William S. Burroughs's *Naked Lunch*. If this is the case, then Barfield's warning about our moving into a "fantastically hideous world" may prove uncomfortably timely. If the imagination of poets can transform inconvenient piles of stone and earth into beautiful mountains, it can also transform everyday reality into a kind of waking nightmare. And as the "bourgeois" public has been taught for decades to accept the visions of the "avant-garde," however unsettling, as the work of genius, the process of transformation may not take too long to complete.[10]

Chapter Twenty-Three

Other Times and Places

Another thinker concerned with the imagination, whose name has already come up several times, is Colin Wilson. Wilson first came to prominence in 1956, when he was only twenty-four, with the publication of his first book, *The Outsider*. It was an immediate bestseller, and the impecunious Wilson, who had written the book at the British Library, while spending his nights in a sleeping bag on Hampstead Heath, became famous overnight. Fame, however, is fickle, and Wilson soon discovered that his notoriety had more to do with an erroneous association with the Angry Young Men— writers like John Osborne and Kingsley Amis—than with the existential ideas at the core of his book. Within six months, he was routinely attacked in the press and has since remained an aptly "outsider" figure himself, never quite accepted by the British literary establishment. (The same was true of Owen Barfield, whose books always sold better in the United States.)

This has had little effect on Wilson's work, and over nearly half a century he has built up one of the most stimulating and wide-ranging oeuvres in Western literature, producing well over a hundred books on subjects as diverse as philosophy, psychology, criminology, sexual deviance, parapsychology, and literary criticism, as well as several novels in science fiction, mystery, and other genres.

As practically all of Wilson's work is related to understanding the mechanisms of consciousness, it is difficult to single out a particular book as the key to his ideas. For readers unfamiliar with his work, *The Outsider* surely is the book to begin with. *Poetry and Mysticism,* mentioned earlier, is a good brief introduction to some of his main ideas.[1]

Wilson began his exploration of human consciousness at the same place Owen Barfield did, with the Romantics of the nineteenth century. But his starting point was different. Like Barfield, Wilson recognized that with the Romantics a shift had occurred in human consciousness. What had happened, he argued, was that suddenly the human mind discovered the powers of the imagination. Of course, people had been aware of this curious ability to focus on what Wilson calls "other times and places" ever since they first sat around a campfire and heard tales of a distant Golden Age, or stories of battle and adventure. If imagination is the ability to focus on "realities not present," then clearly human beings had been doing this for millennia before the Romantics. But something happened toward the end of the eighteenth century that transformed the human imagination so radically, that it was as if it had discovered a completely new power. The difference is like that between a horse-drawn cart and a sports car. Both have wheels and are used for transportation, but the resemblance ends there. The imagination as it began to appear in the second half of the eighteenth century was like a mental Ferrari. Or, perhaps more to the point, like a rocket ship.

There had of course been myths, fairy tales, and stories of gods and goddesses prior to the Romantics, as well as tales of adventures and quests, but these were always tied to very well defined ideas about our place in the world. There was a "great chain of being," and we were only one link in it, a relatively small one. The Romantics rattled that chain, broke it, and blasted off for other worlds. However the space they travelled through was not that of the rotating celestial spheres, but the more mysterious one of their own minds.

With the Romantics, dreams, visions, ecstasies, and wild flights of the imagination became the themes of a new consciousness.

Perhaps the most famous "dream poem" in English literature is
Coleridge's "Kubla Khan," but it is only one example of a new fascination with the "dark side" of the mind and the strange workings
of the unconscious and the irrational. The Romantics discovered
that there was more to human beings than the "daylight" rational
picture of them that had emerged in the Enlightenment. There was
a whole "other world" *inside their own mind,* a world that the
shallow, rationalist Enlightenment picture ignored or suppressed.
The Romantics had discovered an entirely unsuspected universe, a
new dimension of reality, and had taught their readers how to
explore it.

Curiously, Wilson argues that the first of these "mental trav-
ellers"—the phrase is Blake's—was a middle-aged printer named
Samuel Richardson. Richardson was commissioned to write a
book, a sort of do-it-yourself course in correspondence, but he
became so involved in his work that he got carried away and ended
up writing an immense novel about the attempted seduction of a
servant girl by her master. *Pamela* appeared in 1740 and overnight
became the first "bestseller," in our sense of the term. And
although there had been earlier books that we can see as either
novels or the forerunners of novels—like *Don Quixote* and
Robinson Crusoe—*Pamela* was the first that readers today would
recognize as a novel.

Richardson's novel, and his second, even larger work, *Clarissa,*
are not in themselves concerned with the new powers of the mind,
or with any of the themes that would obsess the Romantics. Both
are, in essence, the great-great-grandmothers of the soap opera.
The story of Pamela's unsuccessful seduction—she safeguards her
virginity until she forces her pursuer to marry her—is drawn out
and full of so many coincidences and improbable situations that
today's readers, use to plentiful and highly graphic sex, find it difficult to understand what all the fuss is about. But for the readers
of 1740, it was a revelation. We have to remember that the world
of easily accessible entertainment—books, films, television, CDs,
the Internet—that all of us take for granted is a very recent development. It was only little more than a century ago that anything
like a popular market for reading emerged. In Richardson's time,

practically the only reading material available outside of the cities was the Bible or the weekly sermon. Most people lived lives of inconceivable boredom, and for many the only form of imaginative release from the drudgery of existence was drink. Readers familiar with Hogarth's etchings of Gin Alley know how swiftly that coarse intoxicant filled a hunger among the poorer classes.

Wilson argues that *Pamela* and the other novels that emerged in its wake were like a new kind of drug, but one without the horrific side effects of gin. The story kept readers interested—like all good novelists, Richardson instilled that itch to "see what happens." But aside from the mild titillation of sex, what really attracted Richardson's readers was the sense of having stepped out of the confines of their lives. For a few hours, bored housewives all over England could transport themselves into another world, Pamela's, and forget their own cares and woes. It was, as Wilson writes, "a magic carpet," and soon all of Europe was taking magic carpet rides.[2] Richardson, in effect, had created a new addiction, what the poet and essayist William Anderson later dubbed "bibliomania."

The consequences were as important as Wordsworth's and Coleridge's invention of "nature." What Richardson discovered was that human beings can "take trips" without moving out of their room, an insight that, like many adolescents, I discovered pouring over paperbacks of science fiction and fantasy in my room in the late 1960s and early 1970s. In the Tao Te Ching, Lao Tse says, "Without going out of my door, I can know all things on earth. Without going out of my window, I can know the ways of heaven," and in many ways Richardson's invention of the novel was a practical application of this deep truth. Richardson taught the mind *how to fly*, and soon the writers and poets who came after him used this power to explore other things besides the seduction of a virtuous servant girl. The mind was no longer chained to the earth; it had spread its wings and the effect was staggering. Having tasted of this new power, human beings began to feel a deep dissatisfaction with the "everyday" world. As Wilson writes, one result of this dissatisfaction was the French Revolution, many of whose leaders fueled their revolt through reading Rousseau, whose *New Heloise*, another novel of seduction, outsold *Pamela*, and

Friedrich Schiller, whose play *The Robbers* was perhaps the first in a long literary tradition in which the criminal, the outcast of society, is the hero.³ What was happening was that human beings were discovering their own strengths, a secret power they were unaware of, and were recognizing that they might be something more than "only human" after all. They might, it seemed, be something more like gods. The whole "occult revival" of the nineteenth century, typified by figures like Eliphas Levi and Madame Blavatsky, was one result of this insight.

—

But, as Wilson points out, the Romantics soon discovered they were gods in exile. They discovered that their flights of imagination, their magic carpet rides, did not last. They would be transfigured by some ecstasy, their imagination soaring beyond the highest heaven, and then—they fell to earth. Coarse reality gripped them by the throat and cut their wings. Or they discovered that prolonged adventures in the "other world" left them unfit for the "real world." They became pathetic, ineffectual dreamers, cast ashore in a hard, inhospitable land. Many of them died alcoholics or drug addicts. Coleridge himself had an enormous laudanum habit, as did De Quincey; both lost much of their creative powers in their later years, and Coleridge was famous for accepting advances on the strength of outlines of tremendous works he would never write. E. T. A. Hoffmann, whom Wilson cites as the quintessential figure of the time, drank himself to death. The Romantics came to believe that their visions and dreams were only that, "imagination" in the negative sense, and that the real world of drudgery and boredom was the truth. Like children faced with some task they are unequal to, they sank to their knees and cried. (This was why Barfield called his collection of essays on Steiner's philosophy *Romanticism Come of Age;* he believed that with Steiner the Romantic insights had "grown up.") After an initial explosion of creative fire, the Romantic volcano burnt out, and the generations that followed, like the Symbolists and decadents of the *fin de siècle,* increasingly withdrew from life and its challenges. As Wilson has often quoted, the hero of Villiers de L'Isle-Adam's play *Axel* summed up the late-

Romantic philosophy of life: "As for living, our servants can do that for us."

Wilson was obsessed by this tragic quality of the Romantics and the poets and artists who followed them. Why did so many of the Romantics and other great artists and thinkers of the nineteenth and twentieth centuries either go mad, commit suicide or die prematurely? The list is impressive: Nietzsche, Hölderlin, Maupassant, Ibsen, Nijinsky, Strindberg, van Gogh, and many others: all either died insane, committed suicide, or suffered severe periods of madness. Each of these thinkers was faced with the question of Ultimate Yes or Ultimate No, and each, in different ways, answered in the negative. What drove these "Outsiders" over the edge? And, more importantly, could something have saved them?

In his novel *The Mind Parasites,* Wilson uses the metaphor of a strange race of psychic vampires hidden in the human mind, who have been feeding on it for centuries, as a way of explaining this cultural phenomenon. No one has ever dreamed of their existence, and for ages they have lived off human vitality. But in the Romantics, the parasites recognized a threat. Through them the human race, they saw, was becoming too aware of its own potentials, and would soon realize the existence of the mental vermin who sap their energy. The parasites are the cause of, in William James's phrase, our "habit of inferiority to our true selves," and it is in their best interest that we never discover who we *really* are. If we did, we would throw them off as easily as we do the common cold. And so the parasites decide to wipe out the Romantics and most of the artists and thinkers who followed them, sending waves of despair and depression throughout the *Zeitgeist* of the nineteenth century. The effect is devastating, and the optimism about our infinite potentials, which blossomed with the first Romantics, withers and dies, leaving behind the pessimism of Kafka, Beckett, and, by now, today's postmodernists.

Wilson's metaphor is, of course, only that, but it is a powerful and insightful one. In the novel, the mind parasites are eventually defeated by a band of scientists and philosophers who have learned how to control their consciousness, using methods developed by Edmund Husserl, the father of the philosophical school known as phenomenology. Husserl's basic insight, and the one that is at the heart of Wilson's thought, is that *perception is intentional.* This is essentially another way of talking about the participatory nature of consciousness. Husserl was another philosopher dissatisfied with Descartes' account of the mind, and the mirror theory of knowledge. Rather than simply reflect the outside world, Husserl argued that consciousness reaches out and *grabs* it. Or, using another image, it is as if consciousness was a kind of gun, firing at its target. Both metaphors express the essential *active* nature of consciousness; they also suggest that consciousness may sometimes "miss." We don't always hold onto what we reach out for, and not everyone is a marksman.

Wilson recognized that the failure of the Romantics, as well as that of the existentialists who followed them, was in this *active* quality of the mind. The problem with both, he believed, was that they shared an essentially *passive* attitude to the world.

One thinker associated with the late nineteenth century, however, did not. In Nietzsche Wilson saw the will to health and vitality that is the key to answering affirmatively the Outsider's question of Ultimate Yes or Ultimate No. It is true that Nietzsche died insane, and that throughout his life he was wracked by headaches, dyspepsia, and loneliness. By any common standard, he lived a thoroughly wretched life, moving from pension to pension in a futile attempt to find the right climate to aid his faltering health. But it was precisely his sickness that led Nietzsche to his deepest insight: that beyond the rational intellect there exists a tremendous, vital will to live, an overpowering appetite for life that transcended critical reason. In his periods of recuperation, Nietzsche felt this will rising up in him and, as we have seen, it led him to his vision of the *Übermensch,* the superman. Nietzsche, for all his supposed atheism, was a deeply spiritual man, and given to what have to be called "mystical experiences." But in his case, these were not visions of God or of other deities, but profound insights into this tremendous will to live, into what he called the "Dionysian." During one of these "peak experiences"—to use a phrase from Abraham Maslow, one of the thinkers of stature who recognized the importance of Wilson's ideas—Nietzsche had his vision of "eternal recurrence." When the idea came to him he spoke of being "six thousand feet above men and time."

Wilson asked a simple question: Which was true, a vision like Nietzsche's and the dozens of other examples he collected, or the despair and ennui of the Romantics and existentialists? He concluded that the mystical experience of total affirmation—which could be found in writers like Blake, Dostoyevsky, Goethe, Rilke, and many others—was true, because in such moments consciousness has *increased its intentionality,* its power of reaching out and grabbing the world, and in doing so has become aware both of its own hidden strength and of the objective *meaning* inherent in the world.

This, Wilson saw, is the basic problem of human consciousness. Because we assume that consciousness is simply a passive reflection of the world, we fail to grasp its real function, to act as a kind of laser beam cutting into reality to reveal its meaning. By "meaning" Wilson does not mean any kind of rational argument or explanation, but precisely the same kind of insights that Barfield experienced when he read his favorite poets. Meaning of this kind is an immediate, unreflective appreciation, like that delicious sense of relief when we are thirsty and feel a cold drink going down our throats. It is essentially a sense of grabbing hold of *reality*. It communicates to us the insight that the world is *interesting,* infinitely more interesting than we give it credit for being.

Most of the time, however, we experience the world abstractly, as if a pane of glass separated us from it, and only occasionally do we feel a real, vital connection: on a spring morning, perhaps, as Wilson suggests, or setting out on a holiday. What is dangerous about this is that because we can "see through" the glass, we rarely are aware of its existence and believe we *really are* "in touch" with the world, accepting our spring mornings as delightful and infrequent exceptions. Yet we aren't in touch with it at all; we go through most of our lives never really "seeing" a flower or a blade of grass. The result is that some part of us slowly dies of a kind of "reality starvation."

Wilson has a handy concept to account for our separation from the world. He calls it "the robot." The robot, he says, is that part of us that performs functions unconsciously. It is a kind of automatic pilot. The robot is a very useful and necessary tool, and the fact that we possess highly developed ones accounts for our success as a species; other animals possess robots as well, but they are not as efficient as ours (that's why you can't teach an old dog new tricks and why some species can't be taught any tricks at all). When we learn some new skill like typing, driving a car, playing a musical instrument, or speaking a foreign language, we first struggle with it consciously, painfully practicing it step by step. But then one morning we awake and, miraculously, we can do it. What has happened is that the new skill has passed from our conscious into our unconscious mind. The virtue of this is that it allows our conscious mind to focus on something else. In computer-speak, the robot enables us to be "multitasking." We all see people today driving with one hand while carrying on a telephone conversation. The robot does the driving, allowing them to focus on the conversation, just as my robot is typing these words, freeing my conscious mind to focus on what I want to say. We can all think of other examples: a pianist whose fingers command the keyboard and whose mind is concentrating on interpreting the music, an actor who knows his part by heart and can focus on giving it emotional depth. All of these are examples of Whitehead's observation that civilization advances by making more and more of its functions unconscious, and so freeing up the conscious mind for new developments. The robot is also clearly linked to the philosopher Michael Polanyi's notion of "tacit knowing," knowing *how* rather that knowing *what*. We can tacitly know how to do something, but be incapable of communicating our knowledge. Try telling someone how you ride a bicycle. It's easy to *show* them how, but surprisingly difficult to explain it in words. Without tacit knowing we would all be like infants. If I had to learn how to type every time I sat down to write, this book would never be finished.

But there is a drawback to this. As Wilson points out, one problem with having an efficient robot is that it can be too efficient and start taking over duties I would rather perform myself. It can begin to listen to a Bach fugue when *I* want to, with the result that

I find it a bit dull. It can read a book when *I* want to, with the result that I don't absorb what "it" has read, and I have to go back. It can even make love to my girlfriend, with the result that I find the experience oddly disappointing. Basically, when we approach life with our habitually passive attitude (James's "inferiority to our true selves") we are saying to our robot, "Go ahead and take care of this, it isn't important enough for me to attend to," and the result is that sense of separation from life, of never really touching it, that plagues so many of us in the modern world. But as Wilson points out, a sudden crisis or problem can awaken our urge to "take control" and put the robot in the back seat. I may be driving quite unconsciously, my conscious mind mulling over an argument or thinking about an article I have to write, when a car swerves in front of me. All of a sudden I am *there*; a rush of adrenaline and "I" am driving, not the robot. And, as many of us have noticed, for a short time afterward everything seems a bit more "there" as well. This is because I have taken over the driver's seat, literally in this case, from the robot and am putting my full attention into what is around me. And yet, unless another emergency demands this attention, I will unconsciously relax, and hand the steering wheel back to the robot.

This capacity of crisis to awaken our true will, Wilson observes, is behind the seemingly neurotic choices of many of his Outsiders, their drive, in Nietzsche's words, to "live dangerously." The philosopher Ludwig Wittgenstein inherited a fortune from his industrialist father, but he gave this away and lived in near poverty in a small hut in a desolate part of Norway, in order to live more "authentically." As an adolescent, the novelist Graham Greene suffered profound periods of boredom and depression that could only be lifted by playing Russian roulette. When Greene heard the hammer of his pistol hit on an empty chamber, he experienced an overpowering vision of life's absolute value; the world that before had bored him now appeared infinitely interesting. The philosopher Jean-Paul Sartre said that he never felt as free as he did during World War II when, as a member of the French Resistance, he was liable to be shot at any moment. His philosophical mentor

Heidegger had said that only a deep realization of one's own mortality can instill in a person a true sense of "being," an insight that Gurdjieff agreed with.

All of these examples, as well as the dozens of others Wilson has collected, succinctly drive home the point put by Dr. Johnson that the thought that one will be hanged in a fortnight "concentrates the mind wonderfully." Such an insight is also behind the variety of techniques and embellishments many people employ to "spice up" their sexual relations. A flagging erotic relationship can be revitalized via a little S & M, or other "creative," slightly dangerous, or "kinky" additions, like mirrors or role-playing. The aim of these, as well as "living dangerously," is to get past the robot so that "you" are involved in the act. This is also the aim of other "dangerous" activities, from sports-car racing and mountain climbing to antisocial behavior like vandalism and shoplifting. The "thrill" each affords comes from "you" pushing the robot aside.

Yet, as Wilson makes clear, these self-inflicted crises are slightly absurd. The whole point of civilization is to minimize crisis. We have struggled to get out of the caves in order to make life *more* convenient, not less. But, as Wilson clearly saw, it is inconvenience that stimulates our will, while comfort and security dull us and prompt the most sensitive and intelligent of us to seek out challenges or, failing to find them, to create them ourselves. As Freud argued, there seems to be something inherently neurotic about civilization, so it is no wonder it produces so many "discontents."

Yet Wilson's answer to this is not to abandon civilization. If a "precivilized" state were preferable, surely we would never have bothered to climb down from the trees. Anyway, our immediate response to any kind of inconvenience is to try to *get rid of it*—and this is the basic "shape" of the drive to civilization. Otherwise we would never come in out of the rain. This is also the argument against attempts at "nonrobotic" consciousness that go about it from the opposite end, by putting the robot out of commission. The most obvious and effective ways of doing this are drugs or alcohol. And, it has to be admitted, their initial effects are pleasurable. A glass of wine relaxes the robot's grip, and we suddenly recognize that the world is much more interesting and inviting than we realized. Yet it is also true that overindulgence leads to profound impairment; the robot is so anesthetized that we can barely function at all. The same is true of other drugs. As Aldous Huxley famously said, gazing through the doors of perception at a sink full of "beautiful" unwashed dishes, if everyone took mescaline—as he had—there would be no wars, but there would be no civilization either. Everyone would be too awash in cosmic consciousness to take care of the business at hand.

Obviously there is some drive in us to bring order into our world, to gain some level of *control* over our environment. Yet once we have achieved this, we grow weary of it, and seek out the very inconvenience we have just eliminated. Clearly there is some problem here, and it is directly linked to another curious paradox of human psychology, our inability to appreciate freedom. Wilson notes that one strange trait shared by practically all his Outsiders is that they all have a passion for "freedom" and yet, upon achieving it, they all sink into a profound state of boredom. And this happens because they *have no idea what to do with their freedom once they get it.* We all experience something of this sort: we work all week and dream of what we will do with our weekend, yet when it arrives, the empty day yawns before us and we desperately seek something to fill it with, to, as the saying goes, "kill time," anxious to return to our regular routine. Gone are our plans to study German, listen to opera, finally work our way through Tolstoy, or write that novel we've been dreaming of. Freedom, like the removal of inconvenience, is something we crave yet paradoxically do not appreciate when we get it.

Yet, contrary to the feeling of many who cast a wistful eye at some idyllic dawn age, it is not civilization or the modern world that is at fault; the problem is that we have failed to understand how our consciousness works. Wilson recognized that the attraction of inconvenience and living dangerously is not in the actual problems or challenges they present, but in the *focus and concen-*

tration we bring to bear on meeting them. Heidegger and Gurdjieff hit the nail on the head when they said that the *thought* of one's death can lead to an experience of "being"—the thought, not the actual confrontation. Wilson grasped that one's mind, one's *imagination,* can serve the same purpose as an actual danger. And this, in fact, is the function of imagination: to focus the mind on realities that are not at the moment present. We do this every time we think of what we will do later in the day, or next week, or on next year's vacation. And once this is grasped, one realizes that the solution to "nonrobotic" consciousness lies in *strengthening the power of the mind itself*, not in imagining dangers. A mind sufficiently capable of "pulling itself together" at will would no longer need the trigger of some imaginary challenge, which in any case would soon lose its power of evoking our will. Like all "external" methods, danger can easily lose its charm, just as other means of stimulating the imagination do. This can be easily seen in sex: pornography, kinky fetishes, and erotic fantasies soon lose their power to stimulate, and the jaded palate seeks stronger and stronger devices to stir its appetite, just as a drug addict needs stronger and stronger doses to get the desired effect. Yet a saturation point is reached, and anyone who has ploughed through the Marquis de Sade's *120 Days of Sodom* knows it arrives fairly early on.

But there is no limit to the mental concentration we can develop, as long as we grasp that this is what is necessary and resolve to put our full will into the work. Sex, danger, challenge are all means of avoiding our critical, rational conscious mind and reaching into our unconscious vital reserves—the level of what Barfield calls "figuration" and Moskvitin the "selective forms." Wilson recognized the need to tap these reserves through the conscious mind itself. The mind, he saw, has the uncanny power of stimulating itself. As Bergson said, it has the power to draw from itself more than it contains.

CHAPTER TWENTY-FOUR

Faculty X

One of the powers the mind can draw from itself, Wilson discovered, is a strange ability to transcend time and space, what he calls "Faculty X," the curious ability to grasp the reality of "other times and places." Wilson first formulated this idea in *The Occult*, and it has since been a central theme in all his writing. Along with the notion of the Outsider, it is perhaps his most important contribution to a philosophy of the evolution of consciousness.

We have already seen one example of this in our discussion of Bergson: Proust's famous madeleine. But there are many others. One that Wilson has offered in many of his books is that of the historian Arnold Toynbee. In his classic work *A Study of History,* Toynbee recounts how he was sitting at the ruins of the citadel of Mistra in Greece, meditating on the battle that had taken place there in 1821, which had left the site devastated. As he sank deep into his thoughts, he experienced a "time slip": it was as if he could actually *see* the battle before his eyes. On another occasion he had a similar experience outside the British Museum, in which he seemed to see the whole of human history pass before his eyes in a kind of parade—not too dissimilar, we can see, to what we have heard about the Akashic Record. Examples like these fill the pages of *The Occult* and also its sequel, *Mysteries.*

Wilson also offers somewhat more startling evidence of our strange power to be in "two places at once." Recounting some very radical forms of the "duo-consciousness" we have discussed in this book, Wilson documents some extraordinary cases of what the nineteenth-century psychic researcher F. W. H. Myers called "phantasms of the living": the appearance of the "double" of an individual while the physical body is elsewhere. Relating how the novelist John Cowper Powys "appeared" one evening in the Manhattan apartment of his friend and fellow novelist Theodore Dreiser, while at the same time Powys was sitting in his cottage in upstate New York, Wilson writes:

> We take it for granted that we live in a "solid" world of space and time, advancing from moment to moment according to unchangeable laws, and that we are stuck in the place that we happen to be at the moment. We are, in a sense, "trapped." We feel this particularly strongly when we are bored or miserable—that we are helplessly at the mercy of this physical world into which we happen to have been born. Yet these odd experiences all seem to show that this is untrue. The "real you" is not trapped in space and time. With a certain kind of effort of will, it can rise above space and time and be "elsewhere."[1]

One curious thing about this "time slip" is that, although Powys had predicted to Dreiser that he would "appear" before him that evening, when Dreiser later asked how he did it, Powys declined to answer. And the most probable reason, Wilson believes, is that Powys did not know. Yet, as readers of his novels know, Powys possessed a powerful imagination, and in his extraordinary *Autobiography* he admits to a fascination with magic and occult powers, admitting that he believed he possessed them himself. It is highly likely that Powys "thought" himself into Dreiser's apartment through some unusual feat of concentration. Another writer who shared Powys's fascination with the occult, to the extent of becoming for a period a practicing alchemist, was the playwright August Strindberg; he, too, experienced on several occasions the eerie phenomenon of "dislocation," of transcending the normal limitations of time and space. And Goethe, another poet with an interest in the occult, had this strange power of being able to "project" his "double."[2]

Wilson is clearly fascinated with these and other "paranormal" abilities, but he is more concerned with understanding the mechanisms of "everyday" consciousness. And a little reflection shows that we experience some form of duo-consciousness practically every day. In a certain sense you, as you read this book, are in "two places at once." You are in whatever physical surroundings you happen to occupy, but if I am doing my job correctly and have interested you in these ideas, you also occupy the world of thought and imagination, the "elsewhere" that Wilson mentions above. What happens when I take a book from my shelf, and set off on a trip on Samuel Richardson's magic carpet? I open it, flip through the pages, and idly glance at a paragraph or two, not really reading but just skimming the surface. Then something catches my eye—if it is a book of history, say a description of ancient Athens. I focus more intently on the page and sink back in my chair with the intent to read through the section. A minute passes, then two. I'm *interested*. I forget the solid world I happen to be in and suddenly, the landscape has changed. The walls of my room have disappeared and in their place I am hovering somewhere *outside* space and time. Now, if I am relaxed enough and can muster the concentration, something strange may happen. A particularly well-written passage may trigger it, or I may not be able to link it to any specific cause, but I will suddenly be aware that these events *really happened*. There isn't another way to put it; our language breaks down when we try to define the difference between "knowing" and "*really* knowing," but it exists nevertheless. What has happened is that I have been catapulted centuries back in time, to, say, the trial of Socrates, and I realize that these events actually took place. They aren't just words, a collection of facts, bare data. They are *real*.

—

No animal, as far as we know, can experience this. Animals can't even experience the most rudimentary form of being in two places at once, something millions of people do each night when they watch television. If no one plays with it and nothing else arouses its attention, a cat will stare into space and eventually fall asleep. Compared to it, the viewers of the worst sitcom are virtual Prousts. Years ago a popular book advised its readers to "be here now." All animals follow that sage recommendation. But it is clear that when most human beings find themselves in a physical space that does not demand their attention, the first thing they do is look for something to occupy themselves besides the four walls. They look, that is, for a *mental space* to occupy, an imaginative "here and now," which might be thousands of miles away, centuries in the past.

Wilson believes that the reason human beings crave imaginative experience—a "mental space"—is that we possess two brains. (Readers will recall our discussion of the split brain in chapter 17.) "My own belief is that we have two brains," Wilson writes,

> *so we can be in two places at the same time. Human beings are supposed to be capable of being in two places at the same time. Yet we have not quite discovered the "trick." When we do, we shall be a completely different kind of creature—no longer the same kind of human being who lives out his life so incompetently on this long suffering planet, but something far more powerful and purposeful.[3]*

In books like *Frankenstein's Castle*(1980) and *Access to Inner Worlds* (1983), Wilson spells out his reasons for why our "dual brain" allows us to experience duo-consciousness. Fundamentally it is for the same reason that Schwaller recognized in Egyptian hieroglyphics an expression of a "simultaneity of opposite states." As we have seen, the left-brain "scientist" focuses on the isolated "fact," while the right-brain "artist" absorbs pattern and "meaning." Usually the two are in conflict, and in our own fast-paced, highly outer-world oriented culture, the left brain is dominant, with the result that we "scan" the world, picking out the "facts" and absorbing little "meaning": we see a lot of trees but rarely the forest. Yet, in those infrequent moments when the two brains work together—either at times of deep relaxation or when the right brain, which moves slower than the left, is "speeded up" through interest or excitement—reality suddenly acquires an additional dimension. It becomes three-dimensional and not, as we usually see it, flat, abstract, and dull. In other words, when the two brains work together, the robot is temporarily shut off and we are in touch with *full* reality. That is why events we read of in a novel often seem paradoxically *more real* than those in "real life" and why we ourselves seem to occupy that imaginative world with an almost hallucinatory intensity. It is because we are allowing the right brain to supply the additional dimension. Wilson calls this process "completing," and at its most basic level it is how we "make sense" of the world, linking its disparate elements into a comprehensible whole, what contemporary neuroscientists call the "binding problem."

—

Wilson believes that when we master the "trick" of being in two places at once, of stepping out of time and space, the human race will have made an evolutionary leap. Strangely he sees other evidence for a major shift in human consciousness in an area most of us would consider fertile soil for the exact opposite: the dark world of crime. Earlier I mentioned the humanist psychologist Abraham Maslow, who is most famous for his notion of the "peak experience." Peak experiences, according to Maslow, are sudden bursts of "affirmation consciousness," and he believed they occur to most healthy, active people. They are a kind of psychological indicator that the individual is on the path of what Maslow called "self-actualization," a process of emotional and psychological maturity similar to Jung's "individuation." Wilson saw in Maslow's peak experience a confirmation of his own ideas about consciousness, as well as a corroboration of his belief in the power of the mind to stimulate itself. Maslow believed peaks could not be created at will, but Wilson was intrigued by the fact that when Maslow got his students *talking* about their past peaks, they began to have *more* peaks more frequently. Obviously, simply thinking about peak experiences could help trigger them, a step, at least, in the direction of generating them at will.

Wilson was also influenced by Maslow's idea of what he called "the hierarchy of needs." Maslow believed that human needs are arranged in a kind of ladder, with the most fundamental needs at the bottom, and "higher" needs at the top. Our most basic need, obviously, is for food. Then comes shelter, a home, some kind of "territory" that is our own. After this comes a need for love, sexual relations, the family, and friends. Then comes the need for what Maslow calls "self-esteem," to be *known*, recognized by your peers, appreciated by your workmates and friends. Maslow believed that as each lower need is met, the next higher need appears and makes its demands. So a starving person thinks only of food, but a homeless person with a full stomach pines for a little room, and so on.

Maslow believed that these needs are all recognized by standard psychology and that they are all what he termed "deficiency needs." They are all prompted by a lack of something: food, a home, sex, self-esteem. But he also believed that at the top of the hierarchy, a *different* kind of need appears, one that is not recognized by most orthodox psychologists. After the lower deficiency needs are met, Maslow recognized that in some people—those he called "self-actualizers," who tended to be a minority—a need for some form of *creative expression* became dominant. This could take the form of artistic creation, or it could be something as humble as a hobby—say a fascination with stamps. What characterizes the "self-actualizing" need, Maslow argued, is that it doesn't depend on something *outside* the individual, but is rather an expression of the individual self. Essentially it is an absorption in some activity *for its own sake,* and not as a means to an end—to fulfilling a lack. It is a desire to do something well, to give form to the creative potential of the individual. When Samuel Richardson began writing, it was because he needed money, but when he got carried away with *Pamela,* it was because he became completely absorbed in it and was writing for the sheer pleasure of creation. He was "self-actualizing."

Wilson realized that Maslow's self-actualization could be applied to a society or civilization as a whole. With this in mind, he recognized a curious fact: researching a history of murder, he recognized a clear shift in the *types* of murders he was reading about. Early killings were straightforwardly about gain, and often for something as simple as food. There were, in fact, several cases in which the murderer cannibalized his victims. Then it seemed that most of the murders Wilson researched involved the murderers somehow protecting their lifestyle, their homes and property. An embezzler would murder a business associate who had found him out, an adulterer would murder a mistress who threatened to tell his wife, or a confidence man would murder a string of women he serially married and whose property he would inherit. Then, toward the end of the nineteenth century, a totally new kind of murder appeared: the sex crime, brought to morbid prominence through the courtesy of Jack the Ripper. The Victorians who were shocked by the killings could not comprehend their motive; they spoke of "moral insanity" or saw them as a mad attack on "vice," the victims all being prostitutes. What they failed to see, because they had no previous experience of it, was that the murders were a kind of sex act in themselves, and that the Ripper, whoever he was, was driven by a powerful sexual craving, which could only be satisfied through total dominance over his victims. (Sadly, what was new and unthinkable for the Victorians is now commonplace for us.) And in the twentieth century, another new kind of murder emerged: the murder for fame, for recognition, to "become known." And toward the end of that troubled century, yet another kind of killing appeared, what we call the "motiveless murder," a kind of random, unpredictable spree that most of us lump under the name "serial killing."

Looking at this depressing survey of human inhumanity, Wilson was struck by a sudden insight. The history of murder paralleled Maslow's hierarchy of needs. There it was: food, the home, sex, self-esteem. But where did that leave us? Had we entered the age of the self-actualizing murder, murder as a creative act? Wilson knew, of course, that murder—any sort of crime—and self-actualization are mutually exclusive. Crime, he believes, is essentially a kind of cheating, a shortcut, a choice taken by individuals too weak to actually work for the things they desire. (Like Julian Jaynes, Wilson sees the roots of crime and cruelty in the sudden development of left-brain consciousness.) Most of us who desire recognition or love will take the necessary steps to get them. Criminals, however, don't have the patience or the maturity to do this and so try to "grab" what they want. And this is true not only of actual criminals, but of all weak personalities. Most of us stop short of actual violence, but in some cases the urge to fulfill these needs is so strong that a man will murder a celebrity in order to get his name in the news, or rape a woman in order to have possessed her.

But in each case, the shortcut that satisfied the criminals' needs ends up depriving them of both their freedom and the possibility of further development. No rapist can be seen as a self-actualizer.

Wilson recognized that crime is a kind of Jungian shadow of society, an unfortunate but possibly unavoidable by-product of the evolution of consciousness. And the nightmares of motiveless murders suggests to him that, paradoxical as it may sound, we may be moving into a new stage of development. The obsession with fame and celebrity that characterizes our popular culture is another sign that our society is moving up the ladder of Maslow's hierarchy. Forty years ago, sexual liberation was the battle cry. Today extramarital sex, nudity in films, homosexuality, lesbianism, and even sadomasochism are more or less accepted practices. In the 1960s, Andy Warhol famously said that in the future everyone will be famous for fifteen minutes. Now with television shows like *Big Brother* and countless talk shows where people clamor to reveal their dark secrets, this prediction seems to be coming true. Is it possible that, for all its drawbacks, the New Age movement, with us now for some thirty years, is an indication that we are beginning to move from the self-esteem level to that of self-actualization?

It may seem perverse to point to something as dark as murder to indicate that the human race may be on the brink of a major mutation. Yet, as Alfred North Whitehead remarked, the ideas that advance civilization all but wreck the society in which they occur. In the next section we will look at the work of another thinker who believes humanity is in the midst of a massive shift in its consciousness. One that may destroy our current civilization or that, just perhaps, we may emerge from with a vision of hope and integrity for the future.

PART FIVE

The Presence of Origin

CHAPTER TWENTY-FIVE

The Ascent of Mount Ventoux

Sometime in the year 1336, the Italian poet Francesco Petrarca, known to posterity as Petrarch, did something that no one in history had done before: he climbed a mountain to see the view.

Obviously people before Petrarch had climbed mountains, but it was always for some utilitarian reason. Hannibal crossed the Alps to attack Rome, and Moses climbed Mount Sinai to receive the word of the law from Jehovah. And thousands, maybe millions, of unnamed people before and since must have pushed their way over inhospitable peaks for dozens of reasons—in search of food, to escape marauding bandits, to discover fresh grazing land. But no one before Petrarch had gone to the trouble of climbing an uninviting and dangerous summit simply for what we would call aesthetic reasons. At least we have no record of anyone prior to Petrarch doing this.

As we saw in the last section, as late as the eighteenth century the mountains and other wild landscapes that today's vacationers seek out for pleasure and relaxation were, if possible, rigorously avoided, and the idea of climbing anything more arduous than a hillock would have prompted a groan of complaint from Dr. Johnson and just about everyone else, until Wordsworth and Coleridge made the pastime popular. It is difficult for us to grasp, but something as "obvious" to us as the enjoyment we receive from "taking in the view" of some scenic vista was, in Petrarch's time, utterly unknown. To put oneself at risk in order to do so was considered madness, or worse. For some minds it was even considered demonic.

In a letter to the Augustinian professor of theology Francesco Dionigi di Borgo San Sepolcro, the thirty-two-year-old Petrarch described his historic and unheard of outing. His choice was the formidable Mount Ventoux, an impressive French peak located northeast of Avignon, where the Rhone River separates the French Alps from the Cevennes. Nearby is the principal mountain range of central France, and the area around Mount Ventoux itself is rich in historical and esoteric significance. The Troubadours, the Albigensians, and the Cathars had all thrived in this area, giving the landscape an affinity with Gnostic ideas about the superiority of self-knowledge and experience over ignorance and blind faith. Whether Petrarch had this in mind when he made his ascent is unknown, but it is clear from his account that he believed that in some way he had *transgressed* against the law, both of nature and of God. He knows that what he has done has set him apart from other men. The idea of climbing the mountain has troubled him for years, ever since he was a child; it was a kind of secret dream that disturbed his soul. Now that he has finally done it, he is terrified.

"Yesterday," Petrarch told his friend the professor, "I climbed the highest mountain of our region, motivated solely by the wish to experience its renowned height. For many years this has been in my soul and, as you well know, I have roamed this region since my childhood." The mountain has always been in his sight, he tells the professor, and his desire had increased each day until it became so great that he decided to give way to it.

With his brother Gerardo, who accompanied him, Petrarch met an old shepherd on the way. When he informed the old man where they were headed, the shepherd "in a torrent of words, tried to dissuade us from the ascent, saying he had never heard of anyone risking such a venture." Petrarch ignored the old man's warnings, although as they began to scale the height some foreboding must have crept into his resolve. "While still climbing, I urged myself forward by the thought that what I experience today will surely benefit myself as well as *many others* who desire the blessed life."

It is clear from Petrarch's letter that when he finally reached the top he experienced some sort of emotional and psychic shakeup. The letter becomes agitated; tenses shift, and the language takes on a disturbed character, as if simply the memory of his experience was enough to throw his consciousness into confusion and disarray. The "unaccustomed wind" swirls around him, and he and Gerardo must hold themselves against its force. But more than the powerful wind, what frightens Petrarch with its sublime majesty is the hitherto unseen *space* that opens up around him. He is dazzled by the "wide, freely shifting vistas." Their disturbing expanse shocks him and he is "immediately awestruck."

> *I look: the clouds lay beneath my feet. . . . I look toward Italy . . . and sigh at the sight of the Italian sky. . . . Then I turn westward; in vain my eye searches for the ridge of the Pyrenees, boundary between France and Spain. . . . To my right I see the mountains of Lyon, to the left the Mediterranean surf washes against Marseille before it breaks on Aigues-Mortes. Though the distance was considerable, we could see clearly; the Rhone itself lay beneath our gaze.*

And then, at that moment, Petrarch experiences what is for him a profound synchronicity. Gripped by the vision of space that stretches out before him, feeling—rightly, as we shall see—that he has stepped through a portal into *another world,* he looks for some support, and reaches for his copy of Augustine's *Confessions.* Opening it at random, his eye falls on a passage that reads, "And men went forth to behold high mountains and the mighty surge of the sea, and the broad stretches of the rivers and the inexhaustible ocean, and the paths of the stars, and so doing, lose themselves in wonderment."[1]

It was as if the fates were dotting the i's and crossing the t's: what you are doing now, Petrarch, is not some random, chance event, they said. It is of deep, perhaps even cosmic, significance. After this, things will be different.

—

And this was one time at least when the fates were right. For what Petrarch's terrible ascent of Mount Ventoux—in the true, accurate sense of the world "terrible"—inaugurated was not simply the beginning of ski lodges and vista points in the Rockies and other mountain chains, but a new, unprecedented appreciation of space. If, as Owen Barfield suggests, in medieval times, human beings felt themselves to be part of a tapestry, or felt they wore nature around them like a garment, when Petrarch made his mad ascent of Mount Ventoux, it was as if he were tearing that garment from him and stepping out of the tapestry. The effect must have been as disorienting as that of an inhabitant of Edwin Abbot's Flatland who suddenly popped out into a world of three dimensions. It was not only a crazy thing to do, as the people of Petrarch's time clearly thought; it was also something more. For Petrarch had taken the first step in a completely new understanding of the world—an understanding that we accept without a moment's thought and take for granted, but that, like so much of our experience, is actually the result of a profound change in human consciousness, a shift so radical that the term "evolution" does not truly apply to it. "Mutation" would be more accurate. In this case it is the mutation from the flat, two-dimensional "embedded" world of the Middle Ages to the world that we experience every day, the world of distance, "empty" space, "vanishing points," and receding horizons. The world, that is, of *perspective*. This, and not the Russian orbiting of the satellite Sputnik in 1957, was the true beginning of the "space age."

One of the most important thinkers to recognize the nature of this shift and its significance for human evolution was the Swiss cultural philosopher Jean Gebser (1905–1973), author of one of the most challenging works of philosophy in the twentieth century, *Ursprung und Gegenwart,* translated into English in 1984 as *The Ever-Present Origin.* Although little known in English-speaking countries, Gebser has a reputation in Europe, where his work is seen in the long-standing tradition of polymath cultural theorists, thinkers like Oswald Spengler, Ernst Cassirer, and Erich Kahler. There is something in the German mind that moves irresistibly toward a systematic and holistic view, a drive to see the world as a *totality*. Perhaps the greatest and most well known example of this is the philosophy of Hegel. It is not a style of thought favored by British or American thinkers; in the English-speaking world today, the literary critic George Steiner perhaps comes closest to embodying it.

In recent years, with the rise of schools like deconstructionism and poststructualism, this search for unity has come under severe criticism, and the idea that a single mind can encompass the multiple and diverse elements of contemporary existence has become laughable, when it is not attacked as an expression of intellectual totalitarianism. It is a shame that Gebser did not live long enough to see the unprecedented success that thinkers like Jacques Derrida and Michel Foucault enjoyed in the 1980s, and the influence their work still exerts on academics and the culture at large in the U.S. and Britain. (In their home country of France, however, they have both been considered passé for some time.) For one thing, Gebser's remarks on their philosophies, both centered on fracture, disruption, and the immanent *lack* of totality in human experience, would, we can safely assume, have been rewarding. But even more, their embrace, as well as that of their many followers, of a ruptured, broken, *fragmented* worldview, would have been for Gebser simply more evidence for a belief he put forth decades before anyone had ever thought of "deconstructing" anything.

Gebser believed that since about the turn of the nineteenth century, Western civilization has been in the death throes of what he calls its current "structure of consciousness"—in this case, the structure he calls the "mental-rational." There have been three structures prior to this one (we will discuss these shortly), and we are now at the beginning stages of a fifth, what Gebser calls the "integral" structure. The "mental-rational" structure began, Gebser believes, in Greece around 1225 B.C. and is symbolized by the mythical image of the goddess Athena springing forth "fully grown" from the head of Zeus—a painful *wrenching* of a new form of consciousness out of an older one, reminiscent of the "break-down of the bicameral mind" described by Julian Jaynes.[2] Athena, the goddess of wisdom, bursts forth armed with sword and shield when Prometheus—who stole fire from the gods—splits Zeus's head with an axe. From the beginning, the clear, decisive, *directed* thinking that we associate with rationality is linked to aggression and force. (Again, the link to Jaynes's ideas is clear, also to Leonard Shlain's.) By the beginning of the fifth century B.C., the transition to this new structure of consciousness is complete, one result being the emergence of a new way of thinking, philosophy, out of the older mythical mentality. Gebser notes that the period as a whole coincides with the philosopher Karl Jaspers's "axial age," a time between 600 and 200 B.C. when the fundamental concerns of the Western mind first appeared.

This mental structure, Gebser argued, reached a kind of apex with the rise of perspective—inaugurated with Petrarch's mountain expedition—and has been in a steady decline ever since, notwith-standing the achievements of modern science. The self-reflexive work of Derrida and Foucault, in which, ouroborus-like, Western thought bites its own tail and, in its passion for analysis, begins to *take itself apart,* would have struck Gebser as probably the last gasp of a speedily deteriorating form of consciousness. As we will see, the rise of "postmodernism" in general, with its taste for irony, parody, the disjointed, and the fragmentary, is good evidence in favor of Gebser's argument that at the start of the twenty-first century we are moving headlong into a new form of consciousness, a consciousness he believed would manifest itself in a new experience of *time.*

⟶

Jean Gebser was born in Posen, Prussia, in 1905. As his inter-preter Georg Feuerstein points out, the event was not without coin-cidence.[3] In that year Albert Einstein formulated his special theory of relativity, a theory that would revolutionize science's under-standing of time. Five years earlier, Sigmund Freud had published his first major work, *The Interpretation of Dreams,* which opened a door on a new understanding of the psyche. The same period saw

Max Planck complete his theory of the quantum, which would lead to a total abandonment of classical physics, and Edmund Husserl found the philosophical discipline of phenomenology, which laid the groundwork for later developments like existentialism. Feuerstein also points out that 1905 saw the birth of another philosopher of consciousness, Erich Neumann. For a thinker concerned with sudden changes in human consciousness, Gebser certainly appeared at an apt point in history.

Gebser's life reads like a classic example of an early twentieth-century European intellectual. Like many he was caught up in the chaos of war. Several times it uprooted him, and he felt at first hand the rise of fascism. An early experience helped him deal with the uncertainty that characterized a world ravaged by conflict, economic depression, and the dark forces of totalitarianism. While a young boy at a preparatory school, Gebser learned how to "swim free." Jumping from the high dive, he discovered that his fall into the deep pool was also a leap into the unknown. "It was then," he later wrote, "that I lost my fear in the face of uncertainty. A sense of confidence began to mature within me which later determined my entire bearing and attitude toward life, a confidence in the sources of our strength of being, a confidence in their immediate accessibility. This is an inner security that is fully effective only when we are able to do whatever we do not for our own sake."[4] Years later this confidence in the face of uncertainty would form the basis of Gebser's notion of *Urvertrauen,* "primal trust," the deep sense of well-being and acceptance of life that is the counterpart of *Urangst,* "primal fear," the underlying anxiety that characterizes most of our attitudes toward the world.

Like many who find themselves thrust onto the path of spiritual adventure, Gebser found ample opportunities to test his resolve and equanimity. Born into an aristocratic family who had lived in Thuringia (Duchy of Franconia) for centuries, as a boy he was educated at Breslau, Königsberg, and the renowned preparatory school at Rossleben. His father, thirty-five at the time of Gebser's birth, was a lawyer by profession, but his great loves were literature, writing, and scholarship. His mother, twelve years younger than her husband, was beautiful, charming, and vivacious, yet she displayed a streak of self-seeking and capriciousness that led to much conflict at home. When his father died, the teenage Jean retreated into a world of books and ideas, but this protective cocoon was soon burst; almost immediately after his father's death, Jean was made to leave home and school and begin an apprenticeship at a bank. Although he hated it, the dutiful boy fulfilled his obligations. But two years later, when offered a permanent position, Gebser declined and took his first big step into the unknown, throwing off the comforts of "job security" for the uncertain joys of literature. With a friend, he started a publishing company, and a year later they launched a literary journal, *Der Fischzug,* in whose pages Gebser's early poems first saw print.

Probably the major influence on Gebser at this time was the poetry of Rilke, whose theme of *Herzwerk,* "heart work," is an early example of what Gebser means by "primal trust." When, in the *Duino Elegies,* Rilke calls us "wasters of sorrows," it is the acceptance of the *totality* of life—good and bad—that he has in mind, and this is exactly what Gebser means by his "confidence" in the face of uncertainty. In Rilke's poetry he also discovered a response to an idea that had begun to obsess him: the thought of suicide. Like many young and sensitive men during the dark years of the Weimar Republic, Gebser's "primal trust" was repeatedly put to the test. His family lost their savings in the economic collapse, and the despair and hopelessness that would help put Hitler in power and fuel the rise of pessimistic philosophies like existentialism presented formidable challenges. Rilke's vision of a state of being in which one could affirm *everything*—the *dennoch preisen,* "praise in spite of," embodied in the Angel of the *Duino Elegies*—convinced Gebser that the dark mood engulfing his contemporaries was to be rejected. Likewise a reading of Freud turned his mind away from the provincial concerns of the youth movements of his day—some of which later helped swell the ranks of the Nazis—and introduced an objective, scientific sensibility to complement his growing literary genius. Classes at the University of Berlin, where he came under the guidance of the Catholic philosopher Romano Guardini, helped to broaden his already polymath appetite for knowledge.

In 1929, Gebser had another opportunity to test his "primal trust": a confrontation with Hitler's Brown Shirts convinced him that it was time to leave Germany. The next year saw him traveling to Florence, then back to Germany, then to Paris, then to southern France. At this point, he changed his name from the German Hans to the French Jean—a sign he had rejected his Teutonic past and the nationalism that had overtaken his homeland. Like Nietzsche, Gebser was more European than German; both rejected the obscure, abstract style of thought associated with German thinkers like Kant and Hegel in favor of the clarity and light of the Mediterranean. Gebser's mind, again like Nietzsche's, moved beyond borders and nationalist ideologies in an attempt to embrace a new way of thinking. The Europe of today, seeking to find a new, unified identity, could find in Gebser an articulate and convincing spokesman.

In 1931, Gebser decided to settle in Spain. It was yet another leap into uncertainty; aside from financial worries, he had no command of Spanish, and his first priority was to learn the language. He met the challenge successfully, a clear sign of his natural linguistic ability, and later translated the poetry of his friend Federico Garcia Lorca into German, along with the work of other poets and political writers. Geber's relationship with Lorca was close. At a special gathering in Madrid in 1936, he heard the poet read from "The House of Bernarda Alba," and Lorca later worked with Gebser on a translation of Frank Wedekind's expressionist play *Spring Awakening*. Gebser became fluent enough in Spanish to write a book of poetry in his adopted tongue, *Poesias de la Tarde* (1936); his study of Rilke's experience in Spain, *Rilke und Spanien* (1940), which first mentions his notion of an emerging "aperspectival consciousness," was also originally written in Spanish. He also translated into Spanish the work of another poet in whom he saw signs of the incipient new consciousness, Friedrich Hölderlin. His facility with the language also eased his financial worries by securing him a position in the Republic's Ministry of Education.

Gebser's time in Spain was crucial for another reason. In the winter of 1932/33, he experienced a kind of insight, a "lightning-like inspiration" which later crystallized into the central theme of his *magnum opus*: the notion that a new kind of consciousness was beginning to appear in the West. But his journey through chaos was not yet over, and between 1932 and 1949, when the first part of *The Ever-Present Origin* appeared, there would be several more leaps into uncertainty.

One such leap arguably saved his life: in the fall of 1936, Gebser left Spain for the French border twelve hours before his Madrid apartment was bombed. War had erupted once again, this time between the Republicans and Franco's Insurgents. At the French border he was stopped and arrested, and there is a good chance he would have been executed had it not been for the influence of his Spanish friends. One of these friends did not share his good fortune; Federico Garcia Lorca was brutally murdered by the fascists. Strangely, it was while awaiting a similar fate at the hands of Franco's army that Arthur Koestler had the mystical insight that would lead to his own explorations in the mechanisms of consciousness, brilliantly presented in his seminal work *The Act of Creation* (1963).[5] Like Gebser, Koestler missed a premature death by a hairsbreadth; the experience turned him away from Marxism and political concerns, and focused his mind on science and the question of human evolution. Gebser, too, was changed by his experience. Although a fervent spokesman for personal and political freedom, he found himself occupied more and more with broader, more universal concerns.

When Gebser finally arrived in Paris, he was armed with several of Lorca's poems and surrealistic drawings; he later translated and published the poems with a psychological commentary in 1949. He quickly found himself at home in a circle that included Paul Éluard, Louis Aragon, André Malraux, and Picasso, whose studio in the Latin Quarter he visited. Paris then, just before the occupation, was a bleak, depressed city, home to a unique collection of intellectual and artistic personalities. It was the Paris of Sartre, Camus, and the Surrealists, but also of Gebser's older compatriot Walter Benjamin—then an obscure Jewish critic, now the focus of a worldwide cult. It was also home to the enigmatic Russian teacher G. I. Gurdjieff and his brilliant pupil, the poet René Daumal, author of the spiritual classic *Mount Analogue*. For

Gebser, a German who had rejected his homeland in favor of the defeated country, those years were lean, a time of personal challenge and suffering. His Parisian tenure, however, was brief, and history soon had him moving on once again.

In August 1939, Gebser entered Swiss territory two hours before the borders with France closed. For intellectuals like him, the situation in France was untenable and Switzerland promised safety. He was one of the lucky ones; a year later, after climbing a mountain pass and being arrested at the Spanish border, a depressed and panicky Walter Benjamin committed suicide by taking an overdose of morphine. Switzerland was the last stop on Gebser's decade-long *Wanderjahre,* but it was not the end of his spiritual travels. The Paris he had left behind had been obsessed with politics—with Marx, fascism, and the inevitable splintering and squabbling that plagues revolutionary cliques. (The backstabbing and mudslinging that dominated Sartre and Camus' relationship after the war is characteristic of the milieu.) When he left France, Gebser found not only political and personal freedom; in Switzerland he could discover the inner space necessary to explore the implications of his insight in Spain.

One of the first manifestations of this was an article written in 1941 and later expanded and published as a book in 1944: *Der grammatische Spiegel* (The Grammatical Mirror). In it Gebser collected his thoughts on an insight that had occupied him for many years: the recognition that the grammatical structure of European languages like German and French had in recent times "mutated" and was showing signs of a shift in thinking, indicating the appearance of a new kind of thought in Western consciousness. Like Owen Barfield, Gebser saw that language provided good evidence for an evolution of consciousness. And also like Barfield, he saw the clearest indication of this in poetry—in this case, that of Rilke. But whereas Barfield focused on the past history of language in order to show the roots of our present consciousness, Gebser concentrated on what he saw as an unprecedented form of thought fitfully emerging then, which would soon appear in full as a new "structure of consciousness." As his older contemporary Martin Heidegger said, "Language is the house of being." Like Heidegger,

Gebser would use language itself to spark a recognition of its own possibilities and to turn a sympathetic consciousness to awareness of its own future. Also like Heidegger, he often used gnomic neologisms that can make grasping his insights difficult.

Gebser's polymath mind soon reached out beyond poetry for signs of the new consciousness. In 1941/42, he wrote *Abendlandische Wandlung* (Transformation of the Orient) in which he argued that changes in the sciences, inaugurated by Einstein's revolutionary work in the year of Gebser's birth, showed clear indications of a major shift in human consciousness. In the work of Einstein, Planck, Heisenberg, and Freud, as well as the parapsychological investigations of J. B. Rhine and the depth psychology of his friend C. G. Jung, Gebser saw a break with the linear, mechanistic paradigm of the classical scientific worldview, and a new awareness and expression of the "aperspectival consciousness" rising in the Western mind. That this focus on simultaneity and nonlinear time had already percolated through to modern literature Gebser knew from his reading of novelists like Marcel Proust, Thomas Mann, Robert Musil, James Joyce, and Hermann Broch, all of whom had abandoned the strict linear narrative of the nineteenth-century novel, in favor of a "birds-eye view" approach—a development heralded by Ouspensky's forays into the "fourth dimension." The reality of "other times and places," made tangible by Proust's madeleine, paralleled, Gebser knew, the most recent discoveries in what would soon become known as the "new physics."[6]

Convinced, like R. M. Bucke, that human consciousness was experiencing a breakthrough, Gebser turned his eye to our past, looking for evidence of previous transformations. The result was *Foundations of the Aperspectival World,* the first part of his major work, published as part one of *The Ever-Present Origin* in 1949. Part two, *Manifestations of the Aperspectival World: An Attempt At the Concretion of the Spiritual,* was completed soon after and first published in 1953. For the remaining two decades of his life, Gebser delved deeper and deeper into the implications of his insight in Spain in the 1930s, drawing from that sudden "personal view" an increasingly profound vision of the possibilities open to us on the brink of a planetary transformation.

His last years in Switzerland were filled with lectures, travel, conferences, and symposiums. He visited India, the Far East, North and South America. Just as his reflections on contemporary science were informed by his many meetings with physicists, biologists, and other professionals, the aim of Gebser's "journey to the East" was to give him some firsthand experience of a world whose consciousness, he believed, though very different from ours, complemented that of the West. Indeed, in his book *Asien lachelt anders* (Asia Smiles Differently), published in 1968, Gebser, although sympathetic to "Eastern thought," warned, as C. G. Jung had, against any superficial adoption of it by Westerners—an admonition no doubt prompted by the mass popularity of "Eastern mysticism" among the burgeoning youth culture of the 1960s. That Gebser was no stranger to Oriental thought is clear from his writings, as well as from the fact that he was a familiar face at the celebrated Eranos Conferences, along with Jung, Erich Neumann, Mircea Eliade, Heinrich Zimmer, and other scholars.

The "East" also had another significant meaning for Gebser. In 1961, during a visit to Sarnath in India, the legendary site of Gautama Buddha's first sermon, Gebser had another lightning-like inspiration, this one of a more personal nature. He called it his *satori* experience—a labeling later corroborated by the Zen scholar D. T. Suzuki. As Georg Feuerstein points out, Gebser, for some reason, wanted to keep this experience a secret, and it was not until 1971 that he wrote of it in a letter to Feuerstein. Perhaps he was concerned that Western intellectuals' prejudice again nonrational mentalities would find in this spiritual insight sufficient reason to ignore his challenging ideas. Or, perhaps, as C. G. Jung felt about his interest in the occult, Gebser was concerned with the damage such an admission would make to his academic reputation. Given the unrestrained and guru-seeking atmosphere of the 1960s, Gebser may have wanted to avoid any chance of being seen as a "mystical teacher." In any event, the experience had profound significance for him. He speaks of it being a "transfiguration and irradiation of the indescribable, unearthly, transparent 'Light' . . . a spiritual clarity,

a quiet jubilation, a knowledge of invulnerability, a primal trust. .
. . Since Sarnath I am as if recast, inwardly, since then everything is
in its proper place."[7] As we will see, the notions of "spiritual light,"
"transparency," and "diaphaneity," one of Gebser's neologisms,
hold for him special significance as signs of the incipient aperspectival consciousness structure.

Gebser's *satori,* like his earlier faith in uncertainty, would serve
him in good stead in later years. Recognition of his ideas began to
spread outside his circle of friends and colleagues; but a punishing
work schedule took its toll, as did his awareness that the West
would soon be facing the most demanding challenge of its existence—"The crisis we are experiencing today," he wrote in 1949,
"is not just a European crisis . . . , it is a crisis of the world and
mankind such as has occurred previously only during pivotal junc-
tures." In 1966 Gebser suffered a complete physical collapse; a
progressively worsening case of asthma forced him to curtail his
travels and minimize his work. He was unable to appreciate the
chair in comparative civilizations created for him at the University
of Salzburg in 1967.

Although he never recovered his health, Gebser continued to
produce more books, attempting to convey the central significance
of his ideas to a wider audience. He was aware that a younger generation, eager for guidance and more amenable than their elders to
ideas about other forms of consciousness, had arisen in the last few
years. (Like Nietzsche, Gebser always wrote not only for tomorrow, but for the day after tomorrow.) The work of Sri Aurobindo
and Teilhard de Chardin, both of whom he acknowledged as fellow investigators of the new consciousness, had gained wide readership among the counterculture. Just months before his death,
Gebser wrote in the preface to the 1973 edition of his great work,
"The principal subject of the book, proceeding from man's altered
relationship to time, is the new consciousness, and to this those of
the younger generation are keenly attuned." That he was aware of
some of the retrograde aspects of the counterculture is clear; as we
will see, his reflections on what he called the "magical" consciousness structure and the dangers of "group consciousness," whose

effects he had experienced firsthand during the rise of the Nazis, are applicable to some of the more extreme manifestations of irrationality that arose in the 1960s. But Gebser's "primal trust" shone through powerfully in his last years, and he was convinced that whatever "ominous events" had occurred since *The Ever-Present Origin* first appeared were outweighed by the more positive insights and achievements, which "by virtue of their spiritual potency, cannot remain without effect."[8]

Gebser died on May 14, 1973, convinced that within the next few decades the human race would move toward an event that he believed could "only be described as a "global catastrophe," yet equally convinced that if sufficient will and insight were brought to the task, the crisis could be averted—or, at least, survived. In this respect, his thinking echoes Rudolf Steiner's vision of a coming "Ahrimanic future," an age of total scientistic materialism, bereft of spirit. Since Hiroshima, humankind's Cassandras have increased, both in number and in volume, and it would be easy to relegate both Gebser's and Steiner's warnings and prophecies to the dire rantings of yet another shrill jeremiad. But this would be a mistake. The cliff edge our civilization is moving toward is the end destination of "an increase in technological feasibility inversely proportional to man's sense of responsibility." Yet, a man without hope does not write a massive work of scholarship and insight arguing how our cultural suicide may be avoided. The book, he said, was "addressed to each and every one, particularly those who live knowledge, and not just those who create it."[9] It was not, Gebser meant, a work of scholarship aimed solely at scholars, but an attempt to map out the possibilities and potentials of the future, a guide to help those few who accept the challenge to consciously find their way through the ruins of the old consciousness and the strange landscapes of the new. Thirty years after Gebser's death, we are living the transformation he predicted.

Chapter Twenty-Six

—

Structures of Consciousness

The Ever-Present Origin is a massive work of some six hundred pages, filled with charts, illustrations, a dense etymological appendix, and chapter notes often numbering more than a hundred. It is a work of immense learning, erudition, and wisdom, and assumes the reader has a familiarity with the history and culture of Western civilization, as well as some knowledge of the more esoteric strains of human creativity. Its scope covers religion, mythology, philosophy, literature, science, history, jurisprudence, psychology, and what today we would call the paranormal. Along with presenting a daunting synthesis of all human cultural activity for the last few millennia, it is an attempt to, in Ouspensky's terse phrase, "think in other categories," a confident leap into ontological uncertainty, with little more than poetic insight and intuition and the unwieldy tool of language as guides. Gebser is not alone in recognizing that one of the chief tasks of philosophical thought in the twentieth and now twenty-first centuries is to augment our language—informed, as it is, with the metaphysical bias of our currently deteriorating mental-rational structure—in order to open it to the new *meanings* presented by the emerging aperspectival consciousness. Hence his already rich work is filled with new coinages, whose meanings are not always apparent or, when they seem to be readily comprehensible, are found to be more difficult than anticipated. Further, Gebser, like Martin Heidegger, uses familiar words in an unfamiliar way and engages in lengthy and, at times, abstruse etymological analyses. Readers may at first be mystified by recurring terms like "origin," "aperspectival," "waring," "integrality," "time-free," "diaphaneity," "ego-free," "latency," and many more.

Those coming to the book for the first time will be thankful for the indispensable glossary that Georg Feuerstein has appended to his sympathetic, insightful, and sometimes critical introduction to Gebser's ideas, *Structures of Consciousness*. That there will be many more readers seems apparent. Along with informing Feuerstein's own widely read books on Hindu philosophy, Gebser's ideas are a central influence on another popular writer on the evolution of consciousness, Ken Wilber, considered by many to be one of the intellectual heavyweights of the New Age. Sites devoted to Gebser's ideas can be found on the Internet, and a school of "integral philosophy," including the work of scholars and philosophers like Allan Combs and Noel Barstad, is disseminating them to a wider, English-speaking readership.

The value of this spread of Gebser's philosophy has, however, been questioned. In one of his more recent books, *Coming Into Being: Artifacts and Texts in the Evolution of Consciousness* (1998), the cultural theorist William Irwin Thompson criticizes Wilber's "appropriation" of Gebser, and bemoans the fact that Wilber's California students prefer his self-help version of Gebser's difficult thought to its more demanding source. Feuerstein himself, remarking on the loss that many felt at Gebser's passing, said that "Socratic spirits like Gebser typically live before their time . . . [and] are, therefore, never fashionable. If they were to become fashionable their cause would be lost, for undoubtedly their vision would be vulgarized."[1] In another context, Algis Mickunas, one of the English translators of *The Ever-Present Origin,* has commented critically on the attraction Gebser has for "seekers for a new age and a saving spirituality" and has distanced his own work on Gebser from what he sees as a warranted but limited appreciation.[2]

Perhaps, as Gebser believed, origin is preferable to its later developments. Yet, although he struggled against the very vulgarization that troubled Georg Feuerstein, he was also wary of any kind of "spiritual elite" and warned of any misinterpretation of his work that would include it under the rubric of "Nietzsche and the Gnostics, whose superiority doctrines include claims of power and similarity to the divine."[3] With its Christian stamp—another aspect Gebser shares with Rudolf Steiner—his "integral consciousness" avoids any charge of hubris. Yet, it is also true that the demands placed on one willing to endure the emerging transformation of consciousness are heavy. Gebser warned that if we do not overcome the coming crisis, it will overcome us, "and only someone who has overcome himself is truly able to overcome,"[4] an admonition not readily palatable to a generation bred on psychobabble and the spiritual quick fix. This is the Goldilocks syndrome in another form: vulgarization or elitism, popular movements that appeal to many but lack any spiritual punch, or inner circles of initiates who too easily succumb to notions of evolutionary superiority. Finding the "just right" middle ground between these two is, as can be imagined, not easy.

Gebser, I believe, hoped that his vision of a new consciousness could help transcend this binary trap, the "either-or" paradigmatic of the consciousness structure that, according to him, we are currently exhausting. As the crisis he warned of was inevitable and not limited to the concerns of any esoteric elite, it strikes me that to err on the side of vulgarization, however much our more subtle sensibilities may be offended, is the lesser evil. That more people know of his work today than did thirty years ago can only be a good thing. Hence the inevitably inadequate summary of his ideas that follows is presented in good faith.

In its densely packed pages, *The Ever-Present Origin* charts the history and evolution of human consciousness, from its earliest appearance in protohuman hominids to the cultural achievements of the first half of the twentieth century—and having said that I must immediately add a disclaimer. For Gebser both the notions of "history" and "evolution" as we understand them are charged with the deficient mode of the dissolving "mental-rational" consciousness structure; hence they are radically biased and inadequate to characterize the process by which the different consciousness structures "mutate" and emerge from their perennial source, Gebser's "ever-present origin." To explain the process by which consciousness structures emerge using the deficient vocabulary of only one structure is, as we have seen in our discussion of participatory consciousness, similar to trying to explain the origin of a novel in the contents of the novel itself. "History" and "evolution" are not standpoints outside of the process they are trying to explain; they are products of the modern period (the mental-rational consciousness structure) and are, Gebser argues, characterized by a linear understanding of time, anchored in a "beginning" and moving, in some sense, toward an "end."

To be sure, contemporary historians and evolutionists have abandoned any teleological notion of their subject, and the idea that history "marches on" from its primitive beginnings in a neat, orderly progression to the present, or that evolution has followed a similar trajectory, is no longer considered tenable. Indeed, for some "postmodern" thinkers, "history" itself has ended, not in the sense of Francis Fukuyama, by reaching its "goal"—the globalization of liberalism—but by no longer constituting an intelligible subject of discourse. According to these thinkers, there no longer seems to be a comprehensible entity we can call "history"—a fate that has befallen several hitherto stable concepts, like "the state," "art," "philosophy," even "man." But this is a relatively recent development and, far from being an argument against Gebser's view, is, indeed, evidence for it: our "post-everything" culture is merely the clearest sign that the dominant consciousness structure of the last few centuries is rapidly breaking up. Gebser's view differs from postmodern understandings of history and evolution in that, rather than simply abandoning classical linear notions in favor of random, ruptured, basically meaningless models, he embeds his consciousness structures in an atemporal source, what he calls "origin."

What Gebser means by origin is difficult to convey in a short space—a problem we face with each of his central insights. To understand any one of his coinages we need to understand the others; the definitions and meanings are so intimately interlinked that it could be said that Gebser's entire thought can be drawn out through the process of articulating one of his neologisms. This is so because of the key problem in dealing with "new" modes of thought: language.

In trying to grasp a radically new kind of consciousness using, as we are forced to, concepts forged by our familiar "old" mode of thinking, we are caught in an exercise that seems self-defeating— rather like trying to bang a nail into a wall using the claw end of the hammer. (Ouspensky experienced something of this problem when he recognized that "a man can go mad from one ashtray.") In trying to do this, we are employing the very modes of thought we are trying to "subvert." Nietzsche was perhaps the first to recognize the limits of the "prison house of language," and subsequent philosophers have tried a variety of means to escape from it. (The situation is similar to that presented by Kant and the *Ding-an-sich*.) Wittgenstein was so frustrated by our inability to say anything other than tautologies that he declared philosophy a disease of language. Later thinkers took to more graphic expedients; Derrida's already unreadable "texts" are peppered with "erasures," omissions, and "crossing-outs" in his attempts to avoid a language of "being." The difference here is that, in different ways, both Wittgenstein and Derrida leave "nothing" in place of the "metaphysical" meanings they reject—Wittgenstein retreating into language as it is used "every day" (whatever that may mean) and Derrida into an endless cascade of *difference*. Gebser, however, does not merely "empty" metaphysical language; he fills the old skins with a new, transfiguring wine. He escapes the prison house of language not by retreating into silence or "absence," but by increasing the size of the prison until it resembles something much more like a cathedral.

"Origin," according to Georg Feuerstein, is "the ever-present reality . . . by nature divine and spiritual" out of which the different structurations of consciousness unfold in space-time.[5] It is atemporal and nonspatial, existing outside time and space—insofar as something nonspatial can be "outside." The origin, for Gebser, is "before all time" and is the "entirety of the very beginning," just as the present is "the entirety of everything temporal," including "yesterday, today, tomorrow, and even the pre-temporal and timeless."[6] It is "sheer presence," a primal spiritual radiance whose luminosity is obscured by the lesser light of the consciousness structures that proceed from it. In this sense it is like the Pleroma mentioned earlier, which also exists outside of the created world, and is indeed the source and support of that world.

Some readers may find it helpful to think of Gebser's origin in terms of the physicist David Bohm's notion of an "implicate order," which is likewise an atemporal unity out of which our present universe of space-time—and, Bohm suggests, other universes as well—"unfolds." To "picture" this, Bohm offers an image that may be useful: he suggests that the unmanifest implicate order manifests explicate "worlds," like our own, rather like those Japanese paper toys that, when dropped into water, "unfold" into various shapes. The pellet contains the form, yet the form remains invisible until it is released by the water.[7] Gebser is saying something similar when he speaks of his consciousness structures "unfolding" out of origin. They are contained within it, in a state of "latency," which Gebser calls the "demonstrable presence of the future," a condition that is true of each of the consciousness structures that emerge: each exists in potential in the structure prior to it. For our lives as a whole this is a powerful insight: each of our tomorrows emerges from all of our todays. And, as a student of G. I. Gurdjieff once remarked, the whole point of "work on oneself" is to ensure that your tomorrow is not merely a repetition of today.

Gebser is clear that it is a mistake to think of origin as a simple beginning; it is, as he remarks of the ancient symbol of the yin-yang, "a preforming and primal paradigm of Being . . . not just pre-human, that is pre-mankind, but pre-tellurian, emerging from a 'time' when the earth did not yet 'exist.'"[8] In this sense, Gebser's origin shares much with Rudolf Steiner's contention that "any transformation in the material aspect of the Earth is a manifestation of spiritual forces lying behind matter. But if we go further and further back in time . . . we eventually arrive at a point in evolution where matter first began to exist. This material element developed out of the spiritual. Before this point, only the spiritual element was present."[9] Like Steiner, Gebser believes that the development of consciousness has proceeded through a *progression* away from its source, origin. Hence he rejects interpretations of the unfolding of consciousness structures in terms of "progress" or of the linked idea of "evolution." But also like Steiner, Gebser believes that the ultimate unfolding of his consciousness structures—whose first stages we are currently experiencing—will mean a *return* to origin, to the spiritual sources of being.

For the Viennese satirist Karl Kraus, "Origin is the goal." And for Kraus, as well as for Gebser and other thinker-poets like

Goethe, being "original" means drawing one's creative energies from the primal source. Our own ideas about originality, however, differ from this considerably; since the nineteenth century and the rise of the myth of the avant-garde, being "original" has come to mean being absolutely "new." An "original" idea is one that has "never been done before," and inevitably the gauge of this became how much the bourgeois were shocked by what one produced. (It was precisely this that troubled Owen Barfield when he thought about the future of the imagination.) By now, however, such attempts do little more than numb the audience they are designed to impress, while instilling an appetite for the gross and tasteless— Damien Hirst's dissected animals, far from being "original," are preeminent examples of an exhausted gesture. Origin, for Gebser, has nothing to do with adolescent ideas about being shocking, or with the ever receding horizon of the "new." Origin, he tells us, is something always at hand. Although in a chronological sense the earliest human beings were "closer" to it—as we will see shortly— being atemporal and nonspatial, it is never removed from us. The central characteristic of the emerging "aperspectival integral" consciousness structure, Gebser tells us, is that within it, the preceding consciousness structures are made "transparent," thus allowing the primal "ever-present" radiance of origin to shine through. Just as Steiner's Jupiter, Venus, and Vulcan planetary incarnations will be a recapitulation of "older" forms of consciousness *integrated* with our present Earth "waking consciousness," so Gebser's integral consciousness structure is a harmonizing and reorganization of the previous four structures. (We have seen a similar notion of a recapitulation *plus* in Andreas Mavromatis's speculations on the future of hypnagogia.)

Gebser calls the first consciousness structure to emerge from origin the "archaic." It is "zero-dimensional" and, for all intents and purposes, is practically identical with its source, being little more than the first slight ripple of difference between origin and its latent unfolding. According to Gebser the archaic structure is characterized by the identity of consciousness with the world. It is, in terms of Owen Barfield's account of the evolution of consciousness, a time of complete and total participation, prior to the initial split giving rise to language. Hence, there is little to be said about this structure—not because it is uninteresting, but because the possibility of "saying" had yet to arise. It is a state, as Gebser writes, "akin, if not identical, to the original state of biblical paradise: a time where the soul is yet dormant, a time of complete non-differentiation of man and the universe."[10] It is Erich Neumann's uroboric consciousness, a seamless unity between human being and world. Georg Feuerstein calls it a "fundamental dimness," a "dimly lit mist devoid of shadow."[11] The condition is similar to what Steiner wrote of the "Saturn human being" in *Cosmic Memory*. "The condition of consciousness of Saturn man," Steiner says, "cannot be compared with any state of consciousness of present-day man, for it was duller than that of dreamless sleep."[12] "Dreamless sleep" is precisely what Gebser assigns to his archaic structure. He quotes the Chinese philosopher Chuang-tzu, who lived ca. 350 B.C., as evidence: "Dreamlessly the true men of earlier times slept."[13] Dreamless sleep is also a characteristic of the oldest part of the brain, the reptilian limbic system, prior even to the preconscious hypnagogic condition that Mavromatis suggests may have been a biologically earlier form of consciousness. In this context it is interesting to note that Gebser quotes another source suggesting that the archaic structure may have been similar to what Mavromatis posits as a primal, "nuclear" synesthetic sense (see chapter 12). Gebser refers to a remark by the sinologist Richard Wilhelm. Commenting on early Chinese chromatic symbolism, Wilhelm remarks, "At that time blue and green were not yet differentiated. The common word *Ch'ing* is used for the color of the sky as well as of the sprouting plant." Gebser comments that this nondifferentiation suggests an "unproblematic harmony and complete identity of earth and sky,"[14] perhaps a more "spiritual" way of expressing Mavromatis's notion of a single nuclear sense, which would not yet register the differences we take for granted between green and blue, and the earth and the sky. And although Gebser rejects any suggestion of "primitive color blindness,"[15] we may recall R. M. Bucke's remarks about the lack of color sense in our ancestors (chapter 1). That

synesthesia is also associated with newborns is another consideration linking archaic consciousness with Neumann's uroboric state.

Dating in Gebser is always ambiguous, as Feuerstein himself
admits, so it is not clear exactly *when* the archaic structure held
sway. Because he argued that such questions about "beginnings"—
"when," "how long," etc.—are "linear" expressions of our current
mental-rational structure, Gebser believed they strictly do not
apply to other structures. Yet it is difficult to see how, barring an
insight similar to the one Gebser experienced in Spain, we can talk
about his consciousness structures *at all,* unless we use the concepts
available. We have already pointed out the difficulties involved in
using an inadequate language. Nevertheless, it is the language we
have; it may not be the best tool, but it is clearly better than none.
Ken Wilber suggests that the "archaic period" began three to six
million years ago and lasted until about 200,000 years ago; this
vast stretch of time covered our pre-*sapiens* ancestors,
Australopithecus africanus, Homo habilis, and early *Homo erectus.*

Feuerstein questions the inclusion of *Homo erectus,* arguing
that it is better placed in Gebser's next consciousness structure, the
magical. Surely the point is debatable, but what seems to be clear
is that "archaic" or "Dawn man" (Wilber's term) lacked any sense
of a self separate from the world. They were little more than a reaction to their environment and their own needs and appetites. We
may dream wistfully of some ancient, lost "oneness" with nature,
but the truth is that such oneness precludes our humanity. Archaic
hominids lived in herds, not tribes; were motivated by the pressures
of hunger, thirst, and sexual urges; felt no emotion; and had no
thought of "spirituality." Their "bond" with their fellows was
involuntary and telepathic, not sympathetic. They may have been
closer to origin or the spiritual source than we are, but they had no
awareness that they were—or of much else, for that matter. Their
sense of smell was probably the strongest single source of interaction with the "world," which for them was not the clearly defined
collection of objects it is for us, but something much more akin to
William James's "blooming, buzzing confusion." Lacking a self,
they also lacked memory or any means of symbolic thought. They
lived in a perpetual present, punctuated by eating, excreting, and

copulation. Far from being inhabitants of paradise, our earliest ancestors were the bloody, savage raw material of the future.

—

One step closer to that future were our "magical" ancestors, the bearers of Gebser's next consciousness structure. According to Gebser, the magical structure does not differ greatly from the archaic. Consciousness was still deeply interfused with its environment, and the idea of an "inner" and "outer" world was still to come. Yet at this point a slight separation between human consciousness and world has arisen. Where in the archaic structure human beings were *identical* with the universe, in the magical structure they lived in *unity* with it. There was still no ego-consciousness in the way we understand it; as Feuerstein writes, "For the hominid of the archaic structure the life-world was the self. The bearer of the magical consciousness, by contrast, lived through the 'we' of the horde. . . . The family group was the self."[16] (Again, this seems very close to Steiner's "group soul," the dominant mode of consciousness of the pre–Greco-Roman epoch, which in many ways is still very dominant among less individuated personalities today—both so-called primitives and members of various collectives: political, fashionable, professional.)

In the magical period, our ancestors lived in the consciousness of the group, which was still very much united with nature. Language and the "world" it denotes were yet to emerge, and it is more than likely that communication then took place "immediately," through a kind of telepathy, not of thoughts, but of feelings and impulses. Gebser relates the magical structure to the vital sphere, our visceral, biological life. He writes of the "vegetative intertwining of all living things." Morris Berman, writing of the same time, concurs with Gebser: "Paleolithic men and women took their cues from body feelings and the movements of animals. This was a life governed by shifting moods rather than the demands of the ego."[17]

Throughout *The Ever-Present Origin* Gebser is at pains to make clear that what to us appear as previous consciousness structures are still present and active in our own consciousness. With the rise of our own dominant structure, they have only retreated into latency, yet their influence can still be felt. The archaic structure, he argues, can be felt in some forms of dreams, what he calls "nuclear dreams" and "anticipatory dreams," both of which participate in the atemporal character of origin. The magical structure with its "vegetative intertwining" also remains active within us, and it is this, Gebser suggests, that accounts for the strange, fascinating coincidences we have come to call by C. G. Jung's term "synchronicities." But Gebser came out of the darkness of Central Europe, and for him the "latent" potential of the magical structure seemed to offer more of a threat than anything else. To fully appreciate the magical structure today, he wrote, "requires . . . a sacrifice of consciousness; it occurs in the state of trance, or when consciousness dissolves as a result of mass reactions, slogans, or 'isms.' If we are not aware of this sphere in ourselves, it remains an entry for all kinds of magical influence."[18]

Gebser's remark that magical acts require a "sacrifice of consciousness" is reminiscent of the occult author Gustav Meyrink's aphorism that "Magic is doing without knowing." Another magician, more well known though less succinct than Meyrink, says the same thing. In chapter twenty of his voluminous "confessions" the notorious Aleister Crowley made some perceptive comments about his craft. In remarking on the conditions necessary for a successful magical act, Crowley writes that "success depends upon one's ability to awaken the creative genius," which for him means the unconscious self. "Even the crudest Magic," he continues, "eludes consciousness altogether, so that when one is able to do it, one does it without conscious comprehension, very much as one makes a good stroke at cricket or billiards. One cannot give an intellectual explanation of the rough working involved."[19] Magic, in other words, is a form of "tacit knowing" (see chapter 23).[20]

That magic is best accomplished in a state of un- or nonconsciousness is perhaps the central reason why it is a popular pastime among much of today's youth. Like sex, drugs, and rock and roll (or, for more contemporary listeners, "trance music"), magic aims at and is most successful during an "absence" of self. That the release from the burdens of self-consciousness afforded by a return to an "earlier" structure is often mistaken for an experience of a "higher" state—formulated by Ken Wilber as the "pre/trans falla-cy"—is only one of the confusions attendant upon the dissolution of our current consciousness structure. Much of the "liberation" ethos of the 1960s and '70s was predicated on this misunderstand-ing; a cursory glance at the times shows that magical "group con-sciousness" enjoyed a powerful resurgence then, aided by an impartial advocacy of "mind-expanding" psychedelic drugs. That the time was also one of promise and potential is another indica-tion that it was an expression of the dominant structure's break-down: as the dominant structure collapses, a "free space" is made available, a "spiritual vacuum" that will be filled by either creative or destructive forces. Any sort of leap always includes the possibil-ity of a fall.

Although Gebser must have been aware of this atavism, he had already experienced the effects of a latent magical structure in a more powerful and devastating form. The "vegetative intertwin-ing" that concerned him was the kind he had seen operating in Munich in 1929. A decade later, it had spread across most of Europe. Mass movements like Nazism were less interested in the paranormal effects of synchronicities than in the power of the latent magical structure to overrule conscious critical discernment and bind people into a whole, the *volk*. It is clear that Hitler's ora-tory and Albert Speer's mass spectacles—like the Nuremberg ral-lies, with their dazzling lighting effects—were a kind of "sorcery" aimed at and effective in drowning the lone conscious self in the buoyant waters of "the group." (Again, the similarities to rock con-certs with their mesmerizing "light shows," drug use, and over-powering music are obvious.) In conditions such as these, the ego, already weak and vacillating, is easily overwhelmed; the sheer vital energy of the crowd engulfs consciousness, and one is reduced to being a single cell, in a powerful, massive body. (The book to read on this is Elias Cannetti's *Crowds and Power*.) Such environments are fertile for "magic." The attraction of group consciousness is powerful; the Dionysian energies topple any resistance, and the sheer sense of well-being produced by the influx of vitality obviates any moral or ethical concerns. One needn't participate in totalitar-ian rallies to feel it. An office party or a football game serves just as well, but the dangers and energies involved in these are less than those attached to mass political movements—which don't necessarily need to be "right wing" to warrant concern.

That Hitler's rise to power was the result of some sort of magic is the theme of several sensational books, most famously Pauwels and Bergier's *The Morning of the Magicians.* Yet "serious" writers also considered the possibility. Hermann Broch's disturbing novel *The Spell* tells the story of a strange, persuasive drifter who arrives in a mountain village and, through his charisma and hypnotic speech, fairly soon brings the population under his sway. Broch corresponded with Gebser, and his novels, especially *The Sleepwalkers,* are often alluded to as expressions of the new "aperspectival" consciousness structure. (He and Gebser also shared a mutual friend in the cultural historian Erich Kahler.)

Broch's title *The Sleepwalkers* itself suggests the dim, ambiguous state of a culture on the brink of collapse. Because of the effort involved in maintaining it, self-consciousness is always in danger of succumbing to the ease and latitude of an earlier structure. Writing of the "magical" effects of Nazi mass propaganda, Morris Berman remarks, "Once we recognize that the human being has five (or more) bodies, and that these can get activated in such a way as to generate spiritual or psychic energy ('consciousness') that can actually *float* . . . , then continuity via the history of ideas becomes unnecessary. . . . *Consciousness is a transmittable entity* . . . and . . . an entire culture can eventually undergo very serious changes as the result of the slow accumulation of enough psychic or somatic changes on an invisible level" (my italics).[21]

That much ritual magic involves sex of some sort is also a sign that we are dealing with a loss of self-consciousness and a return to an older, more visceral form of existence. Rudolf Steiner, a member in the early 1900s of the Ordo Templi Orientis—an occult organization focusing on sexual magic—was also aware of the attraction and dangers of this "visceral consciousness," which he believed was the source of trance states, mediumship, and much that we think of as "mysticism." Steiner believed that most of what passes for mystical insight is really a contemplation of subjective visceral activities, and he warned that such practices provide opportunities for "Ahrimanic" entities to enter consciousness, an instance of the "magical influence" Gebser warned of.

Because of his experiences with the Nazis, Gebser is prone to see all "mystics," "occultists," and "esotericists" in the same way, as embodying this dangerous regression to a more primitive consciousness structure. His book is highly critical of figures like Ouspensky and Gurdjieff, although, interestingly enough, he makes no mention of Steiner, of whose work we can assume he was aware. This is unfortunate; as we have seen, there are several parallels between his work and Steiner's, and his ideas intersect at several points with Ouspensky's. Had Gebser's initial encounter with the magical structure been different, he may not have developed so suspicious an outlook.

—

To the archaic and magical structures, Gebser tells us, is added the mythical. The mythical structure is characterized by *polarity;* here the first real separation between consciousness and world occurs, although the two are still intertwined in a way that we find unusual. It is very likely that Owen Barfield's experience of a change in consciousness from reading poetry was at least in part a reactivation of the mythical structure. With the mythic structure comes the differentiation of the unified cosmos into polarities like earth/sky, male/female, god/goddess—or, as we have already seen, into the preeminent mythic formula *yin/yang*. It is during the mythical consciousness structure that the "soul" first begins to emerge. Gebser sees this depicted in the myth of Narcissus, the beautiful boy who fell in love with his own reflection in a pool. Hence for Gebser the *circle* is the archetypal symbol of the mythic structure: here consciousness finds itself by projecting itself into, and returning from, nature. He relates the mythical structure as a whole to water, and in this it is in many ways similar to both Steiner's third post-Atlantean epoch—ca. 2907–747 B.C., during which humankind develops the "sentient soul"—and the consciousness of our Old Moon incarnation.

In the mythical structure, humankind first becomes aware of its inner world, the soul, as it is "reflected" in the outer world of

nature. There is as yet nothing that we can call real *thinking*—
which is not, of course, to say that the people who lived in this
period were "stupid"; merely that thinking in the sense we understand it had not yet appeared. The mythical structure perceives the
world not as an *object* of thought, but as a *subject* of *feeling*. There
is still nothing like a modern ego, but according to Feuerstein the
mythical mode "opened up the dimensions of empathy or more
refined feeling associated with the world." This was a "matter of
rapport and of being collectively flooded by such primary emotions
as fear, anger, sorrow, and pleasure." The mythical mode "still ful-
fills no less a function today, though our Western civilization's pre-
mium on thinking rather than feeling is a sure indication of the
deficiency of the mythical consciousness in our lives."[22]
Nevertheless, a desire to feel the mythical element of our lives still
exists, even in our predominantly mental-rational society, as the
astounding success of Joseph Campbell's *The Power of Myth* and
other works in the 1990s shows.

Stewart Easton, the historian of Anthroposophy, has a passage
that indicates how the mythic consciousness perceived its world:

> *In the age before autonomous thinking, men perceived
> and* interpreted . . . *the world through their feeling. Thus
> to the ancient Egyptian there was no contradiction when
> his literature provided him with many different stories of
> creation and assigned the deed to various gods. When
> Hathor, the cow-goddess, was said to have created the
> world, no doubt the Egyptians recognized what we should
> call the fruitfulness of the world and reverenced it accord-
> ingly; when another god made fast the boundaries of the
> earth and divided it from the heavens, we might say that
> its stability and permanence were accorded their due.
> When the god Ptah had a thought in his heart, and the
> thought was spoken as a word and the world was created,
> the wisdom, order and intelligence behind the world were
> recognized. . . . No contradiction was presented to the
> Egyptians because contradiction belongs to thinking, not
> to the feelings.*[23]

Easton's remarks remind us of Schwaller de Lubicz's belief that the ancient Egyptians saw the world as a *living* being, whose manifestation involved a "simultaneity of opposites states" (see chapter 16) that for us would seem merely illogical and contradictory. But, as Owen Barfield argued, this was in essence a *metaphorical* way of seeing reality. Where we recognize an *abstract* principle—"fruitfulness," "wisdom," "stability"—the consciousness of the mythic structure perceived a living force, the *neters* of the Egyptians: in other words, gods. The gods did not "symbolize" the various aspects of the world associated with them: they *were* those aspects. The philosopher Ernst Cassirer writes that for the mythical consciousness, "The 'image' does not represent the 'thing'; it *is* the thing."[24]

The notion of reflection, symbolized by Narcissus and the pool, suggests that in the mythical structure the mind or soul was beginning to *see* itself. Hence, for Gebser, it is in the mythical structure that language first rises to prominence. Whereas in the archaic and magical structures silence reigns—consciousness remaining in an "autistic" uroboric state *before* the rise of language—in the mythical structure language emerges as a form of sacred power, creating both a "self" and a "world" outside and other than that self.[25] Language then is a medium for polarities. The language Gebser places in the mythic period is not like our own prose; like Owen Barfield he sees this time characterized by a kind of poetry. This "poetic utterance" was propelled by what Gebser calls "oceanic thinking," a circumambulation of images and metaphors, a process of linking new expressions and formulations with previous ones through a kind of verbal labyrinth, an oral "eternal recurrence" whose aim was to maintain and elicit polarities through a kind of spiraling, incantatory declamation. The mythical structure existed in a kind of sacred circle or *temenos,* a self-enclosed sphere containing the polarities of Heaven and Earth, a kind of cosmic egg whose protective shell housed human consciousness well until the time of Copernicus.

The self-enclosed aspect of the mythic structure, Gebser remarks, can still be experienced in our dreams—and as we have seen with hypnagogia, the research of Llinas and Pares seems to offer some corroboration for this. Gebser speaks of the mythic consciousness as a "silent, inward-directed contemplation," which "renders the soul visible so that it may be visualized. . . . What is viewed inwardly, as in a dream has its conscious emergence and polar complement in poetically shaped utterance"—an insight he shares with the French philosopher of the imagination, Gaston Bachelard.[26] The similarity of this to Steiner's Old Moon consciousness, which functioned primarily with images, need not be stressed.

Chapter Twenty-Seven

⌒

The Mental-Rational Structure

With each of the structures emerging—or, as Gebser would say, "mutating"—out of origin, there is an increasing separation from the source, a "progression" away from the atemporal "ever-present." Yet up to the mythic period there is still a strong connection between origin and the unfolding structures; in Owen Barfield's term, they still "participate," and it is perhaps in the mythic structure that a kind of optimum relation emerges: the unity with origin is still strong, yet consciousness has "pulled away" enough to be *aware* of that unity. After this comes a radical break. All three previous structures are very different from our own consciousness—to us, total immersion in any of them would in all probability seem like an "altered state." But now we are touching on the roots of our own form of mind.

The next consciousness structure to emerge is what Gebser calls the mental-rational. As I remarked earlier, its appearance was as profoundly shattering as a natural catastrophe. The ambiguity and uncertainty characteristic of what we call the "postmodern condition" can give us some idea of how people must have felt in the first stages of the mental-rational structure, but I believe the experience for them was much more disruptive—and, if we are to go by Julian Jaynes's account, it was.[1] It really must have been as if a world had been destroyed, for with the rise of the mental-rational structure, the link between inner and outer space was, if not entirely severed, at least made extremely tenuous. We can liken it to when a child first realizes it is a separate being, an independent self, *no longer completely under the protection of its parents*. We may imagine an exhilarating sensation of freedom, but more likely the first manifestation of this is a profound feeling of fear.

For Gebser, the early stage of the mental-rational structure—which, as we remarked earlier, he locates at around 1225 B.C.—brings "the first intimation of the emergence of *directed* or *discursive thought*. Whereas mythical thinking . . . was a shaping or designing of images . . . discursive thought is fundamentally different."[2] What is fundamentally different about this structure is that, unlike the mythical structure, which was still confined and supported by "mythic polarity," discursive thought now, and for the first time, draws its energy from the individual ego. The ties with the group, although still strong in many, begin to loosen, and the "I" begins to emerge. This is the beginning of what Owen Barfield calls "alpha-thinking," thinking *about*. It is also the beginning of what he calls "idolatry," the habit of consciousness to *forget* that the representations it ponders have their source in consciousness itself.

As we have seen, for Rudolf Steiner the development of the ego is the task of the fourth post-Atlantean epoch, the age of the "intellectual soul" (747 B.C.–A.D. 1413), and this coincides roughly with the "ascending" period of Gebser's mental-rational structure. For Steiner, Christ is the archetypal figure here; for Gebser, the rise of Greek philosophy is a clear sign of the new consciousness structure, although its spirit was already presaged in myth, the key figure being Prometheus, whose theft of fire was symbolic of humanity's first attempts to think for itself.[3] As Georg Feuerstein writes, this was the time of "the individual who could brave life, more or less, on his or her own, who did not feel particularly bound by, or even beholden to, the past, but who looked ahead to the possibilities of the future."[4] Indeed, it was at this point that *any* idea of "the future" first emerged. Previously human beings had either been asleep in a spaceless, timeless unity with the world or cradled in the "protective psychic circle" of the mythic structure. But now the

magic circle was broken, and *linear time* began. This is most evident in the Bible: the creation myth posits an absolute beginning,
and Christ's second coming introduces a *final goal* toward which
history is moving. Before this all accounts of creation and time
itself were cyclical, products of the mythical structure.

With the rise of the mental-rational structure, we emerged as
creatures who, for the first time, felt on our own in the world. We
became agents who could make decisions for ourselves, conscious
egos who could *act*. It may be a commonplace to say that *homo
sapiens sapiens* has "progressed" more in the last twenty-five hundred years of "civilization" than in all the millennia before; nevertheless it is true. Jurij Moskvitin's Anthroposphere, which we all
inhabit, with its televisions, mobile telephones, and global communication networks, as well as libraries, hospitals, and interplane-
tary satellites, is the result of that fateful split brought about by the
mental-rational consciousness structure. Whether it was "the
breakdown of the bicameral mind," or the rise of the alphabet—or
some other unknown factor—the kind of unity between consciousness and nature known in places like Çatal Hüyük was gone.

But if this was the beginning of our psychic independence, it
was also the beginning of our estrangement from the world. The
seeds of our later "alienation" were planted then. As Steiner points
out, by the time of the fourth post-Atlantean epoch, consciousness
had become focused strictly on the physical world; "progression"
from origin had reached a point at which the memory of the "ever-
present" was absent, or at best dim. Through each "mutation,"
consciousness had moved away from its spiritual source. Now, in
the mental-rational structure, the luminosity of origin was more or
less completely obscured by the increasingly "hard-edged," opaque
objects of the physical world. Both Gebser and Steiner agree that
this process was absolutely necessary: human intellectual freedom
could only be bought through the sacrifice of the spiritual intimacy enjoyed by earlier ages. Thus arose the possibility of science, the
detailed examination and understanding of the sensible world. But
with this freedom came another, more dangerous possibility—the
potential for consciousness to become *completely cut off* from any
perception of the spiritual worlds, from, that is, any sense of *mean-*

ing. As we saw, this was Goethe's and Steiner's whole argument against the dominance of "scientism," which seeks to account for *all* human experience in terms of the "meaningless" play of matter and motion. Their warnings, however, have had little effect. Some three millennia after Athena first burst forth from Zeus's aching head, a science bent on explaining consciousness—the spiritual—in strictly physical terms seems very strong evidence that this dangerous potential has indeed been actualized.

⸺

This development is an expression of what Gebser calls the "deficient" mode of the mental-rational consciousness structure, a hypertrophying of one aspect of the structure at the expense of others. This is the kind of superrationality that coolly dismisses all "human" considerations from its concerns—the vivisectionist who, in "the name of science," ignores the cries of his tortured laboratory animal; the concentration camp commander who meticulously works out the most "efficient" means of murdering his victims; the philosopher who denies the existence of consciousness because he has "never seen it." This is the affectless, lucid reasoning of the "impersonal" scientists who view the world without a trace of any *feeling* for the living soul of nature, a view that allows them to "take it apart."

The stage of "deficiency" is basically a degrading of a structure, its exhaustion prior to the emergence of a new one, which, as it were, clears a psychic space in which the new structure can arise. For Gebser, the mental-rational structure entered "deficiency" with Petrarch's ascent of Mount Ventoux—with the rise, that is, of perspective. Petrarch's "discovery" of perspective, Gebser writes, ushered in "a new realistic, individualistic, and rational understanding of nature." It was "an epochal event" signifying "no less than the discovery of landscape: the first dawning of an awareness of space that resulted in a fundamental alteration of European man's attitude in and toward the world."[5]

Clearly, the most obvious result of the new "perspectival" perception was the change in how consciousness *represented* the world. Hitherto, the natural landscape and the *human* world took a backseat to the essentially spiritual and religious subjects of paintings. Prior to perspective, the mundane world was merely a reflection of the spiritual realms, a hieroglyphic backdrop to celestial events and figures. But with perspective, this changed. The *represented* world now became what was perceived from the point of view of a single human consciousness. The world was now what we *saw*. One result of this was that, post-Petrarch, the elements of the mundane world began to demand attention for themselves, and the spiritual began to *recede*. As the literary critic Erich Heller writes, with the Renaissance and the rise of perspective, "an abundance of images pressed upon the painters' imagination, claiming their right to significance in the new field of vision. Pillars, towers, gates, trees, jugs and windows demanded to be seen with an intensity as never before."[6] It was as if with the rise of perspective, the everyday world was suddenly *discovered*.

But if this shift from the "pre-perspectival" to the "perspectival" allowed for the objects of our own everyday world to become imbued with a new importance, it also opened the door on the "naturalism," "realism," and "existentialism" that would eventually drain that world of any "transcendent" meaning. Heller has followed this trajectory in his important book *The Artist's Journey into the Interior*. Through an analysis of the poetry of Rilke and the aesthetics of the philosopher Hegel, Heller charts the gradual withdrawal of *meaning* from the external world. First, from the classical mythical symbols that had housed it for centuries, then from the mundane world of nature and human handiwork, until it reaches its final resting place in the *subjectivity* of the artist, typified by Rilke's much quoted dictum, "Nowhere will the world exist but within." Rilke, like other artist-savants of the early twentieth century, recognized that the old symbols of meaning were no longer vital; like exhausted batteries, they could no longer hold a charge. New symbols were needed, and where before tradition would imbue its images with significance, it was now up to poets and artists to fulfill this task. They had to *pour* their own meaning into some *arbitrarily* chosen object—arbitrarily chosen since, with the collapse of tradition (both classical and religious), there was nothing to guide the artist's energies to a suitable vessel. So in the

Duino Elegies Rilke advises us that the Angel will not be impressed by any supernatural display, calling us instead to offer him some *earthly* object: a jug, a rope, a bridge—whatever is at hand. In Proust the transfiguring symbol becomes a piece of cake, a loose paving stone, a lavatory.

Yet, if in Rilke and Proust—and Yeats and T. S. Eliot—we have an example of what the philosopher Arthur Danto calls "the transfiguration of the commonplace," we soon after get the polar opposite: the making commonplace of the transfiguring. Cubist painters used preeminently mundane articles like cigarette packs as subjects for their world; not long after, some artists, like Kurt Schwitters, would use the packs themselves, no longer representing them, but simply fixing them onto the canvas. Dada satirized the whole idea of "art" as any kind of "meaningful" project. The Surrealists who followed "found" art in the street, and saw in the products of the unconscious a kind of "psychic materialism"; they, like the Dadaists, carried on the Great Joke, pulling out the "transcendental" by the roots. Their "found art" exploded into a variety of forms: *art brut, musique concrete,* "word salad." Art was no longer a means of imbuing the everyday world with significance; rather, the whole drift of art in the last century was to bring it down to the everyday—the central icon here, of course, is Andy Warhol's Brillo Box.

The competing ideologies that informed many of these works— existentialism, Marxism, etc.—although different in approach and values, shared one central theme: the absence of any *transcendent* meaning to human existence. No longer was there a single significance to human life, a shared awareness of our place in the cosmos. Meaning, if it existed, was scattered among the interior worlds of hundreds of artists; eventually it would become a purely personal meaning, an arcane, idiosyncratic reading of life, more times than not a foisting of the artist's obsessions on an increasingly befuddled public. And this absence or anarchy of "meaning"—the two are essentially the same—was not limited to art, but included science, literature, philosophy, and all human endeavors, informing the Anthroposphere with a sense of chaos and pointlessness.

—

It may seem a long way from Petrarch's thrilling ascent of Mount Ventoux to Andy Warhol's Brillo Box, but the trajectory is there and it has not stopped yet, as a visit to practically any contemporary art exhibit—or "installation"—shows. The central shift, Gebser argues, is that with perspective, consciousness could now "block off" sections of nature from the whole; it could now focus on particular "slices" of the world and view these as separate realities, apart from the rest of nature. Human consciousness, in a real sense, became the measure of all things, and with the loss of the "transcendent" it was only a matter of time before we would empty out the inventory of our own invention: the uroboric serpent of analysis once again gnawing away at itself. It is the kind of sensibility that Steiner located in the consciousness soul, the presiding "spirit" of the fifth post-Atlantean epoch, whose starting point of A.D. 1413 is very close to 1336, the year of Petrarch's ascent. During the age of the consciousness soul, there is an increasing "objectivity" of thought, a "hardening" and "fracturing" of our perception of the world, a complete break with "participation" and a triumph of what Schwaller de Lubicz calls "cerebral consciousness," which divides, analyzes, and granulates experience. A science that wants to explain consciousness and an "art" that seeks to annihilate its own meaning are two aspects of the same sensibility. Both wish to get rid of anything that goes beyond the immediately given, whether that means neurons or an item from the grocery shop.[7]

That such a situation constitutes a crisis seems obvious. Indeed, the notion that Western civilization is in crisis—or, in a more euphemistic variant, is undergoing a "transition"—has been the punch line of dozens, probably hundreds of books since the beginning of the last century. Oswald Spengler's *Decline of the West,* Ernst Bloch's *Spirit of Utopia,* Hermann Hesse's *Glimpse Into Chaos,* Edmund Husserl's *The Crisis in European Science,* Karl Kraus's *The Last Days of Mankind,* Arthur Koestler's *The Ghost in the Machine,* Robert Musil's *The Man Without Qualities,* José

Ortega y Gasset's *The Revolt of the Masses*, Martin Heidegger's *Being and Time*, René Guenon's *The Reign of Quantity*, Thomas Mann's *The Magic Mountain*, Colin Wilson's *The Outsider*—the list could go on. The above canon, by no means exhaustive, includes novels as well as works of philosophy, literary criticism, and drama—a sign that the concern with what the novelist Hermann Broch called "the disintegration of values" is not confined to academics, but reaches out across the cultural board. Works of art and music, and whole "movements" like Expressionism and Existentialism could be included in this grouping. It would not be too much to say that one of the central themes of the twentieth and now twenty-first centuries has been the imminent collapse of "Western civilization"—for much of the last quarter of the last century its unavoidable demise was not only welcomed but hastened on by members of its most prominent academic establishments.

Even staunch and spirited defenders of the Western mind have little hope for it continuing in any more than a nostalgic or elder statesman role. In a recent book, George Steiner laments, "We have no more beginnings." "There have been previous senses of ending and fascinations with sundown in western culture," he writes, but "nevertheless, there is, I think, in the climate of spirit at the end of the twentieth century, a core-tiredness. . . . We are, or feel ourselves to be, latecomers. The dishes are being cleared."[8] Likewise, the historian Jacques Barzun, at ninety-five a witness to the long sunset of the West, has, in the monumental *From Dawn to Decadence* (2001), charted, over the last five hundred years, the path of our culture's birth, maturity, and now, with what he calls the "Great Undoing," its self-immolation at the hands of chat shows, gangsta rap, and trendy postmodernisms. The great themes of "emancipation," "individualism," and "self-consciousness" that fueled the break with a creaking tradition, Barzun says, are now entangled in an apparently irresolvable morass of competing and contradictory "values." That anything "great" can emerge from this is, he believes, doubtful.

Cassandras, then, have not been hard to find, even if in more recent years their dire warnings have been answered by a chorus of more optimistic, if less convincing, voices. Gebser, too, sees a "new age" approaching. But he is realistic enough to know that it will not be a utopia. "Every consciousness mutation," he cautions, is "a sudden and acute manifestation of latent possibilities present since origin."[9] "Sudden" and "acute" are the key words here, suggesting the equivalent of a civilizational ice age.[10]

The "new factor" that Gebser believes can save us from complete destruction is the emerging "aperspectival consciousness" of the "integral consciousness structure," whose appearance he had recognized during his lightning-like inspiration in Spain in 1932.

Chapter Twenty-Eight

The Integral Structure

Gebser's descriptions of the new consciousness structure provide some of the most unwieldy passages in *The Ever-Present Origin;* here his neologizing reaches an evocative power and a density that will be difficult for all but the most dedicated readers. This is to be expected; what is involved is nothing less than our transformation, our "mutation," into another form of reality. The present "deconstruction" of the mental-rational structure is in preparation for this new dispensation. There is no guarantee that the new structure will emerge before the total collapse of the old—that is up to us. The challenge is whether we will participate in the new mutation consciously, or simply be carried way by its effects.

As its name implies, the integral consciousness structure is characterized by *integration*—in this case the integration of the previous four structures. This recapitulation of "older," more "primitive" forms of consciousness in a new mode is something we have already come across several times in this discussion. For Gebser it means a return to origin after our long progression away from it in the various consciousness structures that have unfolded through time. Such a return means several things for Gebser. One is what he calls the "concretizing of the spiritual." As the word "concrete" suggests, this is a condition in which "the spiritual" becomes actually present and *perceivable*, no longer merely intuited, conceptualized, or "felt." With the "arational integral structure," the actual originary "presence," the primal "uncreated light," is made apparent. The spiritual will be *seen*, not as an object among other objects, but as the inner radiance that has hitherto invisibly supported all objects, rather like the Being Heidegger speaks of, which is itself not a being, but which allows all beings to be. Related to this is what Gebser calls "diaphaneity." The "diaphainon," according to Feuerstein, is "that which 'shines through,' namely the ever-present spiritual origin."[1] This "shining through" is what will become visible to the arational-integral consciousness structure.

Such a consciousness will participate in "diaphaneity" by virtue of its being "ego-free." "Ego-freedom," Gebser warns, is not to be confused with the simple loss of ego, and its "blending" back into its source, characteristic of earlier structures of consciousness and offered as the goal of many so-called spiritual, mystical, or magical paths. Nor is it to be seen as an ascetic denial or negation of the self. Just as the progression of consciousness structures follows a course of "unperspectival," "perspectival," and "aperspectival" consciousness—which we can think of as point, line, and plane—so too does the ego unfold through similar stages: from an egoless condition typical of the archaic, magical, and mythical structures, to an "I" of the mental-rational structure, to, finally, a "transcendence" of the ego in the integral structure. This "transcendence" of the ego is actualized by the "concretion of the spiritual," in which consciousness, in Gebser's term, "coalesces" with origin. Again, the idea is not to lose our sense of "I" by being absorbed into the "whole," but to be aware of the whole and of *ourselves as a part of it* simultaneously, another version of the "double consciousness" we have already encountered. By consciously integrating the four previous structures and mastering their deficient modes—which, of course, would mean to become aware of them and their role in our lives—the "sheaths" or "layers" of consciousness that have obscured the "uncreated light" become "transparent" and are seen as *integral* parts of the ongoing "presencing" of origin, movements of a kind of eternal symphony.

We might say that until the emergence of the integral structure, consciousness, as it were, is in the position of someone viewing a painting with eyes only a few inches from the canvas. From this "perspective" we have an excellent opportunity to analyze fine brush strokes and textures of paint, but only of a small area of the whole. The "painting" itself eludes us. (That much of modern science and philosophy operates in such a position is, I believe, arguable.) With the "aperspectival" mode of consciousness, we can step back and see how the smudges of color form a picture—that is, have *meaning*. And if this is true of a painting, it is also true of our relationship to the whole. From the point of view of our perception and understanding of the universe, we are all smack up against a tiny portion of it, peering suspiciously at a fraction of reality and making our various assessments of such grand affairs as "life" and "the world." It is inevitable that from the vantage points of our limited, mistrustful egos, these assessments are biased, prejudiced, and, for the most part, inaccurate. In order to make any judgments about "life," "the world," or anything else that would in any way be useful—and not merely a series of complaints—we would have to be in a position to see much more of the picture than we do at the moment. This "bird's-eye view," as Colin Wilson calls it, is the central characteristic of the emerging aperspectival consciousness. And although Gebser is at pains to differentiate his insights from previous ideas about "other" forms of consciousness, clearly his "aperspectivalism" is related to various forms of "higher consciousness" we have discussed throughout this book—like Bucke's "cosmic consciousness" and Ouspensky's experiences with nitrous oxide. Bucke, Ouspensky, James, Steiner, Wilson, Mavromatis, Moskvitin, and the others all, like Gebser, see our present "ego-bound" consciousness as part of an ongoing development of consciousness—necessary and indispensable, but not an end goal. In different ways, each arrives at a remarkably similar conclusion. If "perspectival consciousness" is a function of the ego, then an "aperspectival consciousness" and a "transcendence" of the ego are clearly related.

—

Associated with this widening and multiplying of perspective is Gebser's difficult notion of "verition" or "waring." Whereas the mental structure "conceptualizes" the world, the mythic structure "poeticizes" it, and the magical structure "vitalizes" it, the integral structure perceives it "in truth"—not as it appears to a function of a particular structure, but as the source and support of those structures. In "verition" the world becomes "pure statement," its meaning, presence, and being disclosing themselves as self-evident. "Waring" oneself or another reveals what Gebser calls the "itself," the originary presence as it manifests in the human personality, our "apersonal" core, the essence, we can say, of our interiority once we have transcended the ego.

Reading Gebser on "aperspectivity," "waring," and the "integral consciousness structure," one can agree with George Steiner that "our dictionaries lag behind our needs."[2] Although Gebser's experience at Sarnath came after he had written *The Ever-Present Origin,* the strongest impression his account of the new consciouness makes is of its similarity to some descriptions of *satori*— a wordless perception of actual being in all its perfection. In *satori,* as well as in other "mystical" states—including ones induced by drugs—"things," the objects of the world, appear in an irreducible "givenness"; they are so "there," so "real," that language fails before them, and we are left, at best, with the silence that ends Wittgenstein's *Tractatus.* Things seen in *satori* are "im-mediate," not "mediated" through the necessary logical restrictions of language; under the influence of mescaline, Aldous Huxley famously remarked that he saw as Adam must have seen on the first day of creation. There is an inexpressible "innocence of becoming," in Nietzsche's phrase, that we share with children—and that many of us spend the rest of our lives trying to recapture—a freshness of perception that begins to fade as we begin to understand words, although poets have the ability to use words themselves to revive this state of primal glory. Feuerstein's glossary of Gebser's terms is full of words beginning with the prefix "a"—"acategoricality," "acausality," "amensionality," "aspatiality." Like "asexual," which means neither sexual nor nonsexual, but a condition to which the notion of sexuality doesn't apply, all of these "a" terms point to a kind of consciousness that has passed beyond, "transcended," the categories through which we usually understand our experience.

In the integral structure, as in Hindu, Jewish, and Buddhist sacred scriptures, things are "neither this nor that"; they are "before" or "beyond" conceptualization. Likewise, given the Christian provenance of much of Gebser's thought, his notion of the "concretion of the spiritual" has strong similarities with the idea of a "second coming" of Christ, similarities he again shares with Rudolf Steiner, who spoke of a "reappearance of Christ in the etheric." This, for Steiner, did not mean that Christ would "return" in another human body, as many literal thinkers of both a New Age and fundamentalist stamp believe. He meant that in coming years the *spiritual presence* of Christ would become increasingly perceptible to more people—an idea that seems to share much with Gebser's notion of the spiritual becoming concrete. Gebser speaks of a "more intensified Christianity" soon to emerge, after humanity passes through its present "three-day period of descent into hell." With our "resurrection," conditions on our planet will, one assumes, be considerably different.

How and in what way they will be different is difficult to say since, as we have seen, our language is geared to describe *our* world, the way it is now. But that it is therefore impossible, as many mystics and philosophers have contended, to say anything intelligible about a *new* or *different* world is, I believe, untrue. As Owen Barfield makes clear, the language we have now, like our consciousness, has developed over time, and what to us seem everyday figures of speech would have been incomprehensible to people of an earlier age. So there is every reason to believe that a century or two from now, with "aperspectivity" and the integral structure more firmly in place, we may have a language capable of saying what to us is ineffable. And given the accelerating rate of change, such a development may take place sooner than we think.[3]

Given an "accelerated rate of change," there is, however, one aspect of the new consciousness that is already accessible to us—it is, in fact, one that affects our lives immediately and that many of us feel the discomforts (or pleasures) of each day. The meaning of two of the "a" words listed in Feuerstein's glossary should be more open to us: "achronon" and "atemporal" both speak of the changed relationship of consciousness to time. At the opening of *The Ever-Present Origin*, Gebser speaks of our "altered relation to time" as being the central theme of the book. Later he speaks of something altogether more dynamic than a mere alteration. The integral consciousness structure, he tells us, will bring about an "irruption of time."

"To irrupt" means to "enter forcibly and suddenly." We experience something of this quite commonly whenever someone "interrupts" us when we are speaking. Gebser suggests that not only the idea of time, but *time itself* will enter into our lives more radically. It will "interrupt" our lives, break into our experience in new ways. If with Petrarch's ascent of Mount Ventoux Western consciousness entered a "space age," with the turn of the nineteenth century, it had, Gebser argues, entered a "time age."

Just as the different consciousness structures can be characterized by their relationship to space—"unperspectival," "perspectival," and "aperspectival"—so too can they be characterized by their relationship to time. Time as we know it, "linear" time that "moves" from a past through a present and into a future, is, Gebser says, a product of the mental-rational structure. Before that, the "time" of the mythical structure was cyclical: we see this in the Hindu idea of the *yugas* and in the ancient Greek notion of the four ages of gold, silver, bronze, and iron. In linear time the "past" no longer exists and the "future" has not yet happened, but in cyclical time this difference does not apply. "Past" and "future" are meaningless in a circle; in mythical time, events return to the beginning, and the cycle starts again. We experience this with the seasons, although with the changes in weather patterns this "eternal return" may soon be upset. In the magical and archaic structures, there is no "time" at all, neither linear nor cyclical. Everything exists in a kind of pointlike present; we may think of it as a series of disconnected dots or flashes of experience.

(Having written this, it is clear to me that "time" and "self-consciousness" are intimately related. A newborn exists in a timeless state, punctuated by a series of discontinuous "nows" that take up its entire consciousness and recede into oblivion. A two-year-old enjoys a kind of "eternal return," repeating patterns set down in the past—alterations in day-to-day activities meet with much resistance. Only with the emerging "I" does the notion of time in anything like our common sense of it arise, with fledgling ideas of "before," "after," "tomorrow," "yesterday" taking hold. Given this, the fact that most of us remain trapped in linear time throughout our lives seems to suggest that we never grow up. A few get intimations of a kind of time *beyond* time, but usually only toward the end of their lives when they do not have enough time left to make much use of this; and the people they express it to chalk it up to senility and simple-mindedness.)

Gebser points to the beginning of the twentieth century as the starting-point for the new "time consciousness." We have already mentioned Einstein's part in this; we could equally have spoken of Bergson's or Nietzsche's.[4] Einstein, of course, altered "time" more profoundly than either philosopher, precisely because he was a scientist and not a mere "thinker"; in our scientistic age, it takes the voice of a scientist to effect any large-scale change in things. (This was perhaps not so true in the nineteenth century: Hegel's philosophy had as profound an effect on the state of the world as could be imagined; for one thing, it more or less "created" the Soviet Union.)

But Einstein was only one of many thinkers and artists for whom "time" had become a central concern. The cubist visions of Picasso and Braque presented a perception of "simultaneity," of "everythingatonce" rather than "one-thing-at-a-time." Similarly in music Gustav Mahler's Ninth Symphony—a kind of *Decline of the West* in sound—began the "deconstruction" of the traditional symphonic form, a work that would be carried on by Arnold Schoenberg and his atonal and twelve-tone systems, scattering the linear expectations of listeners used to the dramatic, dialectical structure of statement, challenge, and recapitulation.[5] (The process had indeed begun half a century earlier with Wagner's famous

"Tristan chord.") In literature, as we have mentioned, the novels of James Joyce, Thomas Mann, Robert Musil, Hermann Broch, and others, introduced, to varying degrees, the experience of nonlinear time into their narratives, the greatest and most influential of these being Proust; time itself is the central theme of his massive opus. (Not everyone, however, was pleased about this development; in 1927, the artist and critic Wyndham Lewis published *Time and Western Man,* in which he attacked the new fascination with temporal matters. Bergson, Proust, Joyce, and Whitehead came in for particular condemnation, and even Ouspensky received a slighting mention.) Poetry and theater also broke with traditional linear modes; August Strindberg employed the "dream technique" that would become a standard part of Expressionist drama, and T. S. Eliot's jagged and broken verse reflected the discontinuity of experience felt by many.[6] And arguably the most influential work of philosophy in the twentieth century had as one of its central foci time itself: Martin Heidegger's *Being and Time* (1927).

Indeed, the new art forms that arose in the twentieth century used time as the basic element. A painting is static; no matter how explosive its colors or forms, it exists in a kind of timeless moment. Not so cinema. The "moving picture" introduced time into what was an essentially nontemporal realm; when we use the colloquial phrase "the movies" today we are unaware of how radical a break in human consciousness we are referring to. Films could even run *against* linear time, being shown backwards, or flout its remorseless annihilation of experience: anyone today can stop a video or DVD and watch a scene or an entire film again, something many of us would often like to do in "real life." Sound recording, of course, offered similar ways of altering time. A musical performance, unlike a painting, takes place in linear time, and once it is over it is gone, unless the performers play it again. But by the middle of the twentieth century, anyone with a gramophone could put the needle back to the beginning of the record and start again. Today, "multimedia" exhibits and installations using sound, video, and other electronic elements to create an experience of "simultaneity" are a commonplace item in the art world.

These changes are so familiar to us that it is difficult to grasp how new they are. This is also true of the more recent "irruptions of time" that took place as the last century closed. Unless, like myself, you are old enough to remember a time when computers were not a common household furnishing, things like the Internet, World Wide Web, mobile phones, and the other communication wonders that dominate (or enrich) our lives will seem matter-of-fact. No doubt my children will accept them as a given, just as, for me, television was as much a part of "nature"—the world I found when I became aware of it—as a flower or the sun. Children who have grown up with the Web will take "simultaneity" and "multiple perception" for granted. For myself and others forty-something or older, it has been a challenge to adjust my predominantly linear perception to the new models. (Which is not to suggest that the new nonlinear consciousness supposedly engendered by the Web, etc., is a natural, or inevitable successor to the throne; as much as I enjoy my computer and the Internet, most of my adjustment is sheer adaptation for survival.) This may not have been what Gebser had in mind when he thought of time's irruption, but notwithstanding all the hype a new kind of perception *has* been emerging in the last few decades, and it is obvious that it has something to do with the rise of the computer.

———

Another, possibly more immediate, alteration in our experience of time is the sheer increase in the *speed* of everything. We live in an increasingly fast world, a fact that brought the writer Milan Kundera to name one of his novels *Slowness*. It is a cliché that today we move at a tempo our ancestors would have found dizzying—as, indeed, many of us do: in his book *Faster*, science writer James Gleich coins the phrase "hurry sickness." The measurement of time has a long history—the still classic and highly readable book to consult is J. B. Priestley's *Man and Time*[7]—and it is a curious irony that church bells were first introduced to divide the day into sections of time as an aid in synchronizing the meditation of monks. Today, the tables have been turned and the monks' timeless contemplation is a rarity. The bells have won. In our hurrying world, it is time itself that counts.

In 1972, the definition of a second was designated as 9,192,631,770 oscillations of a cesium atom. Since then, this already fleeting segment of time—for all Bergson's arguments, we still speak of time "spatially"—has been sliced into finer and finer bits: the fermata, the nanosecond, the picosecond, the femtosecond—which, at one quadrillionth of a second, reaches a degree of temporal exactitude unappreciable by human consciousness. Just as elementary particles do not "exist" for us—we never have an immediate experience of an electron, let alone a quark—such quantification has no real meaning for us. And yet in our time-obsessed culture, there is a clear compulsion to slice time into smaller and smaller pieces.

The flipside to this is the injunction to "get the most out of your time." We know of "fast food," but that is just the start. The compulsion not to "waste time" has gone beyond the few minutes devoted to nutrition. We speak of "real time," "time-sharing," "multitasking"; time spent with our loved ones receives the hideous honorific of "quality time" ("Okay kids, let's have two hours of loving each other"). The proliferation of amusements and entertainments—twenty-four-hour television offering hundreds of channels—produces the craving to "fill up" a day, or, conversely, to "kill time" between appointments. Instant accessibility produces a frenzy of empty activity. We are afraid of squandering time and do our best to "save" it—but clearly there are no temporal banks into which we can make a deposit. To "save time" simply means either to complete a particular activity faster, or to combine several activities and perform them at the "same time"—one reflection of this being the multipurpose businesses that have become part of contemporary culture: the Laundromat that is also a bakery, the bookshop that provides cappuccino. The idea that one should devote one's attention solely to a single task has, at least in the popular mind, become old-fashioned; some writers, like Camile Paglia, revel in the new "multitasking" sensibility, boasting of their ability to write while listening to the radio, watching the television, keeping an eye on the Internet, and carrying on a telephone conversation, all simultaneously. (How such a regimen influences her writing is, sadly, a question I do not have time for.) We live in a "cut to the chase, been there, done that" world, in which, conversely we do not want to "miss out" on anything. Perhaps this is why the figure of the *flaneur*, the idler on the streets of nineteenth-century Paris, has become such an icon of contemporary cultural theory.

That such a whirligig environment is affecting our perception has, of, course, been a subject of much discussion. For me, brought up on pop culture in the 1960s and '70s, the frenetic, jittery camera style of much of today's television is, quite simply, unwatchable—whether or not the subject matter may be of some interest or value. I do not see the world that way, although I am willing to accept that many people do. (Then again, whether this is an actual shift in representation or a "style" foisted on a passive public by an aggressive market is another matter.) Such nonstop movement may be able to accommodate a great deal of material; but what it gains in quantity it loses in depth. We have heard about the shortened attention span of today's teenagers. This same unwillingness to linger over anything—one wonders how a film by Andrey Tarkovsky would fare today—affects the other "media" as well. Postmodern prose has developed a cynical syntax of the present, a verbal accompaniment to the digital "timepiece" (which, unlike the outmoded clock, displays no past or future—shades of Gebser's "ever-present) and the perpetual rush hour of the information highway. In this "nowspeak," substance, character, emotion, tension, development and plot dissolve into a flat, television-like surface, punctuated by brand names and designer tags, whose immediacy jolts the skim-reader into a brief semblance of attention.

Along with this "will to the now," there is a kind of hoarding of the past, an "archive mania" which, paradoxically, denies the past its true character. In its hands the past becomes a mere source of "information." Unlike true historical scholarship, there is no discrimination between what is worthy of being saved and what is not, what tells a story and what does not. Like Jorge Luis Borges's unfortunate character Funes the Memorius, today's "information junkies" are either unable or unwilling to forget *anything*. The result is an information glut, a clutter of disconnected "facts," the epistemological equivalent of collecting tinfoil, an inability to *throw anything away*, a disinclination to "waste" the smallest bit of "knowledge"—while, of course, at the same time the natural world suffers a daily, mostly unrecoverable, expenditure.

Ally to this the almost automatic "self-reflexivity" of a highly self-conscious culture, in which any new "product," film, book, or performance, generates critical comment almost instantaneously, and you have a milieu in which "works" are increasingly seen as mere triggers for analysis, thus producing a near-continuous flow of verbiage—which, naturally, will add to the already bloated reservoirs of "information."

LAST WORDS

—

Playing for Time

It would be easy to go on with this account of our life in the fast lane; whole books, like Gleich's, have been devoted to it. I have gone on at length about the negative side of time's "irruption" merely to show that, at least on this account, Gebser seems to have been prescient. If this were all there was to it, however, there would be little to look forward to except an increasingly frenetic world. More than likely that will be the case. But other aspects of the time question seem also to have appeared. Not everyone is happy with the pace of things.

Semicomical gestures like the Slow Food Movement, whose emblem is the snail, and more serious organizations like The Long Now Foundation and the Society for the Deceleration of Time suggest that at least some of the population is determined to drag its feet. And in the last few decades questions about time have gained a significant foothold in the popular idea of the physical sciences—the success of Stephen Hawking's widely bought but little read *A Brief History of Time* (1988) clearly shows that. It is an axiom of both classical Newtonian as well as quantum physics that "time's arrow," the relentless progression into the future, is a negligible factor. Time, scientists say, could flow backward, forward or in any direction, with no effect on our understanding of the laws of physics. This atemporality has received many shocks in recent

269

years. Through the work of Illya Prigogine on dissipative structures and the research of the celebrated Santa Fe Institute on chaos theory and complexity, "entropy," the felt movement of time, has become a subject for serious investigation, providing good arguments against the strict determinism of standard physics and for such Bergsonian notions as "becoming" and "novelty." Time is also a central theme in Rupert Sheldrake's controversial work on "morphogenetic fields," as well as in his notion that the so-called laws of nature may not be Platonic constants, but may, like everything else, have "evolved" over time—an idea first presented in the early twentieth century by Alfred North Whitehead. Sheldrake's notion of the "presence of the past," the idea that life forms may possess a kind of "memory" not localized in the strict mechanics of DNA but perhaps housed in a nonphysical field—first presented more than a century ago by Samuel Butler—is, as I remarked earlier, reminiscent of what we have seen of the Akashic Record, as well as of Bergson's idea that the past "still exists" and is still "present to consciousness," requiring but a slight adjustment on our part to be made available.

In a different context, Bergson's ideas about time and consciousness received renewed interest in 1994 when the literary critic Sven Birkerts published his important book *The Gutenberg Elegies*. An inveterate reader, as the work's title suggests, Birkerts was troubled by what he saw as the demise of the book and the triumph of the new "electronic media"—television and film, but most specifically the rise of the computer screen—at the expense of the printed page. A sadness permeates the work, a sense of some irretrievable loss, which unfortunately led some reviewers to chalk the book up to Birkerts's own admitted melancholia. But it is more than a mere exercise in nostalgia; his central concern is with the effect the new "media" are having on our consciousness. He laments the loss of "deep time" and speaks of Bergson's "duration," the meditative, expansive *imaginative* time that accompanies true reading—the time that Samuel Richardson first encountered and introduced to the Western world in 1740. This is the time of Wilson's Faculty X and of the felt change in consciousness Owen

Barfield experienced while reading poetry, not the tick-tock time of a cesium atom.

Birkerts fears that with the rise of the flat computer screen and its much touted "simultaneity," the ability of reading to open up inner depths and to, quite literally, *slow down* time is lost. There is something more to the idea of "sinking into a book" than a mere metaphor for absent-mindedness. (Indeed, if it *is* absent from "here," that mind is also "present" *elsewhere:* in Homer's Troy, Dickens's London, Dostoyevsky's St. Petersburg, or even Birkerts's own elegiac reflections.) For all the Internet's impressive access to "information"—the "world of knowledge" it supposedly puts at our fingertips—such an ability to transport us to "other times and places" is lost to it and its like. Combined with the host of other technological advances, the instant accessibility of the Internet, coupled with the ephemeral "ever-perishing" character of its electronic medium, has, Birkerts asserts, created a unique situation. "In the past fifty years or so, something in the nature of time—or in our experience of it—has changed radically. . . . The shape of the very frame of things has altered." We have reached a condition of "critical mass," the first stages of a unprecedented transition, the upshot of which is that "our old understandings of time—and, therefore, of life itself—are in many ways useless." Birkerts even uses Gebser's preferred term for radical change, suggesting that "the human time experience may be undergoing a fundamental mutation." The similarities of themes and vocabulary are striking. Birkerts speaks of "the sound- and image-saturated *now*," the "cataract of data and imagery."[1]

This focus on the pictorial rather than the literal is of course an expression of the decline of the linear in favor of the simultaneous, a decline that Birkerts, an old-school reader, regards with dismay. Others, however, do not see this shift in such dire terms. As we have seen, in *The Alphabet versus the Goddess* (chapter 18), Leonard Shlain welcomes the return of the image after its millennia-long subjugation by reading, writing, and the "abc's." It was precisely the development of the alphabet with its heightening of left-brain consciousness, Shlain argues, that has led to many, if not all, of the crises confronting us at the start of the twenty-first century. The various forms of simultaneity, and the "image-centered" culture of the electronic media, are, he argues, to be welcomed, not feared, for they presage the advent of a new "participatory," feminine, nonlinear, and hence nonabusive, "concrete" thinking.

The idea that "the next step" in the evolution of consciousness will involve a "return" to a pictorial kind of thinking, or at least to a thinking that exceeds the limits of language, has been a recurring theme in this book. We have seen it in the image of Ouspensky's ashtray. It forms the essence of Steiner's notion of Imagination. It is the principle characteristic of hypnagogia. Owen Barfield wrote of it in his discussion of "beta-thinking" and "representation," as did Jurij Moskvitin in his experience of the "selective forms." A pictorial kind of thinking is more than likely the kind of thinking, if we may call it that, experienced by our early ancestors—a metaphorical, image-based participation in things. It is the kind of thinking Schwaller de Lubicz called the "intelligence of the heart." It is also the "fresh" experience of things we have as children. Colin Wilson's "Faculty X" is the grasp of other times *and places*— sometimes, as we have seen, to the extent of actually being transported there. So there is much to say for this new imagistic consciousness. And if the speculations of the thinkers discussed in this book are only halfway valid, then, whatever our preferences, the species as a whole may be moving in this direction.

So Shlain may be right. But if Birkerts's reflections are sound, then Shlain's welcoming of the return of the image *at the expense of the verbal ego* is at least a bit premature. After all, it was precisely through images and spectacle—not rational, linear arguments—that the Nazi totalitarian regime secured its grip on a people. Linearity and the abstract thinking it promotes undoubtedly have their drawbacks. But the simultaneous, imagistic world of the Internet and electronic media is not necessarily an antidote. As Gebser knew, images and symbols operate at the level of the magical structure, bypassing the critical, reflective mind. The perpetual "now" of the ever-present Internet does not allow for the deep, meditative time in which the mind can focus on values and understand *why* it thinks as it does. A picture may be worth a thousand words, but without the words to tell you, you may not even know what you are looking at—something all good advertisers know. The aperspectivalism and irruption of time offered by our new electronic Anthroposphere may be the first global evidence of a shift in human consciousness—early advocates of the "wired world" were quick to forge links with Teilhard de Chardin and his Omega Point. But it may also be a final efflorescence of our "deficient" mental-rational structure.

Steiner, Gebser, Wilson, Barfield, and others all make a point of stating quite clearly that the ego, while in need of transcendence, is not simply to be jettisoned. An image-based consciousness rooted in the usurpation of language and the rational ego may merely throw the baby out with the bathwater. And in any case, the kind of right-brain-dominant consciousness that Shlain envisions has already been tried; it is a historically *older* form of consciousness, and the left-brain ego developed out of it—necessarily, I would say, as Steiner, Gebser, Barfield, and others do—in order to complement it. A completely left-brain consciousness would be—is—a burden and a mistake: we have seen the effects of such a consciousness in the increasing *loss of meaning* over the last four centuries. But a plunge into a postmodern version of Steiner's Old Moon consciousness or into an electronic version of Gebser's mythical consciousness would have an equally retrograde effect. As in other circumstances, the Goldilocks rule applies here as well. If anything, duo-consciousness and its elusive "just right" have been a central theme in these meditations. The formula "right brain good, left brain bad" that Shlain applies to the history of Western consciousness is, for all the profitable insights he draws from it—and his book has many—in the end simplistic. The Internet, simultaneity, and various other forms of the "return of the image" may indicate a change in consciousness. But they may not be that change itself. As in so many things, only time will tell.

Yet, while the Internet and other electronic advances may not embody the "next step" in human evolution, it is difficult, considering the work of the thinkers I have discussed in this book, to come away without feeling that *some* shift in things is imminent. In various ways, practically all the thinkers we have looked at have argued that human consciousness, at least in the Western world, is

either on its way toward, or is in the first stages of, a radical change
in its mental furnishings. And likewise, practically all of them have
argued that at least part of this change will entail a new experience
of time. I have placed Jean Gebser at the end because he seems to
me to have argued this point most clearly and to have supplied an
enormous amount of evidence for it.

When P. D. Ouspensky began his experiments with the "fourth
dimension," evolution was still a relatively recent idea, and the
new physics was still in its infancy. Today, both ideas occupy a
dominant place in our understanding of ourselves. Indeed, our
grasp of these and other difficult concepts and the success science
has had in applying them have resulted in the hubris of attempts to
explain what, short of the existence of life and of the universe itself,
is undoubtedly the central mystery of our experience: consciousness. Yet, as I remarked in the introduction, to explain consciousness means, in essence, to explain ourselves—and when that core
mystery is gone, something great and powerful will also be lost.
When the mystery of the self, of personhood, is reduced to some
quantifiable formula, whether in terms of atoms, molecules, genes
or adaptive behavior, then the world we live in will no longer be,
as against all odds it still is today, a human one. As the philosopher
Leszek Kolakowski warns, such a world will be one in which a person is not an end in himself, but "is reducible to his function; it will
accept, in other words, that each person is entirely replaceable. Such
a civilization would signal the end of humanity as we know it."[2]

Remarking that we are on the brink of such a transformation
may put me in the company of other Cassandras—less eloquent
and impassioned, no doubt, but more than likely equally as effective. Yet, if we are to avoid the future that Kolakowski envisions,
its dark possibilities must be faced. In different ways, disciplines
and intellectual pursuits as far apart as genetics, neuroscience, the
philosophy of mind, and poststructualism have argued that the
"human being" as we know it—meaning endowed with spirit and
free will and possessed of certain inalienable rights—is an outmoded and obsolete conception, a fallacy of past thinking that our
more rigorous experts have outgrown. Given the thrust of these
ideas and their rapid spread throughout our culture—they are

already mother's milk to a generation of university students—unless some countervision of ourselves arises, their triumph is almost certain to be a fait accompli. Steiner had forebodings of something of this sort, I think, when he spoke of a coming "Ahrimanic future," yet he, and others in this book, offered a way to avoid this. Another transformation seems to be our only chance. As all the thinkers in this book have argued, this must be a transformation of consciousness itself. I have tried to show that the potential for this is available, and that the means of actualizing it are within our grasp.

But this shift itself will not be a picnic. As Morris Berman points out, "It will take a century or two" to arrive at a "new paradigm," and the passage to it "will more than likely include wars, famine, depressions."[3] Not a cheerful thought. But we already have wars, famine, and depressions *without* their leading to any great change; Berman's disturbing vision sounds more like "business as usual"—with the possibility of our arriving at something "different." *How* different is, of course, something we cannot know. History is littered with the ruins of the future, and the fallout of failed prophecy. R. M. Bucke, with whom we began our search for "cosmic consciousness," believed that the onset of the twentieth century would bring an age of unparalleled social and personal fulfillment. Utopia was just around the corner. Clearly, he was wrong. Rudolf Steiner, on the other hand, in the aftermath of one world war and the brief peace before another, spoke ominously of coming catastrophes, of a super-Orwellian age in which spirit would be crushed beneath the scientific-rationalist heel. Steiner's prophecy is chilling and eerily prescient, and, coming from such an optimistic, forward-looking thinker, is doubly unsettling.[4] Yet in our own time, Colin Wilson has seen the possibility of a new, liberated consciousness reflected in the dark glass of serial killing—as unlikely a place as we could imagine for securing the possibility of a coming era of "self-actualization." Surely the ways of the spirit are crooked and unclear, and predictions from "current tendencies" should be taken *cum grano salis*.

Gebser himself warned that we should not lose ourselves in great expectations. As he wrote in one of his last books, "The world will never become a paradise. If it did, its existence would become illusory. Let us not deceive ourselves and succumb to false hopes. The world will not become much better, merely a little different, and perhaps somewhat more appreciative of the things that really matter."[5]

At the beginning of a new millennium, in a time when the mystery of things—and not only consciousness—is fading in the misdirected light of "explanation," a possible future that will be "more appreciative of the things that really matter" is something to look forward to.

NOTES

—

Introduction: Consciousness Explained?

1. Crick, *The Astonishing Hypothesis,* p. 3.
2. Rose, ed., *From Brains to Consciousness,* p. 1.
3. Humphrey, Ibid., p. 247.
4. Searle, *The Mystery of Consciousness,* p. xiv.
5. Ibid., p. 6.
6. Ibid., p. xiii.
7. John Horgan, *The End of Science,* p. 179. Interviewed by John Horgan, Dennett remarked, "We can't explain *anything* to everyone's satisfaction." But, he continued, "the sense of mystery is gone from photosynthesis and reproduction, and I think in the end we will have a similar account of consciousness." I cannot remark intelligently about photosynthesis, but after attending the births of my two sons I can say without qualification that Dennett is dead wrong about reproduction.
8. Searle, *Mystery of Consciousness,* pp. 158, 192, 191.
9. Darling, *After Life,* p. 82. Darling's account is based on a remarkable paper published in 1965 by John Lorber, a specialist in hydrocephalus, "Hydranencephaly with Normal Development," in *Developmental Medicine and Child Neurology,* December 1965, 7: 628–633. A popular account of Lorber's further work, "Is Your Brain Really Necessary" by Roger Lewin, appeared in the December 12, 1980, issue of *Science.*
10. Darling, *After Life,* p. 83.
11. Another remarkable case of hydrocephalus involved the esoteric teacher Rudolf Steiner, who tutored a boy severely retarded by the disease. From being irredeemably mentally deficient, Steiner's student went on to a medical school and became a doctor. His physical condition also improved under Steiner's care. See Steiner, *Autobiography,* pp. 96–99. A brief account can be found in Colin Wilson's *Rudolf Steiner,* pp. 46–47.

12. Singer himself is skeptical of any attempts to explain consciousness. He writes that "those aspects of consciousness that give rise to the so-called hard problems in the philosophy of consciousness, the experience of self-awareness and the notion of the privacy of one's subjective sensations, transcend the reach of reductionistic neurobiological explanations" (in Rose, ed., *From Brains to Consciousness*, pp. 228–229).

13. Zohar and Marshall, *SQ*, p. 62.

14. Similar observations have been made by the Chilean neuroscientists Humberto Maturana and Francisco Varela. See *The Tree of Knowledge, the Biological Roots of Human Understanding*.

15. Moskvitin, *Essay on the Origin of Thought*, p. 50. An excellent summary of Moskvitin's main ideas can be found in Colin Wilson, *Access To Inner Worlds*, pp. 71–87.

16. Barfield, *History, Guilt and Habit*, p. 61.

1. R. M. Bucke and the Future of Humanity

1. Disquietingly, Bucke's psychiatric practice included procedures we would today find unacceptable. Early in his career, endorsing the Victorian belief that masturbation promotes mental disability, Bucke briefly instituted the precedent of "wiring" the penis to prevent his male patients from abusing themselves. The results were equivocal and the practice soon abandoned. Later, he practiced gynecological surgery as a treatment for insanity in women, again with debatable results. His notions, savage to us, were in keeping with the interest in endocrinology popular at the time, and were prompted by a recognized need for more active methods of treating mental illness. Bucke later abandoned surgery and in his last years developed plans for a self-sufficient therapeutic community, an idea years ahead of its time. For different views of Bucke's contribution to psychiatry see Peter A. Rechnitzer, *R. M. Bucke and Victorian Lunacy: Richard M. Bucke and the Practice of Late Nineteenth-Century Psychiatry* (Cambridge: Cambridge University Press, 1986).

2. Bucke, *Cosmic Consciousness*, p. 9.

3. Ibid., pp. 9–10.

4. Sharon Begley, "Religion and the Brain," *Newsweek*, May 14, 2001.

5. Bucke, *Cosmic Consciousness*, p. 2.

6. Ibid., p. 3.

7. Ibid., p. 4.

8. Ibid., pp. 34, 38.

9. Ibid., p. 11.

10. Ibid., p. 61.

11. It is unclear how much Bucke knew or understood of this side of Carpenter's life. Carpenter himself is alleged to have had sexual relations with Whitman and, toward the end of his life, with the astrologer Gavin Arthur, later well known in the counterculture of the 1960s as the popu-

larizer of the "Age of Aquarius." See my *Turn Off Your Mind: The Mystic Sixties and the Dark Side of the Age of Aquarius.*

12. Quoted in *Cosmic Consciousness,* p. 249.

13. For an excellent account of drug experimentation and consciousness exploration in the nineteenth century, see Mike Jay's *Emperors of Dreams.*

2. William James and the Anesthetic Revelation

1. William James "On Some Hegelisms," in *Mindscapes: An Anthology of Drug Writing,* ed. Antonio Melechi, p. 20.

2. Ibid., pp. 21, 22.

3. James, *Varieties of Religious Experience,* p. 304.

4. Melechi, *Mindscapes,* p. 20.

5. James, *Varieties of Religious Experience,* p. 305.

6. Powys, *Autobiography,* pp. 1–2.

3. Henri Bergson and the Élan Vital

1. One of the earliest, most vocal, and incisive of these was Samuel Butler, who summed up his antipathy to the strict mechanical interpretation of Darwinian evolution with the complaint that Darwin had "banished mind from the universe." In a series of brilliant, eloquent and eccentric books— *Life and Habit, Unconscious Memory, Luck or Cunning*—Butler proceeded to make clear the inadequacies of Darwin's hypothesis, drawing on ideas remarkably similar to Rupert Sheldrake's "morphic resonance." Butler's ideas later influenced George Bernard Shaw, another outspoken opponent of strict Darwinian evolution. In an age drunk on the success of science, however, both thinkers were considered cranks and their criticisms had little effect on their contemporaries.

2. Years later, Aldous Huxley, in *The Doors of Perception,* called upon Bergson's notion of the brain as a "reducing valve" to account for the effects of mescaline on consciousness.

3. Bergson, *Mind-Energy,* pp. 47, 77.

4. Ibid., pp. 56–77.

5. Ibid., pp. 27, 41.

6. Ibid., p. 21.

7. Bergson, *Creative Evolution,* p. 136.

8. Bergson, *Mind-Energy,* p. 18.

9. I should at this point address a question that in recent years has put views such as Bergson's out of fashion. The question, that is, if there is any way to judge a species' "superiority" and hence "rank" in the order of evolution, with the corollary that humankind forms no higher species or goal and is merely one among a multiplicity of other living organisms, with no particular meaning or purpose. Indeed, some radical biocentric thinkers

argue that humankind is a degenerate species, one the planet would be better off rid of.

To me, this question seems motivated more by muddled political concerns than by anything else. Clearly an increase of freedom and intelligence, hence choice and creativity, is a valid and worthy gauge by which to judge evolutionary advance, and I accept Bergson's view that in human beings these properties reach a degree of expression that so far seems unattainable by other species. Obviously, the only means I have to judge this is by the very "humanness" whose superiority is in question. But then, it is by the same means that the advocates of "enlightened misanthropy" advance their views. The biocentrists who declare that an owl, bear, or other endangered species is more "valuable" than humankind can only arrive at that thought through their being human. As far as we can tell, no owl or bear or other species can. It is only human beings who are concerned about the dangers of a mistaken appreciation of their value in the scope of life, just as it is only human beings who are concerned about the environment. To say this is not to say that we are not faced with tremendous ecological problems, brought on by our own selfishness and ignorance. Clearly we are. But to argue, for example, that Beethoven is no "higher" than an amoeba is surely not going to do much in the way of this. On the contrary, it is only by recognizing our *responsibilities* as agents of life's creative advance that we can muster the will and intelligence to face this challenge. And if the biocentrist says that I only find Beethoven "higher" and "valuable" because I am human, I can only say that yes, I agree, but that this adds nothing to the discussion, other than the tautology that because I am human I have human values. Yet, what *other* values are there? If we subtract these "human values" we are left with no gauge at all, no means to judge anything, and certainly no way of arguing that we should in any way be concerned about other species. (We would, I believe, be unable to carry on any kind of conversation whatsoever.) Even the biocentrists' ethic that puts animal life higher than the human is itself a human value. They would not think that if they weren't human.

10. A digression here seems in order. Nothing is easier than to point out the lack of evidence for our time exhibiting any "creative advance" over earlier periods, except in the sense of technological progress, which in the last century was the accepted definition of progress itself. Indeed, in many ways we seem to show a good deal of "degeneration" and "decadence"— rising crime rates, looming ecological disasters, social breakdown, the lowering of intellectual and civil standards, "dumbing down," and popular vulgarity, to name just a few. And our tendency to view the achievements of the past as existing on a higher level from which we have slipped—recent postmodern and politically correct sensibilities notwithstanding—remains strong. If the "creative advance" of civilization were

to be judged in a strictly linear, progressive fashion, then these criticisms would have to stand. Indeed, I agree with many of them and it is not my purpose to argue that the early twenty-first century is necessarily more advanced than, say, the fifteenth, tenth, or whichever one you may choose. What I do believe is that what is asked of us is to view the *entire period* of humankind's coming into self-consciousness—the beginning of which varies depending on your sources, but which we may for convenience say was certainly achieved by at least 3000 B.C.—as the time in which the mind or consciousness began to lift itself out of the heavy slumber of matter. Within that period, which is anywhere between five and ten thousand years, we have certainly seen nothing like the simple, neat, and gratifying "progression" from bestial savagery to "modern civilization," so enamored of nineteenth- and early twentieth-century thinkers. What we do see, I believe, are the struggles of consciousness to understand itself and the world, to give expression to that understanding, and to use that understanding to discover and explore new areas of itself and the world. Paradoxically, a study of history, ostensibly of the "past," shows us how closely involved we are with it, and how events seemingly distant from us need millennia to be worked out. The distractions and harangue of a shifting, fleeting "present" conceal from us our link to impulses initiated centuries ago, whose fulfillment may depend on our cooperation.

4. The Superman

1. See also the eagle and snake symbolism of works like *Thus Spoke Zarathustra,* both animals being familiar totems of alchemy. Like Schopenhauer, Nietzsche was aware of Eastern thought, and while denying any kind of "other world," his writing is driven by passionate "spiritual" questions and insights. Nietzsche's attack on Christianity was prompted by the self-serving, hypocritical variety prominent in Europe at the time (and today) and was fueled by a profound need to find a deeper "meaning" for human beings than what it provided. Schopenhauer's "will," incidentally, is the same as Bergson's life force, except that for Schopenhauer, a pessimist, its strivings were pointless. Nietzsche and Bergson were life-affirmers and took the opposite view.

2. There are, of course, some severe problems with this notion. If taken seriously at face value, eternal recurrence cannot be experienced as either eternal or recurrent since, if *everything* recurs again *exactly* as it happens now—and has recurred such throughout eternity—there would be no difference between "this" recurrence and either an "earlier" or "later" one. And being identical, we would have no means of telling them apart, even if we somehow had proof of the reality of recurrence. Each recurrence would appear to us as the "same time," and hence seemingly occurring only once. If recurrence is true and if it is eternal, I could only experience it as such if I had already done so in an earlier recurrence—which means

that I would have to be aware of recurrence "from the beginning," as it were, and so *always* aware of it, or at least aware of it in each recurrence. Which means that if I became convinced of its reality, say, tomorrow, my experience of that conviction must have happened in an earlier recurrence, and will happen again in the next. Add to this the whole problem of "the first time" in a process that is supposedly eternal, and we can see how difficult it is to make sense of it. Which is not to say that the idea does not have transformative power, as it clearly does, and that this was Nietzsche's true interest in it. For all his unconvincing attempts to "prove" recurrence "scientifically" (see the collection of his notes published posthumously as *The Will to Power*), Nietzsche, I believe, was not really concerned with this aspect of the idea, but with whether or not it affected one's attitude toward life. It was, as he makes clear in *The Gay Science,* where the notion first appears, a test of whether one could say "Yes" to life or not. Subsequent writers who adopted the theme, like P. D. Ouspensky and the novelist and playwright J. B. Priestley, abandoned this aspect of it, and focused instead on the possibility of becoming aware of one's recurrence and hence making changes in one's life. For a thoughtful study of the similarities between Nietzsche's recurrence and Rilke's doctrine of "once only" announced in the *Duino Elegies,* see the brilliant essay "Rilke and Nietzsche" by Erich Heller in *The Importance of Nietzsche.*

3. The influential dictum of the notorious "magician" Aleister Crowley, who lifted it from Rabelais' motto of the abbey of Thelema. William Blake also employed it.

4. See James Webb's brilliant but critical histories of occultism *The Occult Establishment* (1976) and *The Occult Underground* (1988), also Joscelyn Godwin's *The Theosophical Enlightenment* (1994).

5. A. R. Orage and the New Age
1. Quoted in James Webb, *The Harmonious Circle,* p. 206.
2. Orage, *Consciousness: Animal, Human and Superhuman,* p. 9.
3. Bergson, *Mind-Energy,* p. 5.
4. Orage, *Consciousness,* p. 25.
5. Ibid.
6. Ibid., pp. 51, 77. See also Jurij Moskvitin's remarks in my introduction.
7. Ibid., pp. 18, 68.

6. Ouspensky's Fourth Dimension
1. The idea is not uncommon in Western philosophy; it can be found in Heraclitus, Pythagoras, and the Stoics. Ouspensky himself discovered it in the writings of the Alexandrian Church Fathers, as well as in the work of Robert Louis Stevenson.

2. A left-wing radical, she would die in the Boutirsky prison in Moscow after the failed revolution of 1905.
3. See Hesse's *Demian*, p. 149. "We who wore the sign might justly be considered 'odd' by the world: yes, even crazy, and dangerous. We were *aware* or in the process of becoming aware and our striving was directed toward achieving a more and more complete state of awareness while the striving of the others was a quest aimed at binding their opinions, ideals, duties, their lives and fortunes more and more closely to the herd. There, too, was striving, there, too, were power and greatness. But whereas we, who were marked, believed that we represented the will of Nature to something new, to the individualism of the future, the others sought to perpetuate the status quo. Humanity—which they loved as we did—was for them something complete that must be maintained and protected. For us, humanity was a distant goal toward which all men were moving, whose image no one knew, whose laws were nowhere written down."
4. Ouspensky, *Tertium Organum*, p. 258.
5. Ouspensky does in fact refer to a lecture by James in *A Pluralistic Universe* in which mention is made of Bergson's argument that science never studies the universe as a whole, only a "time-section" of it.
6. Ouspensky, *Tertium Organum*, p. 137.
7. Hinton also wrote stories about "eternal recurrence" and had an ingenious theory to account for its possibility. He argued that the aether—not yet shown not to exist through the Michelson-Morley experiment of 1887—was like a phonograph record, in the sense that it had "grooves." Matter—the planets, sun, and stars—are "carried" in these grooves and every so often, Hinton believed, they were brought back to their starting point. Time then would repeat itself. No doubt this idea endeared him to Ouspensky.
8. See Rudolf v. B. Rucker's introduction to *Speculations on the Fourth Dimension: Selected Writings of Charles H. Hinton*, p. vi.
9. They also seemed to have presaged the whole fascination with cubist painting and simultaneity in literature that would erupt in the early twentieth century.
10. D. H. Lawrence, a reader of Ouspensky, believed he had it all wrong about animal perception. See James Moore's *Gurdjieff and Mansfield*, p. 197. More recently, the poet Peter Redgrove makes similar critical remarks in his fascinating book *The Black Goddess and the Unseen Real*, p. 19.
11. Ouspensky, *Tertium Organum*, p. 128.
12. Some of Ouspensky's ideas have resurfaced in recent times under the name "punctuated equilibrium."
13. See the work of Graham Hancock and Robert Bauval.
14. Ouspensky, *A New Model of the Universe*, pp. 29–30. One problem with this notion however is how the Inner Circle itself "evolved." If *all* civi-

lization is the product of "artificial cultivation," how did the "first" civilization come about? This, in a different form, is the problem with all
"extraterrestrial-based" theories of the rise of civilization. If civilization
on Earth was started by space beings, who started their civilization?

15. "A new type of man is being formed now and amongst us. The selection
goes on in all races and nations of the earth." *Tertium Organum*, p. 108.

7. The Bishop and the Bulldog

1. In his Notebook for 1768–1771, the Enlightenment polymath Georg
Christoph Lichtenberg said it all with characteristic brevity: "Of all the
animals on earth, man is closest to the ape." Georg Christoph
Lichtenberg, *The Waste Books,* trans. R. J. Hollingdale (New York: New
York Review of Books, 2000), p. 21.

2. Lamarck's notion of inheritance, however, continued to have champions.
For a good account of the Darwin/Lamarck debate, see Arthur Koestler's
The Case of the Midwife Toad (New York: Random House, 1971).

3. Lyell's notion is known as *uniformitarianism*, and it argues that the same
processes taking place now have taken place at the same rate in the past:
the waves that crash against the shore today have done so in the same
way for aeons. Periodically Lyell's dictum is challenged by one version or
other of *catastrophism*, which argues that over the ages, the Earth has
been subject to sudden convulsions of one form or another. One popular
account in the 1950s, Immanuel Velikovksy's best-seller *Worlds in
Collision,* argued that a comet nearly crashed into the Earth, causing terrific damage and, incidentally, accomplishing some of the miracles
recounted in the Bible. There have been less incredible and more convincing arguments for catastrophism, but, for all its provincialism, Lyell's
uniformitarianism is still the approved version of events.

8. Enter the Madame

1. In early December 1877, Samuel Butler published at his own expense *Life
and Habit,* the first of his philosophical works criticizing Darwin's version of evolution; *Isis Unveiled* was published in September of the same
year.

2. Roszak, *Unfinished Animal,* p. 118.

3. Spiritualism's menu of raps, table turning, messages from the dead, floating tambourines, and whatnot strikes us as silly, if not suspiciously morbid. But for a generation told that they were nothing but a collection of
chemical reactions, evolved by chance in a universe doomed to certain
extinction, materializing spirits and levitating mediums seemed to offer
some hope. If such things could be, then science was wrong—or at least
it had left a good deal out of the equation. The idea that only the feeble-
minded were drawn to séances is incorrect, although they participated in
abundance. As we have seen, thinkers as acute as William James and

Henri Bergson were in the thick of it, along with Oliver Lodge, Thomas Edison, Sir William Crookes, Camille Flammarion, and Sir Arthur Conan Doyle. The situation was similar to what we find today with the "New Age": people who are unsatisfied with the "scientific" account of human existence that declares we are either puppets of "selfish genes" or mere assortments of molecules, yet find little solace in recognized religion, seek out alternative routes to personal and spiritual meaning. Much of this is certainly sensation seeking, and the metaphysical marketplace offers a wide selection of spiritual fashions—but not all. The same hunger for meaning and purpose that draws the serious-minded to Tantra yoga or astrology brought their nineteenth-century counterparts to the medium and the mystic.

4. In modern times the idea that the Earth is a living organism was perhaps first proposed by the German psychologist Theodore Fechner. In *Tertium Organum* Ouspensky adapts Fechner's idea to his vision of a "pluralistic" evolution and proposes that the various levels of consciousness represented by the human, animal, and plant world may not have evolved sequentially out of each other, but may instead be the different but simultaneous and interconnected functions of one organism. See *Tertium Organum,* p. 280.

5. Blavatsky, *The Secret Doctrine,* vol. 1, p. 44.

6. Ibid., p. 74.

7. Ibid., p. 68.

8. *Last and First Men* (1930) and *Starmaker* (1937). Blavatsky's influence on science fiction and fantasy writers has been considerable. Her vision of past ages and deep, cosmic time has found its way into the work of pulp giants like H. P. Lovecraft and Robert E. Howard, and Michael Moorcock, whose lapidary tales of decaying imaginary kingdoms brought an uncommon sophistication to a generally adolescent genre, wove Theosophical notions into many of his stories.

9. For an excellent account of Hyperborea ("Beyond the North Wind" in ancient Greek) and the mythology of the Poles, see Joscelyn Godwin's fascinating book *Arktos.*

10. Blavatsky could not have known it, but there is good evidence to suggest that the Earth's crust does indeed experience periodic shifts of a tremendous scale, enough to bring a civilization to an end. See Charles Hapgood's *The Earth's Shifting Crust* (Pantheon: New York, 1958).

9. Dr. Steiner, I Presume?

1. Colin Wilson, *Rudolf Steiner,* p. 27.

2. Steiner's considerable practical abilities are reminiscent of two other "handy" visionaries: Emmanuel Swedenborg and G. I. Gurdjieff. Swedenborg worked as an assessor of mines, among other occupations, and he once engineered the transport of several ships inland, across

mountains. When Ouspensky arrived in Tiflis during the Russian Revolution to work once again with Gurdjieff, he found him setting up a dynamo.

3. Steiner tells the story in *An Autobiography*. This, of course, is the best place to start for accounts of his life; unfortunately, it was left unfinished at the time of his death and only covers the period up to 1907. Besides Colin Wilson's book already mentioned, other biographies include *Rudolf Steiner: Herald of a New Epoch* by Stewart Easton; *A Scientist of the Invisible* by A. P. Sheperd (Edinburgh: Floris Classics, 1983); and *Rudolf Steiner: A Documentary Biography* by Johannes Hemleben (Sussex: Henry Goulden Limited, 1975).

4. Another possible influence was the best-selling *The Great Initiates* by the dramatist and critic Edouard Schuré, published in France in 1889. Schure's book is a massive spiritual history of humankind, told in the form of biographies of its great religious teachers. Schuré argued that all religions share a secret, esoteric side not perceived by the masses, but recognized by those with the requisite insight, and that its message has been handed down, from initiate to initiate through the centuries. Marie von Sivers, whom Steiner met in Berlin in 1900 and who first suggested that it was his destiny to lead a new spiritual renaissance, knew Schuré and was deeply influenced by his book, which she translated. In 1902, by which time she had become Steiner's companion (she would eventually become his second wife), Steiner delivered a series of lectures that would later become the substance of his book *Christianity as Mystical Fact,* part of which advances the view of Christ as an "initiate"—an idea that would not cause much concern today but was radical at the time. Schuré was Steiner's senior by twenty years; nevertheless, he recognized in the younger man a great spiritual power, and soon became a dedicated follower—indicative of the kind of confidence Steiner instilled in those who knew him.

10. From Goethean Science to the Wisdom of the Human Being

1. Quoted in Erich Heller, *The Disinherited Mind*, p. 31.

2. An example of the difference between primary and secondary qualities can be seen in music. For us, what emerges when the hammer of a piano strikes the strings in a certain order is a sonata by Mozart or Beethoven, which we deem beautiful according to our taste and the ability of the pianist. For "scientists" what emerges are silent vibrations of air, which are unaffected by sequence or performance. What is of absolute value to us is, insofar as they are in pursuit of "truth," irrelevant to scientists. Their "reality" likewise leaves us unmoved.

3. A good account of Goethe's ideas on color can be found in Arthur Zajonc's brilliant *Catching the Light,* which can also be read as an account of the evolution of consciousness from the point of view of our

experience of light. Elsewhere he writes, "The qualitative experience of color in humans is incidental to the discipline of physics." But, he adds, "This situation is emphatically not the case for the science of human consciousness. The phenomena at the center of study are precisely the phenomena of conscious experience" (in Hammeroff et. al. eds., *Toward a Science of Consciousness III*, p. 417).

4. From *Goethe's Conception of the World* (London: Rudolf Steiner Press, 1928), quoted in Robert A. McDermott, ed., *The Essential Steiner*, p. 49. The German original was first published in 1897.

5. Also published as *The Philosophy of Spiritual Activity* and, in a new translation, *Intuitive Thinking as a Spiritual Path* (1995).

6. Steiner, *Intuitive Thinking as a Spiritual Path*, p. 5.

7. As with many fundamental philosophical questions, a difficulty arises from the tool we have to grapple with them: language. Steiner was correct to suggest that the phrase "spiritual activity" would be closer in English to the experience he wished to convey than the literal equivalent of *freiheit*, freedom. Yet even that suffers from the blunt, unwieldy necessity of using one word to designate different, but related, experiences. Most of us would argue that simply in reading Steiner's—or anyone's—book, we were being mentally "active." But then, what is the difference between reading a book about Steiner's, or anyone's, life and absorbing the facts, and then reading it and having the sudden vivid realization while reading that this person was not simply a name on a page, but an *actual person* who lived and breathed and to whom these things happened? We do not have a word to clearly and unambiguously denote this difference, yet it is the difference between "merely living" and feeling the unmistakable *reality* of life. I may say that I am a free, active being and acknowledge the truth of that statement. But to *feel* it is something other.

8. Steiner, *On the Theory of Knowledge Implicit in Goethe's World Conception* (1886), quoted in Colin Wilson, *Rudolf Steiner*, p. 166.

9. *Intuitive Thinking as a Spiritual Path*, p. 79.

10. It was apparently to some passages from Fichte that Steiner's unknown mentor (see chapter 9) drew his attention. Also, John Henry Mackay, author of the standard biography of Stirner, *Max Stirner: sein Leben und sein Werk* (1897), was a friend of Steiner's during his Berlin period.

11. Rittelmeyer, *Rudolf Steiner Enters My Life*, p. 61.

12. For the suggestion that Steiner read the Akashic Record during hypnagogic states I am indebted to Colin Wilson. See *Rudolf Steiner: The Man and his Vision*. That Steiner associated hypnagogic states with spiritual perception is clear from remarks he made in a lecture given in 1918, later published as *The Dead Are With Us* (London: Rudolf Steiner Press, 1964). "Besides waking life and sleeping life there is a third state even more important for intercourse with the spiritual world. . . . I mean the

state connected with the act of waking and the act of going to sleep" (pp. 18–19).

11. Cosmic Evolution

1.   Clearly we can see the ancient tradition of the four elements in the first four planetary incarnations: fire, air, water, and earth. But one thing does seem odd. Although one would think that the element of fire, or "heat," should be associated with the Sun, Steiner instead chose Saturn as the initial stage of the cosmic evolutionary process. There is perhaps a reason for this. For Steiner, "matter" evolves out of spirit. Each of the planetary stages he discusses represents an increasing density of matter: from "heat," or fire, to earth is a process of increasing condensation. Heat, as we know, is electromagnetic radiation of a certain wavelength. Its physicality is minimal, so it would make sense to introduce it as the first step in a process of gradual "materialization." And heat makes sense as well in terms of current ideas on the origin of the universe. Big Bang theory argues that the universe began as an inconceivably hot, incredibly dense "point" which—for no apparent reason—"exploded" some ten to twenty billion years ago. So Steiner, who knew nothing of the Big Bang—the idea wasn't mooted until George Gamov and his colleagues first developed the theory in the 1940s and 1950s—made a pretty accurate "guess." In fact, if one ignores his terminology, much of Steiner's account parallels what can be found in scores of popular science books.

But why Saturn? Two possibilities come to mind. One is that Saturn was the ancient god of time, as well as the ruler of the Golden Age, the mythical paradise of the earliest times. According to contemporary cosmological theory, "time" itself began with the Big Bang, so having Saturn at the outset makes at least mythological sense. But there is another possible reason. Saturn is also associated astrologically with contraction, concentration, and constraint; people of a "saturnine" disposition are prone to melancholy and frustration. That the terrific "heat" that preceded the universe was contracted into an inconceivably dense "point" seems a fairly "saturnine" condition, and again Steiner's nomenclature is surprisingly accurate. But this physical contraction has psychological and spiritual parallels. In a series of lectures given in Berlin in 1911, Steiner remarked that the picture of cosmic evolution presented in *An Outline of Esoteric Science* was, although "correct," "deeply immersed in Maya and Illusion" (*The Inner Realities of Evolution* [London: Rudolf Steiner Publishing Company, 1953], p. 21).

Steiner seems to hit the Big Bang nail right on the head when he goes on to say, "Of space there was none in our sense on ancient Saturn. And time first came into being there" (ibid.). But what he is at pains to communicate is that even these abstract yet still relatively "physical" accounts are not the full truth about ancient Saturn. Steiner admits that in his written accounts he had to descend into the trappings of maya in order not to "startle" the public. Given that the account of cosmic evolution presented in *An Outline of Esoteric Science* is fairly startling itself for an unprepared reader, one wonders what it is Steiner was trying to obscure. What the reader of the lectures in *The Inner Realities of Evolution* discovers is that the real character of our previous planetary existences has more to do with certain moral and existential states of consciousness than with metaphors of increasingly dense materiality. Steiner told his audience in Berlin that the true nature of the Saturn condition was that of a "dreadful emptiness into which flows fear" (ibid., p. 11). An initiate seeking to understand the state of consciousness during the Saturn incarnation must be able to feel "his environment tinged and saturated with that which inspires dread and fear wherever he turns" (ibid., p. 10), and also the inner strength and certainty to overcome this fear. Considering that people born "under the sign of Saturn" are usually given an ample share of angst, Steiner's insights seem remarkably appropriate. In the lectures Steiner remarks that he has searched contemporary literature for any sign of an awareness of this "Saturn condition," and declares there is little to be found. This was in 1911. He died in 1925, two years before Martin Heidegger's massive meditation on human beings' "thrownness" into Being, *Sein und Zeit*. When Steiner gave his lectures, Kierkegaard had not yet been rediscovered, Jean-Paul Sartre was five years old, and existentialism, with its chorus of dread, anxiety, fear, and nothingness, would not become an intellectual and cultural fad for at least another twenty years. In his pronouncements on a primordial psychic condition, Steiner seems to have anticipated the spiritual emptiness that would dominate the Western popular consciousness until the revival of the occult and mysticism in the 1960s.

2. Easton, *Rudolf Steiner: Herald of a New Epoch*, p. 271.
3. Steiner, *Cosmic Memory*, pp. 134–135.
4. McDermott, ed., *The Essential Steiner*, p. 172.
5. Bergson, *Creative Evolution*, p. 136.

12. Hypnagogia

1. Ouspensky wrote of his remarkable experiences with both hypnagogia and "lucid dreams," a related phenomenon, in the chapter "On the Study of Dreams and On Hypnotism" in *A New Model of the Universe*. The best account of Swedenborg's familiarity with hypnagogic states can be found in Wilson Van Dusen's books *The Natural Depth in Man* and *The Presence of Other Worlds*. Hypnagogia is also intimately related to the practice of "active imagination" developed by C. G. Jung. One of the books listed in Mavromatis's bibliography is a series of Steiner's lectures grouped together as *The Evolution of Consciousness* (Sussex: Rudolf Steiner Press, 1966).

2. Steiner *Rosicrucian Wisdom,* p. 83.
3. Mavromatis, *Hypnagogia,* p. 259.
4. Experiments with paroptic vision were carried out in the late nineteenth and early twentieth centuries by the scientists Cesare Lombroso and Jules Romains, with startling results. (See Colin Wilson's *Poltergeist* [1981] and *Afterlife* [1987] for an account of Lombroso's work.) The poet René Daumal, later a student of G. I. Gurdjieff, carried out several "blind sight" experiments with a colleague of Romains. For a brief account of Daumal's paroptic vision experiments, see my article "Climbing Mount Analogue" in the September/October 2001 issue of *The Quest,* pp. 167–171.
5. Mavromatis, like other theorists such as Arthur Koestler, suggests that creativity, like hypnagogia, is a kind of "regression" to an earlier, prerational kind of thinking. Given this, it isn't surprising to find synesthesia as a characteristic of several creative individuals. The composer Olivier Messiaen, for example, saw colors while hearing, and even reading, music. The novelist Vladimir Nabokov was a synestheist, as were the poets Baudelaire and Rimbaud. Much of the psychedelic art of the 1960s, associated with the use of mind-altering drugs whose effect is associated with a "regression" to prerational states of consciousness, was synesthetic.
6. Steiner, *The Inner Nature of Music,* p. 14. The synesthetic experiences described by Steiner in these lectures are a central part of Anthroposophy and are discussed in many of his other works, such as *Theosophy* and *How to Know Higher Worlds.*
7. Curiously, Gurdjieff speaks of human beings as "three-brained beings" in *Beelzebub's Tales to His Grandson,* a work written in the 1930s, considerably before the notion of a "triune brain" became popular in the 1960s through the work of Paul McLean.
8. Rittelmeyer, *Rudolf Steiner Enters My Life,* p. 61.
9. The same is true of Swedenborg's accounts of heaven, hell, and life on other planets.
10. Rittelmeyer, *Rudolf Steiner Enters My Life,* p. 62.
11. Mavromatis, *Hypnagogia,* pp. 276, 278.
12. Ibid., p. 281.

13. The Invisible Mind

1. It is true that some forms of inanimate matter show some features that they share with living things. Crystals, for example, exhibit repeated symmetry and organization, and in some schools of thought are considered a kind of "halfway house" between the organic and inorganic realms. I think there are good arguments in favor of this view, but do not believe it affects my remarks above.

14. Cracking the Egg

1. Neumann, *The Origins and History of Consciousness;* von Franz, *Creation Myths.*
2. Neumann, *The Origins and History of Consciousness,* p. 35.
3. Ibid., p. 105.
4. Ibid., p. 24. This is also the message of Nietzsche's famous admonition to "become who you are," and it is likewise the central theme of Hegel's immense narrative of consciousness, *The Phenomenology of Spirit.* To bring to full, conscious articulation what lies latent in potential is one of the central obsessions of the Romantic movement, with its emphasis on growth, becoming, education, and self-cultivation.
5. Neumann, *The Origins and History of Consciousness,* p. 281.

15. The Lost World

1. The fact that Eisler at age six was a refugee from Nazi Germany may account for her particular animus toward thinkers like Nietzsche, whom she associates with Hitler's unquestionably repulsive political views. Nietzsche had indeed been appropriated by Nazi ideologues for a brief time, mostly through the influence of his sister, Elisabeth-Forster-Nietzsche, a rabid anti-Semite, Aryanophile, and promilitarist. But when it became clear that Nietzsche's views on just about everything were as remote from the Nazis' as possible, he was quickly cast aside. Nietzsche was an outspoken *anti*-anti-Semite, an eloquent opponent of German militarism (and militarism in general), and, contrary to Ms. Eisler's remarks, a profoundly spiritual individual. That Eisler repeats many of the stock misrepresentations of his ideas, as well as the standard quotations taken out of context, displays her understandable zeal in promoting her cause, but does little to forward it.
2. *Total Man* (1972), *Personality and Evolution* (1973), *The Neanderthal Question* (1977), *The Paranormal* (1978), *Guardians of the Ancient Wisdom* (1979), *The Double Helix of the Mind* (1980), *The Secret Life of Humans* (1981), *Creatures from Inner Space* (1984), and *Cities of Dreams* (1989).
3. The dates for Neanderthals are much later than what we would suppose for the initial "human beings" who possessed Steiner's Old Moon consciousness. Yet as Steiner makes clear, that consciousness did not end with the evolution of Old Moon into Earth; it lingered on, and it was not until the fourth and fifth post-Atlantean epochs that the kind of clear, rational consciousness we experience today became dominant. So although Neanderthals appeared much later than the time of Old Moon, their consciousness could certainly have shared many of its characteristics. Likewise, the consciousness of the Cro-Magnons who supplanted the Neanderthals seems, at least according to Gooch, to be much more like that of our own, yet, given Steiner's timeline, they appeared during the age

of Atlantis. But just as the Old Moon consciousness continued for a time beyond Old Moon itself, our clear, waking consciousness may have had its beginnings with the Cro-Magnons. It is also possible that the Goddess worshippers of Marija Gimbutas's Old Europe were close descendants of Neanderthals, or of "modern" humans with more Neanderthal "in" them than Cro-Magnon, just as the opposite may have been true for the Kurgan warriors.

On the subject of "Moon consciousness" in general, the idea that an ancient universal religion based on magic and the worship of the Moon predated our own solar, logical civilization was perhaps first proposed by Robert Graves in his classic *The White Goddess* (1948). The idea, of course, has by now become part of the common stock of popular pagan, occult, and esoteric ideas, finding a majority of its adherents in the variety of Wiccan practices available today.

It may be well to comment on the disparity of time periods that may arise when relating the ideas of different thinkers about the evolution of consciousness. This will become more apparent when we discuss the work of Jean Gebser, which in many ways bears important similarities with that of Rudolf Steiner. Rather than attempt an exact chronological correlation, which I believe is not possible nor necessary, what strikes me as important in showing any such relation is to understand the similarity in the kind of consciousness described, and not the supposed historical periods during which they are believed to have existed. That Steiner, Mavromatis, and now Gooch all, in different ways, point to a kind of consciousness that *in a general sense* seems to have preceded our own is, to me, the important thing, and not whether or not they match up chronologically. Having said this, I believe there are enough points of contact between the specifics of their different theories to at least suggest the possibility they are all talking about the same thing.

4. See especially *Cities of Dreams*, pp. 242–249.

5. Ideas about and preferences in sexuality arguably may stem from one's own "consciousness type." Highly "individualized" characters may find the idea of group sex off-putting, although not necessarily for reasons of morality or prudery. I have not had an opportunity to research this in any depth, but it is my intuition—and at this point it is only this—that individuals with a high regard for their "self" or "personality" would find group sex unattractive precisely because such activity operates by *lessening* the distinctiveness between individuals; and as that distinctiveness is valued by strong personalities, anything that subtracts from it is to be avoided. Such individuals set much store by what sets them *apart* from others. Sex, like other bodily functions, is a highly generic activity—as the philosopher Nicolai Berdyaev remarked, the soul resides in the face, not the genitals—and in the abandon of group eroticism, one partner is as good as another.

Characters of a weaker personality would be attracted to group sex for precisely the opposite reasons, because in such activity they would lose what little sense of self they have—which to them is generally a burden, or, in any case, is too weak to be of much value—and gain a greater "identity" as part of a single, mass unit, in which everyone is the "same." There is also less chance of threat: if you and I are "equal"—i.e., reduced to our sex organs, which operate pretty much the same in everyone—then there is less need for me to protect myself from you. People of this second type consider the first "uptight"; those of the first find the second "loose" or "sloppy." It is however a not uncommon observation that there is a kind of inverse ratio between the volume of sexual objects and their aphrodisiacal powers: one naked woman is a more powerful sexual stimulant than a dozen. This is so, I would argue, because the sight of many naked bodies *reduces* them to an uninteresting "sameness." Penises and vaginas *as such* do not differ greatly, and multiple displays can have a dulling effect.

On writing this, it strikes me that herein may lie one argument for the demise of "fertility-based" religions and the rise of 'soul-" or "individual-based" ones—Christianity in particular, with its emphasis on the value and importance of each individual. In the earlier pagan beliefs, what were worshipped were the generative powers—the phallus and vagina. These were of importance, and the individual was recognized solely insofar as he or she was an *expression* of or *vehicle* for these powers, which functioned, as already mentioned, with a reliable regularity. It is a well-known fact that one's sexual organs can easily become stimulated whether one wants them to or not. They are not under the control of the individual—or at least what control we can exert over them is limited. For a religion that argued the importance of the individual *as an individual*, it would be essential to advance those aspects that were under the individual's control and to diminish, or at least to inhibit, those that were not. It may not be sex per se that is proscribed by, say, Christianity, but sex as an *expression of the nonindividual aspect of human nature*. Sexual love, as opposed to lust, can be seen as the "individualizing" of sex, in which indiscriminate copulation becomes devotion to a single beloved. It is also no surprise then that many of the "anti-Christian" activities that are anathema to the church are also anti-individual—the witches' Sabbath, the coven, the satanic orgies. These all may indeed be great fun—it *is* "liberating" to cast off individuality and plunge into some form of "oneness"—but one enjoys these pastimes at the expense of one's self-consciousness. (Of course, the opposite view is that if you can't enjoy these sorts of things, you must be suffering from some "anxiety" about losing your ego.)

In saying this I am not arguing for Christianity and against paganism, only trying to see both in the light of an evolution of consciousness. For if that evolution, at least in part, is concerned with the development of the individual—and I believe history suggests that this is indeed what has taken place—then we are bound to see clashes between a consciousness that values distinctiveness and those that value nondifferentiation. This may turn out to be nothing but a rewriting of Nietzsche's views on Apollo and Dionysus, but it strikes me that this dichotomy may be a basic distinction between character types.

6. Due to the precession of the equinoxes, the position of the Pleiades, as well as the other constellations, changes over time relative to the calendar; today they rise during the spring months; 30,000 years ago they would have risen at the time of the vernal equinox.

7. Some theorists have even suggested that it was precisely some psychoactive substance that set human beings on their higher evolutionary trail. For the late Terence McKenna the "hidden factor in the evolution of human beings, the factor that called human consciousness forth from bipedal ape with binocular vision, involved a feedback loop with plant hallucinogens." See his essay "Mushrooms and Evolution" in *The Archaic Revival* (San Francisco: Harper, 1991). However, other writers on the use of psychoactive substances by prehistoric humans agree that there is insufficient evidence to support McKenna's theory.

8. Rudgley, *Lost Civilizations of the Stone Age,* p. 100.

9. For material in this section I am indebted to Colin Wilson's book *From Atlantis to the Sphinx.*

10. Mary Leakey, *Disclosing the Past,* p. 177.

16. Noncerebral Consciousness

1. For an account of Schwaller's alchemical and political activities, see André VandenBroeck, *Al-Kemi: Hermetic, Occult, Political, and Private Aspects of R. A. Schwaller de Lubicz.*

2. Schwaller de Lubicz, *The Temples of Karnak,* p. 14.

3. In the 1980s a Japanese firm attempted to construct a replica of the Great Pyramid on a smaller scale, using "state of the art" technology. After several attempts ended in failure, the project was abandoned.

4. Schwaller de Lubicz, *The Temples of Karnak,* p. 15.

5. Ibid., p. 8.

6. Schwaller de Lubicz, *Symbol and the Symbolic,* p. 40. Something very similar was argued by Alfred North Whitehead in his little-known but brilliant *Symbolism, Its Meaning and Effect* (1927), in which he discusses our two modes of perception, which he calls "causal efficacy" and "presentational immediacy," or "meaning perception" and "immediacy perception" for short. Whitehead's central insight is that in immediacy perception we perceive things as disconnected fragments, outside of their wider context. This is a necessary expedient for "dealing" with the world, but it distorts and obscures the *relations* between things, and hence when it predominates, as in scientific analysis or in the radically disjointed perception that Sartre called "nausea" and Camus "the absurd," it commu-

nicates a profound sense of meaninglessness, as meaning is dependent on
the excised relations. Meaning perception, equally valid but undervalued
in our immediacy-oriented culture, is, as Ouspensky discovered when
looking at his ashtray, precisely an awareness of the multiple relations
everything has with everything else. And, as Ouspensky discovered, too
much meaning can be as dangerous as too little. The optimum condition
would be what I have called the Goldilocks state, when a balance of "just
right" is maintained—enough meaning to prevent a lapse into nihilism
and the absurd, and enough immediacy to prevent being overwhelmed by
insight. Failing this, the next best would be a mental discipline that would
allow for the easy shift into one or the other, from viewing the world
through a telescope or a microscope, without losing the knowledge of the
reality each mode conveys.

7.   As John Anthony West points out in *The Serpent in the Sky,* the golden
     section is more than a central item in classical architecture. It is the math-
     ematical archetype of the manifest universe, the means by which we have
     an "asymmetrical" "lumpy" world of galaxies and planets, and not a
     bland homogenous sameness, a question that contemporary cosmologists
     are also concerned with. Schwaller linked phi to the orbits of the planets,
     the proportions of Gothic cathedrals, and the forms of plants and ani-
     mals. It is a "form constant," a blueprint for reality, a law of creation.

8.   Schwaller de Lubicz, *Nature Word,* pp. 134, 135.

17. The Split

1.   Shlain, *The Alphabet Versus the Goddess,* p. 65.
2.   Ibid., p. 69.
3.   Ibid., p. 67.
4.   Shlain was not the first to put forth the argument that a direct relation
     may exist between literacy and cruelty. In his essay "To Civilize Our
     Gentlemen" (in *Language and Silence,* pp. 55–67), George Steiner
     advanced the possibility that a highly developed literary mind may foster
     an inability to appreciate the *actual* sufferings of other human beings. The
     German soldiers who daily herded Jews and other "undesirables" into the
     gas chambers and ovens at Auschwitz and Buchenwald relaxed in the
     evening over Rilke and Goethe. Reading the great poets apparently had
     little effect on their treatment of their fellow human beings. Yet the con-
     verse is also true. Dostoyevsky has made his readers profoundly aware of
     human suffering. Dickens's novels depicting the squalor and poverty of
     the working class helped bring public awareness and action to their
     plight, and it is a commonplace that "serious" literature today must con-
     cern itself with some treatment of the socially or politically disenfran-
     chised. As much as literature may be an escape from reality, it is also a
     means of galvanizing our awareness of it, and it is common experience for
     readers like myself that a good writer—not only a great one—can focus

our consciousness to such a degree that the scene depicted is *more real* than it might be in actual reality. This, in fact, is the key to our enjoyment of it, not, I submit, because we have weakened our grasp of reality through reading, but because writing, like all art, succeeds by heightening and modifying that reality, in order to communicate its *meaing* in as concentrated a form as possible. The Germans, we know, were also great lovers of art—images—as their plundering of the great treasures across Europe shows. This love apparently did not inhibit their activities.

5.   Jaynes, *The Origin of Consciousness*, p. 75.
6.   Ibid., p. 86.
7.   Van Dusen, *The Natural Depth in Man*, pp. 86, 91.
8.   Wilson Van Dusen also investigated the voices heard in schizophrenia. In his important chapter "The Presence of Spirits in Madness" in *The Presence of Other Worlds*, a study of Swedenborg, he came to the conclusion that many schizophrenics experience not only the kinds of threatening, demanding, and generally harrowing voices that Jaynes recounts, but also voices of a "higher order," what he came to consider "angelic" or "spiritual guides." These voices showed a remarkable intelligence and insight and often helped the individual as much, if not more, than conventional therapy. Such "intelligent" voices seem related to the comparable phenomena of the more "mature" personalities that often emerge in severe cases of "multiple personality disorder."
9.   Jaynes, *The Origin of Consciousness*, p. 223.
10.   Ibid., p. 225.
11.   Ibid., p. 214.
12.   Ibid., p. 202.

18. The Shock of Metaphor
1.   Barfield, *History in English Words*, p. 18.
2.   Barfield, *Owen Barfield and the Origin of Language*, pp. 2–3.
3.   Clearly there is a sense in which *all* of language and symbolism is metaphorical, in that the word or symbol stands for something else. The word "tree" is not a tree; neither is a picture of one. Yet it is clear that a picture "stands" closer to what it depicts than does its name, so we can perhaps speak of degrees of metaphorical relation, to coin an ungainly phrase. The prehistoric mind that first recognized the hunted animal in its representation ("re-present": to present again) on the cave wall must have been profoundly moved, but the mind that first "saw" (a metaphor) that the word or sound stood for the thing entered a new dimension of reality. A further development, or, as Barfield would argue, a conscious recognition of a primal relation between the mind and the world, would be the kind of analogical thought—read poetic thinking—that constitutes "metaphor" as we understand it: this is to that as that is to that; my anger burns as the fire does.

4. At the time he was writing, Barfield was very much a lone voice; his argument that the mythopoetic habits of early human beings, as well as that of contemporary primitives, were not an indication of lower intelligence, but a sign of a consciousness different from our own, was, to say the least, considered eccentric and had little influence either on the philosophy of language or literary criticism. Since then it has become a commonplace of anthropology, most notably through the work of Claude Lévi-Strauss. Other philosophers also interested in the relation between thought, language, and reality have made a study of the "mythological consciousness" central to their work; two of the most influential have been Ernst Cassirer and Gaston Bachelard.

5. Barfield, *Saving the Appearances,* pp. 116–117.

19. The Participating Mind

1. Quantum "leaps" involve indescribably tiny distances and are really not leaps at all, but a metaphor to describe the odd disappearance of a particle from one orbit and its equally odd appearance in another without covering the space in between, rather as if you popped out of the office and into your home without traversing the streets separating the two. No particle "braces" itself for the jump.

2. Berman *The Reenchantment of the World,* p. 144.

3. Ibid.

4. Heisenberg, *Physics & Philosophy,* p. 58.

5. Berman, *Reenchantment of the World,* p. 145.

6. Blake also remarked on the movement from Poetry to Prose, appreciating it as a retreat of the muses. In his poem "To The Muses," he laments the loss of the inspiration that once filled poets with divine madness. "How have you left the ancient love," he cries. "That bards of old enjoy'd in you! / The languid strings do scarcely move! / The sound is forc'd, the notes are few!"

   Other poets after Blake made the best of the situation. W. B. Yeats, writing in the 1930s, stoically remarked, "Though the great song return no more / There's keen delight in what we have: / The rattle of pebbles on the shore / Under the receding wave" ("The Nineteenth Century and After").

   For a brilliant discussion on this shift in human consciousness, the reader can do no better than to refer to Erich Heller's essay "The Poet in the Age of Prose" in his collection *In The Age of Prose,* and also his extended treatment of the same theme in *The Artist's Journey Into the Interior.*

7. Barfield, *Saving the Appearances,* pp. 135, 71.

8. Ibid., pp. 63, 65.

20. The Tapestry of Nature

1. Barfield, *Saving the Appearances,* pp. 94–95.
2. Ibid. pp. 76–77.
3. Ibid., pp. 77–78.
4. Berman *Reenchantment of the World,* p. 177.
5. In his attempt to clarify some inconsistencies in the philosophy of Kant, the philosopher Fichte seems to have anticipated Barfield's notion of figuration. See Colin Wilson's *Beyond the Outsider,* pp. 54–57, in which Wilson discusses Fichte's notion, presented in *The Vocation of Man* (1800), of a "transcendental ego" *projecting* the world perceived by the perceiving "I." "Instead of the contemplating mind ('I think')," Wilson writes, "looking out at alien nature, there is a far more interesting situation. There are two I's; one is the 'I think,' and the other the 'transcendental ego,' the ego behind the scenes, the cinema projectionist who is projecting nature out there. This metaphor of the cinema described the situation precisely. For if you are sitting in a cinema watching the screen, you assume that what you are watching is happening right in front of you. But in a far more fundamental sense, *it is happening behind you,* in the projection room."
6. Berman, *Coming to Our Senses,* p. 113.
7. Barfield, *Saving the Appearances,* pp. 144–145.
8. Ibid., p. 160.

21. Thinking about Thinking

1. There is a similarity between Moskvitin's Anthroposphere and what the philosopher Karl Popper calls "World 3." Oddly enough, Popper presented his idea in *Objective Knowledge* published in 1972, not too long before Moskvitin published *Essay on the Origin of Thought.* Popper's World 3 is, like Moskvitin's Anthroposphere, a world of human creation. It is the world of ideas—not the Platonic Ideas, which are a kind of archetype, existing in an atemporal "perfect" realm, and which would exist whether or not human beings encountered them. Popper's ideas are the world of human knowledge and creativity, the world housed in the libraries of the world and, as some would hastily say, on the Web. World 1, Popper argues, is the physical world studied by science. World 2 is the world of the human psyche, our subjective, interior world of feelings, emotions, thoughts. World 3, he argues, is not material, although its content is obviously expressed in material media—books, records, even films. It is, however, just as "objective" as the physical world. The similarity to Moskvitin's Anthroposphere seems obvious.
2. Moskvitin, *Essay on the Origin of Thought,* p. 1.
3. Ibid., p. 2.
4. The link between creativity and madness is a hoary theme in the literature on "abnormal mental states," and a representative bibliography would

take us far beyond our subject. In writers we have already discussed, Andreas Mavromatis devotes a significant chapter of his book to the relation between hypnagogia and various mental instabilities, most prominently schizophrenia. Likewise, Danah Zohar's *SQ* devotes an important section to the creative potential of "schizotypic" personalities, "schizotypy" denoting a personality with characteristics often found in actual cases of schizophrenia, but not schizophrenic itself. Outside authors already mentioned, I can recommend *The Anatomy of Creation* (1976) and *Solitude* (1989) by the late Anthony Storr, as well as many of his other works, as excellent studies of the links between creative and disturbed states of mind. Max Nordau's *Degeneration* (1895), mentioned earlier, is a classic example of how a thoroughly "bourgeois" mind is threatened by sensibilities different from its own, and how it typically lumps together the two extremes—genius and madness—that exceed its mediocrity.

5. Moskvitin, *Essay on the Origin of Thought*, p. 1.
6. Ibid., pp. 50, 52, 53.
7. Clearly, Moskvitin's experience is not an uncommon one, especially to individuals who experimented with psychoactive substances. Two early and influential psychic voyagers also reported visions of geometric forms as central to their inner journeys. During his period of "experimental mysticism," Ouspensky recorded a powerfully profound insight, centered around a vision of an enormous flower, "a rose or a lotus the petals of which were continually unfolding from the middle. . . . In this flower was an incredible quantity of light, movement, color, music, emotion . . . knowledge, intelligence, mathematics" (*A New Model of the Universe*, p. 290). And under the influence of carbon tetrachloride, his fellow Gurdjieffian René Daumal recorded a vision of red and black circles and triangles "becoming one another in a geometrically impossible way, this transformation taking place in a non-Euclidean space." See "The Determining Memory" in Daumal *The Powers of the Word* (San Francisco: City Lights Books, 1991).
8. Moskvitin, *Essay on the Origin of Thought*, p. 53.
9. Colin Wilson, *Access to Inner Worlds*, p. 70.
10. Moskvitin, *Essay on the Origin of Thought*, p. 57.

22. The Black Hole of Consciousness

1. Moskvitin, *Essay on the Origin of Thought*, p. 80. However, we should avoid the danger of *relativizing* the value of these different worlds based on the fact that each is a product of different powers of perception. A snail may indeed, and surely does, inhabit a different world from the one we do, but from all we can tell from the snail's behavior, it is a world that includes *less* of the total reality than the one we inhabit. This is not to say that *our* world is the closest approximation to the total world. We have

no idea if it is or not, and most likely beings exist who have a greater perception of the totality than ourselves. The world I see with my glasses on is a different one from the one I see with them off, but I do not believe they are "relatively equal" worlds. In one I can easily avoid being hit by a car; in the other my chances of being hit are amplified. The different worlds revealed by different consciousnesses are not all in an equal relation to the totality of which they are parts. What makes, say, mystical or aesthetic experiences so moving is not merely that they are *different* from our everyday experience of the world, but that what constitutes this difference is in some way *greater* experience. In them we somehow see more of the world than we otherwise do.

2. Ibid., pp. 81–82.
3. Ibid., p. 82.
4. Ibid., p. 83.
5. Ibid., p. 104.
6. See my article "Dreaming Ahead" in the Winter 1997 issue of *The Quest*, pp. 19–23.
7. I am indebted to Colin Wilson for this analogy. The film itself still holds up and is one of the few science fiction adventures that provide ideas as engaging as the story.
8. Barfield, *Saving the Appearances,* p. 137.
9. Ibid., p. 146.
10. On the history of the avant-garde artist as the educator of the "philistine" public, see *The Use and Abuse of Art,* the brilliant series of lectures by the historian Jacques Barzun. His thesis, which he has argued in other books, is that since the nineteenth century the goal of artists has been the realization of an "unconditional life," in pursuit of which they have "educated" average people about their, and their society's, utter worthlessness. As an "unconditional life" is an unobtainable ideal, one result of this has been an increasing "world rejection," culminating in a profound self-effacement and *mea culpa* on the part of nonartists, who are routinely baffled by the increasingly "shocking" productions of their educators. The end of this, of course, is the stridently unaesthetic world of twenty-first–century art, with bisected sheep and manure-covered canvases representing the artistic imagination.

23. Other Times and Places

1. "The Outsider Cycle," beginning with *The Outsider* and running through *Religion and the Rebel* (1957), *The Age of Defeat* (1959) (U.S. *The Stature of Man*), *The Strength to Dream* (1962), *Origin of the Sexual Impulse* (1963), *Beyond the Outsider* (1965), and summed up in *Introduction to the New Existentialism* (1967), forms the foundations for a new existential philosophy, rejecting the pessimism of Sartre and Heidegger, and based on the work of Edmund Husserl and Alfred North

Whitehead. *The Occult* (1971), *Mysteries* (1978), and *Beyond the Occult* (1987) sum up twenty years of research into the paranormal and related areas. His biographies of Gurdjieff, Rudolf Steiner, P. D. Ouspensky, and other central figures in esotericism are good introductions to some of the main themes in the "countertradition" of the West. Novels like *The Mind Parasites* (1967) and *The Philosopher's Stone* (1969) are thrilling expositions of his ideas about human consciousness, using themes from science fiction and the work of the writer of weird fiction H. P. Lovecraft. Sadly, many of these books are now out of print in the U.K. and U.S., and, times being what they are, Wilson is best known to a contemporary audience for his books on criminology and the psychology of murder, the most "philosophical" of these being *A Criminal History of Mankind* (1984). Even here, though, he sees the rise of peculiarly modern phenomena like sex crimes and the so-called motiveless murder as indicators of a shift in human consciousness. As in all his work, the evolution of human consciousness is his abiding concern.

2. For Wilson's full account of the rise of the novel, see *The Craft of the Novel*.

3. Along with Alfred North Whitehead's *Adventures of Ideas* (1937), Wilson's history of the novel is a good argument against the Marxist and positivist notion that history is moved by purely material forces. It is generally argued that the Romantic movement arose in reaction to the Industrial Revolution. Wilson, however, makes a strong case for the counterargument: that the Industrial Revolution itself was a product of the new powers of the imagination unleashed by Richardson's invention of the novel. See *The Craft of the Novel* as well as *Mysteries,* p. 259.

24. Faculty X

1. Colin Wilson, *The Mammoth Book of the Supernatural* (New York: Carrol & Graf, 1991), pp. 19–20.

2. See "Magic—the Science of the Future" in *The Occult,* pp. 37–62. For a longer account of Faculty X, including some of my own experiences of it, see my *Faculty X, Consciousness and the Transcendence of Time,* Colin Wilson Studies No. 8 (West Bridgford: Paupers Press, 1996). For more on Wilson see also my *Two Essays on Colin Wilson: World Rejection and Criminal Romantics and From Outsider to Post-Tragic Man* (West Bridgford: Paupers Press, 1994).

3. Wilson, *The Mammoth Book of the Supernatural,* p. 542.

25. The Ascent of Mount Ventoux

1. Quoted in Gebser, *The Ever-Present Origin,* pp. 12–15.

2. There are also many similarities between Gebser's "structures of consciousness" and Rudolf Steiner's "historical epochs," both in the historical periods covered and in the types of consciousness related to them. See

my article "Rudolf Steiner, Jean Gebser and the Evolution of Consciousness" in *Journal for Anthroposophy* No. 61, Fall 1995, pp. 80–93.

3. Feuerstein, *Structures of Consciousness,* p. 21.
4. Gebser, *The Ever-Present Origin,* p. xvii.
5. For what it is worth, Koestler was another important theorist of consciousness born in 1905.
6. A fascinating account of the remarkable parallels between physics and art since the nineteenth century can be found in Leonard Shlain's brilliant and highly readable *Art & Physics.* Shlain's book can be read as a kind of introduction to Gebser's ideas.
7. Feuerstein, *Structures of Consciousness,* p. 173.
8. Gebser, pp. xxx, xxix.
9. Ibid., p. xxix.

26. Structures of Consciousness

1. Feuerstein, *Structures of Consciousness,* p. 32.
2. Eric Mark Kramer and Algis Mickunas, "Introduction: Gebser's New Understanding," in *Consciousness and Culture: An Introduction to the Thought of Jean Gebser,* p. xi.
3. Gebser, *The Ever-Present Origin,* p. 543.
4. Ibid., p. xxvii.
5. Feuerstein, *Structures of Consciousness,* p. 217.
6. Gebser, *The Ever-Present Origin,* p. 1.
7. Bohm's thought also follows Gebser's in recognizing the need for a new language. See *Wholeness and the Implicate Order,* Chapter 2, "The Rheomode: An Experiment with Language and Thought," pp. 27–47.
8. Gebser, *The Ever-Present Origin,* p. 221.
9. Rudolf Steiner, *An Outline of Esoteric Science,* pp. 119–120.
10. Gebser, *The Ever-Present Origin,* p. 43.
11. Feuerstein, *Structures of Consciousness,* pp. 52, 57.
12. Steiner, *Cosmic Memory,* p. 196.
13. Gebser, *The Ever-Present Origin,* p. 44.
14. Ibid., pp. 44–45.
15. Ibid., p. 45. Gebser comments that the objection that Wilhelm's remark refers to a "case of primitive color blindness is groundless. Application of such a concept here is tantamount to anachronism"—meaning that our notions of color blindness are a product of *our* structure of consciousness and should not be applied to other structures. This is a profitable guideline, as far as it goes. But one problem that can emerge from this policy is that whenever one of Gebser's interpretations of a previous consciousness structure runs into a counterinterpretation, he, or one of his defenders, can pull out this clause as an all-purpose defense against criticism. Exactly why color blindness *must* be anachronistic in this case is unclear.

I am not saying it *is* applicable, only that, aside from Gebser *saying* it is, I do not see any evidence that it *must* be. The situation is common to all "total" accounts, and is most apparent in Marxist or Freudian thought. Both commonly place themselves outside the critical arena by declaring any opposing view to be precisely an expression of what they are "explaining"; i.e., if I disagree with a Freudian about my Oedipus Complex, or with a Marxist about the class struggle, it *must* be because of my "defense mechanisms" and my "false consciousness." In attempting to account for all human endeavors in terms of his consciousness structures, Gebser and his followers run the risk of a similar reductionism. Clearly, my own remarks here can be seen as an expression of a limited, "perspectival" consciousness, and hence their force as *criticisms* would be denied.

16. Feuerstein, *Structures of Consciousness*, p. 62.
17. Berman, *Coming to Our Senses*, p. 69.
18. Gebser, *The Ever-Present Origin*, p. 49.
19. Quoted in Colin Wilson, *The Occult*, p. 353.
20. The idea that consciousness itself is an impediment to perfection is the theme of Heinrich von Kleist's remarkable story-essay "On the Marionette Theater." Briefly put, Kleist argues that human beings lack the grace and beauty of marionettes because, unlike puppets, they are conscious of their actions. It is for this reason that animals appear to us as graceful creatures, exhibiting an ease and "naturalness" unavailable to self-conscious creatures. Kleist however, in a three-part process that bears much similarity to Owen Barfield's account of participation—and that would be employed by M. H. Abrahms in his brilliant study of Romanticism *Natural Supernaturalism*—pictured a future time when humankind will have passed through its awkward state of self-consciousness and so regain, on a "higher" level, the sublime unconsciousness of the marionettes. The "trialectic" of Grace/Fall/Paradise Regained can be seen in Hegel, Steiner, Gebser, and others.
21. Berman, *Coming To Our Senses*, p. 299.
22. Feuerstein, *Structures of Consciousness*, p. 78.
23. Stewart C. Easton, *Man and World in Light of Anthroposophy*, p. 39.
24. Ernst Cassirer, *The Philosophy of Symbolic Forms, Volume 2: Mythical Thought*, p. 38.
25. That magic is associated with silence is the dictum of two of the craft's most famous practitioners. For Eliphas Levi, who inaugurated the magical revival of the nineteenth century, the four cardinal virtues of the magician are "to know, to dare, to will, and to be silent." Likewise, for Aleister Crowley, one of the most powerful ritual gestures is the raising of the right forefinger to the lips, adopting the god-form of the Egyptian Harpocrates, the Lord of Silence.

26. Gebser, *The Ever-Present Origin*, p. 67. On the relationship between poetry and dream, see the introduction to Bachelard's *The Poetics of Reverie*.

27. The Mental-Rational Structure

1. Jaynes and Gebser both present fateful encounters in the sixteenth century between the Aztecs and the Incas and their Spanish conquistadors as paradigmatic examples of the confrontation of two radically different kinds of consciousness. For Jaynes it was a meeting between bicameral (Incas) and unicameral (Spanish) minds; for Gebser, a magical-mythical-unperspectival consciousness (Aztecs) met with disaster at the hands of its European mental-rational conquerors (Jaynes p. 160; Gebser, pp. 5–6). (And, for what it is worth, we are reminded that Freud, an eminently mental-rational mind, spoke of himself as a *conquistador* in his relation to the magical-mythical unconscious he "discovered.")

2. Gebser, *The Ever-Present Origin*, p. 75.

3. The classic work on the shift from a mythical to a mental form of thought in ancient Greece is F. M. Cornford's brilliant *From Religion to Philosophy*. A more recent and equally insightful account can be found in Richard Tarnas, *The Passion of the Western Mind* (see part 1, "The Greek World View").

4. Feuerstein, *Structures of Consciousness*, p. 99.

5. Gebser, *The Ever-Present Origin*, pp. 15, 12.

6. Heller, *The Importance of Nietzsche*, p. 101.

7. As Gebser was well aware, major changes in consciousness are not always unalloyed. The "retreat from the world" and our passing into the "invisible" that Heller charts through Hegel and Rilke has its current "shadow" symbol in the ubiquitous Walkman, icon of mass "interiority." Its popularity argues for a kind of negative "spiritualization," a triumph of subjectivity over the external world, and the loss of any meaningful sense of "public space." Wrapped in our unobtrusive designer headphones, we float, island universes, oblivious of the others around us. The "access to other worlds" discovered by the Romantics has, with consumer humanity, degenerated into the portable personal entertainment center.

    Paradoxically, this most unmistakable agent of social atomism is only one of a flood of *things* that accompany our return to the cave. But these things—the familiar items of our consumer culture—have at best a fleeting significance. They are *made* to be replaced; their function is not to *last* but to be the token fetish in the rituals of consumption. They have no being, no enduring "presence" in the world, and hence can in no way act as a conduit for "meaning." Just as the act of buying something is the true meaning of consumption, and not the thing bought, so the item itself is a necessary element in the process of disposal. We have to get rid of it in order to consume again. Seen this way, we are true "consumers," assimilating our purchases, and then, soon after, excreting them. We no longer buy things to "have." We eat them. No one holds on to last week's breakfast.

With this in mind it is interesting to note that at around the same time Rilke was receiving the inspiration of the *Elegies* and developing the poetic metaphysics of "the invisible" ("We are," he told his Polish translator, "the bees of the invisible"), Rudolf Steiner gave a series of lectures along very similar lines. In 1911 Steiner gave a lecture series called *The Reappearance of Christ in the Etheric* (Spring Valley, N.Y.: Anthroposophic Press, 1983) in which he said that the present Earth was becoming a "corpse," in preparation for its next planetary incarnation as Jupiter. For this to happen, "It is necessary for the earth to be destroyed; otherwise the spirit will not become free" (p. 131). As Rilke was about to declare that "Nowhere will the world exist but within," Steiner was informing his audience that the external world was in the process of passing away so that it may be reborn in a more spiritual form. Both share in the sense of what Heller calls "the loss of significant external reality." See my article "The Fate of the Earth According to Rudolf Steiner" in the Fall 1994 issue of *Gnosis*.

8. George Steiner, *Grammars of Creation*, pp. 1–2. Like Owen Barfield and Jean Gebser, Steiner, too, sees in language a gauge of the evolution of consciousness. Yet what he sees at the beginning of our new millennium is a language "darkened" by the brutalities and inhumanities that crowd the exiting century, a language stamped by the boots of a Hitler, a Stalin, and other totalitarian demigods, and cheapened by the coarse handling of mass media, until it no longer has any reservoir of "future," any potential to throw itself with "hope" into uncertainty.

9. Gebser, *The Ever-Present Origin*, p. 39.

10. Whether it is myth or the dim memory of some actual catastrophe, the story of Atlantis relates how, almost overnight, a powerful, magnificent culture sank beneath the waves. The mysterious ruins and lost cities found over the globe point to once-tangible glories that are now mere tokens of the past. That the same fate can befall our own culture is no longer unthinkable. Casting an eye to the future, Morris Berman writes, "If the west is to survive at all, it will in all likelihood have to pass through a severe crisis, a civilizational breakdown, including plague (already beginning), famine, and massive economic depression, in its transition to a new culture. Anything could happen during such a situation, including the emergence of a Roman-style government, if the period of breakdown is of sufficient intensity and duration" (*Coming to Our Senses,* p. 173).

For many, the scenario Berman depicts seems already in place; clearly since the events of September 11, 2001, the idea that "the West," and specifically the United States, is "safe" is less certain than before.

We may indeed be passing through what the historian Arnold Toynbee called a "time of troubles," the period of challenge and difficulty that precedes the disintegration of a civilization. Toynbee argues that a civilization in peril reacts in specific, recognizable patterns. One is to seek safety by a "return to the past," by reviving a "primitive," "archaic" way of life. The various "back to nature" and fundamentalist philosophies that have emerged in the last fifty or so years suggest something of this sort. Another reaction is the polar opposite, a flight into "the future," something our various cybernauts and technocrats seem to offer. In either case, Toynbee argues, these options fail to meet the challenges presented by the "time of troubles" and, inevitably, the civilizations that follow these routes go under.

28. The Integral Structure

1. Feuerstein, *Structures of Consciousness,* p. 214.
2. George Steiner, *Grammars of Creation,* p. 23.
3. In his elegant and powerful little book *Metaphysical Horror* the philosopher Leszek Kolakowski offers hope that a new vocabulary may soon be emerging: "Language may indeed have suffered a nervous breakdown, but we have reason to believe that the sickness will not be terminal. Language will most likely resume its tireless attempts to cross its own borders and venture into the illicit realm of the inexpressible. The civilization in which we live surrounds our use of words with well-guarded barriers, but it also naturally and continually devises ways of cheating and getting around the wardens. We cannot tell where the invincible spectre of the Absolute will re-emerge and how it will be resuscitated" (p. 55).
4. Charles Hinton's books about the "fourth dimension" (see part 1) seem clear evidence of the "breakup" of the perspectival world, while Ouspensky's work, which brings together Hinton's ideas about "higher space" with speculations on the nature of time, seems a paradigmatic example of the transition from a "space" to a "time" consciousness.
5. A personal note here on Gebser's ideas and their relation to music. According to Gebser, by definition, atonal, serial, tachist, aleatory, twelve tone, and other "modern" developments in music are, insofar as they are expressions of the new "arational" consciousness, more *authentic* than, say Mozart or Beethoven, whose work is an expression of the mental-rational structure. We can say that, according to Gebser, all "postclassical" music—to coin an ugly phrase—is "preferable" to its antecedents because of its relation to the new, emerging consciousness. And the same, of course, can be said of the equally modern developments in literature, painting, sculpture, etc.

One problem with this, however, is that, for all its supposed "time-freedom," most music since, say, 1945, has, along with a great deal of modern "serious" literature, moved further and further away from any immediate appeal. There are, to be sure, devotees of what is today called "new music," just as there are a readership and an audience for "difficult" literature and art. But as a means of expressing the *spiritual quest* in humanity and of actually *moving* its listeners, I cannot see how composers like Stockhausen, Varèse, Boulez, and others, up to Philip Glass and John Cage, exceed, or even equal, the composers of the Classical-Romantic tradition. The works in this tradition are and remain beautiful, and continue to express the deep spiritual longings and striving of Western consciousness. Admittedly, Gebser agrees that the works of the arational structure are not "beautiful" (Gebser, p. 462). They are, he suggests, "spiritual," which, no doubt, is true. Martinu, Bartok, Messiaen—the reader can include his or her own favorites—imbue a powerful spiritual presence into their work. But although I enjoy the work of these composers, I cannot help feeling that the sonata-allegro form, and its *linear* trajectory of theme, variation, and reconciliation, is somehow an archetype of Western consciousness's search for, and discovery of, self.

Linearity can accomplish spiritual acts impossible for the kind of simultaneity that Gebser argues is indicative of the new consciousness. A symphony is linear, one-note-after-another, not all-at-once: were an orchestra to play all the notes of the Jupiter Symphony simultaneously, it would not be music, but noise. Likewise a novel or story or any narrative form; we only need think of William S. Burroughs's "cut-ups" or the "automatic poetry" of the Surrealists to see what is wrong with an "aleatory" approach to writing. Finding out "what happens" is the lure of reading narrative—as we all know, finding out in advance kills the joy of reading or listening. The same is true of philosophy: as Hegel famously pointed out, simply to state conclusions is not enough; the "truth" of thought is in the process of arriving at it. In our desire to escape the "deficient" mode of the mental-rational structure, we must be careful not to abandon those aspects of linearity necessary for perceiving and grasping *meaning*. (Gebser's friend Erich Kahler expressed his concerns about this in his unjustly little-known book *The Destruction of Form in the Arts* [1968].)

And this suggests that, for all their obvious depth and import, it may be wise to take some aspects of Gebser's consciousness structures with at least a grain of salt. In our efforts to make the transition to the new structure, there is the danger that we may develop a new, totalizing (to use a postmodernist phrase) ideology. Just as zealous Marxists are anxious to avoid anything that is "counterrevolutionary" and, "for the good of the revolution," steel their will to go *against* their own preferences, followers of Gebser's ideas may find it more "arational" to listen to alinear, postclassical, aleatory music *because* that is the more "authentic" kind of music for the emerging consciousness structure—not necessarily because they like it. Although I am aware of the various "new" developments in the arts, my own tastes remain for the most part Classical-Romantic, up to early modern. But this does raise a question concerning what we may clumsily call the "historicity of art." Is it "inauthentic" of us to be moved by, say, an ancient Greek statue because it is a product of a passing consciousness structure? Or is there an atemporal realm in which great art exists, outside the changes and modifications of passing time? Is each age equidistant from the "beautiful," or are some closer or farther away from it?

6.   Eliot's *Four Quartets* is one of the great "time" poems of the century. As noted earlier, Eliot was among the cream of London's intelligentsia who attended P. D. Ouspensky's lectures in the 1920s. Eliot's lines, like "Time present and time past are both perhaps present in time future," and "To be conscious is not to be in time," are powerful condensations of some of the ideas he gleaned from Ouspensky's talks.

7.   Priestley, a novelist and playwright sadly out of fashion, called himself a "time-haunted man" and was a devotee of both Ouspensky and the time theorist J. W. Dunne. Priestley's plays *Time and the Conways* and *I Have Been Here Before* deal with notions of eternal recurrence and multiple time. One of his last books, *Over The Long High Wall,* sums up a lifetime of pondering the mysteries of time.

Last Words: Playing for Time

1.   Birkerts, "The Millennial Warp," in *Readings,* pp. 3–4, 5.
2.   Kolakowski, *Freedom, Fame, Lying and Betrayal,* p. 123.
3.   Berman, *Coming to Our Senses,* p. 301.
4.   For an account of Steiner's "Ahrimanic future" and its relation to our own times, see my article "Rudolf Steiner and the Ahrimanic Future," *Journal for Anthroposophy* #56, Spring 1993, pp. 41–50.
5.   Quoted in Feuerstein, *Structures of Consciousness,* p. 166.

SELECTED BIBLIOGRAPHY

Bachelard, Gaston., *The Poetics of Reverie*. Boston: Beacon Press, 1971.
Barfield, Owen. *History, Guilt and Habit*. Middletown, Conn.: Wesleyan University Press, 1981.
———. *History in English Words*. West Stockbridge, Mass.: Lindisfarne Press, 1985.
———. *Owen Barfield and the Origin of Language*. Spring Valley, N.Y.: St. George Publications, 1976.
———. *Poetic Diction*. Middletown, Conn.: Wesleyan University Press, 1987.
———. *Romanticism Comes of Age*. Middletown, Conn.: Wesleyan University Press, 1986.
———. *Saving the Appearances*. New York: Harcourt, Brace & World, n.d.
Barrow, John D., and Frank Tipler. *The Anthropic Cosmological Principle*. Oxford: Clarendon Press, 1985.
Barzun, Jacques. *From Dawn to Decadence*. New York: HarperCollins, 2001.
———. *The Use and Abuse of Art*. Princeton: Princeton University Press, 1973.
Bergson, Henri. *Creative Evolution*. London: The Macmillan Company, 1911.
———. *An Introduction to Metaphysics*. New York: G. P. Putnam's Sons, 1912.
———. *Matter and Memory*. New York: Zone Books, 1988.
———. *Mind-Energy*. London: The Macmillan Company, 1920.
———. *Time and Free Will*. New York: The Macmillan Company, 1910.
———. *The Two Sources of Morality and Religion*. New York: Henry Holt and Company, 1935.
Berman, Morris. *Coming to Our Senses*. London: Unwin, 1990.

————. *The Reenchantment of the World*. Ithaca, N.Y.: Cornell University Press, 1981.

Birkerts, Sven. *The Gutenberg Elegies*. Boston: Faber and Faber, 1994.

————. *Readings*. St. Paul: Graywolf Press, 1999.

Blavatsky, Helena Petrovna. *Isis Unveiled*. London: Theosophical Publishing Society, 1910.

————. *The Secret Doctrine*. London: Theosophical Publishing Society, 1905.

Bohm, David. *Wholeness and the Implicate Order*. London: Routledge and Kegan Paul, 1981.

Bucke, Richard Maurice. *Cosmic Consciousness*. New York: E. P. Dutton, 1966.

Carpenter, Edward. *From Adam's Peak to Elephanta*. London: Sonnenschein & Co., 1892.

————. *Toward Democracy*. Manchester: John Heywood, 1885.

Cassirer, Ernst. *The Philosophy of Symbolic Forms*. Vol. 2, *Mythical Thought* (New Haven: Yale University Press, 1955.

Chalmers, David. *The Conscious Mind*. Oxford: Oxford University Press, 1996.

Cornford, F.M. *From Religion to Philosophy*. Princeton: Princeton University Press, 1991.

Cranston, Sylvia. *The Extraordinary Life & Influence of Helena Blavatsky*. New York: Tarcher/Putnam, 1993.

Crick, Francis. *The Astonishing Hypothesis: The Scientific Search for the Soul*. London: Simon and Schuster, 1994.

Darling, David. *After Life: In Search of Cosmic Consciousness*. London: Fourth Estate, 1995.

Dennett, Daniel. *Consciousness Explained*. London: Allen Lane, 1989.

Devereux, Paul. *The Long Trip: A Prehistory of Psychedelia*. London: Arkana, 1997.

Easton, Stewart. *Man and World in Light of Anthroposophy*. Spring Valley, N.Y.: Anthroposophic Press, 1982.

————. *Rudolf Steiner: Herald of a New Epoch*. Anthroposophic Press, 1980.

Edelman, Gerald. *Bright Air, Brilliant Fire*. London: Allen Lane, 1992.

Eisler, Riane. *The Chalice and the Blade*. London: Harper & Row, 1987.

Feuerstein, Georg. *Structures of Consciousness*. Lower Lake, California: Integral Publishing, 1987.

Gebser, Jean. *The Ever-Present Origin*. Columbus: Ohio University Press, 1985.

Gimbutas, Marija. *The Goddesses and Gods of Old Europe, 6500–3500 BC, Myths and Cult Images*. London: Thames and Hudson, 1982.

Gimbutas, Marija. *The Civilization of the Goddess: The World of Old Europe*. San Francisco: Harper, 1991.

Gleich, James: *Faster, The Acceleration of Just About Everything*. London: Abacus, 2000.

Godwin, Joscelyn. *Arktos*. Kempton: Adventures Unlimited Press, 1996.

———. *The Theosophical Enlightenment*. Albany: State University of New York Press, 1994.

Gooch, Stan. *Cities of Dreams*, 2nd ed. London: Aulis Books, 1995.

———. *Creatures of Inner Space*. London: Rider, 1984.

———. *The Double Helix of the Mind*. London: Wildwood House, 1980.

———. *Guardians of the Ancient Wisdom*. London: Wildwood House, 1979.

———. *The Neanderthal Question*. London: Wildwood House, 1977.

———. *The Paranormal*. London: Wildwood House, 1978.

———. *Personality and Evolution*. London: Wildwood House, 1973.

———. *The Secret Life of Humans*. London: Dent, 1981.

———. *Total Man*. London: Allen Lane, 1972.

Hammeroff, Kaszniak, and Chalmers, eds. *Toward a Science of Consciousness III*. Boston: MIT Press, 1999.

Hancock, Graham. *Fingerprints of the Gods*. London: Heinemann, 1995.

Hancock, Graham, and Robert Bauval. *Keepers of Genesis*. London: Heinemann, 1996.

Heisenberg, Werner. *Physics and Philosophy*. New York: Harper Torchbooks, 1962.

Heller, Erich. *The Artist's Journey into the Interior*. New York: Harcourt Brace Jovanovich, 1976.

———. *The Disinherited Mind*. New York: Farrar, Straus and Cudahy, 1957.

———. *The Importance of Nietzsche*. Chicago: Chicago University Press, 1988.

———. *In The Age of Prose*. Cambridge: Cambridge University Press, 1984.

Hemleben, Johannes. *Rudolf Steiner: A Documentary Biography*. Sussex: Henry Golden Ltd, 1975.

Hesse, Hermann. *Demian*. New York: Harper & Row, 1965.

Hinton, Charles. *Speculations on the Fourth Dimension: Selected Writings of C. H. Hinton*. New York: Dover, 1980.

Horgan, John. *The End of Science*. London: Abacus, 1998.

Humphrey, Nicholas. *Soul Searching*. New York: Basic Books, 1996.

Huxley, Aldous. *The Doors of Perception*. London: Chatto&Windus Ltd, 1954.

James, William. *The Varieties of Religious Experience*. New York: Collier Books, 1977.

———. *The Writings of William James*. New York: Modern Library, 1968.

Jay, Mike. *Emperors of Dreams: Drugs in the Nineteenth Century*. London: Dedalus, 2000.

Jaynes, Julian. *The Origins of Consciousness in the Breakdown of the Bicameral Mind.* Boston: Houghton Mifflin, 1976.

Kahler, Erich. *The Destruction of Form in the Arts.* New York: George Braziller, 1968.

Kant, Immanuel. *The Philosophy of Kant.* New York: Modern Library, 1949.

Koestler, Arthur. *The Act of Creation.* New York: The Macmillan Company, 1964.

Kolakowski, Leszek. *Freedom, Fame, Lying and Betrayal.* London: Penguin, 1999.

———. *Metaphysical Horror.* London: Penguin, 2001.

Kramer, Eric Mark, and Algis Mickuna, eds. *Consciousness and Culture: An Introduction to the Thought of Jean Gebser.* Westport, Conn.: Greenwood Press, 1992.

Lachman, Gary. *Turn Off Your Mind: The Mystic Sixties and the Dark Side of the Age of Aquarius.* London: Sidgwick&Jackson, 2001.

Leakey, Mary. *Disclosing the Past.* London: Weidenfeld and Nicolson, 1984.

Maturana, Humberto, and Francisco Varela. *The Tree of Knowledge: The Biological Roots of Human Understanding.* Boston: Shambhala, 1992.

Mavromatis, Andreas. *Hypnagogia: The Unique State of Consciousness Between Wakefulness and Sleep.* London: Routledge, 1987.

Meade, Marion. *Madame Blavatsky, the Woman Behind the Myth.* New York: G. P. Putnam's Sons, 1980.

Melechi, Antonio, ed. *Mindscapes: An Anthology of Drug Writing.* West Yorkshire: Mono, 1998.

McDermott, Robert A., ed. *The Essential Steiner.* San Francisco: Harper & Row, 1984.

Michell, John. *The View Over Atlantis.* New York: Ballantine, 1972.

Minsky, Marvin. *The Society of Mind.* London: Heinemann, 1987.

Moore, James. *Gurdjieff and Mansfield.* London: Routledge & Kegan Paul, 1980.

Moskvitin, Jurij. *Essay on the Origin of Thought.* Columbus: Ohio University Press, 1974.

Neumann, Erich: *The Origins and History of Consciousness.* Princeton: Princeton University Press, 1973.

Nicoll, Maurice. *Living Time.* London: Watkins, 1981.

Nietzsche, Friedrich. *Thus Spake Zarathustra.* London: Penguin, 1969.

Nordau, Max. *Degeneration.* Lincoln: University of Nebraska Press, 1993.

Orage, A. R. *Consciousness: Animal, Human and Superhuman.* New York: Weiser, 1978.

Ouspensky, P. D. *In Search of the Miraculous.* New York: Harcourt, Brace & World, 1949.

———. *Letters from Russia 1919.* London: Routledge & Kegan Paul, 1978.

———. *A New Model of the Universe.* New York: Alfred A. Knopf, 1969.

————. *Tertium Organum*. New York: Alfred A. Knopf, 1981.

Penrose, Roger. *The Emperor's New Mind*. London: Vintage, 1990.

Powys, John Cowper. *Autobiography*. London: Pan Books, 1982.

Priestley, J. B. *Man and Time*. London: Aldus Books, 1964.

Rechnitzer, Peter A. *R. M. Bucke: Journey to Cosmic Consciousness*. Markam, Ontario: Fitzhenry & Whiteside, 1994.

Redgrove, Peter. *The Black Goddess and the Unseen Real*. London: Bloomsbury, 1987.

Rittlemeyer, Friedrich. *Rudolf Steiner Enters My Life*. London: George Roberts, 1929.

Rose, Steven, ed. *From Brains to Consciousness*. London: Allen Lane, 1998.

Roszak, Theodore. *Unfinished Animal: The Aquarian Frontier and The Evolution of Consciousness*. London: Faber and Faber, 1976.

Rudgley, Richard. *Lost Civilizations of the Stone Age*. London: Century, 1998.

Schwaller de Lubicz, R.A., *Nature Word*. West Stockbridge, Mass.: Lindisfarne Press, 1982.

————. *Symbol and the Symbolic: Egypt, Science and the Evolution of Consciousness*. Brookline, Mass.: Autumn Press, 1978.

————. *Sacred Science*. New York: Inner Traditions International, 1985.

————. *The Temples of Karnak*. Vrochester, Vt., Inner Traditions International, 1999.

Searle, John. *The Mystery of Consciousness*. London: Granta Books, 1997.

Shaw, Bernard. *Major Critical Essays*. Harmondsworth: Penguin, 1986.

Sheldrake, Rupert. *The Presence of the Past*. London: Collins, 1988.

Shlain, Leonard. *The Alphabet Versus the Goddess*. London: Allen Lane, 1998.

————. *Art & Physics*. New York: Quill, 1991.

Shortt, S. E. D. *Victorian Lunacy: R. M. Bucke and the Practice of Late Nineteenth Century Psychiatry*. Cambridge: Cambridge University Press, 1986.

Steiner, George. *Grammars of Creation*. London: Faber and Faber, 2001.

————. *Language and Silence*. New York: Atheneum, 1982.

Steiner, Rudolf. *Autobiography: Chapters in the Course of My Life*. Hudson, N.Y.: Anthroposophic Press, 1999.

————. *Cosmic Memory*. New York: Harper & Row, 1961.

————. *The Inner Nature of Music*. Spring Valley, N.Y., Anthroposophic Press, 1983.

————. *Intuitive Thinking as a Spiritual Path: A Philosophy of Freedom*. Hudson, N.Y., Anthroposophic Press, 1995.

————. *An Outline of Esoteric Science.*, Hudson, N.Y., Anthroposophic Press, 1997.

————. *Rosicrucian Wisdom*. London: Rudolf Steiner Press, 2000.

Tarnas, Richard. *The Passion of the Western Mind*. New York: Ballantine Books, 1991.

Thompson, William Irwin. *Coming Into Being: Artifacts and Texts in the Evolution of Consciousness*. New York: The Macmillan Company, 1998.

Van Dusen, Wilson. *The Natural Depth in Man*. New York: Harper & Row, 1972.

———. *The Presence of Other Words*. London: Wildwood House, 1975.

Vandenbroeck, André. *Al-Kemi: Hermetic, Occult, Political, and Private Aspects of R. A. Schwaller de Lubicz*. Great Barrington, Mass.: Lindisfarne Press, 1987.

von Franz, Marie-Louise. *Creation Myths*. Dallas: Spring Publications, 1986.

Washington, Peter. *Madame Blavatsky's Baboon*. London: Secker and Warburg, 1993.

Webb, James. *The Harmonious Circle*. New York: G. P. Putnam's Sons, 1980.

West, John Anthony. *The Serpent in the Sky*. London: Wildwood House, 1979.

Whitehead, Alfred North. *Science and the Modern World*. New York: The Macmillan Company, 1925.

———. *Symbolism: Its Meaning and Effect*. New York: G. P. Putnam's Sons, 1955.

Wilber, Ken. *Up from Eden*. London: Shambhala, 2000.

Wilson, Colin. *Access to Inner Worlds*. London: Rider, 1983.

———. *Beyond the Outsider*. Boston: Houghton Mifflin, 1965.

———. *The Craft of the Novel*. London: Gollancz, 1977.

———. *A Criminal History of Mankind*. New York: G. P. Putnam's Sons, 1984.

———. *From Atlantis to the Sphinx*. London: Virgin, 1996.

———. *The Mind Parasites*. St. Albans: Pan Books, 1967.

———. *Mysteries*. New York: G. P. Putnam's Sons, 1978.

———. *The Occult*. New York: Random House, 1971.

———. *The Outsider*. Boston: Houghton Mifflin, 1956.

———. *Poetry and Mysticism*. San Francisco: City Lights, 1970.

———. *Rudolf Steiner: The Man and His Vision*. Northhamptonshire: Aquarian Press, 1985.

Zajonc, Arthur. *Catching the Light*. New York: Bantam, 1993.

Zohar, Danah, and Ian Marshall. *SQ: Spiritual Intelligence, the Ultimate Intelligence*. London: Bloomsbury, 2000.

ACKNOWLEDGMENTS

Many thanks are due to Mike Jay and Lisa Jane Persky for their helpful suggestions and warm encouragement, and to my sons Joshua and Max for their indispensable contributions. Special thanks must go to Colin Wilson for generously providing the introduction; to Will Marsh for his care and patience in the copyediting; and to Christopher Bamford, who proposed the idea in the first place. And, as always, I am in debt to the staff of the British Library for their expertise, efficiency, and unruffled cheerfulness. Their unstinting help makes a workplace into something like a second home.

GARY LACHMAN was born in Bayonne, New Jersey, and has lived in London since 1996. He is a full-time writer with more than a dozen books to his name on topics ranging from the evolution of consciousness and the Western esoteric tradition, to literature, suicide, and the history of popular culture. Lachman writes frequently for journals in the US and UK and lectures internationally. Mr. Lachman's books include *Rudolf Steiner: An Introduction to His Life and Work* (2007); *Jung the Mystic: The Esoteric Dimensions of Carl Jung's Life and Teachings* (2010); *The Quest for Hermes Trismegistus* (Floris Books, 2011); *Madame Blavatsky: The Mother of Modern Spirituality* (2012); *The Caretakers of the Cosmos* (Floris Books, 2013); and *Lost Knowledge of the Imagination* (Floris Books, 2017).

A founding member of the rock group Blondie, he was inducted into the Rock and Roll Hall of Fame in 2006. <www. garylachman.co.uk>